THE
EPISTLE
TO THE
ROMANS

A COMMENTARY

KEVIN J. CONNER

Published by City Bible Publishing
9200 NE Fremont
Portland, Oregon 97220

Printed in U.S.A.

City Bible Publishing is a ministry of City Bible Church and is
dedicated to serving the local church and its leaders through the
production and distribution of quality materials.

It is our prayer that these materials, proven in the context of the local
church, will equip leaders in exalting the Lord and extending His
kingdom.

*For a free catalog of additional resources from City Bible Publishing
please call 1-800-777-6057 or visit our web site at
www.citybiblepublishing.com.*

Table of Contents

Bibliography

Introduction

One of the richest of the epistles of Paul is this epistle to the Romans. It is the *foundational* revelation of all God's dealings with man. Nothing else can be received of God as to full salvation without this foundational stone—*justification* by faith. It was the book of the Reformation period, the battle cry of Martin Luther against dead words, legalism, and superstition.

Paul builds three New Testament epistles on the illumination given to him from Habakkuk 2:4— "The just shall live by faith."

* The Just (Romans 1:17)
* Shall Live (Galatians 3:11)
* By Faith (Hebrews 10:38)

This epistle seems to especially answer the questions and pleadings of Job:

1) How can a man be just before God? (Job 9:2; 25:4; justification)
2) The cry for a Mediator (Job 9:32; 33; 16:21; priesthood)
3) God only can bring a clean thing out of an unclean (Job 14:4; 25:4; the Incarnation or Virgin Birth)
4) The cry for a Redeemer (Job 19:25-27; reconciliation)

The epistle was written before Paul had been to Rome (Romans 1:11, 13). It was also written before he went to Jerusalem (Romans 15:26, 31) during the months in Macedonia and Greece on his second (or third) missionary journey (Acts 19:21; 20:1-3, 22; II Corinthians 8:1; 9:1-9). As the collection was ready, Paul finished Romans 15:25. Timothy and Gaius were with Paul when he wrote Romans 16:21, 23. They were also with him in Acts 20:4. Phebe of Cenchrea, the eastern part of Corinth (the chief city of Greece [Acts 20:2]), carried this letter to Rome (Romans 16:1-2). Thus, it seems that Paul wrote Romans in Greece, probably in Corinth, just after the close of his second (or third) missionary journey. The church was in good spiritual condition at the time (Romans 1:8; 15:14; 16:19). Paul desired to see them and confirm them (Romans 15:15, 22-29; 1:9, 10; II Peter 1:12-15: 3:1). Up to this time he had been hindered (Romans 1:13; 15:22). He hoped he would be able to come to them in the will of God (Romans 15:30-32; Colossians 4:2-4; Ephesians 6:18-20). He also desired to correct certain disorders at Rome by this epistle (Romans 16:17, 18; 11:17-18, 25; 14:1-4, 10, 13, 19; 15:1, 2, 5).

There is no record of who began the church at Rome. Neither Peter nor Paul are recorded as beginning it; thus, "apostolic succession" is ruled out. Perhaps some of the Jews from Rome at Pentecost (Acts 2:10) may have begun meetings there. Or, some of Paul's converts from Asia may have started the church. Paul was acquainted with a number of the brethren there (Romans 16:3-16). The Roman church of today is in some ways removed from the truths of this great epistle, especially justification by faith apart from works!

The following diagram gives a general outline of the chapters of Romans.

ROMANS				
DOCTRINAL			NATIONAL	DEVOTIONAL /PRACTICAL
Jew & Gentile Under Sin Condemnation (Romans 1-3)	Jew & Gentile Justification By faith (Romans 4-5)	Sanctification Unto Glorification (Romans 6-8)	Jew & Gentile Election or Rejection (Romans 9-11)	Practical Righteousness Justification in Application (Romans 12-16)

RIGHTEOUSNESS REQUIRED

Romans
The Gospel According to Paul

Righteousness Required
(Romans 1:1 – 4:25)

Salutation (Romans 1:1-7)

Verse 1: *"Paul, a servant of Jesus Christ, called to be an apostle, separated unto the gospel of God..."*

A. Paul declares his own distinct calling and separation to apostleship.

"Paul" – The writer of the epistle. The great Apostle to the Gentiles uses his Gentile name. Paul means "little," in contrast to Saul, which means "destroyer."

"A Servant" – (Meaning "love-slave"; Greek: *Doulos* means "bondslave" [cf. Exodus 21:1-6]) Various kinds of Roman and Hebrew slaves, were branded in the ear. Their ears were "digged." Paul was voluntarily a slave to God's will (Psalm 40:5-8; Isaiah 50:4-6).

"Called" – (cf. verses 6-7) Calling involves commitment, commission, and consecration.

"Apostle" – (i.e., "sent one") (cf. of his conversion in Acts 9). This term indicates the post-ascension gift ministry of apostleship (Ephesians 4:9-16). Paul was especially the Apostle to the Gentiles, though he longed to be one to the Jews. He was a servant first!

"Separated" – (cf. separated *from* [negative]; separated *unto* [positive]; see Galatians 1:15-16 and Romans 1:1.) Vow of the Nazarite (Numbers 6:1-12).

"Jesus Christ" – (Savior anointed) Interpret the names and discover His person and His ministry.

Thus, Paul declares his own distinct calling and separation to apostleship.

B. **"The gospel of God"**

(Note the emphasis on the word "gospel," which means "good news.")
Paul uses this term at least seventy-two times. Note that in each verse
below Paul calls it "my gospel" (Romans 2:16; 16:25-27).

- The Gospel of God (Romans 1:1).
- The Gospel of His Son (Romans 1:9).
- The Gospel of Christ (Romans 1:16).

Note: The same Greek word, "gospel," equals the "good news of God,
to man through Christ." Outside of Christ there is only bad news for the
human race.

In relation to these verses, note the following references:
- The Gospel (Luke 4:18; Mark 16:15)
- The Gospel of the Kingdom (Matthew 24:14)
- The Gospel of Jesus Christ, the Son of God (Mark 1:1)
- That Gospel which I (Paul) preach (Acts 20:24; Galatians 2:2; 1:11)
- The Gospel of the Grace of God (Acts 20:24)
- The Gospel of the Circumcision (Galatians 2:7)
- The Gospel of the Uncircumcision (Galatians 2:7)
- The Everlasting Gospel (Revelation 14:16)
- The Glorious Gospel (I Timothy 1:11)

It is evident that Paul was given a distinctive "gospel of God" according
to and concerning God's son, Jesus Christ. The four gospels of Matthew,
Mark, Luke, and John set forth the Lord Jesus Christ after the flesh (the
historical and eternal Christ), declaring the words and works and ministry
of the Lord Jesus. But to Paul is given the inner revelation of the Christ
"after the Spirit" (refer to "after the flesh" [II Corinthians 5:16-18]), the
very "kernel" of the four gospels. This is wonderfully set forth in the
epistle to the Romans, "glad tidings."

He distinctly calls it "my gospel" (Romans 2:16; 16:25-27). He utters
a terrible curse of anyone who dares to preach "another gospel," which
would trouble and pervert believers, be they angels or men (Galatians 1:6-
10; II Corinthians 11:4). This gospel was not taught to Paul by man, but
given to him by *revelation*, not of the other apostles (cf. Galatians 1:11-12).

It is important to recognize that there is but one gospel! The gospel according to Paul is to declare this: one gospel for both Jew and Gentile—not two or more separate gospels.

The four gospels *fulfill* the Law, the Psalms, and the Prophets, and Paul's gospel interpreted the four gospels, "The Christ after the Spirit" (i.e., the external ordinances of baptism, communion, and the cross are set forth in the four gospels, but Paul's gospel interprets the real spiritual and inner meaning of such. Thus:

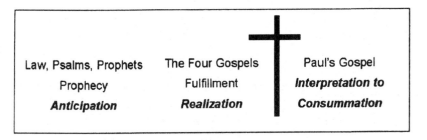

Law, Psalms, Prophets	The Four Gospels	Paul's Gospel
Prophecy	Fulfillment	*Interpretation to*
Anticipation	*Realization*	*Consummation*

Verse 2: *"...(Which he had promised afore by his prophets in the holy scriptures)..."*

A. **The gospel was promised and foretold in the Holy Scriptures.**

The gospel that Paul is about to declare is founded in and on the Old Testament Scriptures and writings of the prophets. Even though Paul was distinctive in his apostolic ministry, called, and declared his revelation as "my gospel," the final court of appeal was the infallible Word of God, the divine rule (Romans 1:2; 16:25-27).

Paul, all through his travels in the book of Acts, entered the synagogues and appealed to the hearers to compare the gospel of Jesus Christ, which he presented to them in its historical and theological context, and to see how it lined up with the prophetic writings of the Old Testament concerning the promised Messiah. He *reasoned* with them *out of the Scriptures* on the Sabbath days. He *opened* the Scriptures, *alleging* that Jesus of Nazareth was indeed the Messiah and that His person, work, ministry, death, burial, and resurrection were the fulfillment of the Holy Scriptures and writings of the prophets.

Jesus Christ was the fulfillment of the Prophets and the gospel veiled in the Old Testament, and Paul's gospel was a teaching revelation and exposition of Him. Jesus Christ is the Gospel of God *personified,* and Paul preached *Him* (Acts 13:5; 14:15-32; 14:1-4; 17:1-4; 17:5, 10-12; 18:24-

28; 19:8-12; 28:23-32, Amplified New Testament). The Old Testament Scriptures are a sealed and veiled book apart from Jesus Christ. Blindness is on the heart of the Jew in the reading of it (II Corinthians 3:13-16). It is a mystery, and Christ is "the key" to the Old Testament. The Scriptures in the Law, the Psalms, and the Prophets have to be "opened" to the eyes, heart, and mind (Luke 24:27, 31, 32, 44, 45). The Jews could search the Scriptures to see whether these things that Paul taught were so (Acts 17:10-12). Paul was willing to be tested by the infallible Scriptures.

Paul's distinctive revelation was the unveiling and revelation of that gospel which was hidden in the Old Testament, hidden in mystery form, and which the prophets themselves did not fully see or understand (cf. I Peter 1:9-12; II Peter 1:19-21; II Peter 3:15-16; Ephesians 1:13; 3:1-11). The gospel of our salvation, or the mystery of Christ and His church, was hidden in God in Christ from the foundation of the world, and was veiled in the Scriptures of the prophets, under symbol, type, shadow, prophecy, and promise, until it was brought out and manifested by revelation in Christ and then interpreted by Paul. Hence, Paul saw that the Holy Scriptures of the prophets had the gospel in them, even though Old Testament Israel and the prophets did not fully perceive such. Paul's gospel answers the cry, pleadings, and questions of Job for a mediator, reconciler, and redeemer, one who could justify man before God.

Note the gospel shadowed forth in the Old Testament:
- The gospel preached to Abraham; he believed it (Galatians 3:7-9).
- The gospel preached to Israel; they rejected it (Hebrews 4:2).
- The gospel in Genesis 3:15 (The seed of the woman; to Adam and Eve).
- The gospel shadowed forth in sacrifice (Genesis 3:21-24).
- The gospel shadowed forth in the five offerings; then in the offering of Isaac (Genesis 15; Genesis 22).
- The gospel of the lamb of God to Israel (Exodus 12).
- The gospel administration in the tabernacle of Moses (Exodus 25-40).
- The gospel in the five Levitical offerings (Leviticus 1-7).
- The gospel in the Day of Atonement (Leviticus 16).
- The gospel in the cleansing of the leper and leprosy laws (Leviticus 13-14).

- The gospel of the red heifer (Numbers 19).
- The Gospel in the brazen serpent (Numbers 21).

The gospel was indeed promised beforehand by God through the prophets in the Scriptures, in type, symbol, prophecy, and promise. The distinctive thought of "the promise" is developed more fully in Romans 4:13-25 (refer to notes).

Verse 3: *"...Concerning his Son Jesus Christ our Lord, which was made of the seed of David according to the flesh..."*

A. **The gospel of God "concerning his Son, Christ Jesus our Lord"**
   Please note: if the gospel of God was promised in the Old Testament times by the prophets in the Holy Scriptures, then verse 3 states the fact that this gospel concerned the Son of God, Christ Jesus our Lord. Thus:
- The gospel was in the prophetic writings.
- The gospel concerned the Son of God.

All God's thoughts toward mankind center in *His Son,* Jesus Christ. Outside of His Son, God has nothing to say to man, nothing good for man—no gospel. God spoke of times past in and by the prophets, but in these last days, He has spoken to us in the person of His Son (Hebrews 1:1-3). The prophets *foretold* the "Good News," even though they may not have understood the full significance of their own prophetic utterances. The Son was the "Good News" *personified.* Hence, Paul calls it "the Gospel of God" in verse 1, but as it concerned God's Son, Jesus Christ, he can truly call it "the gospel of His Son" in verse 9, or "the gospel of Christ" in verse 15. Any gospel that does not concern Jesus Christ is not *the* gospel. Philip began at the same Scriptures and preached from Isaiah 53 concerning Jesus (see Acts 8:5, 26-40). The gospel sets forth the Lord Jesus Christ (Acts 2:36).

"His Son" – Sonship (cf. John 3:16-17; Romans 1:4)
"Christ" – Messiahship, the Anointed One (John 1:41-42; marginal)
"Jesus" – Savior, His humanity (Matthew 1:21-23) (The name of His sinless humanity)
"Lord" – Divinity (cf. Acts 2:34-36; Psalm 110:1; Philippians 2:9-11) (On the basis of His humiliation, He is made Lord.)

B. **"Made of the seed of David"**

In this clause is set forth the fact of His virgin birth. Note the Old Testament progressive revelation of the Gospel concerning Jesus Christ as the promised seed. Covenant man was involved in the covenants of God and salvation.

- The Seed of the Woman (a woman, virgin birth); Adamiac Covenant (Genesis 3:15)
- The Seed of Shem (a man); Noahic Covenant (Genesis 9:26)
- The Seed of Abraham, Isaac, and Jacob; Abrahamic Covenant (Genesis 22:16-18; Galatians 3:16)
- The Seed of Israel (a nation); Mosaic Covenant in this nation (Genesis 28:13-15)
- The Seed of Judah (Genesis 49:8-10; John 7:42)
- The Seed of David (a house); Davidic Covenant; messianic name also (Genesis 49:8-10 with II Samuel 7; Psalm 89)
- The Seed of the Virgin (a virgin woman) (Isaiah 7:14; 9:6-9); that seed, which is Christ (Galatians 3:16, 29)

Note the word "made" used here. It literally means "to become," or "fashioned" (John 1:14). Christ assumed a human body with human limitations (Matthew 1:1).

David was a prophet in his generation (Acts 2:25-36), as well as king, and uttered some of the most remarkable prophecies concerning Jesus Christ our Lord. The gospel in the Psalms is a revelation of the Spirit of God concerning Jesus Christ, foretold hundreds of years before His birth. David was the first of the kings of Judah to receive the covenant of Messiah, the Davidic Covenant, which was an unconditional and unbreakable covenant that the Messiah would be born of David's line. Jesus Christ is the *seed* of David (His humanity; Matthew 1:1) and Jesus Christ is also David's *Lord* (His deity; Psalm 110:1; Matthew 22:24; Acts 2:34-36). As such He is the *root* and *offspring* of David (Revelation 22:16; I Timothy 3:16). Humanity and deity are thus seen in the seed-line promises. He is the King of Kings and Lord of Lords and receives the throne of David (Luke 1:31-33).

C. **"Made of the seed of David according to the flesh"**

This is the Pauline way of stating the doctrine of the virgin birth. If the gospel of God concerning His Son is to be declared, then the whole fact of the gospel depends on the virgin birth.

Paul's gospel will not contradict the four gospels and the historic facts of Jesus of Nazareth. Note these Scriptures:

- "...*Made* of a woman; *made* under the law..." (Galatians 4:4).
- *Made* in the likeness of men, *fashion* of a man (Philippians 2:6-8).
- "...The *likeness* of sinful flesh..." (though not sinful) (Romans 8:3).
- "God was *manifest* in the flesh..." (I Timothy 3:16).
- "...Flesh and blood, he also himself likewise took part of the same..." (Hebrews 2:14).
- "...A *body* hast Thou prepared Me..." (Hebrews 10:5).
- "...Jesus...*made* a little lower [as man was made lower than the angels in verse 7] than the angels for the suffering of death..." (Hebrews 2:9).

In the Greek, *ginomai* means "to become; begin to be" (Galatians 4:4; Philippians 2:6-8). This refers to His humanity, not His deity. Thus, God the Father, by the overshadowing of the Holy Spirit (Matthew 1:21-23), placed the "divine seed" in the womb of the Virgin Mary (Luke 1:31-33) with the "divine blood" (Acts 20:28) in that seed, and Mary supplied the flesh and bones body for the Son of God. In this manner, Jesus Christ was "made of the seed of David" according to the flesh; that is, as pertaining to His physical body.

This sets forth the doctrine of the eternal and pre-incarnate Christ, as the son of the living God in His virgin birth—the incarnation. Jesus had a Jewish body but not Jewish blood!

Verses 1-3: *Summary*

Thus far:

- The gospel was promised in the Prophets.
- The gospel concerned God's Son.
- The gospel involved in its beginning the virgin birth of this eternal and pre-existent Son.

Verse 4:   "...*And declared to be the Son of God with power, according to the spirit of holiness, by the resurrection from the dead...*"

A.   "Declared to be the Son of God"
     (Note verses 3 and 4 of the Amplified New Testament.) Jesus Christ is

declared to be the Son of God with power. This declaration sets forth His eternal sonship.

- In *eternity*, He was the *eternal* Son of God (declares His deity and pre-existence) (Hebrews 1:1-4; John 1:1-3).
- In *time*, He was the *begotten* Son of God (declares His humanity and His virgin birth) (Hebrews 2:9-16; John 3:16).
- On the divine side, He was the Son of God (declares His deity and divine nature).
- On the human side, He was the Son of Man (declares His humanity [as to His human nature]).

Though declared to be "the Son" in Matthew 3:17, the full declaration of that sonship was after His completed vocation by death and resurrection and ascension to the right hand of God (cf. Acts 13:32-37). He was "perfected" in His experience as the Son of Man by sufferings, though He was perfect in His character, nature, and being in regard to His divinity (cf. Hebrews 5:7-9). The resurrection declares Him to be what He is; that is, the Son of God, which identifies Him as deity.

B. "Son of God"

This title is a declaration of the deity and co-equality of the man, Jesus Christ, with His father, God. Many of the Jews accepted Jesus as the Messiah, the Christ, but if they confessed Him as the Son of God they were cast out of the synagogue. This was counted as blasphemy, for *sonship* made Jesus equal with God (cf. John 8; John 4; 9:22, 34-38; 10:27-30; 31-38; 5:17-18).

The truth of His sonship only came by revelation to the human heart. It was for this confession of divine sonship that the religious leaders caused Jesus to be crucified (Mark 14:61-64; Matthew 27:40; John 19:7; Matthew 16:13-17). This sonship involves more especially the fact that *the man* as deity is set forth as the Son of God. He was always the *eternal Son*. Here He is the *begotten* Son, in regard to His humanity.

The four gospels set Him forth as:
- Son of David (Matthew)
- Son of Man (Mark)
- Son of Adam (Luke)
- Son of God (John)

Paul's declaration and distinctive gospel concerns divine sonship. Eternal sonship and the Father's eternal purpose in the Son are declared. This revelation to Paul had its roots in his conversion on the road to Damascus (Acts 9:1-21). Thus:

"Declared" – (Marked out, determined):

- He is declared to be the Son (Romans 1:4).
- He is declared to be the Priest (Hebrews 5:5-6).
- He is declared to be both Lord and Christ (Acts 2:34-36).

"With power" – (Greek: *Dunamei*; also, "divine ability.") This is the power of the gospel (cf. verse 16). All power in heaven and in earth is given to Him as the Son of God (Matthew 28:19-20). Note further the times when His sonship was declared:

- In the virgin birth, His incarnation (Luke 1:30-33)
- In His eternal sonship (Hebrews 1; Hebrews 7)
- At the river Jordan, in His baptism (Matthew 3:15-17)
- At His transfiguration (Matthew 17:1-8)
- In His resurrection and ascension to the throne of God, far above all heavens, far above all things (Ephesians 1:19-23; Philippians 2:9; Romans 6:4; with Acts 13:32-37; with Psalm 2 and Hebrews 1)

This sonship especially involved the *resurrection*: "…Thou art My Son, this day have I *begotten* thee" (Acts 13:33). He was begotten as the firstborn and the firstfruits in resurrection (Revelation 1:5; Colossians 1:8). The Father's great power was manifest in the resurrection of Christ from the dead and when He set Him at His own right hand, far above all things. The Father bestowed on the Son "all power and authority," both in heaven and earth, in the resurrection and ascension to glory. It is on this basis that the command to preach the gospel to the entire world was given (Mark 16:15-20; Hebrews 1:3). The resurrection was the *seal* of His eternal and begotten sonship.

C. "According to the spirit of holiness"

As the Lord Jesus, Christ was absolutely holy and without sin. He was possessed of and by the Spirit of Holiness. He was holy in birth, life, thought, words, and deeds as the perfect man—God manifest in the flesh. Nothing could hinder the power of the resurrection because of His unsullied, untainted holiness of spirit, character, and being. He was raised by the Father, by the Spirit of Holiness (Romans 8:11; I Peter 3:18; I Timothy 3:16; Romans 6:4). This portion of this Scripture perhaps refers to Jesus' own spirit and also to the Holy Spirit. It speaks of His absolute sinlessness and absolute holiness before the Father.

These are the wonderful titles of the Holy Spirit:
- The Holy Spirit is called the Spirit of Truth because He brings us into the truth of Jesus.
- The Holy Spirit is called the Spirit of Christ because He brings to us that same anointing.
- The Holy Spirit is called the Spirit of Holiness because He brings to us the very holiness of God Himself, etc.

D. **"By the resurrection from the dead"**
   Note the great doctrines alluded to in these verses (cf. Acts 13:32-37 with Psalm 2 and previous comments). There are eight profound facts noted here in the gospel:
   1) "Concerning his Son" (divine and eternal sonship)
   2) "Jesus" (His humanity, His earthly name, saviorship)
   3) "Christ" (His anointing for ministry, messiahship)
   4) "Lord" (His deity, glorified and made Lord, Jehovah)
   5) "Made of the seed of David" (His incarnation or virgin birth, Davidic Covenant, messiahship also here)
   6) "Declared to be the Son of God with power" (deity and omnipotence)
   7) "By the resurrection from the dead" (resurrection, the seal of God on His Son)
   8) "According to the spirit of holiness" (His spiritual nature, holiness of character, though human as well as divine)

Verse 5: *"...By whom we have received grace and apostleship, for obedience to the faith among all nations, for his name..."*

A. **"By whom we have received grace"** (cf. John 1:14-17)
   The gospel of God in His Son is the gospel of *grace*. It is the undeserved, unearned, and unmerited favor of God bestowed upon man, the guilty one, though Christ, who is the grace of God personified. The law was given by Moses, but grace and truth came by Jesus Christ. Grace is God's kindness and love in action toward fallen man, through Christ

(Ephesians 2:4-9). (Refer to comments on "grace" in Romans 3:24; 4:4; 5:1-2.)

B. **"And apostleship"** (cf. verse 1)

"Apostleship" means "called to be a sent one in grace, to declare the grace of God amongst the nations" (Matthew 28:19-20). Law was given to one nation. *Grace* is declared to all nations. This ministry of apostleship in the body of Christ is linked with grace, as an expression of grace (the grace-gifts) (cf. Romans 12:1-6; Ephesians 4:1-16; I Peter 4:10) (grace and apostleship) (Ephesians 3:8).

C. **"For obedience to the faith among all nations"**

True grace experienced will deliver mankind from the disobedience in which he lives in, through the fall of Adam, and will bring us back to the obedience from which Adam fell (cf. Hebrews 5:9). Christ came to bring us back to obedience to the will of God. This is obedience of the faith (cf. Romans 16:26). The subject of "obedience" is taken up more fully in the chapter on the "Two Adams" (cf. Romans 5:12-21).

- All nations receive the gospel of grace.
- All nations are to come into obedience.

D. **"The faith"** (Acts 6:7; I Timothy 4:1-4)

That is, the full sum and total revelation of the gospel of truth as in Christ. "The faith once delivered to the saints" (Jude 3).

E. **"For his name"** (cf. Acts 9:15)

"For His name" means the redemptive name of God in our Lord Jesus Christ.

Verse 6: *"...Among whom are ye also the called of Jesus Christ..."*

"Among whom are ye also the called of Jesus Christ" (Greek: *Kleetos* means "called, invited")

- "Paul...called to be an apostle..." (verse 1).
- "...[C]alled of Jesus Christ..." (verse 6).

- "...[C]alled to be saints..." (verse 7). This is the greatest invitation ever given (cf. I Corinthians 1:2) and is made possible by the Holy Spirit. "Saints" mean "holy ones." The words "saint," "sanctify," "sanctification," "holy," and "hallow" are all translations of the same root word. The root idea is that of "separation from" and "separation unto."

Verse 7:   "...To all that be in Rome, beloved of God, called to be saints: Grace to you and peace from God our Father, and the Lord Jesus Christ."

A.   "To all that be in Rome, beloved of God, called to be saints"
Though Paul did not find the church at Rome, he had a great burden to share with its members that which had been given to him (cf. 1:9-15; 15:22-29). The church was composed of Jews and Gentiles. "Called to be saints" means that we are "holy ones"; made possible by the Spirit of Holiness in us.

B.   "Grace to you and peace"
(Cf. apostolic greetings, especially of Paul, in I Corinthians 1:3; II Corinthians 1:2; Galatians 1:3; Ephesians 1:2; Philippians 1:2; Colossians 1:2; I Thessalonians 1:1; I Peter 1:2; II Peter 1:2; Revelation 1:4) Each of Paul's epistles, and also the writings of Peter and John, have "grace and peace" in the salutation.
- "Grace" – The Greek salutation
- "Peace" – The Jewish salutation (Vincent)
In I Timothy 1:2, II Timothy 1:2, and Titus 1:4, the greetings are "grace, mercy, and peace." There is no peace apart from grace. It is the grace of God expressed in Christ that makes peace available with God. The truths of grace through faith, peace with God through Christ, and faith-righteousness are developed more fully as the epistle unfolds (Romans 5:1-2).

C.   "From God our Father, and the Lord Jesus Christ"
- The Father, our Father (Matthew 6:6-9). He becomes our Father only by new birth and is the source of grace and peace.
- The Son, the Lord Jesus Christ (full triune name, interpreted). He is the channel of grace and peace, by the Spirit. The Father has nothing to say to man apart from Christ. The Father's entire heart pours through the channel of His Son.

Introduction (Romans 1:8-17)

Journey to Rome (Romans 1:8-12)

Verse 8: *"First, I thank my God through Jesus Christ for you all, that your faith is spoken of throughout the whole world."*

Thanksgiving (cf. I Corinthians 1:4)
Paul thanks God through Christ for the Roman believers. Their faith was spoken of throughout the known world. We have no record of how this church was planted, except that it was possibly planted through some of the Jewish converts from the first Pentecost (Acts 2:10). Their *faith* was a living testimony. Obedience to the faith was evidenced in them (Romans 1:5).

Verses 9-10: *"For God is my witness, whom I serve with my spirit in the gospel of his Son, that without ceasing I make mention of you always in my prayers; making request, if by any means now at length I might have a prosperous journey by the will of God to come unto you."*

Paul expressed the fact of his continual prayers for the church at Rome and his longing to come to them in the will of God. Note that this epistle was written from Corinth and sent to Rome by Phebe (Romans 15:22-32; 16:1-5a). By comparing Acts 18:1-4, 18-19, 24-28 and Romans 16:3-5, it seems evident that Aquila and Priscilla were Jews of Rome, had a church in their house, were helpers of Paul, and had, no doubt, returned to Rome by this time, as they were also tent-makers.

A. **Verse 9**
(Note: Romans 1:9 [cf. Romans 9:1; Acts 27:23; I Thessalonians 3:10])

B. **Verse 10** (cf. Romans 15:14-33)
For a long time Paul had desired to go to Rome, but this had to be in *God's own time* even though it was *God's will.* He had to go to Jerusalem with certain contributions for the poor there, given by the Macedonian saints and the saints of Achaia, and then he planned on going to Spain via Rome. But note how God overruled all things and directed Paul into His

perfect will and time in going to Rome (Acts 19:21-22). Paul purposed in spirit (by the Holy Spirit) to pass through Macedonia and Achaia, to go to Jerusalem and then to Rome (Acts 18:1-3, 16, and 17-25). On the journey to Jerusalem, as seen in Acts 21:1-4, 7-20, disciples of Tyre said to Paul, through the Spirit, that he should not go to Jerusalem. At the house of the evangelist, Phillip, the prophet, Agabus, came from Jerusalem and foretold Paul's binding at Jerusalem and his delivery over to the hands of the Gentiles. The disciples besought him not to go, but Paul had the witness in his spirit (Acts 20:22-24) that he must go there.

At Jerusalem, he entered into a vow of purification and was delivered into the hands of the Jews and the Gentiles (Acts 21-22). He was held in custody and testified over a period of time to rulers and kings (Acts 23-25, 16 with 9:15). Paul also appealed to Caesar (Acts 25:11-12; 26:32).

In Acts 27-28, we have the account of Paul's trip to Rome and the shipwreck. The angel of God told Paul that he would be brought before Caesar (Acts 27:23-25). In Acts 28:14-16, we read, "And when we came to Rome..." His prayer and theirs were answered. He had "a *prosperous journey in the will of God*," via a shipwreck, and in spite of Jews and Gentiles, kings and rulers. God brought him to Rome in His own time.

It may be questioned as to whether Paul was in the will of God by going to Rome. Did Paul have a ministry to the Gentiles, yet really insist on trying to minister to the Jews, or, in other words, "Jews for Jesus"? (Refer to the *Book of Acts* by Kevin Conner concerning Paul's journey.)

In man's eyes, it was not a *prosperous* journey, nor in *the will of God*. But people were blessed at Mileta, which may not have been otherwise. Paul was delivered from the serpent, and God, in Christ, was glorified. It was truly a prosperous journey in the will of God, from a heavenly viewpoint. Rulers were testified to as well. From Rome, Paul wrote a number of "Prison Epistles" in the providence of God, which may not have been written while Paul was in constant travel in the gospel. It was a "forced vacation" (in God!).

Thus, God deals with His saints:
- Paul in prison writes letters to the churches.
- David in the wilderness writes the Psalms.
- John in Patmos receives and writes the Revelation.
- Moses in Sinai writes the Pentateuch.

A careful study of the Scriptures dealing with Paul's call and its progressive outworking in his life and ministry make it clear that Paul was not only in the will of God, but God set him forth as a pattern for following the example of the Lord Jesus Christ in suffering patiently. Paul followed in Christ's steps.

1) **Acts 9:15-20.** This is Paul's initial call to God's will. He was chosen to bear God's name before kings, Jews, and Gentiles, and to suffer for that name. Wherever Paul would go, this was his will in God and the principles behind his entire life.

2) **Acts 19:21-22.** Paul knew the will of God for himself. He was aware of trouble. Paul purposed in the Spirit to go to Jerusalem.

   - During his journey through the churches, a large collection was taken for the needs of the poor saints at Jerusalem. (Refer to I Corinthians 16:1; II Corinthians 8 and Romans 15:25.) Paul considered his duty and responsibility to take this to Jerusalem (Romans 15:25-27).

   - In Acts 18:21, it is believed that the Feast of Passover was approaching, and, for this reason, Paul felt additional responsibility to go to Jerusalem when he did.

   - Paul adds that after Jerusalem, "I *must* see Rome." He had really been praying about this—*if* it was God's will (cf. Romans 1:10). Paul felt assured that it *was* God's will.

3) **Acts 18:1-3.** Paul knew Priscilla and Aquila, who recently had come from Rome, and he was aware of the treatment of Jews under Claudius.

4) **Acts 18:16-25.** In Acts 18:21, he purposed to keep the feast that was at Jerusalem, when many Jews would be there. He seemed willing to return to Ephesus.

5) **Acts 21:1-20.** In Acts 21:4, disciples told Paul through the Spirit that he should not go up to Jerusalem. In verses 9-11, Agabus, a Judean prophet, took Paul's girdle, bound his own hands and feet, and said that this would happen to the man who owned that girdle and that he would be delivered into the hands of the Gentiles. Agabus was a proven prophet, as seen in Acts 11:27-30. Here, Agabus was here foretelling what would happen to Paul in Jerusalem. This was a witness to Paul's spirit and a confirmation of his original calling. This was the third witness to date. In Acts 21:13, Paul asked them if they meant to break his heart and make him weep. He

confessed that he was ready to go to Jerusalem and die, if needed, for the name of Jesus. Verse 14 indicates that they desired the will of God to be done. Paul felt under constraint of the Spirit to go to Jerusalem. He was bound in the Spirit.

6) **Acts 20:22-24.** Paul was bound in the Spirit, under divine constraint. He was under a continuing direction from the Lord. He did not know exactly what would befall him, but he knew bonds and imprisonment awaited him. The Spirit had already told this to Paul. Paul would not waver. It was a chance for him to testify the grace of God. Thus, Paul was made to realize that he was not just going to take an offering up to Jerusalem, but to be a witness there also. Note again in Acts 21:8-11, God did not use the four daughters of Philip who prophesied, but sent a prophet from Judea to Paul on this matter.

7) **Acts 21:18, 27.** The Lord warned Paul that they would not receive his testimony at this feast.

8) **Acts 25:11-12.** Paul's dual citizenship had its advantages also.

9) **Acts 23:11.** The Lord had told Paul that he would bear witness of Him at Rome.

10) **Acts 26:32; 27:23-26.** Paul appealed to Caesar. God was overruling in everything; otherwise Paul would have been set free. The Lord appeared to Paul and confirmed His will to witness in Rome. These rulers and kings were also tools in the hand of the Lord to send Paul to Rome.

11) **Acts 28:14.** And so Paul went toward Rome.

12) **Acts 28:23-24.** Paul ministered in Rome to the Jews. Paul prayed that he might come in the will of God, with joy. His miraculous preservation in the shipwreck testifies to God's preserving power for Paul to witness at Rome (cf. Romans 1:10-12 and 15:14-33). All things worked together for good (Romans 8:28).

A remarkable comparison between Jesus and Paul is seen in the following (Paul was a pattern believer) (I Timothy 1:16):

- Jesus and Paul hallowed the name of God.
- Jesus and Paul prayed that God's will might be done.
- Jesus and Paul preached the kingdom of God.
- Jesus and Paul steadfastly went up to Jerusalem, even though both knew suffering would come.

- Jesus and Paul both had disciples plead with them not to go to Jerusalem.
- Jesus and Paul were both apprehended by their own nation, and then turned over to the Gentiles.
- Jesus was scourged. Paul was about to be scourged. Both were bound.
- Jesus and Paul stood before kings and testified.
- Jesus and Paul were bound and slain under the Romans.
- Jesus and Paul went to Jerusalem during a feast.

Verse 11:   *"For I long to see you, that I may impart unto you some spiritual gift, to the end ye may be established..."*

A. **Paul expresses his desire for coming to Rome.**
    Here Paul expressed his desire for coming to Rome, though not as a tourist, or sightseer, etc. He desired to *impart* to the saints an impartation of that which he had received of the Lord.

B. **"Spiritual gift" (Greek: Charisma)**
    Spiritual gifts are imparted through apostolic ministry, or the laying on of hands (cf. I Corinthians 12:1-11; II Timothy 1:6-7, 14; I Timothy 4:12-16; I Timothy 1:8, 5:22).
    The *charisma* may be spiritual gifts or ministry by way of the Word of Christ and the anointing of the Spirit. Paul in the Spirit longed to impart "spirituals" to the saints at Rome. Even though Paul recognized that the church at Rome had "spirituals," meaning gifts and ministries (Romans 12:1-8), he longed to supply that which was lacking.

C. **"To the end ye may be established"**
    - Established in the present truth (cf. II Peter 1:12)
    - Established in the gospel (I Thessalonians 3:2)

    "Established" means "to make strong, to set or make fast." Saints need to be strengthened, stabilized. Saints can only receive through the *charisma* (fellowship and fruit).

Verse 12: *"...That is, that I may be comforted together with you by the mutual faith both of you and me."*

Not only did Paul want to impart to them, but he also desired to receive from them. There was a mutual comfort and strength for Paul and the saints. In helping and strengthening them, he also would be helped and strengthened because both he and they were linked together in a mutual faith.

Paul thanked God and took courage when he saw the brethren. No true minister of God can help but be blessed himself by being a blessing and help to others (cf. Acts 28:15). Note that "faith" in Romans 1:5, 8, 12, and Titus 1:4 is a *mutual* faith; a faith shared together in the same Lord.

Testimony to Rome (Romans 1:13-17)

Verse 13: *"Now I would not have you ignorant, brethren, that oftentimes I purposed to come unto you, (but was let hitherto,) that I might have some fruit among you also, even as among other Gentiles."*

Here Paul desires that the believers not be ignorant that he had often times purposed to come to them, but he was "let" (hindered) previously. (Refer to comments on verses 10 and 15:23.) God's *time* and God's *will* must go together.

A. **"Now I would not have you ignorant"**
   This is an expression of Paul (cf. Romans 11:25; 10:3; I Corinthians 10:3; 12:1; I Thessalonians 4:13; II Peter 3:8) and refers to sins of ignorance amongst the believers. God permitted various things to hinder Paul. He felt restraints of God on him concerning going to Rome until God's perfect timing. Such restraints should not be resisted. Saints must not be ignorant of God's overall purposes for His ministers.

B. **"Brethren"**
   Christ's true brethren are those that do the will of God.
   - Compare natural brethren, the Jews, after the flesh.
   - Compare spiritual brethren, Jews and Gentiles, after the new birth, the Spirit.

C. "Oftentimes I purposed"

"Oftentimes I purposed" *to come to Rome.*

D. "Let hitherto"

Paul was hindered; that is, restrained by God's sovereignty and use of circumstances and people (delayed at Ceasarea, shipwrecked, etc.). Sometimes God hinders, sometimes the devil hinders, and sometimes people hinder—yet over and above all God's purpose and timing are in it.

E. "That I might have some fruit among you also, even as among other Gentiles"

Fruit means fruit of spiritual travail—souls born again and brought into Christian maturity (cf. Romans 16:5). The "fruit" of Paul's ministry was the churches he had founded and the saints that had been established. He was an Apostle to the Gentiles (cf. Romans 15-16).

Verse 14:   *"I am debtor both to the Greeks, and to the Barbarians; both to the wise, and to the unwise."*

Please note in verses 14-16:

- "I am debtor..." (verse 14).
- "...I am ready to preach the gospel..." (verse 15).
- "I am not ashamed of the gospel of Christ..." (verse 16).

The gospel was given to Paul, and he felt a charge, an obligation, to discharge to all men. It was a duty to perform and a debt to pay (Amplified New Testament)—a debt of love to God and man. He owed it to the lost. Spiritual privileges bring spiritual responsibility to preach the gospel to every creature.

A. "Greeks"

"Greeks" means the wise, the Hellenistic civilization that was refined (intelligent, cultured, and refined).

B. "Barbarians"

"Barbarians" means the unwise, the non-Hellenistic (the non-thinking, the uncultured).

Verse 15:   *"So, as much as in me is, I am ready to preach the gospel to you that are at Rome also."*

(Refer to comments on Romans 1:8-13.)

Verse 16:   *"For I am not ashamed of the gospel of Christ: for it is the power of God unto salvation to every one that believeth; to the Jew first, and also to the Greek."*

A.   **"For I am not ashamed of the gospel of Christ"**
This was Paul's testimony. He was unashamed (cf. Romans 10:11). If we are ashamed of Him in our day, He will be ashamed of us in that day (Psalm 40:9, 10; Mark 8:38). Shame makes one to disassociate himself from any reproach concerning the gospel (Luke 9:26; II Timothy 1:8, 12, 16; Hebrews 11:16; Romans 5:5) (the reproach of the Cross, glad tidings, the gospel of the Anointed One).

B.   **"It is the power of God unto salvation"**
(Greek: *Dunamis.*) (Cf. Romans 1:4.) The gospel is the dynamite of God unto salvation, full salvation, and for deliverance of the spirit, soul, and body (I Corinthians 1:18). Salvation is based on the ability of God, which negates self-ability to save. ("Salvation" in the Greek is *soteriology.*)

C.   **"Unto salvation to every one that believeth"**
The great requisite to experience this gospel of salvation is believing; that is, faith. It is not available to anyone outside of faith. It is available to all by faith (Matthew 28:19; Mark 16:15-20; Luke 24:47-49).

D.   **"Believeth"**
This is not mental assent, but personal trust, committment, surrender, and complete reliance on the Lord Jesus (Romans 10:9-10, Amplified New Testament). Faith is passive. Believing is active. The ability of God is fully delegated and expressed through His Son by the *gospel* (Acts 1:8).

E.   **"To the Jew first, and also to the Greek"**
(Cf. Romans 2:9-10; Luke 2:30-32; Acts 13:26.) Paul's pattern of preaching the gospel was "to the Jew first, then to the Gentile." Synagogues were first, and then, when the Jews rejected the gospel, Paul turned to the Gentiles. (Note the *Book of Acts* by Kevin Conner.)

"To the Jew first" – (Acts 2; 11:19-21; 13:5, 15; 14:1; 17; 18:5; 19:8; 21:20-21; Romans 10:12; I Thessalonians 2:14-17). Election of grace (Romans 11:4-5).

"Then to the Gentile" – (Acts 9:15; 13:42-48; 15:15-18; 14:2, 5, 27; 18:6; 21:11, 19-25; 28:28). The Gentiles will hear. The Jews counted themselves unworthy of eternal life; thus, God turned to the Gentiles.

Verse 17: *"For therein is the righteousness of God revealed from faith to faith: as it is written, The just shall live by faith."*

A. **"For therein is the righteousness of God revealed"**

This is the whole theme of Romans—faith-righteousness. The gospel sets forth the righteousness of God; that is, faith-righteousness. The relation of being right into which God puts the man whom believes. This was revealed and unveiled in the gospel—God's righteousness and His righteous demands of His creatures.

B. **"From faith to faith"**

"Which springs from faith and which faith receives" (Conybeare & Howson). The righteousness of God is a faith-righteousness, which begins in faith and proceeds to faith—from faith to faith, as from glory to glory and grace to grace.

- Faith towards God (Hebrews 11:6; 6:1)
- Faith towards the Lord Jesus Christ (Acts 20:21)

Thus, going from "faith to faith" may be briefly set forth as follows:

- Saving Faith—unto salvation (Receiving the Word [Ephesians 2:5-8])
- Fruit of Faith—obedience (Obeying the Word [Galatians 5:22, 23])
- Gift of Faith (Speaking the Word [I Corinthians 12:5-9])
- Doctrinal Faith (Teaching the Word [Jude 3])
- Spirit of Faith (The Word Made Flesh [John 1:14; Galatians 3:25-27; II Corinthians 4:13])

C. **"As it is written, The just shall live by faith"**

Originally, this was written in Habakkuk 2:4, "...the just shall live by his [His] faith." This was especially prophetic of messianic times, for the law was not of faith but of works. This is the first quotation in this epistle from Old Testament Scriptures. One of the most remarkable things about Paul's distinctive ministry, and revelation is this: the laying hold of an apparently short and insignificant Scripture in the Old Testament, and, under the anointing and illumination of the Holy Spirit, unveiling untold wealth of truth hidden in that verse, of which we have an example before us.

To illustrate, the Hebrews epistle is founded in the historical and prophetic references to Melchisedec in Genesis 14 and Psalm 110. It is wonderful in its illumination, and it is brought forth by the Spirit, as Paul declares the glories of the priesthood of Christ Jesus.

The same is true of Habakkuk 2:4 (cf. also whole chapters of the Old Testament are interpreted in one verse in the New Testament and the converse is true as well. [John 1:14; 2:20 etc.]). It is worthy to note that before Paul launches into the "gospel of righteousness in Christ," he had a *revelation* text from Old Testament Scripture on which the whole structure was built. The Old Testament shadowed and prophesied the gospel, but it was not brought out to light, nor the mystery fully seen until it was revealed to the holy apostles and prophets by the Spirit (Ephesians 3:1-11; Romans 16:25-27). If the "gospel of righteousness" is to be revealed, then it must be in harmony with and founded upon the Old Testament revelation. It must be the fulfillment of such, and thus, Paul uses this verse to prove, reveal, and unveil the fact that the Old Testament foretold a coming of faith-righteousness, in contrast to the law and works-righteousness. All of this is Amplified in the following chapters of Romans. Hence, the faith-righteousness set forth is not contrary to the Old Testament Scripture and revelation, but is that which they pointed to, that of which the Law and the Prophets prophesied (Matthew 5:17-18; 11:13; Romans 3:21).

Romans 10:3 (Amplified New Testament)
- Right speaking (word)
- Right thinking (thought)
- Right living (deed) (equal to righteousness)

Righteousness is equal to right standing with God (E.W. Kenyon, *Two Kinds of Righteousness*). Thus, we have two aspects of righteousness:
1) Judicial righteousness (Matthew 6:33).

2) Experiential righteousness (Matthew 5:6). The external or experiential righteousness is evidence of the internal or imputed righteousness (Matthew 5:20, 21; 5:6).

The use of the word "just" in this verse is the first use of the word in Romans. It is developed more fully in Romans 5, which is concerning justification. Again, let it be noted how this verse of Habakkuk 2:4 becomes the *foundation stone* for three (or two) of Paul's epistles in the New Testament.

The Scripture, "the just shall live by faith," is quoted three times in the New Testament. The glory of this is that these epistles are built on a part for emphasis. Please note these *three* epistles ("In the mouth of two or three witnessing Scriptures shall every word be established" [Paraphrased]).

"The *Just*" – Romans 1:17c (the truth of *justification* in Christ)
"Shall *Live*" – Galatians 3:11 (the truth of *life* in Christ)
"By *Faith*" – Hebrews 10:38 (the truth of *faith* in Christ)

D. **Verses 16-17: Key Verses**

Verses 16 and 17 are rightly declared to be the key verses of the book of Romans, the gospel according to Paul. It is:

- The Gospel of Christ
- The Gospel of Power
- The Gospel of Salvation
- The Gospel of Righteousness
- The Gospel of Faith ("believing" [Amplified New Testament] [three-fold])
- The Gospel of Justification and of the Just
- The Gospel of Life

A proper understanding of the significance of the words set forth here will be a *key* to the unlocking of the epistle. Christ's power unto salvation is set forth in the gospel. The opposite of all that is listed above is set forth in the fact that man is:

- Lost (in need of salvation)
- Helpless (in need of power)
- Unrighteous (in need of righteousness)

- Unbelieving (in need of faith)
- Unjust (in need of justification)
- Dead (in need of life)

The gospel—the "glad tidings" —sets forth the *answer* to man's *need*. It also involves the questions of the age:

- How then can the lost be saved (Luke 19:10),
- How then can the helpless find power,
- How then can the unrighteous be made righteous before God (Job 15:14; Romans 3:10),
- How then can the unbelieving man find faith (Romans 10:17),
- How then can the unjust be made just before God (Job 25:4, 9:2),
- How then can the dead man receive life (Job 14:14; Galatians 3:21; Ephesians 2:1)?

This is set forth in Romans and becomes the foundational verses on which the whole structure of Romans is built.
1) Man is set forth as lost, helpless, unrighteousness, unjust, unbelieving, and dead (Romans 1:18-32; Romans 2; Romans 3; Romans 7).
2) Man is set forth as in faith-righteousenss, justified, in life, and in salvation through the gospel of Christ (Romans 4; Romans 5; Romans 6; Romans 8; Romans 10).

It is here that the questions of Job are answered, "How can man be justified before God?" (Job 25:4; 9:2). Paul answers Job's questions.
- Just (Job 25:4); Justification (Job 9:2); Righteous (Job 15:4)?
- Mediator (Job 16:21; 9:32-33); Priesthood
- Clean (Job 25:4; 14:4); the Virgin Birth or Incarnation
- Redeemer (Job 19:25-27); Resurrection, Reconciliation

It is the gospel of Christ that answers these age-long questions in the person of Christ. Christ is the Son of God, the only man born of a woman who is clean, the righteous and the just One. Only by faith in Him can man, unclean and unrighteous, be clean and justified in God's sight. Man can be justified, made righteous before God, but only in and through the Lord Jesus Christ. Job longed for a mediator, a daysman, to plead his cause, to come between himself and God. Who could it be? Where could one be found? Not amongst the angels or the sons of man or the saints. Who could plead with God for man? Not God? Not man? It brought forth a cry for a go-between, a redeemer, one having the nature of God and the nature of man, a righteous and just one who could stand between God and man and lay his hands on both. Romans sets forth the One who is the answer, the Lord Jesus Christ, the Son of David, the Son of God and the Son of Man—the righteous and the just One (Job 9:32-33; 16:21; 19:25-27; I Timothy 2:5 [Amplified New Testament, Amplified Old Testament]).

E. **"Righteousness"**
Righteouness here means "uprightness, a right standing with God." This then is Paul's gospel—the burden of it. "My gospel," he calls it. How then can man be in right standing with God? Paul answers—the gospel of Christ...for *therein* is the *righteousness of God revealed.*

G. Raymond Carlson (*Romans*, Teacher's Manual) says:
1) The source of the gospel (verse 1)
2) The dynamics of the gospel—"the power of God"
3) The aim of the gospel—"unto salvation"
4) The extent of the gospel—"to everyone"
5) The condition of the gospel—"that believeth"
6) The reason for the gospel—"the just shall live by faith" (p. 6)

F. **"Unto salvation"**
This is a great and all-inclusive redemptive Word. It involves God's work from justification unto glorification (I Peter 1:5) and deliverance from the penalty, the power, and the presence of sin. We are saved, are being saved, and shall be saved. It includes justification, sancitfication, and glorification. Read these three aspects of "full salvation" also in I Corinthians 1:30, I Thessalonians 1:9-10 and Titus 2:11-13. Salvation belongs to the Lord (Psalm 3:8; Jonah 2:9).

We were saved; released from penalty of sin—*justified* (Luke 7:50; Acts 16:30,31; I Corinthians 1:18; II Corinthians 2:15; II Timothy 1:9).
We are being saved; saved from the power of sin—*sanctification* (Romans 8:2; 6:14; II Corinthians 3:18; Galatians 2:20; 4:19; 5:16; Philipians 2:12-13).
We shall be saved—*glorification* (Romans 13:11; Ephesians 5:25-27; Philipians 1:6; I Peter 1:3-5; I John 3:1-3).

G. **"Righteousness of God"**
This phrase occurs seven times in Romans (Romans 1:17; 3:5; 3:21,22,25,26; 10:3). It is God-provided and imputed (Psalm 32:2; Romans 3:22; 4:3, 8, 21-25; Philippians 3:9).

Righteousness Needed By the Gentiles (Romans 1:18-32)

Romans 1:18-32 begins in earnest to set forth the exceeding sinfulness, or unrighteousness, of man and the great need for righteousness.

Given Up to Uncleanness (Romans 1:18-24)

Verse 18: *"For the wrath of God is revealed from heaven against all ungodliness and unrighteousness of men, who hold the truth in unrighteousness. . ."*

A. **"For the wrath of God is revealed from heaven"**
Paul now begins in earnest to launch forth the condition of the unregenerate man, meaning the man outside of Christ and in need of right standing with God. This section covers Romans 1:18-32 through 3:1-20. It proves that both the Jew and Gentile are under *the wrath* of God, and it proves that *all* are under sin. Note below the use of the word "wrath":

"...[W]rath of God is revealed from heaven against..."* (Romans 1:18). Faith-righteousness is *revealed* in the gospel, and the wrath of God is *revealed* against all unrighteousness.

"...[W]rath against the *day of wrath...*"* (Romans 2:5; cf. Revelation 6:16-17).

*"...[I]ndignation and *wrath...*"* (Romans 2:8; cf. Revelation 15-16 with Revelation 14:9-11). Why is man under wrath?

*"...[T]he law worketh [produces] *wrath*, when broken"* (Romans 4:15, [paraphrased]). Man is under wrath because of the holiness and righteousness of God. All unrighteousness, which is sin, must be judged. God's righteousness, as in *the law*, must be upheld. And the law, when broken, works wrath. Violated or broken law must be judged.

This then shows:

- The *righteousness of God* is revealed (Romans 1:17).
- The *wrath of God* is revealed (Romans 1:18).
- The *love of God* is commended (Romans 5:5-8; cf. Romans 1:7, beloved in God).

Note that the word "love" is not expressly used until Romans 5:5. The key thought in Romans 1, 2, and 3 is that the *wrath* of God is against unrighteousness. God's love cannot be revealed until His holiness has been vindicated and the righteous claims of the law have been satisfied. The law produces wrath. Righteousness demands satisfaction of violated law. Holiness is God's reaction against sin, and righteousness is judgment against sin.

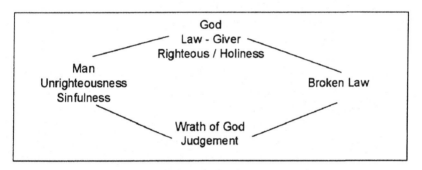

Thus, the holiness of God produces wrath because of broken law against the sinfulness of man. It is the wrath of a righteous and holy God against the sinfulness of man (John 3:17-21, 36 [Amplified New Testament]).

B. **"Against all ungodliness and unrighteousness of men, who hold the truth in unrighteousness"**

"Ungodliness" – Man is not "like God," as God intended Adam to be (Genesis 1:26).

"Unrighteousness" – means "no right standing with God, not upright."

"Suppression of the truth in unrighteousness" – Meaning "holding down the truth, suppression of the truth, or resistance of the truth." The word "hold" means "to suppress the truth." God's truth is held down. Though they know it, they suppress it. The truth is hindered or repressed.

Verse 19: *"...Because that which may be known of God is manifest in them; for God hath shewed it unto them."*

A. **"That which may be known of God"**
    There is a Creator—One knowable to all men. Man knows that there is a God. God has shown this by creation, as verse 20 also affirms.

B. **"Manifest *in* them"**
    Man knows deep inside that there is a God. Every man has this measure of light in him (John 1:9). God has set eternity in the hearts of man. A man's conscience also tells him this (witness of conscience) (Romans 2:15).

Verse 20: *"For the invisible things of him from the creation of the world are clearly seen, being understood by the things that are made, even his eternal power and Godhead; so that they are without excuse..."*

A. **"For the invisible things [persons] of him from the creation of the world are clearly seen, being understood by the things that are made, even his eternal power and Godhead"**
    Thus, the witness of:
    1) Creation – Man may know that there is a God (Romans 1:20).
    2) Conscience – Man knows intuitively that there is a God (verse 19). This is the witness of God to the Gentile world (general revelation).
    3) Scriptures – The Scriptures are a specific and special revelation that was given to the Hebrew nation.

B. **"Invisible things of him"**
    The "invisible things of Him" are the attributes of God, which constitute God's very nature, or, "His eternal power and Godhead." Attributes of omnipotence, omniscience, and omnipresence are essential attributes of God, in Himself, apart from any relationship to His creatures.

    Attributes of God:
    *   Omnipotence – God is all-powerful.
    *   Omniscience – God is all knowing, all seeing.
    *   Omnipresence – God is everywhere and present at all times.

- Immensity of Being – God fills all things, time, and space, and is not limited by such.
- Eternal – God is without beginning or end (timelessness). He is an everlastingly God. He always was, is, and shall be.
- Immutable – God is unchanged and unchanging in regard to His nature and being.
- Self-existence – God exists in and of Himself. He is the only true, independent being. He does not owe His existence or dependence to anything outside of Himself.

C. "Creation of the world"

The creation of the world reveals that there is a God—the witness of creation. Revelation in nature and creation is evidence of God's eternal power and Godhead (Genesis I; Psalm 19:1-6; Job 12:7-10; Romans 10:17-18). Paul refers to the sun, moon, stars, trees, grass, birds, and animals, etc. All the wonders of the world reveal that there is a Creator God. Creation reveals that there is a Creator! Man may understand, by the things that are made, that there is a Power, a Creator, a God, a Designer, and an Architect of the universe and the earth, who is greater than that which He creates.

The *visible* (seen things) reveal the *invisible* (unseen Godhead). Note once again what this verse says, "...the invisible...are clearly seen...being understood by the things that are made...."

D. "So that they are without excuse"

The revelation of God leaves man without excuse.

- In Nature and Creation (the witness for all mankind).
- In Conscience (for all mankind, Jew or Gentile).
- In the Scriptures, Holy Law, and Oracles of God (for the Jew or nation of Israel, especially. This is very clear [Acts 5:41].) The visible reveals the invisible; the seen creation tells us that there is the unseen Creator.

"Godhead" – "Godhead" speaks of the divinity or the sum total of God's divine attributes.

"Purpose" – The purpose is that they might be without excuse. There is *no* excuse.

"Excuse" – (Greek: *Anapologatous* means "answer" [I Peter 3:15]) The fact of creation leaves man without an excuse, without an answer (Romans 2:1). Note now the accumulated facts together in the following verses.

Man is without excuse (Romans 1:20)—he has a conscience and the testimony of creation. No kindred tongue, tribe, or nation is without the "light" of nature, the witness of creation. Creation reveals His invisible nature and attributes, and His power, and His and deity. Design, law and order, beauty, harmony, wisdom, etc., are all revealed in creation. These things show that they could not come from a being less than such. Man does not have the creative ability that is expressed in creation. Man is left without excuse. He is left without any defense or self-justification. Note in Acts 17:16-31 how Paul appealed to the Gentiles by the fact of creation.

E. **Man's Knowledge of God**
The Greeks of Athens were worshipping the *unknown* God. They knew God existed, but to them he was unknown and unknowable. This was during the height of Greek philosophy.
Thus, it is recognized that man knows that there is a God by creation. However, God's power in creation shows that He exists, but it does not reveal God's person, character, nature, or inner being. Hence, the need for further revelation.

Arguments for the existence of God:
- The Cosmological Argument (the systematic and ordered universe)
- The Teleological Argument (design, purpose, and harmony in the universe)
- The Ontological Argument (the intuitive belief in all men that there is a God)
- The Moral Argument (the law of conscience in man that tells him right and wrong)
- The Anthropological Argument (man—the masterpiece of all creation and superior to animals)
- The Biological Argument (the origin of life, as life can only come from a pre-existent life source)
- The Historical Argument (the events of history reveal an unseen hand behind all and governing all nations)

- The Christological Argument (the historical facts of Christ)
- The Scriptural Argument (the origin/preservation of the Holy Bible)
- The Argument from Congruity (the absolute harmony between all the above arguments)

Verse 21: "*...Because that, when they knew God, they glorified him not as God, neither were thankful; but became vain in their imaginations, and their foolish heart was darkened.*"

A. **Man once knew God.**

"Because that, when they knew God" reveals that man did once know God. How did man once know God? God is a spirit, and man is a spirit with a soul housed in a body. Spirit can only be revealed to spirit. God revealed himself in diverse ways—in visions, dreams, and words—in time past (Hebrews 1:1), and in creation and conscience, especially to the Gentile world. Thus, man could know God in this measure—the Creator and creature relationship.

B. **"They glorified him not as God"**

Though men knew there was a God and recognized God behind creation, they did not glorify God as God. They did not honor or give God the glory due Him. The very fact of the Creator-creature relationship meant that the creature was made for and by the Creator and made subject to the Creator, for the Creator's glory and praise. Man did not want to be subject to God. Instead, he desired to be "as God" (Genesis 3:1-6). Insubordination is lawlessness and leads to rebellion. Man is a rebel from God and neither gives God the glory or the thanks for all things—even for his own existence. Even though the creature is dependent on the Creator for his very life, man does not want to give glory to God, but instead takes the glory to himself.

C. **"Neither were thankful"**

Man was not thankful for his very existence, for his life, or for all the providential care of God, in His nature, that was for man's benefit and joy. This was a great sin of unthankfulness and a lack of appreciation.

D. "[They] became vain in their imaginations"
    "Vain" – "Vain" is the Jewish name for idols (cf. Acts 4:25). Ideas and
    concepts of God degenerated into such.
    "Imaginations" – That is, "reasonings" (II Kings 17:15; Jeremiah 2:5;
    Ephesians 4:17).

E. "And their foolish heart was darkened"
    Darkening of the heart is the refusal and rejection of light. God is light
    and is the light that lighteth every man that cometh into the world. Man
    does not want or love the light because his deeds are evil. Light exposes
    what a man is and what he does (John 3:19-30; John 1:1-9). When the
    fool says, "there is no God," his heart is darkened because he says no to
    the One who is the light. Man is in darkness, is a child of darkness, and is
    in the kingdom of darkness.
    "Foolish" – Lack of wisdom and prudence
    "Heart" – The inner man (Ephesians 3:16-17)

Verse 22: *"Professing themselves to be wise, they became fools. . ."*

    Man, professing to be wise, became a fool—or, in other words, "a wise
    fool" (cf. I Corinthians 1-2). The wisdom of this world is foolishness to
    God (Jeremiah 10:14). How many profess to be wise and intelligent but,
    in God's eyes, are fools? Proverbs shows the characteristics of such.

Verse 23: *". . .And changed the glory of the uncorruptible God into an image made like
    to corruptible man, and to birds, and fourfooted beasts, and creeping things."*

A. Man's foolishness is idolatry.
    They changed the glory of the uncorruptible God into an image made
    like to corruptible—also known as fetishism. Man, created by God and
    for God, did not want to retain God in his knowledge; yet, man, who has
    in his very nature the desire and capacity to worship God, turned from the
    true God and made a god of his own. Man was created to worship. All
    men are basically religious and will worship something or someone. Man
    will have a god or make a god to suit his own desires if he will not accept
    the true God. Note the contrasts here:
    Incorruptible God:
    • The Creator
    • The Invisible

Corruptible "Gods," Images:
- Man (image of man, deified)
- Birds (lower then man)
- Beasts (lower then man)
- Creeping Things (lower then man)
- Created Things (lower then man; the lowest form of idolatry)
- The Visible

The Gentile nations, as all mankind, will and must worship something. Man will worship man, or creatures, as birds and beasts. Man changes the glory (cf. Romans 1:23) of the uncorruptible Creator to an *image* of corruptible created creatures. God is a *spirit* and can only be revealed to man's spirit. *Spirit* is incorruptible, in contrast to *flesh*, which is corruptible—according to the fourfold division of flesh in I Corinthians 15:39. The *flesh* of man, beasts, birds, and fish is corruptible flesh. It is corruptible because of sin and death at work in all flesh, since the fall of Adam. God is *spirit*—uncorruptible, incorruptible, and immortal. This is the *glory* of God's own being. Man is spirit, soul, and body (flesh). Animals are soul and flesh-body. Therefore, through sin, man became corruptible and mortal. Animal creation is also mortal and corruptible. The difference between corruptible man and corruptible beasts is that man has *a spirit from God,* and that spirit *may know God* through creative and redemptive revelation. Due to this, man is above the brute creation (Ecclesiastes 3:18-21; 12:7; Zechariah 12:1; Job 32:8; I Thessalonians 5:23; Genesis 2:1-7; Hebrews 4:12).
- The *glory* of man is *flesh*—corruptible (I Peter 1:24).
- The *glory* of God is *spirit*—incorruptible (Romans 1:23).

What does man do? He makes an *image* of the god he desires to worship—the god of his *imaginations* (image...) (verse 21). Rejecting the true God, who is spirit, man makes an image of the god he wants. That "god" may be a man, beast, bird, or creeping thing (vain imaginations, idols). Man makes a god of his own concept—the god of his "image-inations" (the image of the mind of man). This god is what man imagines the god he desires to worship to be like. This is why the nation of Israel was warned not to make any graven images or worship any images of God. God is a spirit, and Israel had beheld no form or likeness of God that they could make into an image or the likeness of God. Any such image is *idolatry*. God is a spirit, and those who worship Him must worship in spirit and in truth (John 4:24; Deuteronomy 4:1-12; 4:14-20, 23, 24, 25-40).

Israel heard a *voice* out of the fire but saw no similitude or form of man, bird, beast, or creeping thing; hence, they were not able to make an idol or graven image of God for idolatrous worship (Exodus 20:1-6). "Thou shalt not make unto thee any graven image, or any likeness of any thing that is in heaven above, or that is in the earth beneath, or that is in the water under the earth..." (Exodus 20:4).

Image worship and the worship of a god behind an image has been in the heart of man since the Fall. It is idolatry. The heathen or Gentile nations worshipped the sun, moon, stars, trees, beasts, birds, stones, sticks, animals, reptiles, creeping things, man, things inanimate, and things animate, and they made to themselves *images*, believing those images were gods. They sought to appease these gods in thousands of ways (cf. Japan, India, Africa, China, etc.). The Crecian, Roman, Babylonian, Egyptian, and Phoenician nations all had gods. This is witnessed to, in abundance, by the idol temples in various nations around the world.

In I Samuel 6:1-18, the Philistines made image-gods of the emerods and mice, believing that the gods who smote them with plagues were like these idols. Heathen believers of the deities are like created things. Hence, the worship of the sun, moon, star, animal, and bird gods. They believed that the gods who created these things—the sun, moon, stars, etc.—created these things in their own image; that is, the sun god must be like the sun, the moon god must be like the moon, etc.

General Bible theme:

- Adam was created in the image of God, not physically but in tri-unity of being (Genesis 1:26).
- All men born of Adam's race bear his fallen image (Genesis 5:1-2).
- Man (especially the nation of Israel) was forbidden to worship any images (Exodus 20:1-6).
- The foolishness of idol or image worship among the Gentiles is evident in Deuteronomy 4:28 and Psalm 115:4-8.
- God has given us a *man* in His image to worship (Jesus Christ) (Colossians 1:15; Hebrews 1:1-7; Romans 8:29).
- All nations worshipped images (Daniel 3-4).
- The world will end up with image worship of the Beast-Man (Revelation 13). Man sinks lower than the Beast!

The man who worships another god is superior to that god he creates. The stupidity of idolatry is exposed in the fact that man, a living creature, makes a dead god, a lifeless image. He who has eyes, ears, nose, mouth, throat, hands, feet, and who was created now becomes the creator of a lifeless god with eyes, ears, nose, throat, mouth, hands, and feet. He then falls and worships the thing he created as his own god. Note the contrast:

The Man – has intelligence (eyes, ears, nose, throat), functions by life, and is the creator of a "god."

The Image – has no intelligence (eyes, ears, nose, throat), has no life, and is a created thing, and is based on a created thing.

If he cared to reason intelligently, the vain, silly, empty, and stupid speculations of the imaginations of man would be exposed to himself. The final deception of image worship is revealed in Revelation 13, where *the image* satanically speaks—an unnatural, supernatural thing. Perhaps this deception comes by the power of Satan. Time will tell!

Some heathen—even the educated and civilized heathen—realize the utter folly of this form of idolatry (that of a dead image) and turn to another form, the "image worship of *a man* (men)," which is as evil or worse. The living man worships and deifies another living man, which is just another form of idolatry. Film stars, sports champions, politicians, games, pop-groups, singers, etc., are all forms of image worship because man was made in the "image of God." Cults such as Father Divine and rock singers become idols. Man sets up another man as his "idol"—his "image"—and worships that idol. Man is also encouraged to, "make his *own* image." The same thing happens in the church, and it becomes "man-worship" and the "worship of ministry," which is idolatry.

B. **Image worship is Devil worship.** (Deuteronomy 4:16)

The folly of idol or image worship is exposed in the fact that the living creature (man) is worshipping the dead creature (idol) that he created. Scripture reveals, though, that there is something subtler behind "image worship"; that is, *demonism*, meaning devil worship and the worship of evil spirits, demons, or devils. Even though man turns from the worship of the true God, he still must worship, for man is a worshipping creature. He turns to worship something or someone—either himself, or a god of his own imagination or making. However, even idolatry itself is insufficient to satisfy the heart-hunger and worship-hunger of man. There must be something or some *spirit* behind the image-idol that can satisfy man's worship-hunger. The image, thus, becomes *a channel,* the *means to an end,* and the *mediator* between man and the unseen spirit-god he knows he must worship. This is the express purpose in idol or image worship. Behind the idol is a spirit, devil, or demon. When the heathen or the idolater worships an image, he worships the spirit or devil behind that image. This is plainly devil-worship. (Please note: I Corinthians 8:1-13; 10:9-13; Daniel 1; Daniel 3; Revelation 9:20; Deuteronomy 32:16-17; Leviticus 17:7; Revelation 13:4, 14).

Note the warnings to believers in Revelation 2:14, 20; 22:15; I Corinthians 10:7, 14, 19-21; and I John 5:21 against all forms of idolatry.

Note below the various subtle forms of idolatry:
- Idols or images of created things (dead or material idols)
- Idols or images of creature things (living creature idols)
- Idols or images of created men (deified man)
- Idol-image of one's own concept or imagination
- Idol-image of selfism, self-worship, self, or the ego within
- Idol-image, or the worship of the Devil or spirits behind an image (occultism, Satanism, etc.)

Verse 24: *"Wherefore God also gave them up to uncleanness through the lusts of their own hearts, to dishonour their own bodies between themselves..."*

Man is given up by God. (Psalm 81:12; Acts 7:42; Ephesians 4:18)
Note the three-fold progression in verses 24, 26, and 28:
1) "...God also gave them up..." (verse 24).
2) "...God gave them up..." (verse 26).
3) "...God gave them over to a reprobate mind..." (verse 28).

This is the divine sequence in God's dealings with man: Man gave God up; God gives man up. Man gave God over; God gives man over. God gave man up because of these things—the things that man chose. It is a divine principle in the Word (cf. Psalm 18:25-26): Man rejects God; God rejects man. Man accepts God; God accepts man. What we do to or with His Son is what God will do or be to us. This does not occur because God is or does evil, for He is eternally holy, righteous, just, and loving, but it occurs because of the divine principle that the actions of men must be dealt with through like actions. Man reaps what he sows. God forgives if we forgive others. This is the *law* of God. This is the *law* of sowing and reaping. God will be to you what you are to Him. (Note Matthew 18:35; 6:12, 14-15.) This is the principle of law. Reproduce after your kind. "...An eye for an eye, a tooth for a tooth..." (Matthew 5:38; Leviticus 24:20). This is not the principle of *grace* but the principle of *law*.

There is no alternative for man. Outside the *grace* of God, man is on the ground of law, and law is the strength of sin (I Corinthians 15:56; Romans 8:2). Man is given up because he has given himself over to idolatry by forsaking the true God and worshipping false gods.

What did God give man up to or over to? What did He hand him over to in the power of sin?

- God gave them up to *uncleanness* (Romans 1:24).
- God gave them up to *vile affections* (Romans 1:26).
- God gave them over to a *reprobate mind* (Romans 1:28).

Or, in other words, God gave them over in:

- Body (Romans 1:24)
- Soul (Romans 1:26)
- Spirit (Romans 1:28)

Verses 24-31 give one of the most horrible and complete lists of sins in the New Testament. These sins will be listed and defined in the following verses. (Please note that verse 24 is repeated.)

Given Up to Vile Affections (Romans 1:24-27)

Verse 24: *"Wherefore God also gave them up to uncleanness through the lusts of their own hearts, to dishonour their own bodies between themselves..."*

"Uncleanness"

God gave them up to uncleanness through the lusts (inordinate and unlawful desires) of their own hearts. Men were dishonoring their own bodies between themselves (I Corinthians 6:8; I Thessalonians 4:4; Leviticus 18:22). Note "lusts of the heart" (Mark 7:20-23). Bodies were dishonored by unnatural uses.

Verse 25: *"...Who changed the truth of God into a lie, and worshipped and served the creature more than the Creator, who is blessed for ever. Amen."*

A. Idolatry

(Cf. Romans 1:18; Romans 2:8; II Corinthians 13:8.) They changed the *truth* of God into a *lie* (Isaiah 44:20; I John 5:20; Genesis 3:1-6). The glory of the uncorruptible God was changed (exchanged) for corruptible gods. The creature (created things) was served more than the Creator was.

B. "Who is blessed for ever. Amen"

The Creator is blessed forever (Amen, so be it). (Note II Thessalonians 2:10-12; John 14:6; 8:32, 36, 44-45 [about God's truth].)

Verse 26: *"For this cause God gave them up unto vile affections: for even their women did change the natural use into that which is against nature..."*

"Vile affections"

Vile affections are passions of dishonor (cf. I Thessalonians 4:4-5). "...[W]omen did change the natural [and proper] use into that which is against nature..." represents lesbianism and other forms of immorality (Leviticus 18:22; Ephesians 5:12) (Greek: *females*).

Verse 27: *"...And likewise also the men, leaving the natural use of the woman, burned in their lust one toward another; men with men working that which is unseemly, and receiving in themselves that recompence of their error which was meet."*

A. Homosexuality

"Burned" in this verse means "a terrible intensity of burning lust." A man with another man is commonly spoken of as "sodomy" in the Bible. The city of Sodom was noted for this corruptible practice (sodomites [Deuteronomy 23:17; I Kings 14:24; 15:12; 22:46; II Kings 23:7]).

B. "Unseemly, and receiving in themselves that recompence of their error which was meet"

("Unseemly" means disfigurement [cf. Genesis 19].) They received judgment suitable to their terrible errors and sins. So also will the judgment of God come on all today, ministers and otherwise, who condone and practice such sins, which are clearly condemned in God's Word, and who also endorse these sins under the cloak of "love and mutual consent" between agreeing parties (Leviticus 18).

Verses 24-27: *Summary*

Thus, verses 24 through 27 reveal the horrible sins of the bodies, souls, and spirits of men and women. Such sins are an abomination to the Lord. Under the law of God in Israel, they were punishable by death. Uncleanness, lusts of the heart, vile affections, and dishonoring the bodies of men and women are unspeakable cases of immorality, and they are on the increase today.

The days of Noah and the days of Lot are being repeated today. The laws of God to Israel and the abominations that were spoken of then are repeated now on a great scale. Immorality is on the increase. Governments and modernists ministers of the gospel seek and pass laws that endorse and legalize these practices that are in direct opposition to God's Word and are condemned to judgment by Him. God has set a price of redemption on the human body. Satan seeks to corrupt and defile the human body with every vile affection and unclean lust of the human heart and nature, which he has exploited for thousands of years. This age will end in a worldwide orgy of sexual sins, and this is the reason why the wrath of God will come upon men (Revelation 9:20; 22:11, 15). The *heart* of man is desperately wicked, and only God can know it (Jeremiah 17:9-10). All that proceeds from it is evil. Christ gives His description of the human heart in Mark 7:20-23. Compare His list with the list in Romans 1:24-32, and also note Ephesians 5:11-12. Paul did not give sordid details of the horrible sins he lists. This is in great contrast to the Greek's descriptions and sordid details of their abominable practices. Sin must not at all be glamorized! It is a shame to speak of those things they did in secret! Note the progression:

- Rejection of the true God leads to *idolatry* (Romans 1:19-23).
- Rejection of the knowledge of God leads to *immorality* (Romans 1:24-28).

Idolatry and immorality are "twins" and lead to devil worship (Numbers 25; I Corinthians 10:6-8; Jude 7; Revelation 2:14, 20; 9:20; Galatians 5:19-21).

Given Over to a Reprobate Mind (Romans 1:28-32)

Verse 28: *"And even as they did not like to retain God in their knowledge, God gave them over to a reprobate mind, to do those things which are not convenient...."*

A. **Willful Ignorance**

"[T]hey did not like to retain God [acknowledge God] in their knowledge..." signifies willful rejection of the knowledge of God (cf. verse 21). They did not want to acknowledge, approve, or consider Him worth having (Amplified New Testament). The vain, empty, silly, and senseless imaginations of man's mind are what result when man does not want to retain God in his knowledge (foolish reasoning and stupid speculations). "The fool hath said in his heart, There is no god" (Psalm 14:1). The so-called atheist is not one who does not believe in the existence of god but one who does not want to retain God in his or her knowledge. Senseless thinking leads and deceives him or her into believing that there is no God. The atheist believes a lie because he or she has no love for the truth. Deception is a life. Turning from the truth of God, an atheist believes the lie and refuses to have God in his or her knowledge. "Did not think God worth knowing" (Vincent); that is, did not allow the rudimentary knowledge or revelation of nature to develop into full knowledge of God. They were given over to a reprobate mind— a mind void of judgment, a condemned mind, a mind given over to a state of continuing depravity—to do those things which are not convenient. (Note Ephesians 5:4.)

B. **"To do those things which are not convenient"**

When man does not want to retain God in his knowledge, he leaves himself open for deception and, finally, a reprobate mind. A reprobate mind is a mind hardened against truth and in rebellion against God. A mind that rejects the truth against itself is open to total depravity (cf. II Corinthians 13:5-7). In such a state of mind, man can only do those things "which are not convenient."

Verses 29-31: *"...Being filled with all unrighteousness, fornication, wickedness, covetousness, maliciousness; full of envy, murder, debate, deceit, malignity; whisperers, backbiters, haters of God, despiteful, proud, boasters, inventors of evil things, disobedient to parents, without understanding, covenantbreakers, without natural affection, implacable, unmerciful..."*

The List of Sins (Man under Sin)

In verses 29-31, we are given a list of sins that man falls into while in such a state of mind—a mind in rebellion against God and His truth. It is the greatest list of sins in the New Testament. It reveals man's terrible "bias" towards evil. Other lists of sins, which could be compared, are found in the following passages, which could be compared:

- Christ's description of the human heart (Mark 7:20-23)
- The deceitfulness of the human heart, only known to God (Jeremiah 17:9-10)
- The works of the flesh (Galatians 5:19-21)   .
- Additional sins (Revelation 22:15; I Corinthians 6:9-10)

Two important things should be noted about the sins listed below, as well as all lists of sins:

1) All of these sins are a violation of the Ten Commandments, or civil commandments of God.
2) They are sins of the spirit, soul, and body and may be grouped under three categories.

A general grouping of them may be as follows:

- Sins of the spirit (verses 21-23)
- Sins of the soul (verses 28-31)
- Sins of the body (verses 24-27)

Please note the following comprehensive list of sins. Violated commandments are suggested after some sins.

Uncleanness (verse 24) – Greek: *Akatharsiac* means "impurity (the state) moral." (A violation of the seventh commandment)

Idolatry (verse 25) – "Idolatry worshipped" means "to venerate, adore, or pay honor; divine honor to any created thing." (A violation of the first and second commandments)

Vile Affections (verse 26) – Greek: *Pathos* means "passion, concupiscence (desire, lust)"; "a diseased condition out of which the lusts spring" (verse 24) (Vine's). This word also refers to "lesbian," "female," "homosexual" (changed of natural [Greek: *Phusikos*] use).

Lusts with Men – (verse 27) "Lusts" in the Greek is *orexis* which means "excitement of the mind (i.e., longing after)"; reaching out for something with the purpose of appropriating it. In verse 29, this word refers to homosexuality. (A violation of the 7th commandment)

Unrighteousness (verse 29) – Greek: *Adikia* means "moral wrongfulness (of character, life, or act)."

Fornication (verse 29) – Greek: *Porneia* means "harlotry (includes adultery and incest)"; illicit sexual intercourse (Vine's).

Wickedness (verse 29) – Greek: *Poneria* means "depravity (i.e. [specifically], malice; plural [concrete] plots, sins)."

Covetousness (verse 29) – Greek: *Pleonexia* means "avarice (i.e. [by implication], fraudulence, extortion)"; (greedy of gain) (A violation of the tenth commandment)

Maliciousness (verse 29) – Greek: *Kakia* means "badness (i.e. [subjectively], depravity or [active] malignity or [passive] trouble)"; (malice, active exercise of a vicious disposition.)

Envy (verse 29) – Greek: *Phthonos* means "ill will (as detraction) (i.e., jealousy, spite)"; desire to deprive another of what he or she has. (A violation of the tenth commandment)

Murder (verse 29) – Greek: *Phonos* means "murder." (A violation of the sixth commandment)

Debate (verse 29) – Greek: *Eris* means "quarrel (i.e. [by implication], wrangling, strife, contention, express enmity)."

Deceit (verse 29) – Greek: *Dolos* is an obsolete verb, probably meaning "a decoy; a trick (bait); figuratively, wile; to bait, snare; craft, guile."

Malignity (verse 29) – Greek: *Kakoetheia* means "bad character (i.e. [specifically], mischievousness)"; "literally, bad manner or character, hence, an evil disposition that tends to put the worst construction on everything" (Vine's). (Misinterpretation of others)

Whisperers (verse 29) – Greek: *Psithiristes* means "a secret calumniator." "To utter maliciously false statements, charges, or imputations about" (Webster's). Note the difference between a whisperer and slanderer: "whisperer" means "clandestine slandering (gossiping; a gossiper and talebearer)"; "slanderer" means "open slandering." (Whisperers are in violation of the ninth commandment.)

Backbiters (verse 30) – Greek: *Katalalos* means "slanderer, talkative against another"; refer to "whisperers." (Violation of the 9th commandement)

Haters of God (verse 30) – Greek: *Theostuges* means "hateful to God, or impious"; to feel and show hate towards God.

Despiteful (verse 30) – Greek: *Hubristes* means "an insulter, or maltreater"; "insolent, one who uplifted with pride, either heaps insulting language upon others or does them some shameful act of wrong" (Thayer's).

Proud (verse 30) – Greek: *Huperephanos* means "appearing above others (conspicuous), (i.e. [figuratively], haughty, arrogant)"; "an overweening estimate of one's means or merits, despising others or even treating them with contempt, haughty" (Thayer's).

Boasters (verse 30) – Greek: *Alazon* means "braggart"; "an empty headed pretender" (Thayer's).

Inventors of Evil Things (verse 30) – "Inventors" in the Greek is *epheuretes*, meaning "inventors, discovers of evil, contrivers"; "morally or ethically evil in regard to qualities, emotions, passions, and deeds" (Thayer's [as used here]).

Disobedient to parents (verse 30) – Greek: *Apeithes* means "unpersuable (i.e., contumacious)"; "stubbornly disobedient, rebellious" (Webster's). (A violation of the fifth commandment)

Without Understanding (verse 31) – Greek: *Asunetos* means "unintelligent, wicked (by implication)"; "stupid" (Thayer's).

Covenantbreakers (verse 31) – Greek: *Asunthetos* properly means "not agreed, (i.e., treacherous to compacts)." Refusing to abide by covenants made; thus, faithless.

Without Natural Affection (verse 31) – "Signifies without...love of kindred, especially of parents for children and children for parents" (Vine's). "Natural" in the Greek is *phusikos*. "Affection" in the Greek is *Astorgos*. (A violation of the fifth commandment)

Implacable (verse 31) – Greek: *Aspondos* literally means "without libation (which usually accompanied a treaty), (i.e. [by implication], truceless)." "This word properly denotes those who will not be reconciled where there is a quarrel; or who pursue the offender with unyielding revenge. It denotes an unforgiving temper" (Barnes). It is also defined this way: "not capable of being appeased, pacified, or mitigated, unalterable" (Webster's).

Unmerciful (verse 31) – Greek: *Aneleemon* means "merciless"; "destitute of compassion" (Barnes).

These sins listed generally relate to violations of the Ten Commandments (Exodus 20:1-20). Sin is transgression of the law (I John 3:4). The Ten Commandments are listed briefly here:

1) Do not have any other gods except Me.
2) Do not worship any graven image.
3) Do not take the Lord's name in vain.
4) Keep the Sabbath day holy.
5) Honor thy father and mother.
6) Do not kill.
7) Do not commit adultery.
8) Do not steal.
9) Do not bear false witness.
10) Do not covet anything that is thy neighbor's.

Verse 32: "...*Who knowing the judgment of God, that they which commit such things are worthy of death, not only do the same, but have pleasure in them that do them.*"

A. **"Who knowing the judgment of God"**

The first use of the word "judgment" in the book of Romans is found here in verse 32 (cf. Romans 1:32; 2:1-3; 5, 16). The answer of God concerning the expression of sin in mankind is that man is under the *judgment* of God. The wrath of a righteous, holy God, outraged by the sin of man, is revealed in judgment upon sin. God must judge sin. God's holiness is outraged if sin is not judged. The judgment of God on sin is *death*. Thus: the *wrath* of God (verse 18); the *judgment* of God (verse 32).

B. **"That they which commit such things are worthy of death"**

This is also the first use of the word "death" in Romans (cf. Romans 5:12-21). "For the wages of sin is death..." (Romans 6:23). They that do such are worthy of death. "...[T]he soul that sinneth, it shall die" (Ezekiel 18:1-6; cf. Genesis 2:17). The stark tragedy of the matter is that man *knows* the judgment of God—that all who do such things are worthy of death—yet persists in doing the same and has pleasure in others who do so also. This is seen in evil, sexual, and occult orgies, and also high-class society group sins. Thus, man sins in the light of divine judgment. Man is seen to be unrepentant, sinning in the light of divine wrath and judgment, without any fear of God (Psalm 50:18; Hosea 7:3).

Summary (Romans 1:18-32)

1) Man knew God and did not want to retain God in his knowledge.
2) Man became idolatrous and worshipped gods of his own making and concept.
3) Man was given up and given over, by God, to the sins he loved.
4) Man's moral, fallen nature is revealed as utterly immoral, lawless, and corrupt. He does what he does because of what he is.
5) Man comes under the wrath and judgment of a righteous and holy God.
6) Man's condemnation is death—the wages of sin.
7) Man knows the coming of divine judgment, yet, he is unrepentant, enjoying the pleasures of sin. He is unrepentant despite the light of creation, the light of conscience, and arguments for the existence of God.

Basically, Paul outlines the condition of the *Gentile world* in Romans 1. The *Jewish world* is dealt with in Romans 2 (refer to Romans 2:9-17).

Dispensationally, Romans 1 may be viewed as a description of the world of mankind, from Adam to Moses. It is a description of the ungodly, unrighteous line of Cain to the time of the flood (which was judgment on that world), and it is a picture of the world after the Flood, from the time of Ham (and the Tower of Babel) to the time of Christ. It also points to Sodom and Gomorrah and the judgments upon those wicked cities, and is applicable to Grecian and Roman times, as well as to our modern days. Dispensationally, Romans 1 could be applied to the ungodly world, from the judgments on the Egyptian world to the separation of Israel and the law of God at Mt. Sinai (which brings us to Romans 2). Thus, we have the following recurring cycle:

- The World of Adam to Noah (then judgments on the wickedness of man) (Genesis 3-9)
- The World of Babel (the judgments on wickedness) (Genesis 10-11)
- The World of Sodom and Gomorrah (judgments) (Genesis 18-19)
- The World of Egyptian Times (judgments) (Exodus 1-14)

All these worlds above reveal the state of idolatry and immorality, and they each came under the wrath and judgments of God. They are set forth as examples of like conditions and judgments in this end of the age—upon both the Jewish and Gentile worlds (Luke 17:22-37; Matthew 24:37-41; Jude 6-7; II Peter 2:4-9; 3:1-14; Revelation 19:20; 20:10-15). The word "wrath" is used about twelve times in Romans. Thus, man is given over to "the impurity of lustful, luxurious, profligate living." More than natural lust, it is bestiality—impurity in the physical. Thus, there is a need for judgment.

Righteousness Needed By the Jews (Romans 2:1-3:20)

Wrath and Judgment on the Jews (Romans 2:1-11)

Verse 1: *"Therefore thou art inexcusable, O man, whosoever thou art that judgest: for wherein thou judgest another, thou condemnest thyself; for thou that judgest doest the same things."*

A. **"Therefore"**
In light of the facts revealed in Romans 1:18-32, all men are left without excuse.

B. **"O man"** (Romans 2:1; 2:3)
This statement is all-inclusive, yet personal and individual. This especially refers to the Jew— "thou art the man."

C. **"Thou art inexcusable"** (cf. Romans 1:20)
No excuse can be offered by anyone—Jew or Gentile. How the heart of man is full of excuses! "And they all with one consent began to make excuse..." (Luke 14:18). This is especially true in regard to sin. Paul especially has the Jew in mind, as he states in Romans 2:1-3. The Jew stood in judgment of the Gentile world for being guilty of the list of sins mentioned in Romans 1; however, in judging the Gentile, the Jew condemned himself, for the Jew was as guilty of these same sins as the Gentile. The Jew's "finger of judgment" pointed to the Gentile, but four fingers of condemnation pointed back to him. Note, in John 8:1-1, that the Pharisees, in judging the woman taken in the act of adultery, condemned themselves—for they were guilty of sin also. Only Jesus Christ, the sinless one, could point the finger. This is developed further in Romans 2:17-23. Here is a divine principle as far as man is concerned: if we judge others for sins and we are doing the very same sins, then we involuntarily condemn ourselves. (Note David's self-judgment in II Samuel 11-12 and Psalm 51. Swift to judge another, he condemned himself.)

D. "Wherein thou judgest another, thou condemnest thyself; for thou that judgest doest the same things"
   The truth must be applied all the way. Do we judge others and do the same things ourselves? In *judging* others, we *condemn* ourselves (II Samuel 12:5; Matthew 7:1-2; John 8:9).

Verse 2: *"But we are sure that the judgment of God is according to truth against them which commit such things."*

   Note the use of the word "judgment" in Romans 1; 2:2-3; 5 with 1:32. God's judgment is according to divine principles. Please note the following in regard to judgment.

According to Truth (Romans 2:2). Judgment according to the truth is true judgment. God judges the facts. He is holy, impartial, final, infallible, and righteous in His judgments. He is the God of truth, justice, and wrath, even as He is the God of love and mercy. God's judgment is contrasted with man's judgment. Man judges another, but he is guilty of doing the same things himself; therefore, his judgment is not according to truth. God alone is perfectly holy and sinless; therefore, His judgment is according to truth "...against them which commit such things" (cf. "judgment and truth" [Isaiah 11:1-5; James 2:12-13; Job 22:4; Psalm 101:1] [God is the perfect judge.]).

According to His Deeds (Romans 2:6) – The "works" of men will be judged. Men will be judged for what they say as well as for what they do.

No Respect of Persons – No impartiality is shown.

Judgment by Jesus (Romans 2:16) – Jesus is the perfect judge. The Father has given all judgment to the Son (John 5).

According to My Gospel (Romans 2:16) – Man is judged for accepting or rejecting Christ.

Verse 3: *"And thinkest thou this, O man, that judgest them which do such things, and doest the same, that thou shalt escape the judgment of God?"*

"That thou shalt escape the judgment of God"
   Judgment is inescapable. There is no escape for Jew or Gentile (cf. Hebrews 2:3; 10:28; 12:25-26). How shall we escape? We shall not escape. Both the Jew and the Gentile are under the judgment of God (Ecclesiastes 11:9; 12:14).

The Jews were like the Pharisees and condemned others (Luke 18:9-14). They were like self-righteous moralists who did not know God's holiness or their own sinfulness. This is self-justification—judging yourself better than others because of culture, race, education, or civilization.

Verse 4: *"Or despisest thou the riches of his goodness and forbearance and longsuffering; not knowing that the goodness of God leadeth thee to repentance?"*

"The riches of his goodness and forbearance and longsuffering; not knowing that the goodness of God leadeth thee to repentance" (cf. Ecclesiastes 8:12)

Since judgment is not executed immediately, the heart of man is set on mischief. The whole purpose of God's delayed judgment is to bring man to repentance. Note:

Riches of God's *Goodness* – (Ephesians 1:7; Romans 11:11)
Riches of God's *Forbearance* – (Romans 3:25)
Riches of God's *Longsuffering* – (Exodus 34:6; Romans 9:22; I Peter 3:20; II Peter 3:9; I Corinthians 13:4)

God is not willing that any should perish but that all should come to repentance (cf. Repentance, II Peter 3:9). He gives all a "space to repent" (Revelation 2:21; Isaiah 30:18). God's goodness precedes His forbearance, which precedes His longsuffering. When these are ended, wrath and judgment come.

Repentance is two-sided:
1) The *divine* side—God convicting man of sin, bringing about a change of mind
2) The *human* side—man responding to this conviction and the subsequent ingredients of repentance

Please note additional "riches":
- Riches of His grace (Ephesians 1:7; 2:7)
- Riches of His glory (Romans 9:23)

All of these riches flow from the very nature of God, which is love. Love is rich in goodness, forbearance, and longsuffering. All creation proves such.

From the very hand of God, creation pours its goodness upon man. God forbears and bears with the wickedness of man. He tolerates such and withholds judgment to bring man to *repentance*.

The longsuffering of God is exemplified in the following:
- In the Days of Noah
- In the Days of Lot
- In the Days of Moses
- In the Days of Israel
- In the Days of the Prophets
- In the Savior's Times (Messianic Period)
- In Our Own Days

Methuselah was the sign-son, and his name means "when he is dead it (the Flood) shall be sent." The longsuffering of God waited in the days of Noah. The oldest man who ever lived demonstrated the longsuffering of God. God seeks to lead—not force—man to repentance. God seeks to lead man to a change of mind, away from a reprobate mind (a mind in rebellion and hardened against God). Man will either *despise* or *repent*. "Despise" means "to do despite."

Verse 5: *"But after thy hardness and impenitent heart treasurest up unto thyself wrath against the day of wrath and revelation of the righteous judgment of God..."*

A. Hardness of Heart
Note the things listed in God's Word that cause hardening of the heart:
- Pride (Daniel 5:13-23)
- Religious Bigotry (Acts 19:8-9)
- Hatred and Wrong Spirit or Wrong Attitudes (Mark 3:5)
- Rationalizing the Word (Mark 8:16)
- Unwillingness to Yield, Deceitfulness of Sin (Hebrews 3:13)
- Unwillingness to Yield (II Chronicles 36:13)
- Disobedience (Zechariah 7:8-12)
- Sin of Unbelief (Hebrews 3:7-12) (H.C.)

B. **"Impenitent heart"**

An impenitent heart is unrepentant—the opposite of repentant. God seeks to lead man to repentance by His goodness, forbearance, and longsuffering. Man becomes impenitent of heart because of various sins he commits.

C. **"Treasurest up unto thyself wrath against the day of wrath and revelation of the righteous judgment of God"**

As the result of a hard and impenitent heart, man *treasures* up wrath. As a man has a treasure box and stores up treasure in it until it is full, so impenitent men store up treasures of wrath because of their hardened and impenitent hearts. Man treasures up wrath, the wrath of God. The wrath of God is the righteous judgment of a holy God against sin. Sin must be judged. Wrath is the reaction of God's holiness against man's sinfulness—divine wrath (cf. Deuteronomy 32:34; James 5:3).

The day of wrath and revelation of the righteous judgment of God (cf. Revelation 20:11-15) is the Great White Throne Judgment where eternal judgment occurs. (Refer to Hebrews 6:2, doctrine of eternal judgment.) The climactic word used by Paul concerning the corruption of mankind, including both Jews and Gentiles, by sin is the word "wrath." Note the use of the word "wrath":

- *Wrath* of God is revealed against all sin (Romans 1:18).
- Treasures up *wrath* because of impenitence (Romans 2:5).
- The day of *wrath*—yet to come (Romans 2:5).
- *Wrath* to be rendered to those who do not obey (Romans 2:8).
- The law worketh *wrath* (Romans 4:15).

As far as God and man are concerned, the ground upon which wrath can be justified (meted out) is the *ground of law*—broken law. As far as God is concerned, the ground of law is in *Himself*—His own sinless, perfect, righteous, and holy being and character. The law of His own being is absolute holiness. As far as man is concerned, the ground is in *law*—God's revealed law and will given, out of necessity, to man. This revealed law is in harmony with God's own divine being. Righteousness, holiness, and goodness are part of the character of God and are part of the characteristics of His law (Romans 7:12, 14; Psalm 19:7-14). The law has the very characteristics of the lawgiver—God Himself. The law was communicated to man. If unkept or broken, then it works wrath. This is exactly what happened. The law was broken, and it worked wrath.

Law and wrath are connected in the very nature of things, in the very nature of God and His dealings with man. (Cf. wrath [Romans 1:18; 2:2-3, 5, 8; 1:32] [wrath and judgment].) Note (transgression):

- Law
- Wrath
- Judgment

The believer is saved from wrath through Christ (Romans 5:9; I Thessalonians 1:10). Vessels of wrath are fitted to destruction (Romans 9:22; cf. Romans 12:19; 13:4-5). Please remember that the word "love" is not used until Romans 5:5. The word "wrath" is used once in John's gospel (John 3:36), but the word "love" is used many times. (Cf. Amplified New Testament; II Timothy 1:12.) The wrath of God is expressed in the wrath of the Lamb (Ephesians 2:3; 5:6; Revelation 6:16-17; 19:15). Vials of wrath are finally poured out on the impenitent (Revelation 15-16). From the divine side, the result of despising (cf. Romans 2:4) God's riches can only bring wrath and judgment.

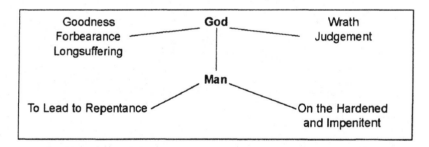

The end of the kingdom will bring men to the Great White Throne of judgment, and also the great Tribulation period is a time of great judgment on men—under the vials of the wrath of God. If men will not accept the goodness and longsuffering of God—or in other words, the love of God and His grace—then they leave themselves under the wrath of God and God's righteous judgment. There is absolutely no other alternative. There is no middle or neutral ground. When man despises, as in verse 4, it brings his heart into a state of hardness and impenitence. Every day of evil, hardness, and impenitence pours its "treasure" into the store. For the righteous, treasures of the love of God are stored. For the wicked treasures of wrath and judgment are stored. There is no chance of mistaken judgment with the divine Judge.

Verse 6: *". . . Who will render to every man according to his deeds. . ."*

Man will be judged according to his deeds.

Man will be judged according to his deeds, actions, or works—according to what he has done (Job 34:11; Psalm 62:12; Proverbs 24:12; Jeremiah 17:10; II Corinthians 5:10). A man does what he does because of what he is. Many Scriptures point to the judgment of our works. Believers and unbelievers, godly and ungodly—none are exempt. The believer's works will be judged at the coming of Christ, at the "bema seat" of Christ—not judged in regard to salvation, but judged in regard to works. Sinners will be judged at the Great White Throne Judgment (Revelation 20:11-15). Dead works, evil works, works of the flesh, good works—all will be on record and brought to account at the throne of God and the Lamb.

Verse 7: *". . . To them who by patient continuance in well doing seek for glory and honour and immortality, eternal life. . ."*

Verses 7-10 give us the two classes in their opposites, as seen below:

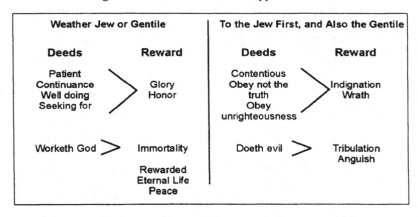

Weather Jew or Gentile		To the Jew First, and Also the Gentile	
Deeds	**Reward**	**Deeds**	**Reward**
Patient Continuance Well doing Seeking for	Glory Honor	Contentious Obey not the truth Obey unrighteousness	Indignation Wrath
Worketh God	Immortality	Doeth evil	Tribulation Anguish
	Rewarded Eternal Life Peace		

Verse 8: *". . . But unto them that are contentious, and do not obey the truth, but obey unrighteousness, indignation and wrath. . ."*

(Refer to II Thessalonians 1:8 and the chart corresponding to 2:7.)

Verse 9: *". . . Tribulation and anguish, upon every soul of man that doeth evil, of the Jew first, and also of the Gentile. . ."*

(Refer to Amos 3:2; Luke 12:47; I Peter 4:17; and chart corresponding to 2:7)

Verse 10: *"...But glory, honour, and peace, to every man that worketh good, to the Jew first, and also to the Gentile..."*

(Refer to I Peter 1:7 and the chart corresponding to verse 7 [whether Jew or Greek].)

Verse 11: *"...For there is no respect of persons with God."*

This verse closes off this section and sweeps away the thought of class distinction, partiality, or favoritism with God.   There is *no difference* between Jew and the Gentile, but there are *advantages* that the Jew had over the Gentile—one of the hardest lessons for the Jew to learn and accept (cf. Romans 3:9; 10:12; 3:1-2; Deuteronomy 10:17; Job 34:19; Acts 10:34; Ephesians 6:9; Deuteronomy 7:6-8; Colossians 3:25).

A. **"Respect"**
   "Respect" can be defined in the following ways:
   - A looking at, respect, regard (from *respicere*, to look at).
   - The act of respecting or noticing with attention; the looking toward, attention.
   - The act of holding in high estimation, deference, or honor; a feeling of esteem, regard.
   - To notice with special attention.
   - "Respect" in the Greek: *prosopolepsia* means "partiality, favoritism."

   Partiality is not to be found in God (Romans 2:11; Ephesians 6:9; Colossians 3:25; James 2:1). To have respect of persons is not good (Proverbs 28:21; James 2:9).

B. **No Respect of Persons—Whether Jew or Greek**
   Paul described the horrible condition of the Gentile world in Romans 1. In Romans 2, he leads up to the same horrible condition of the Jew. The Jew felt that because he was of the chosen race, the elect of God, that he was far superior to those of the Gentile races. Paul is leading up to the fact, and truth, that—whether Jew or Gentile, chosen race or unchosen— all are under sin, hopeless and helpless, and all are, therefore, under wrath. This is developed in the succeeding verses.

The matter of "to the Jew first and also to the Greek" needs to be understood clearly (see Romans 1:16 notes). The Jew exalted himself above the Gentile. The nationalistic spirit of Judaism sought to prevail itself above the grace of God. The Jew felt that he was a "respectable sinner" in contrast and comparison to the Gentile. (Refer again to Acts 13:38-52).

Note in I Thessalonians 2:14-16: "wrath is come upon them to the uttermost." In other words, if it be contended that the gospel is "to the Jew first," then this is exactly what happened. God in Christ came to the Jew first, but the Jews as a nation rejected God; hence, God turned to the Gentiles. However, Paul's language here demonstrates contrasting results. If the Jew received the gospel first and rejected it, then the Jew would get indignation, wrath, tribulation, and anguish first. This is exactly what happened. If this were not the case, then God would be a respecter of persons. Christians need to recognize this and not over-exalt the Jew above the church in our day.

The Law of God – Internal and External (Romans 2:12-16)

Verse 12: *"For as many as have sinned without law shall also perish without law: and as many as have sinned in the law shall be judged by the law . . ."*

A. **"By the law"**
    "By the law" in Scripture generally means the following:
    - The moral law of the Ten Commandments,
    - The civil laws relating both to God and man—in the book of the Law,
    - The ceremonial, or sacrificial law, consisting of the priesthood, tabernacle, offerings, feasts, etc.

    (The context of the text may define any of these referred to above. Generally, "by the law" refers to the moral law or the Ten Commandments.)
    This is the first use of the word "law" in Romans. Paul's emphasis here is to point out the law in relation to the Gentile and the Jew. These are the two main thoughts that Paul takes up in the reminder of the chapter are:

1) Law – (Romans 2:12-16; cf. Romans 3; Romans 7)
2) Circumcision – (Romans 2:17-29; cf. Romans 3:1; 4:1-25)

The Jews boasted of these two things: that they were in covenant relationship with God through the rite of circumcision (Genesis 17; Acts 7:8), and that through Moses God had given to them (as the chosen nation) His righteous law (and all involved in the law and its three main aspects). No Gentile had these things. Gentiles were called the "uncircumcised" (outside the covenant, lawless, and law-breakers) (cf. Ephesians 2:11-12).

The Gentiles – Sinned without the law and, therefore, shall perish without the law.

The Jews – Sinned in the law and, therefore, shall be judged by the law. (The greater the responsibility, with privileges, the greater the judgment.)

Verse 13: *"...(For not the hearers of the law are just before God, but the doers of the law shall be justified."*

This places the Jew and the Gentile into two categories:
1) Hearers but not doers of the law.
2) Hearers and doers of the law (James 1:22; I John 3:7; Matthew 7:24-27) (justified by doing).

Verse 14: *"For when the Gentiles, which have not the law, do by nature the things contained in the law, these, having not the law, are a law unto themselves..."*

Though they did not have the Law Covenant, the Gentiles at times kept some of these commandments; thus, they become "a law unto themselves." Many heathen tribes have laws against adultery, murder, etc. The answer concerning this is in Romans 2:15.

Verse 15: *"...Which shew the work of the law written in their hearts, their conscience also bearing witness, and their thoughts the mean while accusing or else excusing one another;)..."*

A. **"The law written in their hearts, their conscience also bearing witness"**
The "law written in their hearts" is the "law of conscience." The "law

of conscience" is the inner law that every man has had since the Fall. It is internal, not external. How could the Gentiles do the things contained in the law if they were without law? Paul's answer explains it as the work of the conscience. Conscience means "knowing oneself; pertaining to the inward thoughts in a moral sense." Conscience is related to "conscious," meaning "knowing one's own thoughts and actions; the knowledge of what passes in one's own mind." Romans 7:23 speaks of the law of conscience as being "the law of the mind." Two main thoughts are presented here:

1) **The work of the law written in the human heart**—internal law. Man was created a moral being. Moral, in this sense, means that man is a responsible creature and has an internal sense of duty to God and his fellow man. Moral law is in his very nature and being.

2) **The law of conscience witnessing** (moral, the law of conscience or duty). "Conscience witnessing" means an "inward voice; or the inward witness of conscience that tells man right from wrong and convicts him when he has done wrong." All mankind has this inward moral law of conscience—this witness of right and wrong. This is what makes man a moral creature and different from brute creations.

Note, in John 8:1-11, that the Pharisees were under the law and were upholding the law. They stood before Jesus with the guilty adulterous woman and represented Moses and the Law of Ten Commandments (verse 5). Jesus allowed the inner moral law of conscience to do its work (verses 7-9). "…[T]hey …being *convicted* by their own *conscience*, went out one by one…" (John 8:9). They were convicted by their consciences as sinners. The Jew, under law, and the Gentile, without law, have the law of conscience to do its work.

The law of conscience began its work as soon as sin entered in the Garden of Eden (Genesis 3:1-12). Conscience was probably dormant until sin entered the world. It began its work as soon as sin entered, and this is evidenced by the thoughts that began to accuse, or excuse, Adam and Eve. However, the law of conscience is not the final court of appeal in matters of right or wrong. The reason for this is that the conscience may become stifled, scared, and resistant and lose its effect on restraining man from evil. Note these Scriptures on conscience: I Timothy 1:5, 19; 3:9; 4:2; II Timothy 1:3; Titus 1:15; Hebrews 9:8-9.

Thus, man may stifle the voice of conscience—thoughts that accuse or excuse. This varies from person to person. One person's conscience may allow "this" or believe "that" and may feel that his or her conscience is "clear," while another may reject the same thing for "conscience sake." It was because the law of conscience was inadequate and insufficient that God gave the Law of the Ten Commandments. Whether the law is defined as the "moral law of the Ten Commandments" or the "civil law," it is still law—for the civil laws are but expositions, applications, and ramifications of the basic laws in the Ten Commandments. These relate both to God and man.

The law of conscience in relation to sin. The law of conscience may accuse or excuse one man or another in the same evil thing, and its witness is stifled—as it is "written in the heart."

The Law of Ten Commandments in relation to sin. The Law of the Ten Commandments cannot be argued with or stifled. It stands, written on tables of stone, unchanging, unchangeable, uncompromising, and unflinching. It accuses the breaker and does not excuse the one (the Jew) under it. It is a silent, convincing witness and gives the hearer knowledge that is true and divine—knowledge outside of himself—of what sin is (Romans 3:19-20; I John 3:4).

Note:

- By the law is the knowledge of sin.
- Sin is transgression of the law.

The law of conscience is fallible and liable to fail. It can be mistaken and can deceive, or can be deceived, if it is stifled or seared. The Law of the Ten Commandments is infallible, incapable of error, exempt from liability to make mistakes, sound, not liable to fail, and certain because it came as a direct revelation from God to Moses in order to define sin.

B. "While accusing or else excusing one another"

Accusing – Means "to charge with a crime, offence, or fault."

Excusing – Means "justifying, making apology; to free from accusation or fault of blame." (Cf. the witness of creation [Romans 1:20]; the witness of the law [Romans 2:12-14]; the witness of conscience [Romans 2:15].)

Verse 16:   *"...In the day when God shall judge the secrets of men by Jesus Christ
           according to my gospel."*

A. **"When God shall judge"**
    "When God shall judge" refers to the Day of Judgment (II Peter 3:8-
    10; Revelation 20:11-15). (Refer also to notes on Romans 1:32 and 2:1,
    3, 5 [judgment of man].)

B. **"Secrets of men"**
    (Refer to Romans 2:15.) These are the *secret* thoughts, or sins, of
    mankind, which only God sees and knows, and of which only He can be
    the true judge (Ecclesiastes 12:14; Matthew 25:31-46).

C. **"By Jesus Christ"**
    Jesus Christ is the divinely appointed Judge (John 5:20-30). God has
    given all judgment over to the Son.

D. **"According to my gospel"**
    This is the gospel according to Paul—the gospel of justification. Not
    only does the law bring judgment, the gospel does also, even though it is
    the "gospel of the grace of God." In fact, Paul tells us that it will be sorer
    punishment to reject the gospel of the grace of God than to reject that
    which is under the law (note: Hebrews 2:1-4; 4:1-2; 10:26-31; 12:25-29).
    Note also that "Paul's gospel" is mentioned here as it is in Romans 1:9,
    15-16; 16:25-26.

E. **God shall judge.**
    If there is no law, then there can be no justice. Justice demands law,
    and when law goes into operation, it protects justice. God is holy and has
    to prosecute the sinner because of violation of the law. Justice demands
    the penalty to be executed. That penalty is death. Sin must be dealt with
    (I Timothy 1:9-10). If sin is not judged, then God's throne of holiness,
    righteousness, justice, and His law are stake (Romans 6:23; 5:12; 3:23;
    John 5:22; Acts 10:42).

The True Jew (Romans 2:17-29)

Verses 17-20: *"Behold, thou art called a Jew, and restest in the law, and makest thy boast of God, and knowest his will, and approvest the things that are more excellent, being instructed out of the law; and art confident that thou thyself art a guide of the blind, a light of them which are in darkness, an instructor of the foolish, a teacher of babes, which hast the form of knowledge and of the truth in the law.*

Paul now lists the following eleven things concerning the Jew and the things he (the Jew) boasted in (the boastful and proud Jew).

A. **"Called a Jew"**
Called a Jew "after the flesh." (Refer also to notes on Romans 2:28-29 regarding the "true Jew.") Those Jews who reject Christ are of the synagogue of Satan (Revelation 2:9; 3:9; John 8:44). This also refers to nationalistic pride (Matthew 3:9; John 8:33) and pride of race.

B. **"Restest in the law"**
"Restest in the law" refers to "leaning on, trusting in, and depending on the law"—in contrast to the lawless Gentiles (Matthew 13:11; 11:28; Isaiah 48:2). The Jews had false conceit that God gave to their nation the only true law.

C. **"Makest thy boast of God"**
The Jews boasted of their superiority—that God respected them above all Gentile nations and races on earth. The Jews boasted that they alone had the true revelation of God, not the Gentiles. Paul takes the very things they boasted in and shows them that these things actually condemned them more and brought them under greater, stricter judgment than the Gentiles were under. If unkept, the things they "boasted in" actually placed the Jews on the same ground as the Gentiles—on the same level of judgment, and greater.

D. **"And knowest His will"**
God's will is His Word, and His Word is His will (His revealed will in the Law and the Prophets) (Deuteronomy 4:8).

E. **"Approvest the things that are more excellent"**
    "That ye may approve things that are excellent..." (Philippians 1:10).
    Paul is referring to trying the things that differ and having the advantages
    of the law and the Word of God to approve, to disapprove, or to be able
    to discriminate things.

F. **"Being instructed out of the law"**
    "Instructed" in the Greek is *katechoumenes*. Jews were systematically taken
    through catechical and synagogical instruction (cf. Luke 1:4) (formal
    instruction on the basis of their critical dissemination as in the portion of
    verse 18 above).

G. **"Art confident that thou thyself art a guide of the blind"**
    This Scripture is referring to self-confidence. The Jews counted the
    Gentiles blind, and the Jews were the guides. Guiding the blind is a
    wonderful thing, but the Jews failed to recognize that they were blind
    leaders of the blind (cf. John 9:1-41; 15:22-24; Matthew 23:24; 15:14)
    (spiritual blindness).

H. **"A light of them, which are in darkness"**
    The Jews said that they were in the light while the Gentiles were in the
    dark. Blindness, however, places the Jew in the dark with the Gentiles.

I. **"An instructor of the foolish"**
    In this Scripture the Jew is the "instructor," and the Gentile is "the
    foolish." "Instructor" in the Greek is *paideuten*, meaning "the corrector."
    "Instructor" also refers to discipline, training of the Gentile proselytes.

J. **"A teacher of babes"**
    The Jews used the term "babes" in order to designate proselytes or
    novices. Paul uses it to refer to one who is not of legal age (Galatians 4:1)
    (Greek: *Nepien*).

K. **"Which hast the form of knowledge of the truth in the law"**
    This is a rich statement. The Amplified New Testament states it in
    this way: "...having in the law the embodiment of knowledge and truth."
    "The form" is not just the mere appearance, but the scheme—the correct
    embodiment of the lineaments of truth and knowledge in the law.

This statement of the advantages of the Jews after the flesh is interesting: "the *form* of *knowledge* and of *truth* in the law." There was knowledge and truth in the law, but it was in the "form"; that is, it was in the external form. The word "form" used here is the same word used in II Timothy 3:5, "Having a form of godliness [the external form], but denying the power thereof...." This was the tragedy of the Jews in regard to the law: the law to them became a matter of external forms of ordinances, rituals, and ceremonials, but the Jews missed the spirit of the law and the knowledge and truth that was hidden in it (cf. Matthew 5:1-11; Matthew 23:1-32). Jesus Himself so utterly condemned this attitude. Mere formalism (externalism, following the letter of the law), though it was commanding, was only the external. Knowledge and truth are a matter of the heart and spirit, not of the flesh. However, in spite of this fact and in spite of the failure of the Jews by degenerating to externalism in the *form* of the law, there was hidden knowledge and veiled truth.

It is Pauline revelation in "his gospel," written in his epistles, which continually goes back to the law and its externals (forms) and brings into view, brings into full light and revelation, the knowledge and the truth that was concealed therein. This is evidenced especially in the Hebrew epistle concerning the priesthood of Christ and the Day of Atonement ceremonies in relation to the Aaronic priesthood—all of which were external forms in the law. However, within these intricate detailed forms there was wonderful knowledge, truth, and the hidden wisdom of God ordained for our glory (I Corinthians 10:1-11; I Corinthians 5; Hebrews 5-10; II Corinthians 5; Matthew 21:13). Every "jot ant tittle" of the law shall be fulfilled in Christ and in His church (Matthew 5:17-18). It was not fulfilled in mere external form (or in the letter), but it was fulfilled in the spirit of knowledge and truth that was contained within it. The external form that was contained in ordinances of the law was nailed to the Cross (Colossians 2:14-17). The knowledge and truth, hidden within the law, remains for us to experience. We are to come to that knowledge and truth experientially.

At the Cross, Jesus Christ fulfilled and abolished *the form*, but the knowledge and truth hidden in the form remains and is made alive, energized, and quickened in us and to us by the Spirit of Knowledge and the Spirit of Truth. It is "in Christ" that we experience such. The knowledge and truth hidden in the form is the knowledge and truth "in Christ." Christ is the knowledge and truth of God foreshadowed in the external form of the law. The key of knowledge is in Christ (Luke 11:52). The truth is external. The Jews carried on the form and crucified the truth. (Note that in Romans 2:25-29 Paul discusses circumcision as one of these "external forms.")

Verses 21-23: *"Thou therefore which teachest another, teachest thou not thyself? thou that preachest a man should not steal, dost thou steal? thou that sayest a man should not commit adultery, dost thou commit adultery? thou that abhorrest idols, dost thou commit sacrilege? thou that makest thy boast of the law, through breaking the law dishonourest thou God?"*

In verses 21-23, Paul asks five questions.

A. **"Thou therefore which teachest another, teachest thou not thyself?"**
    Do you practice what you preach (cf. Matthew 23:3)? Do you teach yourself while teaching others (cf. Matthew 23:3 again)? Anything else is pharisaical (Psalm 50:16). Every teacher should teach himself as he teaches others.

B. **"Thou that preachest a man should not steal, dost thou steal?"**
    The Ten Commandments are listed in Exodus 20:1-10. The eighth commandment condemns stealing. Stealing includes keeping tithes and offerings, moneychanging, fraud, cheating the Gentiles, etc. (Malachi 3:8). There are thousands of ways to "steal." (See also Matthew 4:17.)

C. **"Thou that sayest a man should not commit adultery, dost thou commit adultery?"**
    The seventh commandment states, "Thou shalt not commit adultery" (cf. John 8:1-11).

D. **"Thou that abhorrest idols, doest thou commit sacrilege?"**
    This portion of Scripture involves the first and second commandments and refers to idolatry (Matthew 23). Anything that comes between the soul and God is idolatry.

E. **"Thou that makest thy boast [in] of the law, through breaking the law dishonourest thou God?"**
    This portion of Scripture refers to boasting in the law, yet at the same time breaking it (James 2:11; I John 3:4). This was typified in Israel (cf. Exodus 32-34). While God was making the Ten Commandments, Israel was breaking them.

Golden calf worship was idolatry. This was dishonoring God who had redeemed them. Another Scripture referring to boasting in the law, yet at the same time breaking it, is found in Romans 2:17.

F. **The Jew and Gentile are under sin.**
Consider Christ's definition of the Ten Commandments in Matthew 5, 6, and 7. Consider both the literal and spiritual aspects of the sins involved in breaking His commandments (with relationship to God and man). The law is holy, just, good, spiritual, and perfect. The Jews broke the spirit of the law as well as the letter of it.

The Jew "In the Law"	The Gentile "Without the Law"
In the Law (vs 12)	Without the Law (vs 12)
Sinned in the Law (vs 12)	Sinned with Law (vs 12)
Judged by the Law (vs 12)	Shall Perish without Law (vs 12)
Rests in the Law, Boasts in God (vs 17,23)	Have Not the Law (vs 14)
Knows God's Will, Instructed Out of the Law (vs18)	Doing by Natue the Things in the Law (vs 14)
Form of Knowlege and Truth in the Law (vs 19-20)	Are a Law unto Themselves (vs 14)
Breakers of the Law (vs 21-23)	Show work of Law Written in Their Hearts (vs 15)
	Conscience (Law) Bears Witness, Thoughts Now Accuse or Excuse (vs 15)

As seen in the diagram, we have the state of the Jew "in the law" and the Gentile "without the law." Both the Jew and Gentile stand as sinners, with or without the law. The law did not make them sinners. It only exposed their sin even more. They were already sinners—born in sin and shaped in iniquity. The *doers*, not the *hearers*, of the law are justified. Hearing and doing the law were the only means of justification unto life (Romans 3:20-30). The man that "doeth" all things written in the book of the law shall live in them (Galatians 3:10-12, 21-22; Deuteronomy 27:26). However, "by the deeds of the law shall no flesh be justified in God's sight" (Romans 3:19-20). Paul is exposing the Jews to themselves by the very law in which they boast. Paul is hedging them up in the fact that they have not, could not, and did not keep the law, and therefore, they cannot be justified by the law. They have been hearers only, not doers, and they stand as unjustified as any Gentile (Galatians 2:15-16). The law condemned the Jew even more—the more the light, the greater the judgment. To whom much is given much is required.

The matter of the law is very important to understand and much confusion exists over the subject—to believer and unbeliever alike. The epistle to the Romans gives the greatest and most important facts concerning the law in the New Testament. The theme of the law is developed in this epistle in a remarkable manner (refer especially to "law" in Romans 7). The main reason Paul introduces the law here, after his preceding statements, is to convince the Jews "in the law" that they also are sinners, like the Gentiles "without the law," and it is the law that works wrath (Romans 4:15). Sin is transgression of the law (I John 3:4). Hence, both the Jew and the Gentile are under sin.

Verse 24: *"For the name of God is blasphemed among the Gentiles through you, as it is written."*

"For the name of God is blasphemed"

The third commandment states, "Thou shalt not take the name of the Lord thy God in vain; for the Lord will not hold him guiltless that taketh His name in vain" (Exodus 20:7). The people of Israel alone, of any nation, had the revelation of the name of the true God given to them by Moses, in Exodus 3:15-16, and then this name was invoked upon them in the Aaronic blessing (Numbers 6:24-27). However, the prophets came to lament over the sins of Israel for the blasphemy and reproach brought upon the name of God because of the way the nation lived. The people of Israel actually became worse than the Gentile nations surrounding them. They say, "Are these the people of the Lord, whose name is called upon them?" (Jeremiah 7:8-16, 30; Ezekiel 20:9, 14, 22; 36:21-23, 20). It is even more serious for the Christian to take the name of God, as revealed in the name of the Lord Jesus Christ, in vain in water baptism by not walking according to the life of that name (Romans 6:3; Matthew 28:19; Acts 2:38). This is truly "taking the name of the Lord in vain." This goes beyond cursing, swearing, and using God's name in vain. The name of God is blasphemed today by the way that some Christians *live*. Unbelievers sometimes question and ask, "You call yourself a Christian?" "...Let everyone that nameth the name of Christ depart from iniquity" (II Timothy 2:19-20). (See also II Samuel 12:14; Isaiah 52:5.)

Verse 25: *"For circumcision verily profiteth, if thou keep the law: but if thou be a breaker of the law, thy circumcision is made uncircumcision."*

A. Circumcision

Here Paul discusses circumcision as an example of an "external form" —one in which the Jew boasted, especially with regard to a Gentile proselyte. This is the first mention in the book of Romans of the rite of circumcision. Paul introduces the subject here and also discusses it further in Romans 3:30 and 4:9-12. This follows in sequence of thought with the name of God mentioned in verse 24. The name of God and circumcision were vitally related in the nation of Israel.

The covenant of circumcision (Acts 7:8) was given in Genesis 17. It involved three things:

1) Blood shedding (cutting away of the flesh) (flesh and blood).
2) Cutting of the flesh and invocation of the child's name.
3) The ceremony took place on the eighth day.

Circumcision was *before law*. It was given to Abraham while he was in grace and faith-righteousness (Genesis 17). Circumcision was confirmed *under law*. It was given to Israel, both in grace and under the Law Covenant (Exodus 12:43-45; Joshua 5:1-9). So important was this rite of circumcision that not one uncircumcised male was permitted to eat of the Passover lamb (Exodus 12:44-48). And again, even though God appeared to Moses in the burning bush and gave him the revelation of His redemptive name, God sought to kill Moses because he had not brought His children into covenant relationship with Himself through this rite (Exodus 4:24-26). The Jews themselves would even violate the Sabbath day by circumcising a man in order to bring him into the Abrahamic and Mosiac Covenant relationship (John 7:19-23). Only by circumcision was a child brought into the covenant relationship with God and entitled to the promises, privileges, and blessings of this covenant (Luke 1:59; Acts 7:8; Philippians 3:5; Leviticus 12:3 Joshua 5:1-12).

B. "Thy circumcision is made uncircumcision"

Circumcision of the Gentiles so that they could receive the blessings of Abraham was a great issue in the early church (Acts 15:5; 16:3; 21:21). The Jews looked upon the Gentiles as "uncircumcised dogs" (Philippians 3:2-3), outside of the covenants of promise, without God, without hope, and without Christ in this world. The Jews boasted that the law and the covenant of circumcision made them superior to all nations. However, in this verse, Paul lets the prop of the law, which the Jews leaned upon, pierce them. He also causes the prop of circumcision to snap under them, leaving them as helpless and hopeless as the Gentiles Circumcision, because it was a sign and a seal (Romans 4:11), would be profitable only if the law was kept (cf. Galatians 5:3). If the law was not kept, then the circumcised in the flesh became as uncircumcised in the spirit—in the sight and mind of God. Circumcision becomes uncircumcision if the law is violated.

Verse 26: *"Therefore if the uncircumcision keep the righteousness of the law, shall not his uncircumcision be counted for circumcision?"*

"Counted for circumcision"
Thus, if the Gentile keeps *the righteousness of the law*, his righteousness is counted for true circumcision. Uncircumcision becomes circumcision if the law is kept (Acts 10:34-35).

Verse 27: *"And shall not uncircumcision which is by nature, if it fulfil the law, judge thee, who by the letter and circumcision dost transgress the law?"*

"Judge thee"
Thus, if the Gentile, uncircumcised in the physical sense, fulfills the law, he becomes the judge of the Jew who follows only the letter of the flesh of circumcision yet transgresses the law (Matthew 12:41).

Verses 28-29: *"For he is not a Jew, which is one outwardly; neither is that circumcision, which is outward in the flesh: but he is a Jew, which is one inwardly; and circumcision is that of the heart, in the spirit, and not in the letter; whose praise is not of men, but of God."*

Summarizing Verses 28 and 29
In summarizing verses 28-29, we set forth the contrast between the true and false Jew. "Jew," etymologically, means "a praised one" (cf. Genesis 49:8). "Judah" means "praise" (see also I Corinthians 4:5). Note the differences below:
The True Jew
- The Spiritual Jew
- Inwardly

- Circumcision in the Heart (inward)
- In the Spirit
- Praise of God
- Keeper of the Law

The False Jew
- The Physical Jew
- Outwardly
- Circumcision in the Flesh (outward)
- In the Letter
- Praise of Men (Judah)
- Transgressor of the Law

Verses 25-29: *Summary*

The True Jew and True Circumcision

In verses 25 through 29, Paul declares the *true Jew* and *true circumcision*. They are not of the flesh or of external form. Please also note that Paul is not stating this of himself, or even by revelation, but he is simply giving illumination to that which was in the Old Testament itself and which the Old Testament said and foretold. He is taking the Old Testament revelation and amplifying it in regard to circumcision. That is, the Old Testament Scriptures plainly spoke of both literal and spiritual circumcision and also pointed to true spiritual circumcision of the heart. The Mosaic or Old Covenant and Abrahamic Covenant simply pointed to the New Covenant circumcision. The flesh pointed to the spirit, the external to the internal. The tragedy was that the Jews became caught up in the external form of the rite and missed what it pointed to—of the heart. They gloried especially in Gentile flesh (Galatians 6:13).

The Old Testament Scriptures spoke of:
- Circumcision of the *heart* (Deuteronomy 10:16; 30:6; Jeremiah 4:4; Leviticus 26:41),
- Circumcision of the *lips* (Exodus 6:12, 30),
- Circumcision of the *ears* (Jeremiah 6:10; Acts 7:51),
- Circumcision of the *flesh* (Genesis 17; Ezekiel 44:7-9).

The New Testament simply confirms true circumcision to be of the heart and in the spirit—not in the flesh. It is internal, not external. (See Colossians 2:11; Galatians 5:1-6; Colossians 3:11; I Corinthians 7:18-19; Ephesians 2:11; Galatians 6:15.) Therefore, fleshly circumcision profited if one kept the law because it was a sign and seal of that fact that "the flesh" had been "cut off." Paul, however, proves that the Jew had not kept the law; therefore, the Jew's circumcision had no profit or gain because, in breaking the law, his circumcision became uncircumcision. In other words, the Jew is made as an uncircumcised Gentile—Gentilized and a lawbreaker under the judgment of God. The "letter" (Old Testament & New Testament) kills, but the Spirit gives life. The Jews kept the letter (form) of the law but missed the spirit of the law. Within the letter was, and must be, the Spirit. They preached the letter and thus, stifled the Spirit. This is seen in their boasting of Jewishness and circumcision but missing the fact of inward Jewishness and inward circumcision of the heart. What actually occurs is that the Gentile becomes as if he had been circumcised—a true spiritual Jew—if he keeps the righteous law, and the Jew becomes as if he had been uncircumcised— a Gentile person—if he breaks the righteous law.

In these verses, Paul leaves the Jew without law and without circumcision to lean upon for self-righteousness. He fully shows that both the Jew and Gentile have violated God's laws. "Conscience" and "commandments" condemn all. The Jew stands uncircumcised before God, which leaves him in the same helpless condition as the Gentile. (Refer also to the notes on 3:1, 30; 4:9-13.)

Note below Jeremiah 9:25-26:
- Circumcised Punished with the Uncircumcised
- Nations Uncircumcised (in the flesh)
- House of Israel (uncircumcised in the heart)

The diagram on the following page brings into focus the general, overall view of the Old Testament "covenant of circumcision."

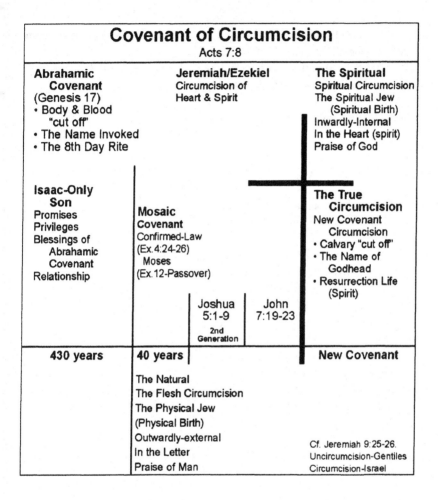

The Advantage of the Jew (Romans 3:1-8)

After casting down the Jew's self confidence in the law and circumcision in Romans 2, Paul anticipates their questions. He answers the five following objectives in Romans 3:1-8:

1) "What advantage then hath the Jew?" (Romans 3:1). *The advantage of having the Word of God.*

2) "What profit is there of circumcision?" (Romans 3:1). *There is an advantage if the law is kept. It is a sign and seal to them.*

3) If man's sin brings glory to God, how can God be just to punish man? (Romans 3:5). *God must be and is just.*

4) Does the unbelief of the Jew destroy the validity of God's Word? (Romans 3:3). *No, God's Word is true.*
5) If God gets greater glory through my life and sin, then why does He judge me as a sinner? (Romans 3:7-8). *God is holy and must judge sin.*

(Please see the following Scripture verses for greater explanation.)

Verse 1: *"What advantage then hath the Jew? or what profit is there of circumcision?"*

A. **"What advantage then hath the Jew?"**
    The Jew had the Word of God as an advantage.

B. **"What profit is there of circumcision?"**
    Paul's answer to this question is that there is much profit in every way. Paul also lists the advantages that the Jews had above the Gentile nations (note verse 2 with Romans 9:4-5). The things listed profited, and were privileges of, the Jews and therefore, they were also responsibilities the Jews were accountable for. Circumcision profits if the law is kept (cf. 2:25). It was a covenant relationship with God. It was to them the sign and seal of their righteousness. Thus, the greatest advantage was to have the promises and benefits of the Abrahamic Covenant, of which circumcision was the sign and seal in the flesh (Psalm 147:19; Deuteronomy 4:7-8).

Verse 2: *"Much every way: chiefly, because that unto them were committed the oracles of God."*

"Oracles of God"
    The chief advantage of the Jews, and the highest, precious privilege and responsibility given to them, is the fact that they received the oracles of God. Note the use of the word "oracle" in Scripture:
*   "[E]nquired at the oracle of God..." (II Samuel 16:23).
*   The holiest was the oracle of God (I Kings 6:5, 16, 19-31; II Chronicles 3).
*   "[L]ift up my hands toward thy holy oracle" (Psalm 28:2).
*   The lively oracles given to Moses (Acts 7:38).
*   Oracles of God committed to the Jews (Romans 3:2).
*   "The first principles of the oracles of God" (Hebrews 5:12).

- "If any man speak, let him speak as the oracles of God..." (I Peter 4:11).
- The ark placed before the holy oracle (II Chronicles 3:16; 4:20; 5:7, 9).

The "oracle" means "the speaking place" from where the voice of God came. It was actually the holiest place in the tabernacle or temple—the place where God spoke from off the bloodstained mercy seat in the cherubimed ark of the covenant.

Thus, we have:

- **The lively oracles** (the Ten Commandments given to Moses at Mt. Sinai)
- **The oracle** (the cherubimed mercy seat in the tabernacle and temple) (God spoke from there.)
- **The living oracle of God** (personified in Jesus Christ)
- **The oracle of today** (God speaking in Christ in His church)

The oracles were committed to the Jews. That was both a privilege and a responsibility. The Jews were privileged, above all nations, to hear the voice of God (Deuteronomy 4:5, Exodus 19:20), and they were also responsible, above all nations, to be guardians of the Word of God—the Holy Scriptures, the Oracles of God. All of this was prophetic and symbolic of the Lord Jesus Christ, who today is *the Oracle* of God to man (Hebrews 1:1-2 [Amplified New Testament]; John 1:1-3, 14-18). God has nothing to say to man apart from Christ. Christ is *the speaking place* of the voice of God. Whoever hears Christ hears the Father, for it is the Father's words that He speaks. God was in Christ (Hebrews 1:1-2). (Refer also to John 14:1-11; Deuteronomy 18:18; John 10:30-41; 12:44-50; Colossians 1:19; 2:9; II Corinthians 5:19 and John 1:1-14.)

Verse 3: *"For what if some did not believe? shall their unbelief make the faith of God without effect?"*

"Shall their unbelief make the faith of God without effect?"
The Jews' unbelief is dealt with more fully in Romans 9, 10, and 11. Even though the Jews had the advantage of having the oracles of God, they failed to believe. The fact of faith is brought to greater view in Romans 4:25-5:2 and 10:17-18. Romans 10:17 states, "...faith cometh

by hearing, and hearing by the word of God," or, in other words, by the *oracle of God*. Hence, the Jews could have had faith—letting the oracle of God create faith (Hebrews 4:1-2)—but they fell into the slough of externalism and formalism so that no faith was evident in the spirit of the Word of God. Moses lamented over this in the Scriptures (Deuteronomy 32:20) when he said that they were "children in whom there is no faith."

There are only two specific uses, according to the King James Version's translation, of the word "faith" in the Old Testament. One of the uses is in a negative sense (Deuteronomy 32:20), the other is in a positive sense (Habakkuk 2:4). Habakkuk 2:4 is quoted by Paul as the foundation text for this epistle (Romans 1:17). However, even though some of the Jews did not believe the oracles of God, their unbelief did not make the faith (or faithfulness) of God of no effect. Unbelief will hinder man from receiving blessings that God has for him, but man's unbelief in no way affects the character of God and His faithfulness. God is faithful. "If we believe not, yet he abideth [remaineth] faithful..." (II Timothy 2:13). He cannot deny Himself (II Timothy 2:13). Unbelief hindered Jesus Christ—the oracle of God—in His earthly ministry of blessing to the others, yet He Himself was faithful, unchanging, and unchangeable (Matthew 13:58; Mark 6:6). Unbelief negates faith in man.

Verse 4: *"God forbid: yea, let God be true, but every man a liar; as it is written, That thou mightest be justified in thy sayings, and mightest overcome when thou art judged."*

A. "God forbid"

In this verse, Paul answers the question posed in Romans 3:3—"God forbid." The unbelief of the Jews, or the whole of mankind, cannot make the faith of God without effect. Why? Because God is true, and every man is a liar (cf. verse 7). This is why the unbelief of man cannot affect the faith of God. God is as true as ever, as commented in verse 3. The liars of mankind can never alter or affect the truth of God. Truth is truth, regardless, and is as God Himself—unchanging and unchangeable. We can do nothing against the truth (II Corinthians 13:8). Man may twist it, pervert it, and cause it to become error, but truth itself can not be overcome. It is eternal and incorruptible because it is spiritual.

B. **"Every man a liar"**
    The original temptation to the woman (and all mankind represented) by the serpent was a lie. This is the nature and character of Satan to speak, act, live, and believe a lie. (See also John 8:44-47; II Thessalonians 2:1-12; Psalm 62:9; 116:11). It is impossible for God to lie (Hebrews 6:18a).

C. **"As it is written, That thou mightest be justified in thy sayings, and mightest overcome when thou art judged"** (cf. Psalm 51:4)
    Paul quotes this section from Psalm 51:4b. This psalm is not only a confession of *sin* in its outworkings in David's life, but also a confession of the very heart of the problem of sin. This is stated in Psalm 51:5, "Behold, I was shapen in iniquity; and in sin did my mother conceive me." In Psalm 51:4, he states, "Against thee, thee only, have I sinned [not just Uriah's wife, Bathsheba], and done this evil in thy sight: that thou mightest be justified when thou speakest, and be clear when thou judgest." Two great, important facts are recognized and confessed here by David, relative to the portion of Scripture Paul quotes in Romans 3:4:

1) All have been conceived and born in sinfulness—in a sinful state.
2) All sin is against God, directly or indirectly. God desires this truth in the inward parts. (Psalm 51:6).

    These two facts give God ground to speak to man as He does. God is indeed justified in His Word, in His sayings to and against man, and in His judgment of man. Man cannot justify himself by any of his sayings before God. "Behold, I am vile; what shall I answer thee? I will lay mine hand upon my mouth" (Job 40:4) (Job 40:1-5). It is wise for man to do so; that is, lay his hand over his mouth (cf. Romans 3:19).

Verses 5-6: *"But if our unrighteousness commend the righteousness of God, what shall we say? Is God unrighteous who taketh vengeance? (I speak as a man) God forbid: for then how shall God judge the world?"*

"Is God unrighteous who taketh vengeance?...God forbid: for then how shall God judge the world?"
    (Cf. Amplified New Testament.) Romans 3 through 8 show the line of argument that Paul takes up to offset the carnal reasoning of the Jews. The context of these verses is that man cries out against the truth of the

judgment of God against the world, and God takes *vengeance* (II Thessalonians 1:9-10) against the ungodly, and, whatever man does, the character of God remains unaffected. The carnal reasoning behind these verses, though, is that, if God remains faithful and true, in spite of and regardless of the unrighteousness, unfaithfulness, and lies of man, then why should God judge man and take vengeance on him? The Jews argued that man's unrighteousness commanded (established, exhibited) the righteousness of God. They argued that God *became* unrighteous to take vengeance on man. However, God's character remains unchanged— despite what man does.

This same principal is argued from the angle of the truth of the grace of God in Romans 5:20 and 6:14-15, where the Jews could figuratively say, "If grace abounds where sin abounds, then the more we sin, the more we experience the grace of God." This is the same line of carnal reasoning against the character of God relative to the judgment of God that is seen here in these verses under consideration. If this carnal reasoning is true, then God cannot even judge the world, let alone the Jews! This reasoning comes from a lack of understanding of the very nature and character of the Holy God.

Verse 7: *"For if the truth of God hath more abounded through my lie unto his glory; why yet am I also judged as a sinner?"*

"Why yet am I also judged as a sinner" (cf. 9:19; 3:4)

This is the same line of argument continued from Romans 3:5-6. This carnal reasoning is restated, "The more lies a man tells, and every man is a liar (verse 4), then it just makes the truth, and the fact that God is true (verse 4), more manifest." The Jews' argument was that it actually abounds to the glory of God (read also Amplified New Testament). And, once more this reasoning states, "If through our falsehoods God's integrity is magnified, is advertised, and abounds to His glory, then why am I still being judged as a sinner?" And, another example: "Just as black makes white stand out, and actually makes the white appear whiter, so does the unrighteousness and lie of man (the black) make the righteousness and the truth of God (the white) appear more glorious." This was the carnal line of reasoning Paul had to deal with. If this reasoning is correct, then why is man judged as a sinner? Note "judgment" in the following verses (Romans 1:32; 2:1-5; 2:12,16,27; 3:5-7):

- God shall judge the world of mankind (Romans 3:6).

- God shall judge the sinner (Romans 3:7).
- Jew or Gentile—God is Judge (Romans 1:32).
- Sin and sinners must be judged (Romans 2:1-3).
- There is a Day of Judgment (Romans 2:16; 2:5).

Verse 8: *"And not rather, (as we be slanderously reported, and as some affirm that we say,) Let us do evil, that good may come? whose damnation is just."*

A. **"As we be slanderously reported, and as some affirm that we say"**

This verse states that this slanderous report that had been leveled against Paul's teaching of the grace of God—"Let us do evil that good may come"—is the same evil doctrine of "Let us sin that grace may abound." To slander means "to tell the truth in such a way as to give the false or lying impression" (Charles Finney). These were false accusations against Paul's message.

B. **"Damnation is just"**

God's vengeance—judgment unto damnation upon sinners—is indeed just.

Verses 3-8: *Summary*

In verses 3 through 8, opposites are set against each other as seen below:
- The unbelief of man – The faith of God (verse 3)
- The lie of man – The truth of God (verses 4 and 7)
- The unrighteousness of man – The righteousness of God (verse 5)
- The evil of man – The good of God (verse 8)
- The sin of man – The grace of God

Verses 3 through 8 really deal with the arguments and objections of the Jews against the judgment of God against them. They, however, had the oracles of God and so were without excuse.

Romans 1 through 2 has set forth the character and nature of man—both Jew and Gentile—as seen in the words listed above, and, in contrast, the opposite words are listed that show forth the character and nature of God. God is totally opposite to all that man is (his evil nature and character), and God must deal with all that is opposite to Himself. If He does not, His throne of holiness would be at stake!

The Divine Verdict – All the World Is Guilty (Romans 3:9-20)

The summary of Paul's arguments so far will be found in this following section. The Gentiles (Romans 1) and the Jews (Romans 2) are *all* under sin!

Verse 9: *"What then? are we better than they are? No, in no wise: for we have before proved both Jews and Gentiles, that they are all under sin..."*

"Both Jews and Gentiles, that they are all under sin"

The question of unrighteousness among both Jews and Gentiles has been settled—both are unrighteous. Now Paul shows that both are also guilty before God because both are under the dominion of sin (Galatians 3:21-22). The expression "under sin" suggests that everything is held down by and subject to sin's power (Amplified New Testament) (i.e., we are ruled over as helpless and hopeless slaves to sin). All men are under, subject to, ruled over, and enslaved by sin. They are helpless to deliver themselves from sin's tyranny apart from God's grace. Sin *reigns* as king over every man (Romans 5:21). (Cf. verse 9, under sin; verse 19, under the law.) Verses 10 through 19, which follow, are founded upon the fact that all are under sin.

Verses 10-18: *"...As it is written, There is none righteous, no, not one: there is none that understandeth, there is none that seeketh after God. They are all gone out of the way, they are together become unprofitable; there is none that doeth good, no, not one. Their throat is an open sepulchre; with their tongues they have used deceit; the poison of asps is under their lips: whose mouth is full of cursing and bitterness: their feet are swift to shed blood: destruction and misery are in their ways: and the way of peace have they not known: there is no fear of God before their eyes.*

A. Aspects of the Divine Character of God

In the passages under consideration, we see God speaking as: a judge (verses 10-12), with at least six sweeping charges of guilt; a physician (verses 13-15), with a diagnosis of man's sick condition; and a historian (verses 16-18). These are three aspects of the divine character of God dealt with in Romans 3:10-18.

B. **Old Testament Scripture References**

Paul now appeals to Scripture references of the Old Testament. In Romans 3 we have at least seven Old Testament quotes, as seen in the following:

- Romans 3:4 from Psalm 51:4
- Romans 3:10-12 from Psalm 14:1-3
- Romans 3:13a from Psalm 5:9 (Jeremiah 5:16)
- Romans 3:13c from Psalm 140:3
- Romans 3:14 from Psalm 10:7
- Romans 3:15-17 from Proverbs 14:16 and Isaiah 59:7-8
- Romans 3:18 from Psalm 36:1

Thus, Paul weaves his context together with Old Testament revelation of man's condition. Note the universality of guilt. The statements given below are all-inclusive of sinners—Jew and Gentile, none are exempted.

- Jews and Gentiles—all under sin.
- "...There is *none* righteous, no, not one..."
- "...There is *none* that understandeth..."
- "...[T]here is *none* that seeketh after God."
- "They are *all* gone out of the way..."
- "...[T]hey are *together* become unprofitable..."
- "...[T]here is *none* that doeth good, *no, not one.*" Thus, none are excluded. None are exempted. Both Jew and Gentile are all on the same level in God's sight.
- "For *all* have sinned and come short of the glory of God..." (Romans 3:23).

Man is a sinner by nature (what he is), a sinner by action (what he does), and a sinner by his own choice (what he wills). Thus, God must crush man in mind, heart, and being in order to make man realize his own condition and recognize his need of God.

As G. Raymond Carlson states in *Romans* (Teacher's Manual) (p. 22-23) that God speaks as a judge (verses 10-12), as a physician (verses 13-15), and as a historian (verses 16-18).

Verses 10-12: *". . .As it is written, There is none righteous, no, not one: There is none
that understandeth, there is none that seeketh after God. They are all gone out
of the way, they are together become unprofitable; there is none that doeth good,
no, not one."*

A. **Jews and Gentiles—*all* are under sin.**
   All nations, chosen or unchosen, are held under the power, sway, and
   dominion of "King Sin."

B. **"None righteous"**
   Before Paul can declare the righteousness of God in the gospel (1:16-
   17)—the righteousness that he is about to lead into in verses 3:21-25 and
   4:1-5—he must declare the universal fact that no man is righteous—no,
   not one. The self-righteousness of the Jews and the unrighteousness of
   the Gentiles must be dealt with. None are righteous, no, not one. Before
   man will hear the gospel of the faith-righteousness of God in Christ, and
   before he will be able to receive it, he must be utterly stripped of every
   vestige of self or other righteousness and be shown as he is—unrighteous
   before God.
   Not only must he see that he is unrighteous in God's eyes, but he must
   also see that he is incapable of making himself righteous before God in his
   own eyes. "Can the Ethiopian change his skin, or the leopard his spots?
   then may ye also do good, that are accustomed to do evil" (Jeremiah
   13:23). The answer is evident. Fallen man, like the Ethiopian and the
   leopard, cannot change himself. He cannot do good in and of himself.
   (Note the word "unrighteous" in Romans 1:18, 29; 2:8; 3:5.)

C. **"None that understandeth"**
   "None that understandeth" is referring to spiritual dullness or, in other
   words, a lack of spiritual perception or insight (cf. 1:21). Sin blinded the
   mind and understanding of man in relation to spiritual things. Man ate of
   the Tree of Knowledge of Good and Evil, and his understanding became
   darkened (Ephesians 2:1-3). (Refer also to "understanding.")

D. **"None that seeketh after God"** (cf. Psalm 14:2)
   Man, of himself, would not seek the Lord God. This is seen in the fall
   of Adam. God sought man; man did not seek God (Genesis 3:1-10). If
   God had not come seeking man, it is certain that man would not have
   sought after God. It is not in man.

The reaction of sin is to hide from the voice of the Lord, to hide behind some garden tree (Genesis 3). The Son of Man came to seek and to save that which was lost. Man basically does not want God, nor does he have any desire to seek after God because he is under the power of sin. God came, in *grace*, to seek man.

E. "They are all gone out of the way" (cf. Psalm 14:3; Isaiah 53:6)
    "Gone astray" means "aside, off the divine path" (Psalm 14:3). "All we like sheep have gone astray; we have turned every one to his own way..." (Isaiah 53:6). "There is a way which seemeth right unto a man, but the end thereof are the ways of death" (Proverbs 14:12). (Also see Proverbs 15:9.) These Scriptures aptly describe man going out of God's way and going his own way, as with Adam and Eve. Adam did what we would have done—the whole race was in him. He prefigures us (cf. 16-17).

F. "They are together become unprofitable" (cf. Psalm 14:3)
    "None profitable" also refers to men being all together filthy (stinky). They were unprofitable to God in their stinking state of corruption (Isaiah 1:5-6). This is the main condition of man before God. There is nothing good in man, and nothing profitable can proceed from man. Man is useless in sin.

G. "None that doeth good" (cf. Psalm 14:1-3)
    How can man *do* good if he is *not good* in himself? All that proceeds from unrighteous man is evil or tainted with evil. Man is not a sinner because he sins; he sins because he is a sinner by nature. Man *does what he does* because of *what he is*. None do good because none are good. Only God is good.

H. "For all have sinned and come short of the glory of God" (Romans 3:23; I John 3:4)
    Sin is transgression of the law. The glory of God is His righteous character and standard—His holy character and being. Man sinned and fell short of the glory of God.

Thus, in these verses, Romans 10-13 with Romans 3:23, we have eight charges of God as the Judge.

Verses 13-18: *"Their throat is an open sepulchre; with their tongues they have used deceit; the poison of asps is under their lips: whose mouth is full of cursing and bitterness: their feet are swift to shed blood: destruction and misery are in their ways: and the way of peace have they not known: there is no fear of God before their eyes."*

Now in Verses 13 through 18, the diagnosis of the Great Physician is listed. There are six deadly things mentioned in this diagnosis of God concerning man. Note the use of the physical members of man's being that are used to describe his spiritual condition.

A. **"Their throat is an open sepulchre"**

Jesus called the Pharisees "white-washed sepulchres" —white washed but not washed white (cf. Matthew 23:27). Their outward appearance was beautiful; however, within was as if they were full of dead man's bones (rottenness, stinkiness) (Luke 11:44; Acts 23:3). Corruption can only proceed from an *open* sepulchre because of that which is within it. Naturally speaking, the throat (mouth) reveals the condition of the inward parts. Man is "death" within, unless the vileness and pollution of the throat, that stinks, is dealt with (Mark 7:14-23).

B. **"With their tongues they have used deceit"**

They have tongues of deceit that are opposite to the truth. "Deceit" means "opposed to truthfulness." (Also note the "tongue" chapter in James 3.)

C. **"The poison of asps is under their lips"**

The bite of the serpent or asp injects the deadly poison hidden within them (James 3:8). The lips of men are full of deadly poison—poison that flows through the whole human race. A serpent, with forked tongue, injected the poison of sin into the human bloodstream (cf. Genesis 3:1-6).

D. **"Whose mouth is full of cursing and bitterness"**

Cursing is the opposite of blessing. Cursing and blessing can come out of the same tongue (James 3:9-10), as can bitterness or sweetness (James 3:11). The mouth is the entrance and exit of the sepulchre.

E. "Their feet are swift to shed blood: destruction and misery are in their ways: and the way of peace have they not known"

Feet that are swift to shed blood speaks of murder and death-dealing. Men have gone the way of destruction and misery and are out of God's way (cf. verse 12a). The way of peace they have not known. God's way is the way of peace.

F. "There is not fear of God before their eyes"

Men are fearless—unafraid of God or His judgments against sin and sinners. Sin hardens, sin brazens, and sin defies God. There is no reverence or fear of God involved in it. Sin brought fear, but it also hardens the heart in its outworking so that man ceases to fear God (note Genesis 3:9-10).

G. Summarizing Verses 13 through 18

Thus, the members of the physical body are used, figuratively and literally, in a bad sense. All of these described members were used in the fall of man (Genesis 3:1-6). Paul refers, in Romans 6:19, to the yielding of such members as servants of sin. Eve saw (eyes) that the forbidden tree was good and pleasant to the sight. She walked (feet) to the tree and partook (ate, the mouth, also lips, tongue, and throat) of the forbidden fruit, and every evil in the human race sprang from that initial sin.

Verses 10-18: *Summary*

Thus, sin is in human nature (verses 10-12), and sin is in human conduct (verses 13-18). What is inside shows on the outside, in the heart, and then in the members. (See also Proverbs 6:16-19.)

Verse 19: *"Now we know that what things soever the law saith, it saith to them who are under the law: that every mouth may be stopped, and all the world may become guilty before God."*

A. "That every mouth may be stopped"

"That every mouth may be stopped," means "closed, shut up, with absolutely nothing to say, not a word in self-defense." Man stands speechless, silenced before God. This is a guilty world, subject to the judgment of God. The law has done its work, and there is no hope for man outside of grace.

B. "All the world may become guilty" (The Divine Verdict)

After the exposure of man (as he is) in verses 9-18, verse 19 closes with the fact that the Jews and Gentiles are all under sin and that the "divine verdict" for their lives is "guilty!"   Rephrased, this verse says, "Whatsoever the law says (i.e., Psalms, Scriptures of Old Testament, etc.), it says to those (the Jews) under its rule and authority." The Gentile, without the law, is indeed guilty and is fully proven so by his evil deeds, but the Jew, ever trying to excuse himself and his guilt as having the law, is also proven guilty by that very law he boasted in. Paul uses the Jews' own Scriptures to convince them of sin, righteousness, and judgment (cf. John 16:9-11). The Scriptures Paul quotes were written to the Jews—not to the Gentiles—so by *their own* Scriptures Paul shows them their guilt before God. Jew and Gentile—whether under law or without law—are all are under sin. Every mouth is stopped, and the *entire world* is guilty before God. If the Jew excuses his own guilt and pleads "not guilty," the verdict of God Almighty is still "guilty." "For whosoever shall keep the whole law, and yet offend in one point, he is guilty of all" (James 2:10) (James 2:8-13). Note, especially, the laws concerning the Levitical offerings, also called the "sin and trespass offerings," and the use of the word "guilty." Here we have the often-repeated statement, "If a soul sins, through ignorance, against any of the commandments of the Lord, though he must (know) it not yet is he guilty" (Leviticus 4:2, 13-22, 27; 5:2, 4-5, 17, paraphrased). The law of God is clear. Whether a man knows it or not—whether he sins ignorantly or knowingly—he is *guilty* before God. Innocence or ignorance is not bliss in this sense! Notice how often the word "guilty" is used in Leviticus 4-5 concerning these related offerings.

Sin and *trespasses* make men guilty before God. Paul has proven the Jew and the Gentile to be such (Galatians 3:22). It is only when a man recognizes his guilt before God that he can throw himself on the *grace* and *mercy* of God (cf. verses 24-25). Joseph's brothers had to reconcile, or recognize, their guilt in relation to their brother before they could come to the ground of grace, forgiveness, and reconciliation (Genesis 42:21). The sinner must come before God and Christ in the same way. The purpose of the law was to reveal man's guilt (cf. John 8:1-10). The conscience at work brings about guilt over the broken law, exposes man, and casts the Pharisee out of the presence of the sinless Christ. Thus, whether it be the law of conscience or the Law of the Ten Commandments, both bring man to a realization of his guilt before God.

C. The Tabernacle of Heaven's Court Case Scene

The scene depicted before us in Romans 1-3 is that of the "divine court case," with the Jew and Gentile on trial—heaven's court case against rebellious man. The verdict of Almighty God is "guilty," and the penalty is "death." The court case has come to a close—there is no difference between Jew and Gentile. No soul dare plead for justification. The proof is clear and convincing. There is no appeal and no reversal. Note the tabernacle of heaven's court case scene:

Tabernacle of Heaven's Court Case Scene

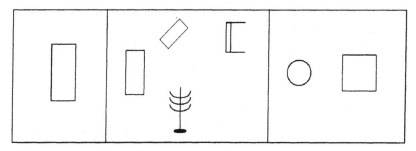

- Who is the judge? *God*
- Who is the prosecutor (attorney)? *The Holy Spirit Convicting (John 16:9-11).* A prosecutor is one who pursues formed charges against an offender to bring him to final judgment.
- Who is the advocate? *Jesus Christ*
- What are the books? *The Old and New Testaments (books of the law, book of works, code ethics)*
- What are the two witnesses against the Gentile world? *Creation and Conscience*
- What are the further witnesses against the Jewish world? *The Law and the Prophets, Angels Also*
- Who is the accused? *Mankind—Jew and Gentile*
- What is the significance of the Jews? *Divine Government, Angelic Hosts*
- What are the charges against the accused? *Sins, Violation of the Law (1 John 3:4), High Treason (Romans 1)*
- What is the court verdict? *Guilty (Romans 3:19; Leviticus 4-5), Case and Trial*
- What is the penalty? *The Death Penalty (Romans 6:23)*
- Who is the adversary? *The Devil (Zechariah 3:1-6)*

Verse 20: *"Therefore by the deeds of the law there shall no flesh be justified in his sight: for by the law is the knowledge of sin."*

A. **"There shall no flesh be justified in his sight"**

As Paul has said, the entire world (Jew and Gentile) is guilty, and it is impossible for anyone to be justified on the ground of the law in the sight of God. Why? What does this Scripture mean by "justification"? Why can no flesh—Gentile or Jew—be justified by the deeds of the law?

It is important that a clear understanding of Romans 3:20 is seen because of its relation to the law and the two great opposing doctrines, which are listed below:

Justification by Works (deeds of the law; what a man does) (Romans 2:13, also dealt with in 3:19-31; 4:1-5)

Justification by Faith (hearing by faith; what God has done in Christ) (Romans 1:17; Romans 5)

Here Paul resumes his apparent digression on the introduction of the subject of "law" and "justification" from Romans 2:12-29 and 3:19-21. To the Jewish mind, the Gentile was already condemned. Hence, Paul concentrates on the Jew in relation to the law and proves, by the very law that the Jew boasted in, that the Jew did not and could not keep the law. Therefore the law condemned him. The law could not justify him or put him in right standing before God. Before Paul can deal with the glory of his foundational text of Romans 1:17—"The just shall live by faith"—he must show the utter impossibility of anyone being justified by works of the law, and he must show the futility of *trying* to be justified by such (Acts 13:39). Note the statements below:

* None can be justified by the law.
* The utter futility of trying to be justified by the law is evident (Acts 13:39).
* The law is not of faith but of works.
* To seek to be justified by the law is to seek justification by works (what man can do).
* There is no ground of justification in man himself (Psalm 14:2-3).
* None can be justified by the law, whether it be moral, civil, or ceremonial law.

Let us follow the importance of these statements and the doctrine of "justification by works (deeds) of the law." See further explanation below:

- "...[I]f a man *do,* he shall even *live* in them" (Ezekiel 20:11).
- "...[I]f a man *do,* he shall *live* in them..." (Leviticus 18:5).
- "For Moses describeth the righteousness which is of the law, That the man which *doeth* those things shall *live* by them" (Romans 10:5).
- "...For not the *hearers* of the law are just before God, but the *doers* of the law shall be justified" (Romans 2:13).
- "...Cursed is every one that continueth not in all things which are written in the book of the law to do them. But that no man is justified by the law in the sight of God, it is evident: for, The just shall *live by faith.* And the law is not of faith: but, The man that *doeth* them shall *live* in them" (Galatians 3:10-12).

The law says, "do and live!" The gospel says, "live and do!" (believe, live, and do—grace). The emphasis in these verses above is on *doing.* "The man that *doeth* them shall *live* in or by them" (Ezeziel 20:11, paraphrased). Life, based on the law, is granted upon the basis of doing—upon the basis of works (what man has done, what man can do) (cf. Luke 10:28; Nehemiah 9:29). This emphasis upon "do" is clearly manifested in Exodus 19 and Exodus 24, at the giving of the "law of covenant." Note that Exodus 19:8 states, "...All that the Lord hath spoken we will do...." Also Exodus 24:3-7 states, "...and all the people answered with one voice, and said, All the words that the Lord hath said we will do." However, life was not to be gained by the law. "...[I]f there had been a law which could have given life, verily righteousness should have been by the law" (Galatians 3:21; also see 3:22).

In order to fully appreciate the importance of these verses just quoted (in that the Lord took the people of Israel at their word, and in that the Lord promised them *life* if they would *do* His commandments [Leviticus 18:5; Ezekiel 20:11; Nehemiah 9:29]), it is necessary to gather a few prominent facts concerning the background of the giving of the law, and concerning the law which is called "the law of works" (Romans 3:27; 10:5).

When the Lord sent Moses to Israel, the nation was in hopeless bondage and slavery to the nation of Egypt. The people of Israel were unable to be delivered or to deliver themselves from the utter misery of their condition. There was absolutely nothing that they could *do* to release themselves from this slavery and oppression. If works could have delivered them, they would have worked until death, but nothing they could *do* could free them from the Egyptians. What then could be done? From man's viewpoint, nothing; but from God's viewpoint, everything. Hence, God came to Israel entirely in grace (Romans 3:24-27) and mercy and told Israel that He would save them if they would trust Him, believe Him, and wholly cast themselves on Him, His power, and His ability.

Through the call of Moses and the ten plagues that followed in Egypt, God revealed His judgments and grace. The people of Israel did nothing but trust and rely wholly upon the great I Am. They could do nothing. Thus, God, by His own power, brought them out of Egypt, through the Red Sea, and led them by the cloud to Mt. Sinai.

All of this was done through the grace and power of God. Israel had done nothing. There were no works, deeds, or activities on their part; they only had simple faith and obedience to God's Word (Exodus 1-15).

The Abrahamic Covenant was a covenant of grace and faith. The Feast of Passover was in grace. At Sinai and the Feast of Pentecost, God revealed His purpose for the nation (Exodus 19:1-6).

At Mt. Sinai, though, a great change took place. Israel moved from the *ground of grace* to the *ground of law and works*. Israel moved from what God had done and could do for them (based on their obedience) to what they could do by works to earn things from God. "...All that the Lord hath spoken we will do..." (Exodus 19:8). Immediately they repudiate the grace of God (what God has done) to come over to the ground of law of works, to what they could do.

The Passover Feast in Egypt and the preservation through the plagues of judgment on Egypt were experiences in the grace of God—what He did and could do for them. All they did was trust and obey. At the Feast of Pentecost at Sinai, however, their experience falls to the ground of law and works (deeds, what they could do for God). God gave the law and said (paraphrased), "This do and thou shalt live." He promised them life on the basis of their works or deeds. For fifteen hundred years God let a nation demonstrate to the world, and to themselves, that no flesh can be justified by the deeds of the law. When Israel said, "All that the Lord hath spoken we will do," in effect God said, "Have a try—I will let you prove to yourself and to the world what you can do."

Hence, the Scriptures under the law covenant—a covenant of works—emphasize, "the man that *doeth* them shall *live* in them" (refer back to Ezekiel 20:11). The deeds of the law consist of all the works pertaining to the law—ceremonial, sacrificial, or moral law. In fact, a man could keep the external commands—ceremonial and moral—but never be justified by them. Note Paul's own experience in Philippians 3:1-8, "...touching the righteousness which is in the law, blameless...." Morally and ceremonially a man could keep the law but would not be justified. The real heart of this matter is dealt with in Romans 7. The summary of it is that works of the law cannot justify anyone.

B. "For by the law is the knowledge of sin"
"...I had not known sin...except the law had said, Thou shalt not covet" (Romans 7:7). The law was not given to justify man—for it could not. No man could be justified by the deeds of the law because of the reason dealt with in Romans 7. (The matter of the law will be taken up more fully in Romans 7.) But for the present, it is important to recognize the purpose of the law as well as what it was *not* given for. We will look at both the negative and positive sides of the purpose in giving the law.

On the negative side:
- The law was not given to men as a means of *regeneration* or *salvation*; that is, it was not a means of quickening men, regenerating men, or making men alive. The law could not give life (Galatians 3:21). It ministered death.
- The law was not given to make men *righteousness* or to *justify* them—it could not do these things. Men could not gain right standing before God by keeping the law. None could, or did, keep it.
- The law was not given as a way of holiness or a means of *sanctification* by sanctifying those whom God had saved.
- The law, with its accompanying ceremonials of priesthood, feasts, the tabernacle, and the sacrificial system, was not given as the final and complete model of worship. These things were typical and temporal until the spiritual and the real came in Christ.

Thus, the law condemns, curses, and kills instead of regenerating, justifying, or sanctifying (Galatians 3:10).

On the positive side:
- The law was given to show God's holiness.

- The law was given to bring out Israel's badness, not it's goodness. The law was designed to expose sinfulness and unrighteousness (Romans 7:8) and to show the weakness of the flesh in the fulfilling of its requirements (Romans 8:3). God knew these things, but Israel did not know them and only found them out by self-effort (Leviticus 18:5; Ezekiel 20:11; Luke 10:28).

- The law was given to impart to Israel a proper knowledge, or definition, of sin (Romans 3:20; 7:7). The law gave Israel knowledge and commands but no power to fulfill it forever.

- The law was given to show man that he was a slave to sin and was under the death penalty—for the wages of sin is death (Romans 6:23; 7:8-9). It was a ministration of death (II Corinthians 3:6). The law required obedience, yet it was powerless to help achieve it. The law did not create sin but was given to expose the presence of sin, to reveal sin's nature, and to reveal man's guilt.

- The law was given to shut the mouths of all men—man was guilty before God and under wrath. It brought condemnation (Romans 3:19; 4:15).

- The law was given as a schoolmaster to bring Israel (and all men) to Christ (Galatians 3:22-25). The law was given to turn man from works to faith, from law to grace, from Moses to Jesus, from Sinai to Calvary. The law was given to prepare for grace (see John 1:17).

- The law was a temporary arrangement to restrain transgressions until the Messiah came (Galatians 3:19; 4:3-5). It was not a permanent arrangement (Hebrews 8:13; Matthew 27:51; 11:13; Luke 16:16; Galatians 3:24-25).

These are the main purposes of the giving of the law to Israel. From Adam to Moses, there was no definition of what sin actually was. "For until the law sin was in the world: but sin is not imputed when there is no law" (Romans 5:13). Adam had one commandment (Genesis 2:17). There were also verbal commandments of the Lord given to the patriarchs—Abraham, Isaac, and Jacob. Unless it became seared, the law of conscience also told mankind what was right and wrong. However, from Adam to Moses, we have no express definition of sin. The only things that could give a reasonable knowledge of sin were the conscience or a verbal revelation from God to man, defining what was sinful. A reasonable knowledge of sin did not come until the time of Moses. Sin was in existence, as has been stated, but the law given to Moses defined sin and gave knowledge of what sin was. Man could not have a clear definition or knowledge of sin unless God Himself defined it. Man is an ignorant, yet guilty, sinner. The purpose of the law was to enlighten this ignorance and define sin, as stated in Romans 3:20, "For by the law is the knowledge of sin." Please note that sin is the transgression of the law (I John 3:4), and where there is no law, there is no transgression (Romans 4:15).

The Law of the Ten Commandments is developed more in the civil laws given to Israel. There were three main areas of the laws of God in Israel.

1) **Moral Law** (Ten Commandments, written on tables of stone) (Exodus 20:1-17)
2) **Civil Law** (written in the "book of the law" and placed in the side of the ark) (Exodus 21-24)
3) **Ceremonial Law** (the whole of the Mosaic economy in the rituals) (Exodus 25-40)

Verses 19-20: *Summary*

Thus, the primary purpose of the law was to give man knowledge of sin and an infallible standard of God. The purpose was not to justify them but to give them knowledge and enlighten their ignorance. The law was the only clear definition of sin given in the Old Testament. The law of conscience is infallible because of man's fallen state and because of his defiance of the voice of conscience. No man could set up laws to define sin because he has a biased point of view and only has the basis of the knowledge which conscience gave him. Therefore, if sin was to be defined, *God* must do it. He defined sin in the Ten Commandments. Thus, in verses 19 and 20 we find that every mouth is stopped, and the entire world has become guilty before God. The law closes everyone's mouth and reveals his or her guilt. The law condemns all. (See also 4:15; 5:13-14.) Man is shut up now to the grace and mercy of God. This can be seen typified in Luke 10:30-37, in the parable of the Good Samaritan. The priest and the Levite (representation of the law and ceremonials) beheld "the certain man" (the sinner) half dead and they each passed by on the other side. However, the Good Samaritan (grace in Christ) came, poured in the oil and the wine (word and spirit), and took him to the inn (church) where he was looked after, at the Samaritan's (Christ's) expense, until he (Samaritan, Christ) should come again.

Righteousness Provided (Romans 3:21-31)

Righteousness by Faith in Christ (Romans 3:21-26)

Verse 21: *"But now the righteousness of God without the law is manifested, being witnessed by the law and the prophets..."*

A. "But now"

"But now," meaning from Romans 1:18 to 3:20, Paul has expressed and exposed to man his condition as a helpless sinner—under wrath, under judgment, unjustified, guilty, condemned, and under the death penalty. This is what man is. "But now," Paul turns to what God is and what God has done. Paul has described man, for what he is and for where he is, and has shown what the law has done for man. Now Paul brings in God and shows what God does about the whole sick, pitiful condition of man. Here Paul again takes up the text of Romans 1:16-17, "...the righteousness of God revealed from faith to faith..." concerning the gospel of Jesus Christ. He takes up the "good news." So far it has been only bad news man's state, condition, and helplessness under sin and under law. Man's living was under wrath and judgment of death, without the gospel. There is need for some good news.

B. "The righteousness of God without the law is manifested" (Romans 1:17; 2:5; 3:5; 3:22, 25-26)

Note the use of the word "righteousness" (the righteousness of God, His righteousness) in these verses. Righteousness is developed more fully in Romans 4 under "faith-righteousness," which man receives. What, though, does the righteousness of God mean? What is righteousness? The righteousness of God is the very antithesis of man, who is unrighteous (Romans 1:18, 29; 2:8; 3:10). Without sacrificing His righteousness, God found a way to bestow His righteousness on man.

"Right" or "righteousness" means "justice or just; the quality of being righteous; exact; restitute; purity; godliness." It is righteousness of principle or action (practice), according to either divine or human law. "Righteous" means "just, upright, doing that which is right, free from sin." "Right" means "upright, perfect standard of truth, freedom from error, justice, state of being right." The righteousness of God therefore may mean "character" or "gift." A righteous man is one who conforms to God's law. Since man cannot conform by himself, he is literally perverse, crooked, and unable to straighten himself out. He is standing in need of justification.

"Manifested" means "appeared, brought out where it may be seen, revealed."

"Without the law" means "apart from or independently of the law" (Amplified New Testament).

It will be seen that "righteousness" and "justification" have a similar meaning; nevertheless, God uses each of these different words with its own particular emphasis. God is just. God is righteous in all He is, all He does, and in His very character, nature, being, and actions. He is perfect, upright, holy, just, and right.

The question arises: Are there two kinds of righteousness? Romans 10:3-6 states that there are two different kinds. The Jews, ignorant of God's righteousness, tried to establish their own righteousness. As far as God is concerned, there is only one acceptable kind of righteousness. "For Christ is the end of the law for righteousness to every one that believeth" (Romans 10:4). These are the two kinds of righteousness:

1) The righteousness of the law (law-righteousness)
2) The righteousness of faith (faith-righteousness)

The righteousness of the law has already been defined as the "law of works" (Romans 3:27). It concerns what man can do (works and deeds of the law). In fact, a Jew could have law-righteousness, as Paul's experience shows. "...[T]ouching the righteousness which is in the law, blameless...not having mine own righteousness, which is of the law..." (Philippians 3:6-9) and "...[G]oing about to establish their own righteousness..." (Romans 10:3). These two Scriptures show that a Jew could have this law-righteousness by the law of works—what he could do—yet it was only an *external* or *outward* righteousness. It never dealt with the man himself or the real problem—what he *was*. The problem is on the inside of man (this is dealt with in Romans 7). In other words, a Jew, like Paul, could keep the externals of the Ten Commandments (except the tenth, Romans 7) and could be counted in man's sight, and his own sight, as moral and self-righteous. The law-righteousness—the law of works—is a picture of moral and self-righteousness. A man may be able to restrain, by self-effort, the outworking and expression of the sin principles that would break these commandments. This restraint, though, is self-righteousness (law-righteousness), and though it makes one acceptable to himself and others, it does not satisfy the heart of God. In light of these facts, however, one should not willfully violate the Ten Commandments.

Two examples of law-righteousness are seen in Paul and the rich young ruler who came to Jesus. Paul himself exemplified law-righteousness. He was a moral man who kept the commandments, or the outward expression of them, and was blameless. He exemplified righteousness of the law, but his righteousness was as filthy rags before God (Isaiah 64:6). Jesus said, "...except your righteousness shall exceed the righteousness of the scribes and Pharisees..." (Matthew 5:20). The Pharisee was a self-righteous person who had external righteousness. The Pharisee fasted, tithed, and kept the moral and ceremonial law externally, but internally he was unrighteous (Matthew 23:1-39; 27-28). As was mentioned before in Matthew 23:27, Jesus called the Pharisees "whitewashed sepulchres"— outwardly beautiful but inwardly full of corruption, uncleanness, and hypocrisy.

The rich young ruler, in Matthew 19:16-22, was also a moral man. Touching the righteousness of the law, he was blameless (externally). He wanted to *do* something to inherit eternal life. In talking with him, Jesus quoted some of the commandments, which the young ruler had kept from his youth. The problem came when the ruler was asked to give up everything he owned and follow Jesus. In asking this, Jesus touched the real man, the internal person. The ruler went away sorrowful. This is also an example of Christ's indictment on pharisaical righteousness (cf. Leviticus 18:4-5).

B. **"Witnessed by the law and the prophets"**

The Law and the Prophets witnessed the righteousness of God manifested in Jesus Christ. The Law and the Prophets witnessed and testified as "two witnesses." Though the righteousness of God is manifested without the law, it is not contrary to the law or against it. Rather the Law and the Prophets witnessed it. That is, it was attested to and born witness to by them. "In the mouth of two or three witnesses shall every word be established (paraphrased)" (Deuteronomy 17:6; 19:15; Hebrews 10:28; Matthew 18:16; II Corinthians 13:1). Thus, we have the witness of the Law and the Prophets. The Old Testament actually attested to the righteousness of God, to come personified in Messiah.

The witness of the law to the righteousness of God (Isaiah 51:4-5). The law, in itself, is righteous and is a witness of the righteousness of God. There was nothing wrong with the law in itself (Psalm 19:8; Romans 7:12, 14; I Timothy 1:8; Psalm 119:144, 172; Deuteronomy 4-5). The problem was in man. The ceremonies in the law showed man's need of cleansing from sin.

The witness of the prophets to the righteousness of God (Isaiah 51:4-5, 5; 58:8; Daniel 9:24; Psalm 45:7; 85:10-13) (the Lord our righteousness). The prophets also spoke of the righteousness of God and prophesied of the "Lord our righteousness"—the righteous Branch, to be raised up in the last days (Jeremiah 23:6; 33:16). These things were prophesied, through the prophets, by the Word of the Lord. The prophets upheld the spirit of the law, while the law sets forth the letter.

Christ came not to destroy (unloose) the Law or the Prophets but to fill them up (Matthew 5:17,18). Not one jot or tittle of the law would pass until all was fulfilled in Christ. Note:

- All of the Law and the Prophets prophesied until John the Baptist (Matthew 11:13).
- The Law and the Prophets witnessed (Romans 3:21).
- By the law is the knowledge of sin (Romans 3:20).
- The form of knowledge and truth was in the law (Romans 2:20).

Hence, even though God has revealed His righteousness apart from the law, that righteousness is not contradictory to the law or against it. It was actually attested to by the Law and the Prophets, and it is in Christ—the fulfillment of them both. In fact, it confirms, upholds, and establishes the law. (Refer to notes on Romans 3:31 and 8:4 [Amplified New Testament].) Even so, as far as man is concerned, he cannot be justified or made righteous by what he can keep of the law. As far as God is concerned, the Law, Prophets, and Christ set forth the righteousness of God. As far as man is concerned, the law cannot make him righteous or impart to him the righteousness of God. Moses (the Law) and Elijah (the Prophets) pointed to Jesus Himself (cf. Matthew 17:1-7).

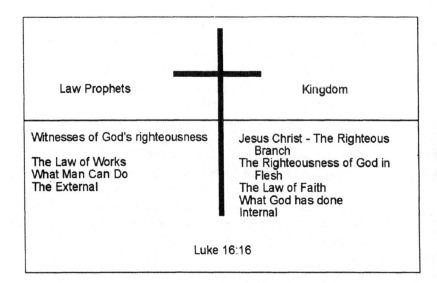

Luke 16:16

Law Prophets	Kingdom
Witnesses of God's righteousness	Jesus Christ - The Righteous Branch
The Law of Works	The Righteousness of God in Flesh
What Man Can Do	The Law of Faith
The External	What God has done
	Internal

Verse 22: *"...Even the righteousness of God which is by faith of Jesus Christ unto all and upon all them that believe: for there is no difference..."*

A. **"The righteousness of God which is by faith of Jesus Christ unto all and upon all"**

Compare the word "righteousness" in the following verses:

- "...[R]ighteousness of God revealed from faith to faith..." (Romans 1:17) ("revealed in the gospel" [Romans 1:16])

- "...[R]ighteousness of God which is *by faith* of [in] Jesus Christ..." (in other words, faith-righteousness) (Romans 3:22).

- "But the righteousness which is of faith..." (Romans 10:6).

- "...[I]n him, not having mine own righteousness, which is of the law, but that which is through the faith of Christ..." (Philippians 3:9).

- "For Christ is the end of the law for righteousness to every one that believeth" (Romans 10:4).

- "Even the righteousness of God which is by faith of Jesus Christ..." (Romans 3:22).

- "To declare, I say, at this time his righteousness...of him which believeth in Jesus" (Romans 3:26).

- "...Abraham believed God, and it was counted unto him for righteousness" (righteousness which is received by and through faith) (Romans 4:3).

- Righteousness is by faith "of Jesus Christ" (as also "in Jesus Christ") from God. Thus, faith is the gift of God to the repentant sinner who believes in and on Jesus Christ (Ephesians 2:8-9; Romans 4:16).

Jeremiah calls the Lord "Jehovah Tsidkenu" or "the Lord our righteousness" (Jeremiah 23:6; 33:16). This is His redemptive name. Also note in I Corinthians 1:30, "...Christ Jesus, who of God is made unto us wisdom, and *righteousness*..." We have a call to turn from unrighteousness (Gentiles) and self-righteousness (Jews) to the faith-righteousness of God in Christ. It is a call to turn from works of the flesh and works of self-effort to the work of God in Christ.

"Unto all" – Meaning "worldwide in its outreach, to the entire world; wheresoever."

"Upon all" – Meaning "all exclusive in its application, to every soul; whosoever."

B. **"Them that believe"**

Faith (believing) is the channel of receiving this righteousness of God (Romans 1:16-17; 10:6). Faith is personal trust, confidence, and reliance upon Jesus Christ (Romans 3:22, 26 [Amplified New Testament]). The law itself was righteousness and upheld righteousness, but it could not impart righteousness to the one who endeavored to keep it. God, though, imputes righteousness to the one who simply believes on Jesus.

This believing, or faith, in Jesus Christ is not just mere mental assent, but as the New Testament clearly states, "...Believe on the Lord Jesus Christ, and thou shalt be saved..." (Acts 16:31). "Believe," in this sense, means, "to adhere, cleave to, trust in, to have faith in, to rely on." Acts 16:31 of the Amplified New Testament reads, "...Believe in and on the Lord Jesus Christ—that is, give yourself up to Him, take yourself out of your own keeping and entrust yourself into His keeping, and you will be saved..." This version explains exactly what it means to "believe in Jesus."

The sinner realizes his condition—that he can never gain an acceptable righteousness by the law of works, or self-righteousness, and that he cannot be justified by self-effort in the law—so he comes to God through Christ. He gives himself up to Christ. He takes himself out of his own keeping and entrusts himself to Christ's keeping. He adheres to, cleaves to, and relies upon Jesus, and because of this, he receives the righteousness of God. He is brought back into right standing with God in Jesus, and righteousness is appropriated by faith. This righteousness is obtained—

not attained or earned. The Bible does not allow any of man's claims to merit righteousness or God's favor (Ephesians 2:8-9; Romans 11:6). To base righteousness on human merits is to displace the righteousness of Christ and His vicarious sacrifice for sin, which is the one and only ground for a sinner's acceptance by God.

No man can be justified on the basis of what he is or what he has done. That condemns him. Justification is on the basis of what Christ has done for man. Righteousness is not a type of power given to overcome sin and produce personal holiness. Righteousness is demanded by God, absolutely fulfilled in the God-man (Christ), and imputed to us as we receive Christ as Lord and Savior. This is Bible believing—Bible faith.

C.   "For there is no difference"

"No difference" means "no distinction (Amplified New Testament); no respect of persons with God, no partiality or unfairness with God." With God, one person is not different from another (Deuteronomy 10:17; II Chronicles 19:7). Whether Jew or Gentile, there is no difference or distinction. In Exodus 11:7, where it states, "...that ye may know how that the Lord doth put a difference between the Egyptians and Israel," the Lord only states a difference between the two nations because of the blood of redemption. Salvation, though, is available by faith for all (Romans 10:12; Acts 15:9). There is no difference. God gives to man His righteousness in Christ, and this alone qualifies and fits man for heaven. How could God accept unpunished sinners into heaven? There is an absolute demand for righteousness.

Romans Teachers Manual (Carlson, pp. 27-28) states:
- There is no difference in the fact of sin. There may be degrees of sin, but evil is evil regardless of the amount or intensity. Poison is poison. The wicked are to be judged according to their works.
- There is no difference in the fact of God's love for us. God does not love men because of what they are, but because of what He is. His nature is love. Sin does not affect God's love for us, but it makes us incapable of receiving the blessings of that love.
- There is no difference in the power of Christ's death for all.
- There is no difference in the way of appropriation. All must come the same way.

Verse 23: *"...For all have sinned, and come short of the glory of God..."*

A. **"All have sinned"**

All are guilty; there are none exempt or excluded. The term "all have sinned" is all-inclusive—all are lawless, all have transgressed (I John 3:4). This includes the Jews within the law and the Gentiles outside of the law. (Refer also to notes on Romans 3:9-19.)

B. **"And come short of the glory of God"**

Man was created to express the glory, honor, and desire of God, and to please God. Man was created for God's pleasure (Revelation 4:11). "Come short," means "fallen and falling short, none measure up." The divine measuring rod reveals that all have, and all do, come short of the perfection of God, the glory of God, and the divine standard of God's righteousness.

Verse 24: *"...Being justified freely by his grace through the redemption that is in Christ Jesus..."*

A. **"Being justified freely by his grace"**

"Justified" – Note the use of the words "just" and "justified" in verses 24 and 30. "Justified" means "made righteous, acquitted; made and declared right, freed from guilt and blame, and therefore, freed from the penalty and punishment of sin's guilt."

"Freely" – (Greek: *Dorean* means "gratis, for naught" [same use in Matthew 10:8]). This is the only place this word is found in the book of Romans. After all, man has nothing to pay.

"By His grace"– Meaning "gift, favor." Grace is undeserved, unmerited, and unearned (cf. Romans 4:16). When the Greeks wanted to give a gift out of pure generosity of heart, without any thought of reward, the word they used for gift was "grace."

God acts *justly* and *graciously*. He is perfectly balanced in His attributes (Psalm 85:10). He is *just*, yet waits to be *gracious* to the sinner, at Calvary. At Calvary, the *law* was honored, *sin* was judged, *death* was meted out, and *pardon* was made available. Thus, God was *gracious* without being *unjust*, and *just* without being *ungracious*.

B. "Through the redemption that is in Christ Jesus"
    "Through the redemption" – means "the buying back, out of the forum,
        out of the market place, with a price."
    "That is in Christ Jesus" – means "provided in and through the
        Anointed Savior, our Kinsman-Redeemer."

Verse 25: *". . . Whom God hath set forth to be a propitiation through faith in his blood,
    to declare his righteousness for the remission of sins that are past, through the
    forbearance of God. . ."*

A. "Whom God hath set forth"
    "Whom God hath set forth" means "foreordained" (marginal) (cf.
    Revelation 13:8; Exodus 32:32; Revelation 21:27; Ephesians 1:4). Christ
    was foreordained as the Lamb from, and before, the foundation of the
    world (John 1:29, 36; I Peter 1:19-20; Revelation 5:6-13; 7:17).

B. "To be a propitiation"
    "Propitiation," in the Greek, is *hilasterion*, meaning literally "a mercy
    seat" (also "atonement"). The tabernacle of Moses and the ark of the
    covenant prophesied Christ as a propitiation. The mercy seat itself was a
    symbolic representation of Christ, foreshadowing God's foreordained plan
    concerning Christ and Christ's sacrificial blood and body.

C. "Through faith in his blood"
    This was the first mention of "blood" in the book of Romans, and it
    refers to the sacrificial blood of Jesus—the blood Atonement. There is
    only propitiation through His blood.
        It should be remembered that faith, though vitally involved, is not the
    cause of justification. Rather, it is grace—the pure grace of God alone—
    that is the source of justification. Salvation by grace removes the dangers
    of self-righteousness, or self-effort, and the fear of being unable to meet
    God's demands. This grace is evidenced in the sacrificial blood of Jesus
    Christ (John 1:17).

D. "To declare his righteousness for the remission of sins that are past"
    "Remission" means "passing over" (marginal) (cf. Exodus 12, the
    Passover). God has passed over and ignored former sins, often times
    without punishment.

For four thousand years, God seemed to pass over the sins of the human race without meting out the punishment that sin deserved. At times, there was manifest judgment, but generally speaking, God passed over and seemed to ignore sin (Acts 17:30). How then could He be righteous but not judge sin? The answer is in the following clause: "through the forbearance of God" (Romans 3:25).

E. **"Through the forbearance of God"** (cf. Romans 2:4 and notes)
    "Forbearance" means "holding back" or, in this case, "the restraint of God." God held back the punishment for sin, in the full sense, even though unpunished sin was a challenge to His justice and His righteousness. God did not ignore sin; however, he did not inflict the full penalty due, or the human race would have been wiped out. Further, God withheld full punishment on sin and sinners because there was a mercy seat, propitiation in the sacrificial system under the law in the tabernacle administration. Here sin was, and could be, covered by sacrificial blood. This propitiation was actually a revelation of the grace of God, even under the law to Israel. God withheld His punishment because of His longsuffering, forbearance, patience, and goodness in order to lead men to repentance. God is gracious. Righteousness calls for punishment of sin, and grace provides a plan of pardon for sinners.

Verse 26: "...To declare, I say, at this time his righteousness: that he might be just, and the justifier of him which believeth in Jesus."

A. **"To declare, I say, at this time, His righteousness"**
    The Amplified New Testament states this verse this way, "...to demonstrate *and* prove at the present time (in the now season)..." All former ages pointed to "this time." "At this time" means "affixed time or season" (Young's). This is the time that the Law and the Prophets looked forward to and pointed to (I Peter 1:10-11; Romans 13:11; II Corinthians 6:2; Ephesians 1:10; I Timothy 2:6; Titus 1:3). In due time Christ died for us. Hebrews speaks of "the time then present" (Hebrews 9:9) and "the time of reformation" (Hebrews 9:10). Peter calls it "the last time" (I Peter 1:5; I Peter 1:20, last times). Paul also refers to "the fullness of time" (Galatians 4:4), "the due time," or "according to the time" (Romans 5:6). It was fixed, in the counsels of the Godhead, when the righteousness of God personified in Christ was to be revealed.

Old Testament sacrificial blood was only a temporary arrangement and covering in "time past" until God brought in "this present time" or "this present arrangement in the New Covenant." Note below:

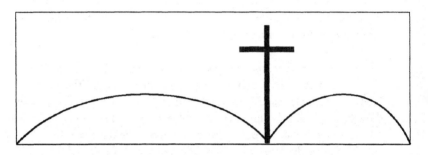

B. **"That he might be just, and the justifier of him which believeth in Jesus"**

With all that is said on the wonderful grace of God in fully justifying the sinner and acquitting the guilty, there is the great problem of justification. How can God be *just* and the *Justifier* of him who believes in Jesus? How can God justify the guilty and sinful man? Is this consistent with God's divine nature and character? Is God just in freely pardoning guilty man? What of His unalterable and irrevocable Word? How can God disregard sin? His Word is at stake! He has issued the decree, the death sentence, upon sin, and now He seems to go back on His Word. Or does He? The answer should be clear by now. Sin must be judged. Justice must reign in the throne of God—the "just Judge." How can God inflict the punishment for sin and at the same time cancel it? The law demanded this (Exodus 34:7). The answer is found in the person of His Son, Jesus. Man sees the great gulf between himself and God (Job 10). If God acquitted the guilty, He could not be just. If He went back on His Word of sentence and judgment of sin, He could not be just. This is the problem.

However, in God, grace and love found a way. Certainly this way was not found in man (John 3:16). Not only is God just, holy, and righteous, but He is also *love*. Love found a way whereby God could be just and at the same time be the Justifier of sinful man. What was this way? How did God keep His Word and, at the same time, justify the believing sinner? The answer is seen in the Lord Jesus Christ. God reckoned Jesus as a sinner on Calvary and dealt with Him as a sinner (Isaiah 53:6; Matthew 27:46; Galatians 3:13-14; II Corinthians 5:21).

C. **"Which believeth in Jesus"**

Believing in Jesus is the one condition for justification in Christ. This is available to all men freely, but there are God's terms to be considered— God's terms in the sense of repentance, which leads to faith. God can be the *Justifier* of those who believe in Jesus. This is received and appropriated by faith. It is a fact—an eternal reality. Whether man believes it or not, he can never alter the fact of what God did for man in Christ at Calvary. Believing or not believing will not, in any way, affect Calvary's work of redemption. No man can take from this work, add to it, or disannul it. Calvary's work happened in the counsels of the Godhead and is forever settled and established in heaven. It is not a matter of this work being so only if man believes. From God's viewpoint, it took place at the Cross, once and for all, and it is a finished work (John 19:30). Nothing can change that fact.

But from man's viewpoint, there is only one way of having experientially what God did judicially in Christ. There is only one way to know that God is just and is the Justifier of him who believes in Jesus. That way is by faith (to believe in Jesus [Amplified New Testament]). Faith is totally opposite of works. Man always wants to do something to justify himself before God. Romans 3 has revealed that there is nothing man can do. No one can be justified by the works of the law. Man can only be justified before God by faith ("to them that believe in Jesus"). God has done it all in Christ. "Even the righteousness of God which is by faith of Jesus Christ unto all and upon all them that believe..." (Romans 3:22; note especially Galatians 3:22-26 fully.) All that pertains to redemption and propitiation, from the God-ward side to man, shows that there is nothing in man that deserves, earns, or merits redemption. It is all based on grace. God redeems and accepts man in His Son. It is all of God and by God to man and for man. It is based on grace—rich and free.

If man is to receive the benefits of the Atonement, the words "faith" and "believing" need to be God's terms (Romans 3:22, 24-28; 5:1). The words "faith" and "believing" have become so meaningless today. Multitudes hang their hope of salvation upon a wrong concept of these words. It must be remembered, as has been noted before, that faith is not the means of justification, but the channel by which man receives it. The means of justification is the redemptive, sacrificial, and propitiatory work of Christ at the Cross and at the throne of God. The channel of justification is faith in the work of Christ—faith in Jesus Christ and in His blood.

Note below the difference between Mt. Sinai and Mt. Calvary:

MT SINAI	MT CALVARY
Servant Moses	Jesus - The Son
Do and Live	Believe and Live and Do
The Secondary Level	The Higher Level
Justified by Works	Justified by Faith in His Blood
Natural. Old Covenant	Spiritual. New Covenant

Verses 25-26: *Summary*

Within these two verses are tremendously rich words that are relatively important to understand in order to appreciate what Paul is setting forth here. The theological implications of the following words will be considered in this summary of verses 25 and 26.

- Grace
- Redemption
- Justification
- Propitiation
- Blood
- Remission
- Righteousness

A. "Grace"

Grace is the foundation of the whole plan of redemption (as far as God and man are concerned). It was exemplified through the mercy seat in Moses' tabernacle. Grace is free (Romans 3:24). God is gracious. Grace involves words such as "mercy," "love," and "kindness."

B. "Redemption"

"Redemption," meaning "to buy back again out of the hands of another; a transition." It involves the following:

- To free by avenging and repaying (Exodus 6:6; Deuteronomy 7:8)

- A separation and redemption (Psalms 111:9; 130:7)
- A redeemer—one who frees (Job 19:25; Isaiah 44:6, 24)
- The right or price of redemption; the kinsman-redeemer (Ruth 4:7; Jeremiah 32:7-8).
- A loosing away (Luke 21:28; Romans 3:24; Ephesians 1:7, 14)
- To acquire out of the forum (Revelation 5:9; Galatians 3:13; 4:5)

"Ransom" is a word that is closely linked with "redemption." The "ransom" is the price actually paid in the transaction of redemption.

C. "Justification"

"Justification" means "to declare right, or righteous." In these verses and also in Romans 3:19-21 and Romans 4, we are brought to the burden of the textual theme stated in Romans 1:16-17; that is "the just shall live by faith," or, in other words, justification by faith. Paul has hauled away every prop that man could possibly lean upon in order to show the glory of God in justification by faith, which is made available for sinful man. Please note below the most prominent facts of these verses. These facts are an assistance in grasping more clearly what Paul is about to present concerning justification by faith.

- "...[B]y the deeds of the law there shall no flesh be justified in His sight..." (Romans 3:20).
- "...[J]ustified freely by His grace..." (Romans 3:24).
- "...[T]hat he might just, and the justifier of him which believeth in Jesus" (Romans 3:26).
- "...[J]ustified by faith without the deeds of the law" (Romans 3:28).
- "...[J]ustify the circumcision by faith, and uncircumcision through faith" (Romans 3:30).
- Doers of the law are justified before God (Romans 3:31).

The whole emphasis is on justification by faith. Previous verses have established certain facts concerning justification. See those facts below:

God is a just and holy God (Romans 3:26).

He is upright, righteous, straight, and perfectly right. God, in His nature, being, character, thoughts, words, and deeds, is just.

God is a just Judge and must pass judgment on sin (Romans 2:1-10).

God, being holy and just, must be a just Judge. He must deal with sin according to His own righteous character. He must execute sentence on all sin and sinners. A judge is one who sits on the bench of a court, hears and determines a case, tries and decides an accused person (to pass a sentence), condemns this person as guilty or absolves him as innocent, gives the decision of the court, and discerns or distinguishes between guilt or innocence. "Justice" means "impartiality, equity, rendering to every one his due right; it is conformity to truth and reality; the quality of being just." "Judgment" means "the act or process by which the mind forms an opinion or comes to a decision; discernment; decision of a court, a decree, order, entrance or doom pronounced and effected." Justice must be seen, and judgment must be declared.

God is a just Judge. He has passed sentence on sin and sinners. He knows all the facts of every case. His justice is perfect, and His decisions are infallible. The verdict on the whole world from the court of heaven is "guilty" (Romans 3:19). The sentence is the death sentence (Romans 6:23; 2:6-9). This is man's doom. The decree has gone forth (Genesis 2:17). God cannot acquit the guilty until, or unless, sin is dealt with; otherwise He would not be just. He must act in a judicial manner. Sin is lawlessness (I John 3:4).

- "...[T]he wages of sin is death..." (Romans 6:23).
- "...[I]n the day that thou eatest [sin] thereof thou shalt surely die" (Genesis 2:17).
- "...[T]he soul that sinneth, it shall die" (Ezekiel 18:4, also 18:20).
- "...[I]t is appointed unto men once to die, but after this the judgment..." (Hebrews 9:27).

God's Word is infallible and irrevocable (Romans 3:2-8).

God has proclaimed His Word and His law. His Word is eternal in its principles of truth, for truth is spiritual. God cannot lie. He cannot go back on His Word justly, or alter what has gone out of His mouth. His Word is irrevocable, immutable, and infallible (Hebrews 6:18; Malachi 3:6a; Psalm 89:34). It is not subject to mistake or error. It must come to pass. He will watch over His Word to perform it (Jeremiah 1:12). He is bound by the limits of His own Word.

Man is unrighteous and in a helpless and hopeless condition.

- Man is an ignorant and guilty sinner (Romans 3:9, 19).

- Man is under the sentence of death (Romans 6:23).
- Man is helpless to save himself from death, the penalty of sin (Romans 3:19-20). How can man be just before God? "...[I]n thy sight shall no man living be justified" (Psalm 143:2; Job 10:14).
- Man cannot justify himself (Job 9:20; Luke 16:15).
- Man cannot be justified by deeds or words of the law (3:20, 27-28; Galatians 2:16).
- Man cannot be declared right or just, cannot be freed from blame or guilt, cannot absolve himself or make himself right. Man cannot do it himself. How then can man be justified before God? He cannot of himself. It leaves him in the most pitiful condition—under sin and death, with no way out. Romans I, 2, and 3 set this forth clearly.

The God of grace alone can justify man (Romans 3:21-30).
In man's hopeless condition, God comes to him in grace. Grace is God coming to man, not man coming to God. Grace is the undeserved, unearned, and unmerited favor and gifts of God to man. God offers this *justification freely* for man. "Being justified freely by His grace..." (Romans 3:24) "...[T]hat he might be *just*, and the *justifier* of him which believeth in Jesus" (Romans 3:26). When God justifies a man, it means that He pardons and absolves that man from guilt or punishment. From man's side he is "made or declared right" (Romans 5:1, 8). He is absolved, pronounced just, vindicated, and freed from blame and guilt. Justification is a judicial sentence, a declaration of being right, and a setting right. It is absolution, the remission of sin, and the remission of guilt and of punishment. God has proclaimed man free from the guilt of sin and, therefore, free from punishment. This is all based on God's grace (what God does for man), for man could do nothing for, or of, himself. Man cannot earn justification; otherwise, justification would be a reward (i.e. "works"). Man cannot merit it; otherwise, it would be a reward. Man cannot deserve it; otherwise, it would not be grace.

However, God could not display His love and compassion to sinners if He had not dealt with sin in Christ. In justification, we have the legal sentence of the Judge of heaven. That sentence declares the guilty sinner righteous before God. He is *accounted* righteous by God. Righteousness is put to his account. God looks on him as righteous in Christ. It is righteousness—imputed and imparted (II Corinthians 5:21). The sinner is acquitted of the guilt and punishment of sin and righteousness is restored. However, the pardon is not valid unless it is accepted. For example, remember the prisoner on the cross who refused to accept a free pardon? He therefore had to die for the law he had broken.

D. "Propitiation "

Another great word used by Paul, and vitally linked in the plan of salvation, is the word "propitiation." This word is only specifically translated as such in three places in the New Testament (I John 2:2; 4:10; Romans 3:25) by the apostles John and Paul. See below:

- "...[H]e is the propitiation for our sins..." (I John 2:2).
- "...God sent his Son to be the propitiation for our sins" (I John 4:10).
- "...Christ Jesus, whom God hath set forth to be a propitiation..." (Romans 3:25) (foreordained as such).

"Propitiation" has two different rendered words from the same Greek root. These different words present two different and special thoughts. See below:

- Greek: *Hilasmos* means "what appeases, propitiate" (I John 2:2; 4:10).
- Greek: *Hilasterion* means "place of propitiation, or appeasement" (Romans 3:25; Hebrews 9:5).

The two different thoughts rendered from this word are "what, or that, which appeases (object of appeasement)" and "the place of appeasement." Consider these thoughts below concerning the doctrine of the propitiation:

The Object of Appeasement

The object of appeasement is what Paul has been dealing with in Romans 1:18; 2:5, 8 and 4:15. The *wrath* of a Holy God against sin has to be appeased and satisfied. The object of appeasement must be an offering for sin, a sacrifice. Sin must be judged by a righteous God. God's wrath must fall on sin. Sin can only be dealt with by death. Death is judgment upon sin. This only will satisfy God. Death is the divine wrath and judgment on sin. God told Adam he would die in the day he sinned (Genesis 2:17). Sin and death have been in operation since Adam sinned, and they are passed on to Adam's entire race. God cannot justify the sinner in his sin. However, in God's time element, between the day Adam died spiritually and the day he died physically, God, in grace, introduced the plan of salvation. This plan of salvation began typically in the animal sacrifice for sin and shadowed forth the sin offering of His only begotten Son.

This plan of redemption was typically in progress in the Old Testament (and in the gospel in types), as has been seen. In due time, the Son of God came as the Kinsman-Redeemer, and *He* became the object of appeasement—the propitiation. The Redeemer enters, as the advocate, when the court has declared man guilty and under the death penalty. How? He took upon Himself, in the Father's will, the sin of the world (John 1:29, 36) by being made sin and by being a sin offering for us (II Corinthians 5:21). The moment He was "made sin" for us and the moment all the sins of the world were laid upon Him (Isaiah 53), He became our sin offering (Leviticus 4-5). The wrath of a righteous and holy God—a sin-hating God—fell upon Christ, the sinless substitute. The wrath ended in *death*, for "the wages of sin is death" (Romans 6:23). Christ died for our sins according to the Scriptures (I Corinthians 15:3). God's wrath was appeased. He was and is satisfied. Sin had to be dealt with by a just God, and God dealt with sin through His only Son. God dealt with sin in Christ on the Cross—not Christ's sin, as He Himself was sinless, but the sin of the world. Christ Jesus was the *object of appeasement*. He was foreordained, and set forth, by God as our propitiation. God's appeasement is in Christ, who was judged for our sin by death. Death is the end of sin. Once sin has been judged by death, that is the end of judgment.

When God forsook His Son (Psalm 22:1) in the three hours of darkness, Christ endured the wrath of God against sin. He became the object of the Father's wrath. Who needed appeasing? Who needed to be pacified, quieted, and satisfied? God—who is holy, just, and hates sin. Sin is an attack on the holiness of God. Holiness in reaction against man's sinfulness produces wrath. Wrath needs appeasing. Once wrath was executed on sin, the law of God, which was broken and demanded punishment, had been upheld. The law, upheld by justice, can do nothing more once the penalty against it has been executed. After Christ's sacrifice, God's wrath was appeased, His law was upheld, His holiness was no longer at stake, and His righteousness was vindicated.

The Place of Appeasement

In the Old Testament, the one and only place of appeasement was the brazen altar in the court of the tabernacle. This was the only place where death took place and where all sacrifices were slain. At this altar of brass (significant of judgment against sin), death took place. It was the only place of acceptance for offerings. Any other place was an abomination. Here the innocent victim—the animal—suffered the wrath and death of the broken law that was due the sinner. Sin was typically laid on the sacrifice, and the sacrifice was treated as sin itself and received death—the wages and penalty of sin. Not only did death take place, but the evidence of that death had to be sprinkled about the altar, touched on the horns, and/or brought within the tabernacle and sprinkled before the veil, touching the horns of the golden altar as well. Beyond that, the greatest feast in Israel was the Day of Atonement. It was the only day out of the year that the high priest entered within the veil. The priest could only enter by *blood*, which was brought within the veil and sprinkled on the mercy seat of the ark of the covenant between the gold cherubim. This was the *place of appeasement*. Note in Exodus 12:12-14, "...the blood shall be to you a token...when I see the blood..." The blood was taken from the brazen altar, where it was shed and where death took place, and taken within the veil into the Most Holy Place—the place of appeasement. Blood on the mercy seat was evidence to God of death. Death is sin judged and judgment is the wrath of a holy God whose law was broken against sin. The mercy seat was the place of appeasement, and when God saw the blood, He was satisfied. He knew that sin had been dealt with in the sacrifice at the brazen altar and the blood was evidence of this. He could not withhold peace from His people now. God could speak from between the cherubim of glory, from off a blood-stained mercy seat (Numbers 7:89).

The brazen altar, where the blood was shed, and the mercy seat, where the blood was sprinkled, were now linked together with the same blood. This was also the case for all other offerings (Leviticus 1-7, 16; Exodus 12; Numbers 19, 28-29). The prophetic implications and truth in this are profound. The word "propitiation" used here in Romans 3:25 is the same Greek word translated "mercy seat" in Hebrews 9:5. "...Whom God put forward (before the eyes of all) as a mercy seat *and* propitiation by His blood—the cleansing and life-giving sacrifice of atonement and reconciliation..." (Amplified New Testament).

Note also, in Luke 18:13, the prayer of the publican in comparison
with the prayer of the Pharisee. The publican prayed, "God be merciful
(Greek: *Hilaskamai*) to me a sinner." The same word "merciful" is used in
Hebrews 2:17 and means "to be propitious, appeased." The publican,
with this attitude, came to God, to the place of appeasement. He came to
the place of the mercy seat—the place of reconciliation. In reality he
prayed, "God be *mercy seated* to me a sinner." He came to the place of
mercy, and, as a result, he went down to his house justified (Luke 18:9-
14). The Pharisee, though, was self-righteous and self-condemned and
did not return justified. This story also illustrates the truths presented by
Paul, the Pharisee, and Paul, the sinner who became justified by faith in
the blood of Jesus. (Also contrast with I Samuel 6:19).

As an illustration, picture God and the sinner meeting together at the
mercy seat in the tabernacle. Blood is sprinkled on the place of
appeasement, and the sinner is reconciled and justified before God. Note
that in Solomon's temple the mercy seat was called "the place of the
mercy seat" (I Chronicles 28:11). Note the translations from the same
Greek root in the verses below:

- Greek: *Hilasmos* means "propitiation" (I John 2:2; 4:10).
- Greek: *Hilasterion* means "mercy seat" (Hebrews 9:5; Romans 3:25
  [translated "propitiation"]).
- Greek: *Hilaskomai* means "reconciliation" (Hebrews 2:17).
- Greek: *Hilaskomai* means "merciful" (Luke 18:13).

All of this pointed to the *Cross*—God's brazen altar—which was the
one and only place of appeasement, sacrifice for sin, bloodshed,
propitiation, expiation, reconciliation, and mercy. At the Cross, sin was
judged, and death took place. *Christ* was the *object* of appeasement as He
endured the wrath of God against sin, but *Calvary* was the *place* of
appeasement. It does not finish there, though. Today there is a place of
appeasement, which is the mercy seat of heaven, where men may come.
Heaven's throne is the place of mercy that is available for all (Hebrews
4:16). It is a blood sprinkled throne and mercy seat. God has set forth
Jesus Christ to be a mercy seat through faith and His blood (Romans
3:25). Redemption is through His blood (Colossians 1:14). Animal
blood could not deal with the sin problem. It had to be heaven's blood,
the blood of God in Christ (Acts 20:28).

Thus, as has been explained, we have the propitiation blood and the mercy seat blood. The blood of Jesus Christ on the throne of heaven is evidence to God that His Son's sacrifice is vicarious and that sin was judged in His death. Today, this is the only place of appeasement—our propitiation. Christ Jesus is the mercy seat and we come to God by Him (John 14:1, 6; Hebrews 7:26).

The Result of the Appeasement

The result of appeasement is *reconciliation* (Romans 5:10; 11:15; 5:11; II Corinthians 5:18-20). "Reconciliation" means "to expiate, to make satisfaction or reparation for." It also means "the expiation, the atonement, the reconciliation after enmity or controversy; to bring together parties at variance into renewed fellowship; to restore to friendship, or favor, after estrangement; to adjust, to settle, to cover, to change thoroughly; to offer or receive a sin offering is the result." The word is translated once as "atonement" but is more correctly translated "reconciliation" (Romans 5:10, 11).

E. **"Blood"**

This word has been covered fully enough in the area of "appeasement." Blood is the evidence of death. The blood on the mercy seat is the evidence to God of the sacrificial death of His Son, Jesus. The sinner must have faith in that blood.

F. **"Remission"**

Remission involves the word "pardon." God acquits (pardons) the sinner who believes in Christ, and He declares him just—not innocent. To declare the sinner innocent would be a judgment contrary to the truth. The judgment declares that the demands of the law have been satisfied the sinner is now free from condemnation. It is pardon from God—the Judge. It is forgiveness to the sinner. It is remission of guilt and, therefore, remission of punishment. God can pardon the sinner now because of all that Christ did in the propitiatory work at Calvary and because of Christ's work as a mediator in heaven (on the basis of His blood there). Christ's blood was shed on earth and taken to heaven, just as within the tabernacle, the blood was shed at the brazen altar (Calvary) and taken within the veil (heaven's sanctuary).

G. **"Righteousness"**

"Righteousness" means "to declare right, to justify," and specifically, "to be in right standing with God." In justification there are two main elements: 1) pardon, or remission of the punishment; 2) justification, or restoration to favor. Justification is more than remission or acquittal. This would leave the sinner simply in the position of a discharged criminal. God's law, however, demands a positive righteousness, as well. Besides deliverance from punishment, justification involves and implies God's treatment of the sinner as if the sinner was, and had been, personally righteous. The justified sinner receives not only remission of sins and the penalty, but also the rewards promised to the obedient. (Refer to *Strong's Systematic Theology*, p. 854.)

In other words:

- In justification, the sinner is pardoned, or acquitted, of guilt and punishment for past sin (negative side), and the sinner is counted righteous in God's sight and receives right standing with God (positive side) (Romans 3:24, Amplified New Testament).

- In justification, Christ bore our guilt and punishment and provided a pardon. In righteousness, Christ brings us into right standing with God, clothes us with righteousness, and makes us righteous before God.

- In justification, man is acquitted in the same way that a criminal is discharged. In righteousness, man is in right standing with God and restored as a citizen (Romans 5:1, 9, Amplified New Testament).

- The sinner who believes in Christ is justified in Christ. The sinner who believes in Christ is made righteous in Christ.

H. **Summary of Verses 25-26**

"Christ set forth as a propitiation [atoning sacrifice] through faith in His blood, to declare His righteousness for sins past, through His forbearance [apparent delays in judgment did not mean that God winks at sin], declare His righteousness [his way of making sinners right], that He might be just [inflict punishment for sin] and the justifier [remove the punishment of sin] on him which believes in Jesus."

Verses 21-26: *Righteousness by Faith in Christ: A Summary*

There is a logical order in the use of various words in Paul's epistle to the Romans. They are placed in the following order and will then be superimposed in the tabernacle of Moses. The tabernacle of Moses beautifully illustrates the theological implications in typical-symbolic form (Romans 2:20). (Refer to *Hebrews*, by Seiss.) Note the following words:

Righteousness of God

The Law

Transgression

Wrath

Judgment –means "justice."

Propitiation – means "sin-offering, appeasement" (blood shed at the altar and brought within veil [cf. Leviticus 16; II Corinthians 5:17-21]).

Redemption – means "to buy back again, out of the hands of another, out of the forum."

Ransom – means "the price actually paid to redeem."

Justification – means "put in right standing, declare righteous."

Righteousness – means "restore to right standing before God."

Reconciliation – means "making of friends those who were at variance before" (result of the atonement).

Atonement – The actual and official presentation of the blood of Jesus, by Jesus, at the throne of God in heaven. Before man could be reconciled, he must be justified. Before he could be justified, he must be redeemed. Before he could be redeemed, he must be averted from the wrath of transgressed law against the righteousness of God through propitiation. Thus, God found a way to be just and to be the Justifier of him who believes in Jesus.

Grace – "undeserved, unmerited, unearned favor of God bestowed on man"

Note the following scenario. A son breaks his father's *law*. The *righteous* anger of the father is *wrath*. He has given his word, and the *penalty* must be paid. The son is sold into slavery, prison, and bondage. He needs *redemption*. He cannot redeem himself. Someone else (a person) pays the price of his redemption—the *ransom*. He is ransomed, and the person who paid the price dies instead. This is substitution. The father and son, though, still have to be reconciled. They are reconciled by the death of the person who paid the ransom. The evidence of this death is given to the father. This is *atonement*. We are God's by both *creation* and *redemption*.

GRACE OF GOD UNDER LAW COVENANT

The Atonement
vs 25.
The Reconciliation

The Blood, vs 24

The Law of God -
Righteousness
in the Ten
Commanements
vs 3:20.
Ark - Glory of God.
vs 23. Throne of
Justice.
The MercySeat -
Faith in Blood
vs 24.

BrazenLaver

Righteousness

Brazen Altar
By Faith, vs 26

Redemption
Ranson
Substitution
Appeasement
Israelite

All Guilty

Israelite justified by faith in the sacrificial blood which the
High Priest took within the Veil on the Day of Atonement and sprinkled
on the MercySeat -Propitiation.

Righteousness Apart from Works of the Law (Romans 3:27-31)

Verse 27: *"Where is boasting then? It is excluded. By what law? of works? Nay: but by the law of faith."*

A. **"Where is boasting then? It is excluded"**

If a man can only be justified by faith in what God had done, boasting is excluded, banished, and ruled out entirely. Man loves to boast, in pride, concerning what he is and what he has done. Man would like to boast that he is able to earn his salvation from God; however, none can vaunt themselves. "Boasting" means "to say or speak of oneself all the time with pride, vainglory." Boasting is what self-effort and the works of the law produced in the Jews (Romans 2:17, 23; II Timothy 3:2).

Note "boasting" and "boasters" in Psalms 10:3; 49:6; 52:1; Proverbs 20:14; Romans 11:18; Ephesians 2:8-9; James 3:5; and Psalm 94:4. Our boast is in God (Psalms 44:8; 34:2). Faith rules out boasting. There is no credit, virtue, or merit in faith itself; it is what Christ has done. The exercise of faith is the exercise of dependence upon another. The law of faith completely excludes boasting.

B. **"By what law"**

"By what law" is also translated "on what principle" (Amplified New Testament). For a fuller treatment of the subject of law, refer to Romans 7 notes. The word "law" means "a rule of order or conduct established by authority; the regular method or sequences by which certain phenomena or effects follow certain conditions or causes; one of the rules or principles by which anything is regulated." Paul introduces here another law. After dealing with the law of conscience, and then the law of Moses (law of works), he brings in a higher law—the law of faith. It is by this law that man may be justified.

Note the comparison between the law of works and the law of faith:

- The law of works is the principle of doing good. The law of faith is the principle of believing in what another has done.
- The law of works means trusting what you can do and having to justify yourself before God. The law of faith means trusting yourself wholly over to Christ, what He has done, and what He can do for you in order to be justified.

- The law of works produces boasting of self-efforts and self-results. The law of faith excludes, shuts out, and stops such boasting from entering, but causes us to boast in God.
- The law of works is a never-finished work. (How great an amount of works could man do to justify himself before God?) The law of faith is a finished work (cf. John 19:30; 17:2-6). (Also cf. "no servile work" in the feasts and Sabbaths of the Lord [Leviticus 23:7-8, 21, 25, 30-31, and 35-36].)

John 6:28-29 states, "...What shall we do, that we might work the works of God? Jesus answered and said unto them, This is the work of God, that ye believe on him whom he hath sent." The Jews, under the law of works, knew little or nothing about the law of faith.

The law of faith is that divine rule, or principle, by which the justified shall live. Romans 4 expounds on this fact. Laws govern the entire universe. Laws do not make things; they simply govern their operation. The law of faith governs all that we receive from God through Christ. The believer's whole life is governed by the law of faith, for "...whatsoever is not of faith is sin" (Romans 14:23, also 14:6). Faith is not the *ground* of justification. If that were the case then faith would be meritorious. Faith is the *method* (channel) of receiving justification. Unbelief is sin (John 16:8-11).

Verse 28: *"Therefore we conclude that a man is justified by faith without the deeds of the law."*

(Refer again to notes on Romans 3:20, 26.)

Verse 29: *"Is he the God of the Jews only? is he not also of the Gentiles? Yes, of the Gentiles also..."*

A. **"Is he the God of the Jews only?"**
Note the following statements taken from Scripture:
- Jews and Gentiles are all under sin (Romans 2:9).
- Jews and Gentiles are to be judged by God (Romans 2:9-10).
- There is no respect of persons with God (Romans 2:11).
- The gospel is the power of God unto all who believe (Romans 1:16-17).

- There is no difference between Jew or Gentile, for the same Lord is rich unto *all* that call, whether Jew or Gentile (Romans 10:12-13).
- Whosoever shall call on the name of the Lord shall be saved (Romans 10:13).

B. **"Yes, of the Gentiles also"**
If God were only the God of the Jews, He would be a nationalistic, sectarian God. Theologically, if God were not the God of the Gentiles, as He is God of the Jews, then there would be two "Gods"—two "infinities." The doctrine of *one true God* rules out any other "god." The one God fills all things and is present everywhere at all times. He could not be so if He was not the only one true God. This truth rules out all boasting, pride, attitudes of seclusion, and sectarian spirits of the Jews towards the Gentiles. Acts 10-11 demonstrates this. God's visitation of the Spirit on the Jews and Gentiles, with the same gospel, baptism, and Spirit, places them into the same body (Ephesians 4:1-16; 2:12-22; I Corinthians 12:13). God is the God of all flesh.

Verse 30: *"...Seeing it is one God, which shall justify the circumcision by faith, and uncircumcision through faith."*

"One God, which shall justify the circumcision by faith, and uncircumcision through faith"
One God justifies:
- Circumcision (Jews *by* faith) (channel of faith)
- Uncircumcision (Gentiles *through* faith) (channel of faith)

God justified *by faith* for the Jews because the seed of that faith was in Israel and because the Jews began *with the father*, Abraham, as Paul is about to introduce in Romans 4:1. God justifies *through faith* for the Gentiles because they came into faith *in Christ*, and the gospel was presented to them (Acts 14:27). The door of faith was opened to the Gentiles. In both cases, it is faith, whether circumcised or uncircumcised (cf. Ephesians 2:10-12).

Verse 31: *"Do we then make void the law through faith? God forbid: yea, we establish the law."*

A. **"Do we then make void the law through faith?"**

Paul anticipates, in this verse, Jewish objections and questions. There seems to be an apparent contradiction between law and faith. The argument is this: if a man cannot be justified through the law, but only by faith, then faith makes void the law (Amplified New Testament). Romans 3:31 restated: "Do we then (by this) faith make the law of none effect, overthrow it or make it a dead letter? God forbid, yea, we establish the law."

B. **"God forbid: yea we establish the law"**

Paul's answer to his previous question is "...Certainly not! On the contrary, we confirm and establish and uphold the Law" (Amplified New Testament). What does this mean? What is the apparent contradiction between law and faith? Does faith rule out the law, or does law rule out faith? The answers to those questions are relative to the verses that have proceeded them concerning the law of works and the law of faith in Christ. We have the law. We have Christ. The law pointed to Christ (Matthew 5; 11:13). Christ Himself did not come to destroy the law, make it void, overthrow it, or rule it out as a dead letter of no effect. He came to fulfill the law. By fulfilling it, He *magnified* it and made it honorable (Isaiah 42:21). Christ did this by perfectly keeping the law in letter and in spirit and by being the fulfillment of it. The law was fulfilled in Christ, who is the author and the finisher of our faith.

There is no conflict between law and faith. The law made the way for faith and prepared sinners for faith, but when faith came, personified in Christ, the law had fulfilled its purpose, function, and ministry. It ended in Christ. Christ is the *end* of the law (Romans 10:4). "...[B]efore faith came, we were kept under the law, shut up unto the faith which should afterwards be revealed" (Galatians 3:23, also 3:17-25). The law was a schoolmaster to bring us to Christ, that we might be justified by *faith*. Once faith came, we were no longer under the schoolmaster (guardian of a pupil to bring him to the teacher). Thus, there is no conflict between the law of Moses (not law!) and faith. Law has not been made to no effect and is not purposeless, overthrown, or a dead letter. It has been confirmed, upheld, and fulfilled in Christ.

Wherefore then serveth the law? (Galatians 3:15-20). The following diagram illustrates:

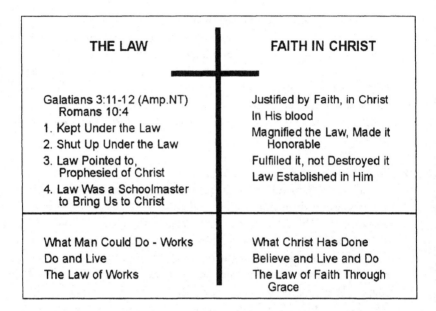

THE LAW	FAITH IN CHRIST

Galatians 3:11-12 (Amp.NT)
Romans 10:4
1. Kept Under the Law
2. Shut Up Under the Law
3. Law Pointed to,
   Prophesied of Christ
4. Law Was a Schoolmaster
   to Bring Us to Christ
	Justified by Faith, in Christ
	In His blood
	Magnified the Law, Made it
	   Honorable
	Fulfilled it, not Destroyed it
	Law Established in Him

What Man Could Do - Works Do and Live The Law of Works	What Christ Has Done Believe and Live and Do The Law of Faith Through Grace

If Christ has fulfilled the law and the righteousness of the law, then whosoever believes and receives Christ (in the biblical sense), the righteousness of the law is fulfilled in him (Romans 8:1-4). (Note: "Christ in us, the hope of glory" [cf. Romans 8:4; 13:8-10] and Romans 7 on "the law" [and notes].)

Righteousness Confirmed (Romans 4:1-25)

Abraham and David – Two Old Testament Witnesses (Romans 4:1-12)

In this section, Paul brings in two Old Testament examples of people who had a faith-righteousness.

- Abraham – before law (Romans 4:1-5) (developed in Romans 4:9-25)
- David – after law, under law (Romans 4: 6-8)

Compare Romans 4 with Galatians 3. The whole burden of Romans 4 is "imputed righteousness." Imputed righteousness is the "key" phrase of this chapter (imputed, reckoned, counted).

Verse I: *"What shall we say then that Abraham our father, as pertaining to the flesh, hath found?"*

A. **"Abraham our father"**

In Romans 4 and 5, Paul deals with two fathers as shown below:

- Abraham – the father of all whom believe (Romans 4)
- Adam – the father of the entire human race, of whom all are born (Romans 5)

From the time of Adam to Abraham, we have the dispensation of the Father God—two thousand years. Paul goes back to Abraham—to the very beginning, to the source and foundation of the Hebrew race. As far as the Jews were concerned, there was no greater "father" than Abraham (and also Isaac and Jacob). The Jews had their beginning in Abraham.

In Luke 3:8-9, John the Baptist exclaimed to the multitude, "Bring forth fruits worthy of repentance, and begin not to say within yourselves, We have Abraham to our father..." He then goes on to speak, in verse 9, about the axe that was laid at the root of the trees. Nationally speaking, Abraham was that root, source, and foundation of the chosen nation. The axe, spiritually speaking, was laid right at the root, and the trunk and the branches (i.e., the whole nation of Israel and Judah) were cut off. This thought is also taken up in Romans 9-11 on the national aspect concerning the symbol of the olive tree.

Jesus Himself also applied the axe of truth in John 8:1-59 concerning Abraham "their father." The whole chapter is a conflict over "fathers." Jesus spoke of His heavenly Father. The Pharisees spoke of Abraham, their father (John 8:39), and even claimed God as their spiritual Father (John 8:41). Note the facts that Jesus told them in John 8:33, 37. He said, and agreed with them, that they were Abraham's seed—after the flesh (as Romans 4:1 also says, "...Abraham our father, as pertaining to the flesh..."). This pertained to the natural, national, and fleshly birth as the seed of Abraham. Jesus plainly said, "If ye [truly and spiritually] were Abraham's children [seed], ye would do the works of Abraham [your boasted natural father]" (John 8:39). Again in John 8:42, He said, "If God were your [heavenly] Father, ye would love me..." Also in John 8:44, Jesus plainly told them who their real spiritual father was: "Ye are of your father the devil..." (murderers and liars, not abiding in the truth). (The entire chapter should be read to understand this matter.)

Abraham was the father of the chosen race. All the covenant promises from God originated with him. He is the source, the foundation, the beginning, the covenant holder. The Abrahamic Covenant is a covenant of faith and grace, and the promised seed of the Messiah was founded in him. Only those born of Abraham's line, through Isaac, Jacob, and Jacob's twelve sons, were counted before God as "the seed." Only in Abraham could they receive blessing. Hence, the Jews' boasting of Abraham their father pertains to the flesh. Now Paul asks, "What shall we say then [to the fact] that Abraham our father...hath found?"

By bringing in Abraham, Paul brings in the pivotal man of the race— the very one in whom they boasted (Isaiah 51:2; Matthew 3:9; John 8:33; II Corinthians 11:22). Paul takes them to their foundational father—to their very beginning—to show them that the man in whom they boasted, and whose seed they claimed to be, was justified by *faith*, not of works or of the law. Abraham knew and experienced the *truth* and reality of justification by faith.

B.   **"Pertaining to the flesh"** (cf. Romans 9:5-8)
     "Pertaining to the flesh" refers to the national, natural, and fleshly birth (John 3:3-5) (that which is born of the flesh is flesh, whether Jewish or Gentile flesh).

Verse 2:   *"For if Abraham were justified by works, he hath whereof to glory; but not before God."*

Abraham was not justified by works or by the law.
     Abraham's lifetime was 430 years before the law came. He was not justified by the law or by works of the law. He was not justified by works at all (Romans 3:20, 27). Abraham could not, and did not, do anything to justify himself before God. As was Adam's entire race, he also was born in sin and shapen in iniquity. If he had been justified by works, he would have had something in which to boast, something in which to glory (but not before God). He could only boast in himself before others, but certainly not before God. God does not count, or accept, any man on the basis of works. No flesh shall glory in His presence (I Corinthians 1:26-31). "...Not of works, lest any man should boast" (Ephesians 2:4-5, 8-9; Romans 3:27). (Note Amplified New Testament.) What works or amount of works could a man do to be justified before God? Abraham is a witness to the Jews that he was not justified by works or by the law.

Verse 3: *"For what saith the scripture? Abraham believed God, and it was counted unto him for righteousness."*

A. **"For what saith the scripture?"**

The final "court of appeal" is the Scriptures. The doctrine of justification by faith was found in the Jews' own sacred writings in which they boasted (John 5:38; II Timothy 3:15-16; II Peter 1:20; II Peter 3:16). This means of justification in Christ's death was foreshadowed in every Old Testament sacrifice.

B. **"Abraham believed God"** (Genesis 15:6; James 2:22; Galatians 3:6)

This Scripture is quoted from Genesis 15:6: "And he [Abram] believed in the Lord; and he counted it to him for righteousness." The whole, surrounding context in this chapter of Genesis is wonderful in its significance and prophetic implications. Note also that this verse (Genesis 15:6) is the first use of the word "believe" in the Scriptures (King James Version). (This is not to imply that faith is not present. Hebrews 11 shows that, from Abel on down, faith was the underlying principle in the lives of the Patriarchs.) However, in this verse, the word "believe" is expressly translated in connection with Abraham. Here Paul calls him the "father of us all [them who believe]" (Romans 4:16).

The word "believe" means "trusted in." Belief is not mere mental assent or agreement to some statement of truth from God, but it is the casting of the self wholly upon God and His Word and trusting God and His Word fully with the heart. This is what Abraham did. (In Genesis 12, Abraham is called and the promises of the seed and the land are given to him. Genesis 13 furthers the promises to him. Then, in Genesis 14, the revelation of Melchisedec is given, and Genesis 15 refers to "faith.") The ground for Abraham's belief—the only ground—was the *Word of Promise* that God gave him (Genesis 15:1-21, 5). The promise was that Abraham's seed would be as the stars of heaven in number.

This promise came when Abraham was old and his wife, Sarah, was old and barren. It was impossible from a human and natural viewpoint. But this Word of God came to Abraham (Abram), and he believed, trusted, relied upon, had faith in, and cast himself wholly upon God and His Word. (This is the one and only basis and foundation for true faith.) Note especially in Romans 10:17: "…faith cometh by hearing, and hearing by the word of God."

C. "It was counted unto him for righteousness"

This "believing" was reckoned, or credited, to Abraham's account as righteousness; that is, "right living and right standing with God" (Amplified New Testament).

Also, this believing in Abraham's life was not just a single act, done once for all, but it was actually a life-principle. That is why God could reckon (count) it to him for righteousness (right standing and right living with God). The only way of right standing and right living before God is through this life principle of faith (believing God). Abraham believed God all through his life. At times, there were lapses in his faith, but he was a man of faith, and he believed God right through to the end. He went from "faith to faith" (Romans 1:17). He was a man who lived by the *faith*-principle—the law of faith (Hebrews 11:8-16). Faith is not a single act or momentary attitude of the heart, but it is a continuous act and state of the heart. Abraham believed God; this was the principle by which he lived. "The just shall live by faith," and Abraham was a faith-righteous man—a justified man.

Note how Paul builds up this short example of Genesis 15:6, in the same way that he built upon "the just shall live by faith" from Habakkuk 2:4, and in the same way that Hebrews builds upon Psalm 110 and Genesis 14 (concerning Melchisedec).

Verse 4: *"Now to him that worketh is the reward not reckoned of grace, but of debt."*

"To him that worketh is the reward...of debt"

If people work, then they are rewarded for that work. The person for whom they work (their employer) owes them wages—their reward. The employer is, in every way, in debt to the employees. This is just. The natural sequence is works, debt, and reward. If people work for a master, then the master is indebted to them and must reward them for their work in order to be just in his or her dealings. The employees, therefore, are justified in taking wages for their work.

In other words, the workers earned the wages. Therefore, if Abraham worked for salvation (to be justified), then God was in debt to Abraham. God owed him a reward. But Abraham was not justified by works or by the law of works (Romans 3:27). He should not, and did not, *earn* salvation, justification, or right standing with God. God was not indebted to Abraham, and neither is God indebted to any of Abraham's race. God did not have to reward Abraham at all. Neither can the Jew work to be justified. It is of grace, through faith, that one is justified and accounted righteous. It is not of law or of works. Note the theme: grace or works—one or the other, but not both (Romans 11:6).

Verse 5: *"But to him that worketh not, but believeth on him that justifieth the ungodly, his faith is counted for righteousness."*

A. **"To him that worketh not"**
   Note the contrasting verses in Romans 4:4 and 4:5:
   * "...[T]o him that worketh..." (Romans 4:4), referring to the "law of works, "...justified by works..." (Romans 4:2).
   * "...[T]o him that worketh not..." (Romans 4:5), referring to the "law of faith, "...justified by faith..." (Romans 5:1).

   Compare the above with:
   * Grace through faith (Romans 4:4-5). (Grace, the free gift [Romans 3:24])
   * Debt and reward through works (Romans 4:4). (Debt, reward earned and given)

   The thought of giving is in both Romans 4:4 and 4:5. A reward, earned by works, is a debt paid. However, grace is giving also, but grace is a gift, freely given, that is not earned but gratuitously bestowed on another because of the nature of the giver. The gift of grace is not the result of anything in or done by the recipient. Note:
   "Worketh" (Romans 4:4) – Compare Cain—justified by works, as Jew or Gentile seeks to be (Genesis 4).
   "Believeth" (Romans 4:5) – Compare Abel—justified by faith, as Jew and Gentile may be (Genesis 4; Hebrews 11:1-6).

   Working and believing are totally opposite. This matter of working and believing was actually the greatest stumbling block to the Jew—as it is to all mankind. The moment Adam sinned, the law of works came into operation, for Adam felt that he must do something to make himself presentable to God (to be justified before God for his action). The fig leaves were the outcome of the law of works. What can man do? Works!

The Jews said to Jesus, "…What shall we do that we might work the works of God?" Jesus replied, "…This is the work of God, that ye believe on him whom he hath sent" (John 6:28-29). This is the very thing the Jews did not want to do. They refused this work of God and continued to carry on the works of the law—the works of self-effort. The Jews boasted that Abraham was their father, yet Abraham was a justified man—a faith-righteous man. Abraham believed God. He went from faith to faith. The true seed of Abraham would also believe (John 8:31-59).

Note that rich young ruler wanted also to do something to inherit eternal life (Luke 18:18-27). This law of works, of man desiring to earn blessing from God, is a constant test in a believer's life. No man can earn or merit salvation, the baptism of the Holy Spirit, or any of the blessings and promises of God. Salvation is a free gift. The Holy Spirit is the gift of God. Redemption and all its attendant blessings are of the free grace of God. Nothing can be earned. Nothing man can do, by way of works, can earn these things apart from God. Therefore, God asks man to believe, to trust wholly, and to rely upon God through Christ. Note:

- The Law of Works – means "what man has done, what man can do" (law).
- The Law of Faith – means "what God has done, what God can do" (grace).

For man to believe in Him who justifies the ungodly is for him to cast his entire personality on God.

B. **"His faith is counted for righteousness"**
   Note the following verses:
   - This righteousness of God is manifested without the law (Romans 3:21).
   - The Law and the Prophets (Romans 3:21) witnessed it.
   - It is righteousness by faith in and of Jesus Christ (Romans 3:22).
   - It is a faith-righteousness (Romans 4:3, 5).

   Note the word "counted" in Romans 4:3 and 5. "Counted" in the Greek is *logizomai*. This Greek word is used eleven times in this chapter. It is translated in the following ways:
   - Counted (Romans 4:3, 5)

- Reckoned (Romans 4:4, 9-10; 6:11; 8:18)
- Imputed (Romans 4:4:6, 8, 11, 22-24; II Corinthians 5:19; James 2:23; Psalm 32:2)

"Counted" means "to reckon, number, account." Christ was "reckoned amongst the transgressors" (Luke 22:37). He was "numbered" with them. The key truth here in this chapter is "imputed righteousness."

Romans 3:21-31 declares that the righteousness of God has been manifested without the law (being witnessed by the Law and the Prophets). The righteousness of God has been perfectly expressed in the Lord Jesus Christ Himself (Jeremiah 23:5; 33:14-15). But Romans 4 declares how the righteousness of God is imputed to us. It is imputed (reckoned, accounted) to us on the basis of faith and faith alone. It is not imputed on account of works. Righteousness was imputed to Abraham by faith (Romans 4:3, 5). Righteousness may be imputed to us—whether Jew or Gentile—if we believe on God who raised Jesus from the dead (Romans 4:22-25). Righteousness may also be imputed to (reckoned to and put to the account of) Abraham's seed by faith (Romans 4:11-12). Righteousness is imputed by faith; that is faith in what God has done and not in anything that we have done or could do. (Refer to notes on Romans 4:8.) Thus, Paul brings in Abraham, of whom the Jews boasted that they were his seed, and Paul shows them that Abraham was a justified man (a righteous man). His justification was based entirely on faith and grace and not on the law of works. Note below clarification on the subject of "works" between Paul and James:

Justification by faith—not of works. There is no conflict between Paul and James on this subject of justification. Paul's emphasis is that a person is justified by faith and not by works. The reason is as follows: man is dead in trespasses and sins; therefore, any works done by man before salvation or to earn salvation are dead works. These dead works, done in self-effort (religious works and ceremonial works of the law), can never justify man. A spiritually dead man can only do dead works. These have to be repented of. "I know thy works..." (Revelation 1-3). (See also Romans 4:1-8; Ephesians 2:8-9; Hebrews 6:1-2; 9:14.) Works done before salvation are dead works which call for repentance. However, Paul does not eliminate works after salvation. Continually, in his epistles, he exhorts the believer to "maintain good works."

Justification by works of faith. James' emphasis is that of a person already justified by faith but whose faith is manifest in works of obedience (James 2:14-26). Faith without works is dead. Faith without obedience is dead. The believer is saved by grace, through faith, not of works (Ephesians 2:8-10); yet he or she is created "...unto good works, which God hath before ordained that we should walk in them" (Matthew 5:16; I Timothy 6:18; Titus 2:7; Hebrews 10:24; I Peter 2:12). Works done before salvation are dead works. Good works after salvation—works of a person alive in Christ—are ordained of God as evidence of faith. "I know thy works...repent and do the first works" (Revelation 1-3). Thus, Abraham was justified "by faith" and "by works."

Verse 6: *"Even as David also describeth the blessedness of the man, unto whom God imputeth righteousness without works..."*

King David as an Example of Faith-Righteousness
In this verse, Paul brings in another testimony of "faith-righteousness" —King David. Note below:
- **Abraham** – Abraham was before the law and under grace. He was justified through faith without works. The Abrahamic Covenant was made with him, and he was the first to receive specific seed promises.
- **David** – David was after, and under, the law, yet also experienced justification by faith and grace apart from works of the law. The Davidic Covenant was made with him, and he was the last to receive specific seed promises. Jesus Christ was of Abraham and David (Matthew 1:1).

To the Hebrew mind, there was no greater king then David. Both Abraham and David were covenant men, and both received the promises of the covenant concerning the Messiah seed. The Messiah was descended from both of them. Jesus Christ was the seed of Abraham and the seed of David, after the flesh.

Abraham lived over four hundred years before the law of God was given, and David lived several hundreds years after the law was given; yet, both of these men knew the blessedness of justification and of faith-righteousness. David, under the law, broke the law of God and deserved wrath and judgment. The law condemned David as a murderer and an adulterer. Yet he came to know the grace of God, even under the law (cf.

II Samuel 11-12; Psalms 32, 51). If a man breaks one commandment, he is guilty of all and comes under the death penalty (James 2:8-12). Thus, the law, or the works of the law, could not justify even David. David could do nothing, by way of works, to be justified before God. Absolutely nothing! Abraham was justified by *faith*, without works, before God. Abraham was justified by *works*, after faith, before man. David was justified by *faith*, without works, before God also, yet his works of faith followed.

Verse 7: *"...Saying, Blessed are they whose iniquities are forgiven, and whose sins are covered."*

Paul quotes these two verses (Romans 4:7-8) from a testimonial Psalm of David (Psalm 32:1-2). David here describes the blessedness of imputed righteousness.

A. **"Blessed are they whose iniquities are forgiven"**
    "Blessed" – means "happy, fortunate and to be envied" (Amplified Old Testament).
    "Iniquity" – means "perverseness of spirit, lawlessness."
    "Sins" – means "transgression, error; to pass across a given boundary (I John 3:4).
    "Forgiven" – Hebrew: *Nasa* means "to lift up or away" (Psalm 32:1, 5; 25:18; 103:3). Greek: *Apoluo* means "to send away, or let go" (Luke 6:37). Greek: *Charizomai* means "to be gracious to" (Colossians 2:13; Ephesians 4:32). Greek: *Aphiemi* means "to send or let off or away" (Romans 4:7). Greek: *Aphesis* means "a sending away, letting go" (Acts 5:31; 13:38).

Forgiveness is part of the New Covenant promises (Jeremiah 31:31-34). As seen in the definition above, there are various shades of meaning for the word "forgiveness." Forgiveness is the "lifting up and away" of the heavy load and burden of sin. It is the "sending away or the letting go" of all our sins and the loosing of the one enslaved to sin. Forgiveness is the grace of God—the free gift of God bestowed on the judgment-deserving sinner who believes. God forgives sin on the basis of sin being judged.

Note in Leviticus 4:20, 26, 31, 35; 5:10, 13, 16, 18; 6:7 and Numbers 15:25, 26, 28: "...it shall be forgiven him (them)." Forgiveness is the "letting away" of sins through the Atonement upon one's confession (Leviticus 5:5, 10). The same Greek word, *aphesis*, is translated "remission" in Matthew 26:28; Luke 1:77; 24:47; Acts 10:43; Hebrews 9:22; 10:18; Romans 3:25. It is typically seen in the scapegoat (azazel), which was (literally) "the goat for going away." The scapegoat had all the sins, iniquities, and transgressions of Israel confessed and laid on it by the laying on of hands. It was then sent away, bearing all the sins of the nation of Israel into an uninhabited land (Leviticus 16:7-10, 20-26). The scapegoat ministry speaks typically of "forgiveness" or "remission of sins."

B. **"Whose sins are covered"**
    "Sins" – means "transgression, error; to pass across a given boundary" (I John 3:4).
    "Covered" – Hebrew: *Kasah* means "to cover or conceal" (Psalm 32:1). Greek: *Epikalupto* means "to cover over" (Romans 4:7).

Let us note the blessedness of this "covering of sins," for it is of God. The Scriptures plainly teach that man is not to cover his sins, but they are to be forsaken and confessed that God may cover them. Note the contrasting Scriptures below:

- "He that covereth his sins shall not prosper: but whoso confesseth and forsaketh them shall have mercy" (Proverbs 28:13).
- "If I covered my transgression as Adam..."(Job 31:33; also see Isaiah 55:7).
- "Thou hast forgiven the iniquity of thy people, thou hast covered all their sin. Selah" (Psalm 85:2).

David is describing his own experience in Psalm 32:5 when he says, "I acknowledged my sin unto thee, and mine iniquity have I not hid. I said, I will confess my transgressions unto the Lord; and thou forgavest the iniquity of my sin. Selah." David did not cover his sins; he did exactly what Proverbs says to do. He confessed them, forsook them, and found the mercy of God (II Samuel 12:12). Thus, he knew the blessedness of iniquity and sins forgiven—sins covered by the blood of atonement. Sins that are unforsaken and unconfessed cannot be forgiven or covered. God can only forgive and cover that which is confessed and forsaken. Then God can justly judge sin and forgive it. God cannot just forgive sin without judging it. This explains the Scripture "...love covereth all sins" (Proverbs 10:12; James 5:20). The word "atonement" in Old Testament Hebrew is "*kaphar*," meaning "to cover" (Exodus 30:10-16; 32:30; Leviticus 4:20-35; Leviticus 16). It is the blood of atonement which covers and conceals all our sins and iniquities from God's sight (Romans 3:24-25). This explains the Lord's goat that is used as a sin offering and whose blood makes atonement for the sanctuary and for all Israel (Leviticus 16:7-19). Anti-typically the two goats (the Lord's goat and the scapegoat) may be seen as follows:

The Lord's Goat – represents the blood atonement, the covering of sins by the blood. Jesus Christ, in His death, was the Lord's goat or the goat for Jehovah. Note: "Whose sins are covered."

The Scapegoat – represents the result of the Atonement; the forgiveness and remission of sins by sending away all our sins and iniquities. Note: "Blessed are they whose transgressions are forgiven," meaning "sent away, loosed, lifted up and away."

David could sincerely describe the blessedness of the grace of God. He was guilty of murder and adultery and was condemned by the Law of the Ten Commandments. He was under the death penalty. Nothing he could do, by works of the law, could earn forgiveness. No works or amount of works could justify him before God. His mouth was stopped. He was guilty before God. However, David confessed his sin (II Samuel 12:13; Psalm 51:4; Proverbs 28:13; Psalm 32:5), and he knew the blessedness of forgiveness (II Samuel 12:13; Job 7:21; Psalm 32:1; Micah 7:18; Zechariah 3:4; Psalm 51). David could have gone and offered a sacrifice according to his position as king (Leviticus 1-7; Psalm 51), but he knew forgiveness of sin went deeper than all the external forms of animal sacrifices. He offered unto God a broken and contrite spirit, acknowledged his sins and iniquities, and pled for mercy and cleansing (Psalm 51). Boasting was excluded. The law of works profited nothing. David knew the law of faith, and God justified him and imputed righteousness to him apart from works. The Jews could also know this blessedness if they came God's way by believing in Jesus Christ (Romans 3:24-26). Note the following summary concerning David's sin:

- David was guilty of murder and adultery. Sin is transgression of the law (I John 3:4).
- According to the Law of Ten Commandments, which he had broken, he was under the death penalty.
- His sin was pointed out to him. He confessed it and pled for mercy.
- God forgave him, covered his sin, and had mercy on him. His sin was "covered" by the "Atonement" (typically).
- Thus, David was justified by faith and grace—not of works. The free grace of God was experienced.
- However, God did punish David and his household (II Samuel 12:7-14).

Thus, we have the witness of Abraham, before law, and David, under law, as two men justified by faith.

Verse 8: *"Blessed is the man to whom the Lord will not impute sin."*

A. **"To whom the Lord will not impute sin"**

The key word in this chapter, as has already been noted, is the word "impute." This chapter is dealing with the truth of imputed righteousness. This verse is also from Psalm 32:1-2: "Blessed is the man unto whom the Lord imputeth not iniquity...." The Amplified New Testament translates Romans 4:8: "Blessed *and* happy *and* to be envied is the person of whose sin the Lord will take no account nor reckon it against him." "Impute" means "to reckon to another what is not theirs." As noted in comments on Romans 4:5, the same Greek word, *logizomai*, is translated as "counted," "reckoned," and "imputed" in this chapter. In verse 8, it is translated "imputed." Find below the development of this great truth of imputed righteousness in the following verses of Romans 4:

- "...Abraham believed God, and it was *counted* [imputed, reckoned] unto him for righteousness" (verse 3).
- "...[R]*eckoned* [counted, imputed] of grace..." (verse 4).
- "But to him that...believeth...his faith is *counted* [reckoned, imputed] for righteousness" (verse 5).
- "...David...unto whom God *imputeth* [reckoned, counted] righteousness without works" (verse 6).
- "Blessed is the man to whom the Lord will not *impute* [reckon, account] sin" (verse 8).

• "...[F]aith was *reckoned* [imputed, accounted]...for righteousness" (verses 9-10).

• "...[T]hat righteousness might be *imputed* [reckoned, accounted] unto them also..." (verse 11).

• "...[I]t was *imputed* [reckoned, accounted] to him [Abraham] for righteousness" (verse 22).

• "...[I]t was *imputed* [reckoned, accounted] to him; but for us also, to whom it shall be *imputed* [reckoned, accounted], if we believe on him that raised up Jesus..." (verses 23-24).

All mankind, Jew or Gentile, have been "under sin" and there is "none righteous, no not one." The righteousness of the law has condemned all those under it who tried, or did not try, to attain its standard, and thus, the entire world is guilty before God. Every mouth is stopped. All are under judgment, worthy of death, helpless, and unable to do anything to justify or acquit themselves before God.

Then, God comes in grace in Christ Jesus. God brings in His Son as the manifested righteousness of God; that is, God brings in His Son as "the Lord our righteousness" —Jehovah Tsidkenu. Jehovah Tsidkenu is God's redemptive name (Jeremiah 23:5-6; 33:15; I Corinthians 1:30). God presents His Son, His righteousness personified and the righteousness of the law fulfilled, to guilty man, and says, in effect, to man, "In grace I present My Son to you. He is the righteousness of the law. He is My righteousness personified. If you will accept Him and all that He is and believe in and upon Him—taking yourself out of your own care and keeping and casting yourselves wholly upon Him and all that He is and all that He has done—then I will accept you in Him. In Him you shall be justified. In Him you shall be made righteous. He will be your righteousness, and the channel of receiving is by faith. I will impute, reckon, and account to you all that My Son is. Accept My Son, My righteousness, and you will be in right standing with me. You will be the righteousness of God in Christ." This is the *Word of God*. Either man believes and accepts it, or he disbelieves and rejects it. *Unbelief* in Christ is counted for *unrighteousness*. *Faith* in Christ is counted for *righteousness*. This Word of God may sound wonderful and beautiful in theory and doctrine, yet it can be so unreal to the heart that lacks the experience of its truth. Still, this is the revelation of the gospel according to Paul. Questions immediately arise out of such a revelation. The chief questions are: "How can God impute righteousness to those who believe on Jesus Christ? How can God impute righteousness to a guilty sinner? How can God impute, reckon, or account to us His righteousness?" The answer is found in the word "impute."

Let us consider the following facts in order to appreciate the blessedness of Romans 4:8:

Sin is not imputed when there then is no law (Romans 5:13). Where there is no law, there is no transgression (Romans 4:15). Sin is the transgression of the law (I John 3:4). Sin is lawlessness. (Note also the Amplified New Testament on Romans 5:12-14.) The strength of sin is the law (I Corinthians 15:56). Sin cannot be charged to man's account if there is no law to transgress. Hence, if sin is imputed and charged to man's account, it is because of the transgression of the law. Man (or Israel as a nation), under the law, violated the law, and therefore, sin was imputed to him (or to Israel).

God, in Christ, was reconciling the world unto Himself, not imputing their trespasses unto them (II Corinthians 5:18-21.). God made Christ, who knew no sin, to be sin for us. "...And he was *reckoned* [numbered, accounted] among the transgressors [lawless]..." (Luke 22:37). When God made Christ to be sin for us, God *imputed, reckoned,* and *accounted* all the sins, transgressions, and iniquities of the world to Christ's account. God charged Him as being guilty of all the sins, transgressions, and iniquities of the world. He treated Him as a transgressor—a lawless one—and dealt with Him according to the penalty for sin, which is death. Thus, God dealt with sin in Christ. The claims of the law have been upheld and satisfied. Death, which is judgment on sin, has been meted out, and the law can exact no further penalty than death.

Imputed righteousness (II Corinthians 5:18-21). The purpose of all that was described in the preceding paragraph was to show that God may now impute righteousness, without works, to all who believe in Jesus. God imputed sins to Christ that He might impute Christ's righteousness to us. "...[T]hat we might be the righteousness of God in him" (II Corinthians 5:21). "...[B]lessedness of the man, unto whom God imputeth righteousness without works, saying, Blessed are they whose iniquities are forgiven, and whose sins are covered. Blessed is the man to whom the Lord will not impute sin"(Romans 4:6-8).

B. Imputed Righteousness

God can impute righteousness to us because He imputed our sins to Christ (refer to notes on Romans 3:25). Thus, God can be just and can be the Justifier of him who believes in Jesus. This is the only righteousness that God will accept—righteousness in Christ. The righteousness of Christ is the righteousness of God manifested. It is faith-righteousness. It is righteousness by *grace*, through faith, not of ourselves. It is the *free gift* of God. Note the two aspects of this righteousness, which are as follows:

1) "Imputed righteousness" means "righteousness inwrought, positional righteousness, legal and judicial" (Romans 4:6).

2) "Fulfilled righteousness" means "experiential and practical righteousness; righteousness outworked" (Romans 8:4; 6:19).

Imputed righteousness is that which God reckons to us in Christ. When we accept Christ, He is our righteousness—our imputed righteousness. It is all that He is because of what He has done. However, the righteousness of Christ has to be *outworked* in us, not by works, but by Christ living His life (His righteous life) in and through us. This is outworked or fulfilled righteousness. Otherwise, the subtle doctrine of "sinning that grace may abound" may creep in (Romans 6:14-15). If Christ is our imputed righteousness, then Christ will fulfill that righteousness in us. Grace can only reign through righteousness (refer to notes on Romans 5:21). Outworked (fulfilled) righteousness will be dealt with in Romans 8:4.

Verse 9: *"Cometh this blessedness then upon the circumcision only, or upon the uncircumcision also? for we say that faith was reckoned to Abraham for righteousness."*

A. "Cometh this blessedness then upon the circumcision only, or upon the uncircumcision also?"

Here Paul resumes his thought on circumcision from Romans 2:25-29 and 3:1. As if to answer an argument arising out of the fact that Abraham and David were covenant men, of the circumcision, and that this is why they knew the blessedness of justification, Paul answers the question with this question in Romans 4:9 (paraphrased): "Is the blessing of justification (imputed righteousness) for the circumcision (the Jew) only or for the uncircumcision (the Gentile) also?" Paul is now about to take

Abraham's experience in uncircumcision and circumcision to prove that the blessedness was for both the Jew and the Gentile—the circumcision or the uncircumcision. He has already dealt with the matter of *true* circumcision in Romans 2:25-29. The circumcision is made uncircumcision if he breaks the law. The uncircumcision is made the circumcision if he fulfills the law.

A Jew is not a Jew outwardly, but one inwardly. A Gentile, by nature, is a Jew inwardly if he knows true circumcision of the heart in the spirit. And a Jew is a Gentile inwardly if he does not know the true circumcision of the heart. If a Jew only knows the circumcision that is fleshly and natural, then he is a Gentile. He is a true Jew if he knows the inner experience represented by the physical fact. In other words, a Jew (circumcision) can be a Gentile (uncircumcision) inwardly, and a Gentile (uncircumcision) can be a Jew (circumcision) inwardly (Jeremiah 9:25). Only the new creature in Christ Jesus is acceptable to God, and neither circumcision nor uncircumcision avails anything (Galatians 6:15; Deuteronomy 10:16; 30:6). The Lord prophesied that He would circumcise the foreskin of the *heart* and that this circumcision of the *flesh* pointed to that of the *spirit*. The Jews became caught up in circumcision of the flesh and missed the circumcision of the spirit (Jeremiah 4:4; I Corinthians 7:18-19; Galatians 2:3; 5:1-3, 6, 11; 6:12-13; Colossians 2:11; Ephesians 2:11; Philippians 3:3; Colossians 3:11).

B. "For we say that faith was reckoned to Abraham for righteousness"
    (Refer to notes on Romans 4:3, 5.) Abraham knew the blessedness of faith-righteousness—faith in God, in who He is, in what He has done, and in what He will do. Faith-righteousness is not self-effort, which is faith in self, in what self is, and in what self can do.

Verse 10:   *"How was it then reckoned? when he was in circumcision, or in uncircumcision? Not in circumcision, but in uncircumcision."*

"How was it then reckoned?...Not in circumcision, but in uncircumcision"
    Paul now proceeds with another argument concerning circumcision. He has shown what true circumcision is in Romans 2:24-29. Now he takes this experience of Abraham, in the state of both uncircumcision and circumcision to show that it really shadowed forth "the Jew and the Gentile" in a faith-righteousness before God.

How then was this righteousness reckoned or imputed to Abraham? When he was circumcised or when he was uncircumcised? The answer is that this faith-righteousness was reckoned to him when he was uncircumcised—when he was in a "*Gentilized*" *state physically*. The first call and promises of God were given to Abraham in Genesis 12:1-4, which was before circumcision. It is worthy to note Paul's argument here and his application of Abraham's experience before and after circumcision.

Abraham	
Gen 12:1-4	
Abram	**Abraham**
Uncircumcised Rom.4:10	Circumcisied. Gen 17
Received call and promises of God. Gen.12	Received Covenant of circumcision Acts 7:8
Has altar, tent Gen.12.8	New Name given The"H" of Jehovah.
Meets Malchisedek, Gives tites and receives bread and wine Gen.14	Intercession before the Godhead.Gen.18
Abraham believed God. Promises given in a vision.	Promises confirmed again, after Isaac's offering Gen 22:15
Abraham believed God Gen.15	Abraham believed God. Faith perfected. Jam.2:17-23
Counted to him for righteousness	Imputed righteousness, Fulfilled righteousness, Sign & Seal,
Abraham in "Gentilized" state physically	Abraham in " Hebrew state"
Abraham in uncircumcision,	Abraham in circumcision
Father of many nations. Gen.4:18	Father, one chosen nation Gen.4:1 The circumcision

What Paul explains in the verse would have been very repugnant to the biased Jew, especially because Paul, a Jew, wrote it. Thus, Paul uses Abraham's experience (the experience of the Jews' boasted father), both before and after circumcision, to show that God was making Abraham the *father of all who believe*—Jew or Gentile, circumcision or uncircumcision.

Consider the following diagram that shows the things that happened in Abraham's life (in both his uncircumcised and circumcised states) as a faith-righteous man:

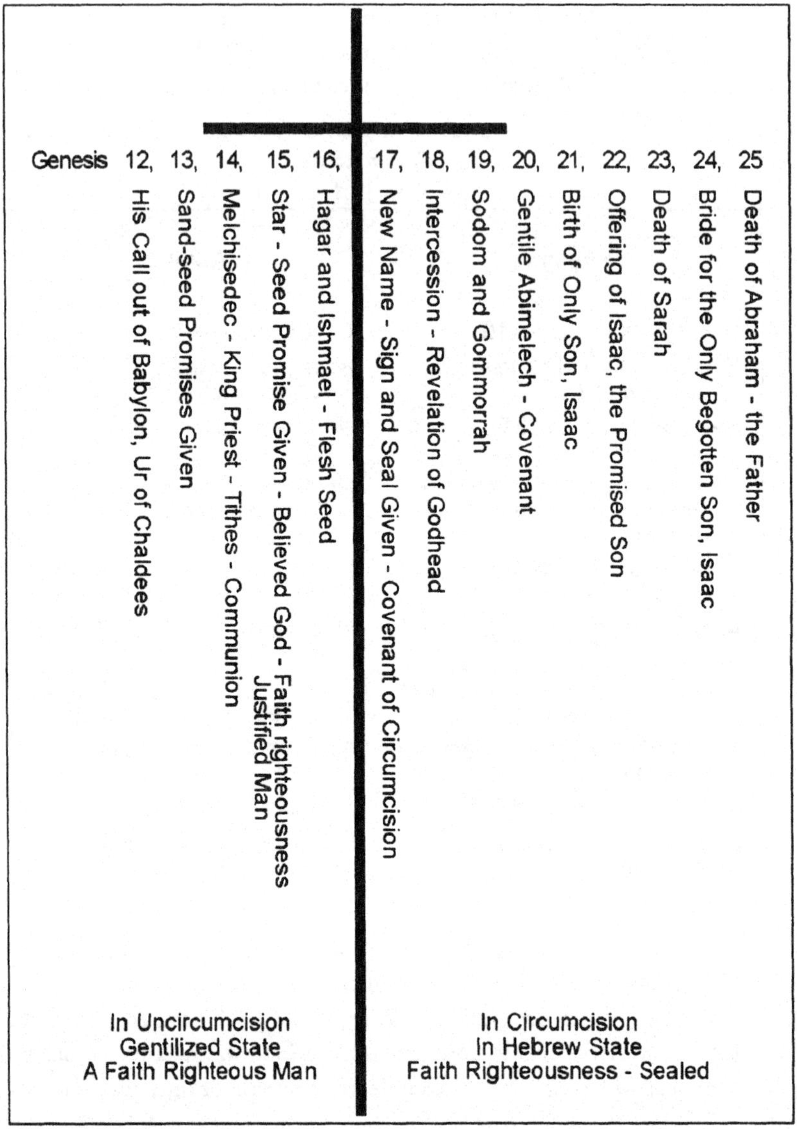

Genesis 12, 13, 14, 15, 16, | 17, 18, 19, 20, 21, 22, 23, 24, 25

- His Call out of Babylon, Ur of Chaldees
- Sand-seed Promises Given
- Melchisedec - King Priest - Tithes - Communion
- Star - Seed Promise Given - Believed God - Faith righteousness Justified Man
- Hagar and Ishmael - Flesh Seed
- New Name - Sign and Seal Given - Covenant of Circumcision
- Intercession - Revelation of Godhead
- Sodom and Gommorrah
- Gentile Abimelech - Covenant
- Birth of Only Son, Isaac
- Offering of Isaac, the Promised Son
- Death of Sarah
- Bride for the Only Begotten Son, Isaac
- Death of Abraham - the Father

In Uncircumcision
Gentilized State
A Faith Righteous Man

In Circumcision
In Hebrew State
Faith Righteousness - Sealed

Verse II: *"And he received the sign of circumcision, a seal of the righteousness of the faith which he had yet being uncircumcised: that he might be the father of all them that believe, though they be not circumcised; that righteousness might be imputed unto them also..."*

A. **"He received the sign of circumcision"**

Genesis 17 gives us details concerning the covenant of circumcision. Note the outstanding points concerning this covenant. It was a "covenant," meaning "an arrangement" (Acts 7:8; Genesis 17:2, 4, 7, 9-11, 13-14, 19-21). Through this covenant, God confirmed again to Abraham all the promises that He had previously given. He changed Abram's name to "Abraham" and Sarai's name to "Sarah." God took the letter "H"—the fifth letter of Hebrew alphabet—and added it to their names. Abram and Sarai became partakers of the name of God. God took the JHVH (YHVH), and Abram He called "Abraham," and Sarai, "Sarah." "Abraham" means "high father, father of many nations" or "father of a multitude." "Sarai" means "contentious," and "Sarah" means "princess of a multitude." Nations and kings were to be born of them, and God promised to establish His covenant with their seed. God asked Abraham to walk before Him and be perfect. The *token* of the covenant between God and Abraham was circumcision (Genesis 17:11). It was to take place on the eighth day of life, and failure to keep the rite of circumcision was regarded as breaking the covenant. This rite initiated Abraham's seed into covenant relationship with God.

God put a sign in the body through which the seed line would come. Without this rite the Jews were not entitled to the blessings and promises of that covenant. Circumcision made them covenant people of the Lord. All the seed that would be born of Abraham would come through a circumcised channel and vessel. Isaac, the beginning of the seed, was born through this circumcised channel, as was the whole nation, in order to be counted for "the seed." Circumcision itself was not the actual covenant. The Word of the promises was the actual covenant, and circumcision was the token, the flesh token, of that covenant. Note the words below that were used to describe circumcision:

- A Token (Genesis 17:11). In Hebrew, this word means "a sign." It carries the same meaning as the rainbow of the Noahic Covenant (Genesis 1:14-19; 9:12-13, 17).
- A Sign (Romans 4:11). Greek: *Semeion*, means "a mark, a signal" (New Testament word).

- A Seal (Romans 4:11). Greek: *Sphragis*, (Strong's number 4973, probably strengthened from 5420, "to fence") means "a signet (as fencing in or protecting from misappropriation). (By implication, the stamp impressed [as a mark of privacy, or genuineness], literally or figuratively—seal.)

A Token – The rainbow was the token of the covenant to Noah (Genesis 9:12-13, 17). God gave a token to Moses as a sign that he was sent from God (Exodus 3:12). The blood was a token of the Passover deliverance (Exodus 12:13). (See also Psalms 65:8; 86:17; Joshua 2:12; Numbers 17:10; Exodus 13:16; Psalm 135:9.) In the same way, circumcision was a token of the covenant to Abraham (Genesis 17:11).

A Sign – This is the same word used to refer to many of the signs and miracles of Christ and the apostles. Refer to these Scriptures: Matthew 12:38-39; 16:1-4; 24:3, 24, 30; Hebrews 2:4; Mark 16:17-20; Luke 2:12, 34; John 20:30; Acts 2:19-22, 43). Speaking in tongues was a physical sign (in a member of the body) by which the seed life would life come to those around (I Corinthians 14:22).

A Seal – A seal is an impression or inscription. The same word is used in I Corinthians 9:2; II Timothy 2:19; Revelation 5:1-9; 7:2-8; 9:4; Matthew 27:66; John 3:33; 6:27; II Corinthians 1:22; Ephesians 1:13-14; 4:30.

The great covenants of the Bible consisted of three parts, or features. (Refer to *The Covenants* by Kevin Conner and Ken Malmin.) This is seen in the Adamic, Noahic, Abrahamic, Mosaic, Palestinian, Davidic and New Covenants.

Those parts are as follows:
1) The Words of the Covenant (the promises, the Father God)
2) The Blood of the Covenant (the sacrificial blood, the Son of God)
3) The Sign or Seal of the Covenant (the Holy Spirit)

In Abraham's experience, which Paul is using here to illustrate this truth, these three main features were present in his life as a covenant man:
1) The Words of the Covenant (the promises of God) (Genesis 12-22)

2) The Blood of the Covenant (by sacrifice) (Genesis 15, Genesis 22)
3) The Sign or Seal of the Covenant (token of circumcision) (Genesis 17)

The same three parts are fulfilled in the believer's life. Let it be remembered that Abraham was a justified man, a faith-righteous man, and a believer. Circumcision was just the seal of the covenant to him. He was already a believer in Genesis 15 and was in covenant relationship with God. He had already been called, chosen, and redeemed by covenant blood, and then this seal of circumcision was given to him. This seal was a sign in the body (the flesh) and was a seal of the faith-righteousness that he had when he was still uncircumcised. It is the same in the New Covenant, which is the fulfillment in Christ of all the covenants.

Note:

- There are promises, or words, of the New Covenant (Hebrews 8).
- There is the blood of the New Covenant (Matthew 26:26; Hebrews 8-10). The blood is from the sacrifice of Jesus at Calvary, where He was "cut off," as in circumcision. His body and blood were shed.
- There is the seal of the New Covenant in the invocation of the name of the Godhead (the Lord Jesus Christ) and the resurrection power in the baptism of the Holy Spirit. (Note a sign of physical manifestation as in Acts 2:4. Otherwise a person may be "uncircumcised in lips, heart, and ears" [cf. Exodus 6:12, 30; Jeremiah 6:10; 9:26; Leviticus 26:41; Acts 7:51].)

Each covenant had its own sign or seal, and God never took the sign or seal of a previous covenant to place on another. All previous signs, seals, and covenants find their fulfillment in the New Covenant, which has its own special sign and seal.

Note the diagram on the following page.

OLD TESTAMENT CIRCUMCISION	NEW TESTAMENT CIRCUMCISION
• Blood shed/cutting off the flesh (body & blood involved)	• Water Baptism (Identification with death of Christ)
• Invocation of the child's name	• Invocation of the name of God ("Cut off" from old life [flesh])
• The 8th day rite. Covenant children were then entitled to promises, blessings, privileges in the Covenant	• Holy Spirit seal of New Covenant (Acts 2:4).
• Literal, physical circumcision	• Spiritual circumcision, heart and spirit

CALVARY'S CROSS

- Christ "cut off" (Body and Blood)
- Resurrection 8th day by Spirit
- Godhead Name given Him - New Covenant Seal

B. "A seal of the righteousness of the faith"

Circumcision pointed to Calvary. For believers in Christ, circumcision finds its spiritual fulfillment in the "cutting off" of the flesh life, identification with Christ at Calvary (the body and blood of Jesus), invocation of the name of the Godhead bodily in water baptism, baptism of the Holy Spirit (the seal of God), and the sign of speaking in other tongues (the token of the New Covenant). One who believes in Christ is circumcised in the heart (in the spirit) and has praise of God, not praise of the flesh, the letter, or man (Romans 2:29). As it was for Abraham, so it is for the believer in Christ. The seal, baptism of the Holy Spirit, is given because of faith-righteousness already imputed, because the believer is already in covenant relationship with God (Acts 7:8).

FOR THE ISRAELITE	FOR CHRIST THE HEAD	FOR THE BELIEVER
1. Blood Shed, Cut off the Flesh	1. Calvary, Death & Burial	1. Cut off In Water Baptism, Dead & Buried with Him
2. The 8th Day	2. The Resurrection, 8th Day	2. Rise to Walk, Newness of Life.
3. Invocation of the Child's Name	3. The Triune Name Given Him	3. Invocation of Godhead Name; Mt 28:19; Acts 2;36

Thus, Gentiles and Jews who believe are the seed of Abraham and are in covenant relationship with God through Christ. They have faith-righteousness.

C. **"That he might be the father of all them that believe, though they be not circumcised"**
The very fact that Abraham was a faith-righteous man when he was uncircumcised made it possible for him to be the "father of all who believe." He was the "father of the uncircumcision" who believe in Christ, as well as the Jewish believers in Christ. The Gentile believers, though called "uncircumcision" in the flesh, are not of the seed of Abraham. They are Christ's because they believe in Him (Galatians 3:16, 28-29). Abraham believed when he was uncircumcised, and he was then justified. Gentiles, though uncircumcised, believe and are also justified.

D. **"That righteousness might be imputed unto them also"**
Abraham believed God. It was imputed to him for righteousness, even though he was uncircumcised. The Gentiles also believed God, and righteousness was imputed to them, as well, even though they were uncircumcised. (Circumcision and uncircumcision was the whole issue in Acts 10-11 and Acts 15. Note, in Acts 11:1-18, that the Spirit fell on the Gentiles and was the seal of God (the sign) and the token to Peter and the brethren that *righteousness* (faith-righteousness) had been imputed to the Gentiles as well as to the Jews.

Verse 12: *"...And the father of circumcision to them who are not of the circumcision
only, but who also walk in the steps of that faith of our father Abraham,
which he had being yet uncircumcised."*

A. Abraham—The Father of All Who Believe

Abraham is the father of all who believe—Gentile or Jew, circumcision
or uncircumcision. The emphasis is on believing, not on circumcision or
uncircumcision (of the spirit, not of the flesh). Abraham is the father of
circumcision; that is, he is the father not only in the physical sense, but
also of the true circumcision of the heart. Believers are the circumcision
who:

- Worship God in the Spirit (cf. I Corinthians 14:15-16),
- Rejoice in Christ Jesus (I Peter 1:18-19),
- Have no confidence in the flesh (cf. Ishmael, Philippians 3:3).

(Note, in Philippians 3:3-14, that Paul had all "these things," in the
flesh, in which to place his confidence if he desired.)

B. "Walk in the steps of that faith of our father Abraham"

Abraham went from "faith to faith" (Romans 1:17). He lived the life
of faith, step by step—and then his faith was made perfect (James 2:21-
24; II Corinthians 5:7). It is Abraham's walk of faith that we, as believers,
look to and follow one step at a time (the steps of faith) (Isaiah 51:1-2).
These steps of faith in Abraham's life can be traced to Genesis 12 and
Genesis 25. Note below concerning Abraham:

- By faith, when he was called, he went out (Hebrews 11:8).
- By faith he lived in a tent, looking for a city which God built
  (Hebrews 11:9-16).
- By faith he paid tithes and had communion with Melchisedec
  (Genesis 14, especially 14:18-20).
- By faith he accepted the Covenant (Genesis 22) until he offered up
  Isaac and his faith was perfected (cf. Genesis 15 and Genesis 22 on
  the "seed promises").

Each chapter shows steps of faith. If we are Abraham's seed, through
Christ, then we also will have a walk of faith (steps of faith, one step at a
time) as God leads us. We shall then go from "faith to faith."

The Law Versus Faith (Romans 4:13-15)

Verse 13: *"For the promise, that he should be the heir of the world, was not to Abraham, or to his seed, through the law, but through the righteousness of faith."*

A. **"For the promise"**

In this verse, Paul takes up another thought concerning Abraham—this thought pertains to the promise. The first use of the word "promise" in Romans is in chapter 1, verse 2, and it is developed more fully in this verse. (Note also Galatians 3, particularly noting the words "law," "faith," "grace," "works," and especially "promise.")

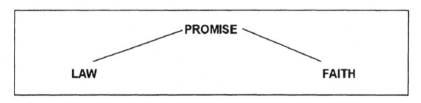

In the previous chapters and verses, Paul has proven, by Abraham's experience in uncircumcision and circumcision, that it was faith that was counted to him for righteousness and that faith-righteousness is the only thing that God accepts today. His terms are the same, either for Jew or Gentile, circumcision or uncircumcision. Paul now goes back to the backbone of faith, the very ground and foundation of faith itself. (This subject will also be taken up and developed further in Romans 10:17. Romans 10:17 is actually a continuation of Romans 4 on the subject of faith-righteousness.) What was the foundation, or ground, of Abraham's faith, the faith that was accounted unto him for righteousness? There is only one ground for true faith and for faith-righteousness—*the Word of God.* "...[F]aith cometh by hearing, and hearing by the word of God" (Romans 10:17). It is for this reason that Paul introduces the thought of "the promise" relative to "the faith of Abraham." Faith must be linked, united to, and grounded upon the promises of God—His Word. Note the mention of the word "promise" in the following verses:

- "...[T]he promise that he [Abraham] should be the heir of the world..." (Romans 4: 13).

- "...[T]he promise made of none effect [through the law]..." (Romans 4:14).
- "...[T]he promise might be sure to all the seed [of faith]..." (Romans 4:16; cf. Romans 9:4, 8, 9; 15:8).
- "He [Abraham staggered] not at the promise of God through unbelief..." (Romans 4:20).
- "...[W]hat he had promised, he [God] was able also to perform..." (Romans 4:21).

Note again the connection of "the promise" with "faith":
- The promise – through the righteousness of faith (Romans 4:13).
- Faith made the promise void (of none effect) if through law (Romans 4:14).
- Of faith, by grace, that the promise might be sure to all the seed (Romans 4:16).
- Strong in faith, in the promise (Romans 4:20).
- Fully persuaded (faith) what God had promised, He performs (Romans 4:21).

Thus, we have faith in the promise! The foundation of Abraham's faith-righteousness was the promise of God. Abraham believed God (Romans 4:3), and when he believed God, he believed the Word and promises of God (God and His Word). There can be absolutely no faith apart from the Word and promises of God. Faith must have a foundation; hence, Romans 10:17 is of paramount importance relative to the "faith chapter" in Hebrews 11. These "faith heroes" of Hebrews 11 had their faith in and upon the Word and promises of God. (Note especially Hebrews 11:11, 13, 17, 33, 39-40 and the use of the word "promise" [Hebrews 10:36]. Without exception there will be found some Word of God, or some promise of God, given to each, and thus, "by faith" they were able to be what they were, to do what they did, and to endure.)

Thus, Paul introduces the thought of "the promise" over "the law." This is evidenced by the fact that Abraham was a faith-righteous man and was the father of all who believe (the father of all the faith-righteous, be they Gentile or Jew). It is in this section that Paul goes beyond faith itself to the very source or foundation of faith—the promise of God. How did

Abraham get to this point of faith? Where did the faith come from? What is the basis of faith? The answer is found in Romans 10:17, which states, "So then faith cometh by hearing, and hearing by the word [*rhema*] of God." In other words, Abraham received this faith by hearing the Word from God. He heard the promise. The fact that Paul's whole intention in this section is concerning "the promise" (the foundation of Abraham's faith and his faith-righteousness) cannot be over-emphasized. Hearing and believing the Word of God is the one and only source of faith (faith in the promises and Word of God).

In Romans 1:1-3, Paul briefly mentioned the gospel, which God had promised before by His prophets in the Holy Scriptures concerning His Son, Jesus Christ. In Romans 9:4, Paul speaks of Israel's privileges in receiving "the promises" and in being "the children of the promises" (Romans 9:8-9).

B. **"For the promise that he should be the heir of the world"**

The promise here included both the seed and the land for the seed to dwell in. In the promises of the Abrahamic Covenant, the seed and the land were always associated. If Abraham is to have seed, then the seed must have land in which to dwell (Genesis 12:1-3; 13:15-18; 15:13-21; 17:1-8; 22:15-18). These promises were confirmed to Isaac and Jacob, as well.

C. **"Heir of the world"**

Note that one of the promises of God to Abraham was that he would be "heir of the world." "World" in the Greek is "*kosmos*," meaning "orderly arrangement." By implication, the use of this word refers to the world (in a wide or narrow sense), including its inhabitants. Its use actually goes beyond the land of Canaan and really includes the whole world, even as the seed promises do. Partial fulfillment of this promise is seen in Abraham and his seed after the flesh; that is Isaac, natural Israel (and its possession of the land of Canaan), and Israel and Judah (and their possession of other parts of the earth). Ultimate fulfillment is seen in Abraham and his seed after the spirit. Spiritually, Christ (Isaac) and the church will together posses the whole earth in the "one thousand years" aspect of the kingdom (cf. Hebrews 11:8-16) (the heavenly Canaan-land; the saints possess the kingdom [Daniel 2, 7; Hebrews 3-4]).

The earthly Canaan was only the shadow of the millennial kingdom rest when Abraham and his seed (all who believe) will possess the earth as the promised inheritance (Revelation 20:1-6; Jeremiah 32). Abraham, Isaac,

and Jacob are heirs, and if we are Christ's, then we are Abraham's seed and
heirs of the same promise (Galatians 3:27-29; 4:1-7; Hebrews 6:12-20;
Romans 8:14-17). We are joint-heirs with Jesus, the seed of Abraham
(Galatians 3:16).

D. **"Was not to Abraham, or to his seed, through the law, but through the
righteousness of faith"**
Note below:

- Abraham and His Seed, After the Flesh (natural Israel, through Isaac)
- Abraham and His seed, After the Spirit (spiritual Israel, through
Jesus)

Note from above that the "natural" is temporal, and the "spiritual" is
eternal (first the natural, then the spiritual). The promise of God was not
given to Abraham through, under, or on the basis of keeping the law of
Moses. This promise was given before the law and would be fulfilled in
those who believed God—through faith-righteousness.   In Galatians
3:16-18, Paul says, in effect, "...the covenant (made to Abraham) that his
seed had the promises made to them, was not through the law (covenant),
which was 430 years after the Abrahamic Covenant, and it cannot
disannul the promises, that it should make the promises of none effect.
For if the inheritance be of the law, it is no more of promise, but God
gave it to Abraham by promise" (paraphrased) (read also the Amplified
New Testament).

Verse 14: *"For if they which are of the law be heirs, faith is made void, and the promise
made of none effect..."*

**"If they which are of the law be heirs, faith is made void, and the
promise made of none effect"**
The argument here is based on the relationship between the promise
and the law. Is the law against the promise of God? God forbid! The
point here is concerning the proper heir. If the promise was made under
the law, then it means that the Jews (Israel) under the law covenant are the
heirs. This belief would exclude Abraham himself and all believers. Faith
would be made void (nullified), and the promise would be made of none
effect. The promise, however, was given to Abraham *before* the law (cf.
Galatians 3:16-18, 21-22). Thus, the promise was before the law, and
faith was before the law.

Abraham believed the promise, given before law, and received faith-righteousness, before law. The promise was made to him, and this makes him and his seed the heirs—the true seed. The law is not against the promises of God. The law actually had nothing to do with these promises. The law covenant cannot disannul, add to, take away from, or in any way affect these promises. The law was added on for a limited period of time (Galatians 3:15-29, Amplified New Testament) until the seed (Messiah) came to those with whom the promises were made. Thus, two covenants are involved—the Abrahamic Covenant and the Mosaic Covenant. By implication, the New Covenant is involved as well. The following diagram illustrates the weight of the argument here.

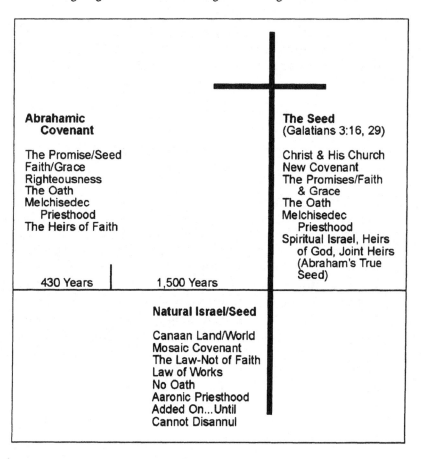

Abrahamic
  Covenant

The Promise/Seed
Faith/Grace
Righteousness
The Oath
Melchisedec
  Priesthood
The Heirs of Faith

430 Years | 1,500 Years

The Seed
(Galatians 3:16, 29)

Christ & His Church
New Covenant
The Promises/Faith
  & Grace
The Oath
Melchisedec
  Priesthood
Spiritual Israel, Heirs
  of God, Joint Heirs
  (Abraham's True
  Seed)

Natural Israel/Seed

Canaan Land/World
Mosaic Covenant
The Law-Not of Faith
Law of Works
No Oath
Aaronic Priesthood
Added On...Until
Cannot Disannul

Verse 15:   *"...Because the law worketh wrath: for where no law is, there is no transgression."*

A. **"The law"**

"The law" refers to the Mosaic Law (broken moral or civil law) (Romans 5:13-14). Transgressed law—natural, spiritual, and moral law—brings wrath on man. God's universe operates on natural laws. God's creatures live and operate upon spiritual, moral, and physical laws. Natural law is fixed and consistent. The laws of the universe are for man's good and protection. These laws are no respecter of persons, good or evil (i.e., law of gravity). To disobey or violate these laws brings self-destruction, death, and wrath. To obey and follow them brings life. It is the same with the spiritual or moral laws. The very nature and being of God demands that there be a law. Without law everything would be in a state of disorder and lawlessness—crime and confusion would be the result. God is just and justice requires law. God is the Lawgiver and Lawmaker.

B. **"Worketh wrath"**

Refer again to "wrath" in Romans 1:18 and 2:5-8. The basis of wrath is God's broken law.

C. **"For where no law is, there is no transgression"**

If there is no law, there can be no lawlessness because "sin is transgression of the law or sin is lawlessness" (I John 3:4). Only where there is law is there the possibility of man breaking it. Hence, "the law" to Adam was one commandment (Genesis 2:17). He could not have transgressed this one law, or commandment, if he had not been given it. God did not make Adam an automated robot. God created man with the power of choice. God took "a calculated risk"—to speak as a man—and made men freewill beings. A creation that could not keep or break a given law would not be a freewill creation. Paul refers to the result and effect of Adam's choice and transgression of the law in Romans 5:12-21. The progression and logical sequence here is found below:

1) Law (spiritual or moral)
2) Transgression (violation of law)
3) Wrath (result of broken law [refer to notes on Romans 7])

The Palestinian and Mosaic Covenants deal with the promises of the land given under the Abrahamic Covenant. The Jews dwelled in this land on God's conditions; otherwise, they would have been cast out of this land of promise (cf. Deuteronomy 27-32).

Thus, the promise was not given under law, through works, but it was confirmed there. It was given under the Abrahamic Covenant and received by faith. When the events of Numbers 13-14 occurred, that generation actually rejected the Abrahamic Covenant promise of the land, for it could only be entered by faith in the promise, not through the law (cf. Hebrews 3-4).

Abraham—The Father of All Who Believe (Romans 4:16-22)

Verse 16: *"Therefore it is of faith, that it might be by grace; to the end the promise might be sure to all the seed; not to that only which is of the law, but to that also which is of the faith of Abraham; who is the father of us all..."*

A. **"Therefore it is of faith, that it might be by grace"**
   "Of faith" – means "trusting and believing God" (Romans 3:26-31; 1:16-17) (not works).
   "By grace" – means "undeserved, unmerited, unearned favor of God bestowed on sinful man" (Romans 1:7; 3:24; 5:1-2; 11:6) (believing and receiving, not working and earning).

B. **"To the end the promise might be sure to all the seed; not to that only which is of the law, but to that also which is of the faith of Abraham"**
   The promises in the Abrahamic Covenant belong to *all* of Abraham's seed—Jew or Gentile, circumcision or uncircumcision—who believe unto faith-righteousness. Galatians 3:16-29 has made this clear. Promises that were made to Abraham and his seed were also made to Christ and His church (composed of Jew and Gentile). It is a many-membered seed, yet it is one seed!

C. **"Who is the father of us all"**
   "Father" is a key word in this chapter. Note the use of the word "father" in the following verses of Romans 4:
   • Father Abraham, as Pertaining to the Flesh (verse 1)

- Father of All that Believe (verse 11)
- Father of the Circumcision (verse 12)
- Faith of Father Abraham (verse 12)
- Father of Us All (verse 16)
- Father of Many Nations (verse 17, also verse 18)

As noted earlier in Romans 4:1, Paul allows no false boasting to arise in the Jews concerning the name of Father Abraham (Matthew 3:5-19; Luke 3:8; John 8:12-59; Romans 9:7). As noted before, there is a twofold sense in which "father" is used of Abraham:

1) Father in the Natural (after the flesh, natural and national seed, Israel, natural birth through Isaac)
2) Father in the Spiritual (after the spirit, spiritual birth through Christ, true Israel, faith, grace [which God alone accepts])

Verse 17: *"...(As it is written, I have made thee a father of many nations,) before him whom he believed, even God, who quickeneth the dead, and calleth those things which be not as though they were."*

"I have made thee a father of many nations" (cf. Genesis 22:18; 17:1-8).

Abraham was "made the father" of *many nations*, not just the chosen nation of Israel, or the Jewish nation. This included the nations of the Gentiles who believe. Those out of every kindred, tongue, tribe, and nation constitute the many nations of Abraham's seed and of whom he is the father. He is the Father of all who believe. "And many nations shall be joined to the Lord in that day..." (Zechariah 2:10-11; cf. Matthew 28:18-20). Many of the Old Testament prophecies speak of "the nations" that will come to the Lord in messianic times. God said, "I have" when Abraham had no seed (cf. Genesis 17:1-8). God counts the things not done as though they were done, and Abraham believed God. To God (the Eternal, the "I Am"), all of the past, present, and future are seen before Him as complete and as one eternal omnipresence. There is a divine principle of promise here: God counts things done once He speaks; He calls things that are not as though they actually are.

Verse 18: *"Who against hope believed in hope, that he might become the father of many nations, according to that which was spoken, So shall thy seed be."*

"Believed in hope"

Note below:

- Abraham's Faith (Romans 4:3, 9, 12-13, 16)
- Abraham's Hope (Romans 4:18; cf. 5:1-2)

Hope is an essential ingredient of faith. "Hope" means "a confident and quiet expectation." There is a place for hope as well as for faith (cf. Romans 8:24-25; I Corinthians 13:13) "Now faith is the substance of things hoped for, the evidence of things not seen" (Hebrews 11:1). Hope is the assurance. We are saved by faith (Ephesians 2:8-10), and we are saved by hope also (Romans 8:24; 5:4-5). Naturally speaking, when God made the promise to Abraham that he would have seed as numerous as the dust, the sand, and the stars (Genesis 13 and 15), the whole situation looked very hopeless. Abraham and Sarah were hopeless. They had hoped for a child, yet time passed on. With the promise, faith and hope prevailed. Against hope and hopeless physical conditions, Abraham believed in "the hope" that God had given him. This faith and hope were born out of God's Word—"so shall thy seed be."

"That he might become" – refers to "manward aspect, faith and hope, yet to be done."

"I have thee" – refers to "Godward aspect, counted it done; in God's mind it was done."

Verse 19: *"And being not weak in faith, he considered not his own body now dead, when he was about an hundred years old, neither yet the deadness of Sarah's womb..."*

"Not weak in faith"

"Not weak in faith" refers to the fact that Abraham did not consider his and Sarah's body conditions. Compare this with Romans 4:20 that states that Abraham was "strong in faith"; that is, he considered the promise of God.

Note the words "death" and "consider" below:

- The *Deadness* of His Own Body (Abraham) (Hebrews 11:12; Genesis 17:17; Romans 4:19)
- The *Deadness* of Sarah's Womb (Hebrews 11:11; Romans 4:19)

- God, Who Quickens the *Dead* (Romans 4:17)
- Isaac, the Only Begotten Son (offered up, and then raised from the *dead* in a figurative sense) (Hebrews 11:17-19; Genesis 22). "...I and the lad will go yonder and worship, and come again to you" (Genesis 22:5).
- Jesus, Our Lord, Raised From the *Dead* (Romans 4:24-25)

In each case above, the physical condition was death. Death was stamped upon Sarah, Abraham, and Isaac. If Abraham had considered this he would have been weak in the faith. Abraham's faith was in the God of resurrection—the God who quickens and who makes alive. Resurrection life was, thus, experienced typically in Abraham, Sarah, and Isaac. This resurrection life shadowed forth Jesus' resurrection from the dead (cf. Romans 4:24-25) (note the Amplified New Testament). Do we consider (contemplate, meditate, look upon, or gaze at) the promises of God or the physical conditions? Promises strengthen faith. Physical conditions weaken faith.

Verse 20: *"...He staggered not at the promise of God through unbelief; but was strong in faith, giving glory to God..."*

Abraham's Faith
"Staggered not" – means "did not waver." Abraham did not look at the physical conditions.

"Unbelief" – the besetting sin. Unbelief is distrust (cf. unbelief of the Jews and the faith of Abraham) (cf. Hebrews 12:1-2).

"Strong in faith" – Abraham considered the Word of God (Romans 10:17). (Note: "consider" in Hebrews.)

"Giving the glory to God" – Abraham did not give glory to Sarah or to the flesh. He gave glory (praise and adoration) to God.

Verse 21: *"...And being fully persuaded, that, what he had promised, he was able also to perform."*

"What he had promised, he was able also to perform"
God performs! This is full assurance of faith in God's promises (II Corinthians 1:20; Hebrews 6:12-17). God backs up and is able to fulfill what He promises. Man often makes promises and has no ability to perform; however, this is not the case with God. Thus, there is no room

for works. All Abraham could do was to believe God. Works produced Ishmael. (Paul deals with that subject in Galatians 3-4.) Faith produced Isaac. Through faith, Sarah conceived (Hebrews 11:8-16).

Verse 22: *"And therefore it was imputed to him for righteousness."*

"It was imputed to him for righteousness"
Romans 4 covers Abraham's life of faith ("...the just shall live by faith" [Romans 1:17]). In this brief panoramic view of his life, Genesis 12 through 22 are covered and divided into two parts. Romans 4 covers Abraham's uncircumcision and circumcision; thus, he is typified as "Gentilized" and then "Hebrewized." Therefore, he is the father of all who believe—Jew or Gentile, those without law, those under law. He is the father of all who know faith-righteousness (imputed to them by believing God) in the Lord Jesus Christ.

Faith Imputed Righteousness (Romans 4:23-25)

Verses 23-24: *"Now it was not written for his sake alone, that it was imputed to him; but for us also, to whom it shall be imputed, if we believe on him that raised up Jesus our Lord from the dead..."*

"Not written for his sake alone"
Abraham's experience is written for our admonition and example. The righteousness that was imputed to him because he believed God and His Word is the same righteousness that will be imputed to us if we believe in the God of the resurrection.

Verse 25: *"...Who was delivered for our offences, and was raised again for our justification."*

A. Isaac and Jesus
Note the death and resurrection of the Lord Jesus Christ:
   • Typified in Isaac, the only begotten son and seed, who was, in a figurative sense, raised from the dead (Hebrews 11:17). Abraham believed in the God of the resurrection (Genesis 22). Thus, faith imputed righteousness to him.

- Fulfilled in Jesus, the only begotten Son of God and the seed, who was actually raised from the dead by God the Father (John 3:16-17; Romans 1:4). Abraham did typically with his son what God would do actually with Jesus. Abraham believed, and all who believe in the resurrection receive faith-righteousness.

Note below concerning Jesus:
- "Jesus" – Jesus is the name of His sinless humanity.
- "Christ" – He is the Christ by reason of the anointing.
- "Lord" – He is Lord by ascension and glorification (Psalm 110:1; Acts 2:34-36; Romans 10:8-9; 14:9). Confess Him as Lord.

B. **"Delivered for our offences, and was raised again for our justification"**
    "Delivered" – Jesus was delivered to the Jews and Gentiles (Matthew 20:19; 26:15; Mark 10:33) and turned over to them for the Cross (Luke 23:25).
    "Offences" – (Cf. Romans 5:14-21.) Note the offense of Adam passed onto all men, then death.
    "Raised again" – Jesus was raised again in the resurrection (Romans 1:3-4).
    "For our justification" – Jesus was raised again for our justification in order to declare and to put us in right standing before God.

Summary (Romans 4:1-25)

The theme of Romans 4 is "imputed righteousness" (Romans 4:12-24). Faith-righteousness is imputed righteousness (Romans 4:1-11). The doctrine of imputed righteousness by the channel of faith was a great stumbling block to Jewish pride (cf. Romans 10:1-5). There is no possible way to become righteous except through faith imputed righteousness.
- There is none righteous, no, not one (Romans 3:9-10, 19-20).
- The law exposes self-righteousness in the Jew (Isaiah 64:6; Philippians 3:9; Matthew 5:20).
- Therefore, God must impute righteousness, on His terms, to those who believe in the death and the resurrection of His Son.

RIGHTEOUSNESS
RECEIVED

Righteousness Received
(Romans 5:1 – 8:39)

The Reconciliation (Romans 5:1-11)

Verse 1: *"Therefore being justified by faith, we have peace with God through our Lord Jesus Christ..."*

A. "Therefore"
"Therefore" means "in the light of all that has gone before and in view of the foregoing" (cf. Romans 5:1; 8:1; 12:1).

B. "Being justified"
(Refer to notes on Romans 3-4.) Paul has answered Job's age-old question: "How then can man be justified with God?" (Job 25:4). Note:
- Man cannot justify himself (Luke 10:28-29; 16:15; 18:9-14).
- Man cannot be justified by works of the law (Romans 3:20).

Man is justified in the following ways:
- Justified by *God* Himself (Romans 3:20; 8:30, 33)
- Justified by His *grace* (Romans 3:24)
- Justified by *faith* (no room for doubt) (Romans 5:1; 3:27-28)
- Justified by His *blood* (Romans 5:9; 3:25)
- Justified by the *name* of the Lord Jesus Christ (Galatians 2:16; I Corinthians 6:11)
- Justified by the *Spirit* of God (I Corinthians 6:11)
- Justified by works of *obedience* (practical righteousness) (James 2:21-26)

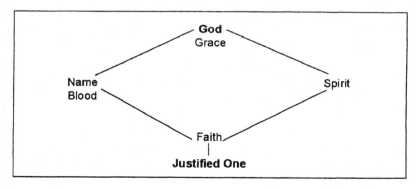

C. **"By faith"**
    (Cf. the "faith chapter" [Hebrews 11].) The men listed in Hebrews
    11 were faith-righteous men. They knew righteousness by faith. Note:

- Abel (righteous) (Hebrews 11:4)
- Enoch (Hebrews 11:5-6)
- Noah (heir of faith-righteousness) (Hebrews 11:7)
- Abraham and Sarah (righteous by faith) (Hebrews 11:8-19)

D. **"We have peace with God through our Lord Jesus Christ"**
    The first eleven verses of Romans 5 cover the benefits of justification.
    The last verses cover what we inherited in Adam in the Fall (cf. faith and
    peace, Romans 1:7; 5:1). There is no peace between God and sinners
    until sin is dealt with and man is clothed in righteousness and is in right
    standing with God. Sin is the enemy of God and man. Note:
    Melchisedec was king of righteousness and king of peace (Romans 14:17;
    Isaiah 32:1, 17; cf. Hebrews 7:1-2; Psalm 85:10). Righteousness and
    peace kiss each other at the Cross (Colossians 1:20). We are being made
    righteous through faith and are being granted peace. Peace is not mere
    tranquillity of mind, but cessation of hostility. God grants peace of heart,
    mind, and spirit to us through the Cross. The Lord Jesus Christ is our
    propitiation (Romans 5:10 also).

Verse 2: *"...By whom also we have access by faith into this grace wherein we stand,
and rejoice in hope of the glory of God."*

A. **"Access"** (cf. Ephesians 2:18)
    In the Old Testament there was no access into God's presence except
    for the high priest once a year. The veil was rent after the Cross
    (Matthew 27:51), and now there is access into God's presence for both
    the Jew and the Gentile (Hebrews 10:19-20).

B. **"By faith"**
    "Faith" means "not feelings, but faith of facts, in a person, not merely a
    doctrinal fact" (Romans 1:16-17). The justified live by faith. The whole
    life of a believer is in faith.

C. **"Grace"**
    "Grace" means "undeserved, unmerited, unearned favor of God bestowed
    on sinful mankind through Christ" (cf. 1:7; 3:24; 4:16; 5:15, 17, 20-21).

D. **"Wherein we stand"**

"Wherein we stand" means "our standing." Righteousness is "right standing" before and with God. Man could not stand in His presence in an unrighteous state.

E. **"Hope of the glory of God"**

"The glory of God" means "the restored glory of God." The full glory of God is to be revealed in us (Romans 8:18-25). Man has fallen short of "the glory" (Romans 3:23). In Christ Jesus the hope of this glory is restored. Believers rejoice in this hope (I Peter 1:21).

Verse 3: *"And not only so, but we glory in tribulations also: knowing that tribulation worketh patience..."*

A. **"Tribulations"**

Note (also from Romans 5:2 above) we:

- Rejoice in hope of the glory of God (the ultimate glory).
- Rejoice in tribulations—the immediate trials that lead us to the ultimate glory.

The Scriptures speak of two aspects of tribulation (cf. Acts 14:22; John 16:33; I Thessalonians 3:4; Revelation 2:9). Note below:

"Tribulations" – means "trials, tests, persecution, etc.; all that the saints experience in measure, in this present age" (cf. *"tribulam,"* referring to a Roman flail used to get rid of the chaff of wheat).

"The Great Tribulation" – the final time of trouble and tribulation immediately proceeding the second coming of Christ (Revelation 7:14; Matthew 24:21, 29; Daniel 12:1-2, 12; Revelation 13). The Great Tribulation is a period of three and one half years during the last days and is also called "the wrath of God against ungodly men." The same period is called "the Tribulation" (the great one) because it is the final persecution of the saints, some of whom will fail to overcome in the last days.

One must distinguish between "the wrath of God" and "tribulation." Tribulation is for the saints and is the wrath of Satan and enemies against believers. Wrath is for the ungodly, the sinners, and Satan and his hosts. The saints will experience tribulation, but they are not appointed to wrath (I Thessalonians 5:1-10).

B. **"Tribulation worketh patience"** (cf. Hebrews 6:12-15; James 1:2-4; 5:7-11; II Peter 1:6)
The purposes of tribulations (trials) are to work patience in believers. In a believer, impatience with God brings tragic results. (See God's theme on patience.) God gives the promise, then tribulations are the preparation to meet any problems until the provision comes.

Verse 4: *"...And patience, experience; and experience, hope..."*

A. **"And patience, experience"**
"Experience" means "the process of trial; proving," as in II Corinthians 8:2, or "the result of trial; approvedness" as in Philippians 1:22. In Romans 5:4, the meaning can only be the latter: "the result of trial; approvedness" and can also refer to "a tried integrity; a state of mind, which has stood the test." The process has already been expressed by tribulation. In other words, "patience worketh proof of approval, after probation." (Vincent)

B. **"Experience, hope"**
(Cf. Romans 4:18; 8:24-25; I Peter 1:21; 3:16; refer also to Romans 5:2 and notes.) The hope is "the glory."

Verse 5: *"...And hope maketh not ashamed; because the love of God is shed abroad in our hearts by the Holy Ghost which is given unto us."*

A. **"Hope maketh not ashamed"** (cf. Romans 4:18; Luke 13:17; I Peter 2:6; 3:16)
"Maketh not ashamed" means "not to be put to disgrace or dishonor" (cf. Romans 4:18). Against hope, Abraham believed in hope, and hope did not make him ashamed, disgraced, or dishonored.

B. **"Because the love of God is shed abroad in our hearts"**
This is the first mention of the word "love" in Romans (also see Romans 5:8). "Shed abroad" means "poured out" (cf. Titus 3:6; Acts 2:33; 10:45; Jude 11).

C. **"By the Holy Ghost which is given unto us"**
This is the first mention of the Holy Spirit in Romans. (Refer especially to Romans 8 on the work and ministry of the Spirit in the

believer.) The Holy Spirit is the gift of God, given to us, because we are now in right standing with God. We are justified.

Verses 1-5: *Summary*

Note the following fourteen blessings, mentioned in Romans 5:1-5, that are given in connection with the justified man:

1) Peace
2) Access into this Grace
3) Grace
4) Rejoicing in Hope
5) Glorying in Tribulations
6) Patience
7) Experience, or Approvedness
8) Hope
9) Not Ashamed
10) Love of God
11) The Holy Spirit
12) Reconciliation
13) Saved from Wrath
14) Joy in God (verses 1-11)

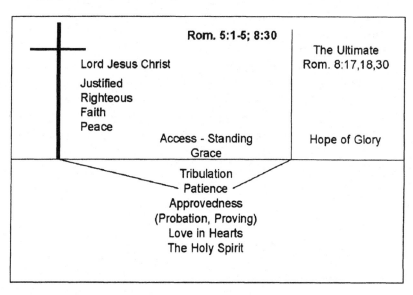

Verse 6: *"For when we were yet without strength, in due time Christ died for the ungodly."*

A. **"For when we were yet without strength"**

Sin leaves man weak, helpless, and hopeless apart from God. It leaves man without strength. Man is utterly unable to lift up or save himself. As a weak baby—born in sin and unable to do anything for itself—so is man without Christ Jesus.

B. **"In due time"**

"In due time" means "according to the time"(marginal). Compare the following:

- "The fullness of time" (Galatians 4:4)
- "Set forth" (foreordained) (Romans 3:25)
- "The set time" (I Peter 1:18-21), meaning "the end of the ages of the Old Testament" (cf. I Corinthians 10:6, 11; Ephesians 1:10; I Timothy 2:6; Titus 1:3; Hebrews 9:26).

God had a specific timetable concerning the plan of redemption. Man died when Adam sinned, but God had set aside and foreordained His plan of redemption that has been, and will continue to be, manifested in these last times. Note also that the Passover lamb was to die after four days in the set time (cf. Exodus 12:1-12).

C. **"Christ died for the ungodly"**

Christ died for both the Jew and the Gentile (cf. Romans 1-2). "For" in the Greek is *huper*, meaning "on behalf of" or "instead of." Either of these meanings could be applicable in light of the whole body of truth concerning Christ's death (Galatians 3:13; Romans 14:15; I Peter 3:18).

Verse 7: *"For scarcely for a righteous man will one die: yet peradventure for a good man some would even dare to die."*

"For a good man some would even dare to die"

There are three classes of men mentioned in Romans—the righteous man, the good man, and the sinner. It is possible that someone would be willing to die for the first two but not for the latter (cf. John 15:13).

Men find it difficult to die on behalf of a righteous man, let alone a sinner or an ungodly person. Some "off event" may cause a person to die for a righteous man. Christ, however, died for the sinner—the ungodly. This is not natural or human love—it is divine love. In the natural sense, there is nothing worthy in dying for the ungodly. To love the unlovely is divine love. Though one may die for the upright—and it might be justified for a good, noble man—it was divine love that caused Christ to die for sinners.

Verse 8: *"But God commendeth his love toward us, in that, while we were yet sinners, Christ died for us."*

A. **""God commendeth his love"**
    God commended His love; he did not force it on us. Love cannot be forced or legislated (cf. Acts 20:32). God's love is demonstrated and manifested in the death of Christ (John 3:16). (Refer also to "love" in Romans 5:5, 8.) God's love is commended to us in the death of Christ. God is love. After all the emphasis on wrath against sin in the previous chapters, Romans 5 shows that God's wrath has been appeased in the sacrifice of Christ. Through the sacrifice of Christ, sin was dealt with, the law was satisfied, and holiness was upheld so that God could commend His love toward us, the sinners. Note the nature of God:

- God is holy and righteous and, because of these attributes, must deal with sin in wrath. Sin is transgression of His holy law, and its claims must be upheld and satisfied.

- God is love and is graciously inclined to the sinner. Calvary shows the revelation of the wrath of God against sin (Romans 1-3) and the love of God toward the sinner (Romans 5).

Note:
- The wrath of god is revealed (Romans 1:18; Ephesians 2:3).
- The love of God is commended (Romans 5:8; Ephesians 2:4).

Note the diagram on the following page.

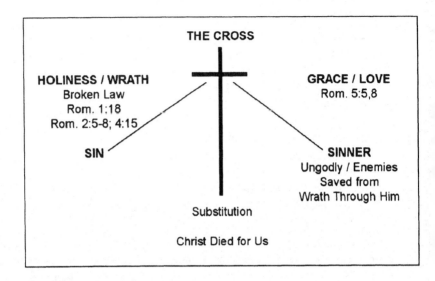

B. "While we were yet sinners"
   Note:
   • Christ died for the ungodly (Romans 6).
   • Christ died for us, sinners (Romans 8).
   • Christ died for His enemies (Romans 10).

   (Cf. Ephesians 2:1, 5; Romans 5:6.) Christ's death displays His love.
   Christ did not die for the righteous or the godly, but for the sinners—the
   ungodly, the strengthless. In His sacrifice, love is indeed shown for God's
   enemies, not for His friends (Romans 5:10).

C. "Christ died for us" – The Doctrine of Substitution
   The doctrine of substitution is laid out in this verse. This doctrine
   shows the wrath of God against sin and the love of God for the sinner.
   How could God deal with sin and yet manifest grace to the sinner? The
   doctrine of substitution was His answer.
   The whole chapter of Romans 5 can be summed up in this word
   "substitution." Christ died for (in behalf, instead of) us. The doctrine of
   substitution begins in Genesis and is continually revealed in Israel in the
   sacrifices at the brazen altar, in the tabernacle, and in the temple. The
   ritual pointed to Israel's repentance. Ritual without repentance is a mere
   valueless form. Israel offered up imperfect sacrifices through imperfect

priests until Jesus, the Sacrifice and the Priest in one person, came to fulfill and abolish these rituals. (Refer also to notes on Romans 3:24-26 again.)

However, animals used in sacrifices were irresponsible creatures. They were unwilling sacrifices, sinless, amoral, and could not atone for man (a rational being) made in the image of God. David saw this, as did the prophets (Psalm 51; 1 Samuel 3:14; Hebrews 10:1-14). These sacrifices pointed to the human sacrifice of the New Testament—the sacrifice of Jesus Christ—who was the very opposite of all that an animal sacrifice was in Old Testament times. Old Testament animal sacrifices were good, but the New Testament sacrifice of Jesus is better. Note this order: God, angels, beasts, man, and then the Lord Jesus Christ. An angel caused man to fall, so God used an animal (next in sequence) to die for man unto the death of His Son. Note the doctrine of substitution in the following:

- The innocent, guiltless, sinless animal died instead of Adam and Eve. Through this substitutionary death, Adam and Eve were clothed in faith-righteousness—clothed through the death of another (Genesis 3:21; Leviticus 1-7).

- The sacrifice of Abel that was offered in faith was a substitutionary victim (the body and blood of a lamb between God and Abel) (Genesis 4; Hebrews 12:4; 11:4). Abel was a faith-righteousness man.

- The sacrifices on the altar of Noah (Genesis 8-9).

- The sacrifices of Abraham (Genesis 15).

- Isaac—the sacrificed typical son (Genesis 22) was a revelation of Calvary. The substitute ram in the thicket was offered instead of Isaac (the only son). At Calvary this was reversed. The Son was offered instead of animals. With Isaac, an animal replaced the son. At Calvary, the Son replaced animals (Hebrews 11:11-19).

- The Passover lamb (Exodus 12).

- The five Levitical offerings (Leviticus 1-7).
  - The burnt offering – the sacrifice of worship (Leviticus 1).
  - The meal offering – the sacrifice fellowship (Leviticus 2).
  - The peace offering – the sacrifice of reconciliation (Leviticus 3).
  - The sin offering – the sacrifice of atonement (Leviticus 4).
  - The trespass offering – the sacrifice of restitution (Leviticus 5).
- The morning and evening sacrifice (Exodus 29; Numbers 28).

- The great Day of Atonement; the Feasts of the Lord (Leviticus 16; 23; Numbers 29).
- The red heifer (waters of separation) (Numbers 19).
- The Lord Jesus Christ Himself—the Cross. Christ died for (instead of, in behalf of) us. This is also illustrated in the fact that Christ died instead of Barabbas, the thief.

The three crosses on Calvary's hill illustrate the glorious truths of Romans 1-5 and the doctrine of substitution.

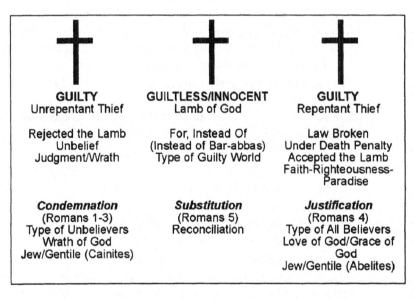

GUILTY	**GUILTLESS/INNOCENT**	**GUILTY**
Unrepentant Thief	Lamb of God	Repentant Thief
Rejected the Lamb	For, Instead Of	Law Broken
Unbelief	(Instead of Bar-abbas)	Under Death Penalty
Judgment/Wrath	Type of Guilty World	Accepted the Lamb
		Faith-Righteousness-Paradise
Condemnation	*Substitution*	*Justification*
(Romans 1-3)	(Romans 5)	(Romans 4)
Type of Unbelievers	Reconciliation	Type of All Believers
Wrath of God		Love of God/Grace of God
Jew/Gentile (Cainites)		Jew/Gentile (Abelites)

Each person in the world will find himself or herself aligned with one of the crosses on either side of Christ. Where they align themselves will determine their eternal destinies. A person's attitude toward the Cross and Jesus will forever settle his or her destiny in eternity. Illustrations are:

- Joseph and the Two Prisoners (one to life, one to death) (Genesis 40).
- The Brazen Altar and King Solomon, with Adonijah and Joab (one to life, one to death) (I Kings 1:50-53; 2:28-34).
- The Two Thieves on their Crosses (one to life, one to death). (Note: II Corinthians 2:15-17. So it is in the gospel).

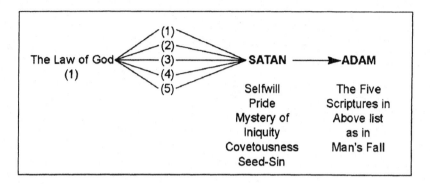

Note the way in which the above diagram relates to the following one.

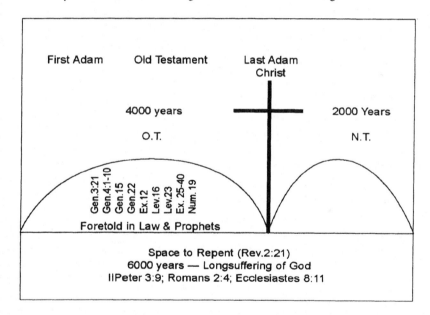

Verse 9: *"Much more then, being now justified by his blood, we shall be saved from wrath through him."*

A. **"Much more"**

Paul's use of "much more" in this chapter includes:

* Much more then...salvation (verse 9)
* Much more...life (verse 10)
* Much more...grace (verse 15)

- Much more...reign in life (verse 17)
- Much more...abounding grace (verse 20)
- (Cf. also Hebrews 9:14)

B. "Being now justified by his blood"

(Refer to Romans 5:1 comments, Romans 8:30, 33, and blood on the mercy seat [cf. Romans 3:25].) Blood is the evidence of Christ's death and outpoured life. Blood is the only remedy for sin. The dominant truth of substitution is bloodshed for another. Note the following:

- "...[W]hen I see the blood..." (Exodus 12:13).
- "I have given the blood as atonement for the soul" (Leviticus 17:11-14) (paraphrased).
- Other Scriptures include Colossians 1:14, 20; I John 1:6-7; Matthew 26:26; Revelation 12:11; I Peter 1:18-21; Hebrews 9:7-14; 15-22.
- Refer also to the Bible themes of "blood atonement."

C. "We shall be saved from wrath through him"

After being *under* the wrath of God because of the sins of Romans 1 through 2, we are now saved *from* wrath through Jesus Christ (cf. Romans 1:18; 2:5-8; 4:15; 5:9). The wrath of God fell upon Christ when He died for us. Wrath is appeased and law is satisfied. The claims and demands of the law of God have been met in Christ. Therefore, by accepting His death and resurrection, we are saved from future wrath (cf. I Thessalonians 1:10; Revelation 15-16; 6:16-17). The day of wrath that is to come, as well as the wrath of God in the end times, is included in this meaning. The believer is not saved from "tribulation" but is saved from God's "wrath" (cf. Romans 5:3 and 5:9). The phrase "the blood of the Lamb" (Revelation 7:14) can be termed "the wrath of the Lamb" (Revelation 6:16-17). However, it refers to the same Lamb and the same God.

Thus, the believer is saved from wrath through Christ because in Christ he has a faith-righteousness and right standing with God. The believer is no longer counted a sinner, an ungodly person, or an enemy, but is considered a new creature (II Corinthians 5:17).

Verse 10: *"For if, when we were enemies, we were reconciled to God by the death of his Son, much more, being reconciled, we shall be saved by his life."*

A. **"Reconciled to God by the death of his Son"**
   Christ died for us:

   - While we were without strength (Romans 5:6),
   - While we were yet sinners (Romans 5:8),
   - While we were yet enemies (Colossians 1:21 [enemies]).

   "Reconciliation" means "to become friends, those who were once at variance" (Colossians 1:20-21; Daniel 9:24; II Corinthians 5:18-21; Ephesians 2:16; Hebrews 2:17). (Refer again to the words listed in the summary of Romans 3:25-26.)

   Note the order in Romans 5:

   - Substitution (verses 6-9)
   - Reconciliation (verses 10-11; Romans 8:32)

   We are reconciled by Christ's death (Genesis 2:17; Romans 6:23). Christ had to die. It was not His life—the perfect, sinless, and blemishless life of the Lamb—that saved us, but His death (Exodus 12:12; Leviticus 1-7). Christ's death was a substitutionary death. Note the emphasis on "death" in Romans 5:6-10, 12, 14-15 and 17. Note also the distinct use of this word "death" in relation to Jesus Christ. The wages of sin is death. Christ had to die; that was the penalty for sin.
   Abraham, Sarah, and Isaac had the stamp of death on them (cf. Romans 4:17-18, 24). Christ's death is the death of all deaths (Romans 5). It was substitutionary. All the deaths of mankind combined could not compare with Christ's death. It was unique, substitutionary, and perfect. (Refer to *Foundations of Christian Doctrine* by Kevin J. Conner.) Note below what made Christ's death unique in the universe:

   - His death was the chief purpose of the incarnation.
   - His death was a free act.
   - His death was an accomplishment.
   - His death was of infinite value.
   - His death was a penalty.
   - His death was a satisfaction.
   - His death was complete and final.
   - His death was of supreme interest to heaven.
   - His death is prominent in the New Testament.
   - His death is essential to salvation.

- His death is the fundamental theme of the gospel.
- His death was a manifestation of divine love.
- His death was for the whole world.
- His death was a glorious conquest.
- His death is essential to Christianity.
- His death was the chief and central fact His life. He knew it was the Father's will.
- His death by crucifixion should be distinguished between the Atonement. (Refer to *The Foundations of Christian Doctrine* by Kevin Conner.)

B. **"Much more, being reconciled, we shall be saved by his life"**
    This is the first use of the word "life" in Romans. (See also Romans 5:17,18, 21.) Note:

- First, it is Christ's saving *death*.
- Then, it is Christ's saving *life*.

We are saved in this order:
1) From wrath (Romans 5:9)
2) By His death (Romans 5:10)
3) By His life (Romans 5:10)

Christ's perfect, sinless life on earth condemned man (even as the law condemned man) and His perfect, substitutionary death saves man (which the law could not do). To uphold the life of Christ without His death is to totally condemn man (even as the law was unto condemnation). This is why the gospel is in the order of His death first—His substitutionary death for the sinful—and then His resurrection life. Therefore:

- Christ died for sinners (His death).
- Christ lives for sinners (His resurrection life). (See John 14:6; Colossians 3:1-4; II Corinthians 4:10-12; Romans 8:2; II Corinthians 5:17-18.)

Christ died and now lives to save us (John 14:19). Note that the Holy Spirit is the Spirit of Life. Jesus Christ lives in heaven, in the power of an endless life, and it is His risen, ascended life that He, by the Spirit, communicates to the believer day by day (Romans 5:5). Life in the Spirit is dealt with in Romans 8. (Read also I John 1:1-2; 2:25; 5:11-13, 20.) This life is found in the Son of God.

Verse 11: *"And not only so, but we also joy in God through our Lord Jesus Christ, by whom we have now received the atonement."*

A. **"Lord Jesus Christ"**
    Concerning the saving death and life Christ, Major Ian Thomas says:
    1) He had to be what He was (perfect) to do what He did (redeem).
    2) His sinless life made possible or qualified Him for the death He died. If He had been anything less than righteous, He could have only died for His own sins, not ours.
    3) He had to be what He was to do what He did (redeem), that we might have what He is (life), to be what He was (perfect). We must have what He is (life) to be what He was (perfect).
    4) We will be what He was (perfect) only in the measure we allow Him to be what He is (perfect).
    5) The death He died qualified Him for the life He received.
    6) He died not only for what we did, He died for what we were.
    7) The life He lived nineteen hundred years ago condemns me, even as the law condemned me. He was born sinless, inhabited by God, uninhabited by sin.
    8) The life He lives in us now is the life that saves us. The Christian life is the life Christ lived then, lived by Him now in you.
    9) Thus, being saved by His death, we are now much more saved by His life.

B. **"Joy in God"** (cf. Romans 5:11)
    "Joy in God" is spiritual joy and kingdom joy (II Corinthians 7:2-4; Romans 15:13; 14:17). We rejoice in the hope of the glory of God (Romans 5:2), not in our accomplishments or in ourselves. We rejoice through Jesus Christ because of all that He has done and by virtue of who He is.

C. **"Received the atonement"**
    This verse is the only place where this word is translated "the atonement" in the New Testament. The Greek word for "atonement," *katallage*, is the same Greek word translated in Romans 5:10 as "the reconciliation." Note the great "Day of Atonement" in Leviticus 16. Note also the use of the words "atonement" and "reconciliation" in this chapter of Leviticus, as no other chapter on offerings.

Note the two goats below:
1) **The Lord's Goat** – The goat for Jehovah (the blood is brought within the veil) died to reconcile.
2) **The Scapegoat** – The goat that was sent into the wilderness *lived* to reconcile.

Christ and His church (two yet one) are both involved in the ministry of reconciliation (II Corinthians 5:18-21). Note that the two goats speak of Christ:

- In His death, He died to reconcile (the Lord's goat).
- In His resurrection, He lives to reconcile (the scapegoat).

"Atonement" in the Old Testament means "to cover." "Reconciliation" in the New Testament means "to bring together those formerly at variance." The New Testament message does not speak of covering sin but cleansing it. Animal blood could only temporarily cover sin; it could not cleanse it. Jesus' blood eternally cleanses sin; it does not merely cover it. The mercy seat was that "covering" in Moses' tabernacle.

Note below concerning the Atonement (the reconciliation):
- It was *ordained* in heaven (Revelation 13:8; I Peter 1:19-20; Titus 1:2; Acts 2:23).
- It was *instituted* on earth (Exodus 12:3-6; Leviticus 1-7; Leviticus 16; Numbers 29). Old Testament animal sacrifices were good for the time in which they occurred; however, the New Testament sacrifice of Christ is eternally better.
- It was *necessitated* by God' holiness and man's sinfulness. God's holiness versus man's sinfulness manifested itself in wrath—the reaction of a holy God against sin. This wrath could only be averted through atonement.
- Its *nature* is seen at Calvary in Christ's death. Christ's death was a ransom, redemption, substitution, propitiation, and atonement.
- Its *efficacy* is seen in its results. Man may now receive pardon from death, freedom from sin, reconciliation, justification, sanctification, glorification, and eternal life.

The Two Federal Men (Romans 5:12-21)

The Two Adams – Adam and Christ, First and Last Adams, Representative Men (Romans 5:12-14)

Verse 12: *"Wherefore, as by one man sin entered into the world, and death by sin; and so death passed upon all men, for that all have sinned. . ."*

A. **"By one man"**

In this verse, Paul goes back to the beginning—back to the first man, Adam—and gets to the very root and source of the problem of sin. All that mankind is, as seen in Romans 1:18-32, is because of what is written in Romans 5:12—because sin entered into the world by one man. In Adam we received a terrible heritage of sin, offense, disobedience, judgment, condemnation, and death. A key word in this section of Romans 5:12-21 is the word "one," and it is used about twelve times. Paul has dealt with Abraham—the father of all who believe—in Romans 4. He now deals with Adam—the father of all mankind—in Romans 5.

Adam Covenant Man	Dispensation of the Father God	Abraham Covenant Man
Sin / Death / Unbelief Father of all Mankind "In Adam"		Grace / Faith Death / Substitution Father of all Belivers "In Abraham"
	2000 Years Covenants	
ROMANS 4		**ROMANS 5**

Adam is the first man—the one man who is the federal and representative head of the human race (I Corinthians 15:21, 46-47). He represents the whole before God. All are in Adam, the one man.

B. **"Sin entered into the world"**

Sin entered into the world from outside of the world. It entered through Satan who is the original sinner in heaven. Adam is not the original sinner. Angelic hosts who fell with Satan were part of this original sin. After this fall, sin entered earth through the Serpent (Genesis 3:1-6).

C. **"Death by sin"**

"For the wages of sin is death..." (Romans 6:23). Sin and death are linked together (Genesis 2:17). The key thought in Romans 5:12-21 is "death." The key thoughts in Romans 7 are "law," "death," and "sin." "...[T]he soul that sinneth, it shall die" (Ezekiel 18:1-4).

D. **"So death passed upon all men"**

If Christ died for sin (Romans 5:6-8, 10), then for whom did He die? The answer is for sin and for sinners. Death was necessary because death is the penalty for sin.

E. **"By one man"**

Adam was the first living soul (Genesis 1:26-29, 3:1-6, I Corinthians 15:47). Note below that man was made in the image of God in:

- Triunity of being,
- Character,
- Likeness,
- Dominion. (Man was set over the works of God's hands [Psalm 8; Genesis 1:26-28].)

Adam knowingly transgressed a given law and commandment. He was not deceived. Eve was deceived; Adam disobeyed (I Timothy 2:13-14; I John 3:4). Hence, the sin is charged to the man, not to the woman. Sin did not enter the world by one woman, but by one man. God saw Adam as the federal head of the whole human race. He was the representative man. In his loins, as yet unborn, was the whole race of mankind. Thus, when Adam fell, the entire race fell in him. When he sinned, we all sinned, for all the unborn generations were in him.

F. "For that all have sinned"

The Amplified New Testament states, "In whom all have sinned" (marginal). Note that the devil (the Tempter, the Deceiver) is not specifically mentioned here though he was the original sinner in heaven. Satan is the first sinner and the source of all sin. Sin personified in him is not mentioned expressly until Romans 16:20. Romans 16:20 speaks of the final "bruising" that comes for him based on what was prophesied to Eve in Genesis 3:15.

Note the principle of "in" as used by Paul and the writer of Hebrews. Note in Hebrews 7:1-10, Levi paid tithes to Melchisedec. "And as I may so say, Levi also, who receiveth tithes, payed tithes in Abraham. For he was yet in the loins of his father [as yet unborn], when Melchisedec met him" (Hebrews 7:9-10). This was the subjecting of the Aaronic and Levitical priesthoods to the greater priesthood of Melchisedec.

The entire race was "in" Adam when he sinned, and this subjected the entire human race to sin, sickness, disease, and death, and it subjected Satan to the judgments of God as well. Thus, in Adam, all sinned. In Adam, all died. When Adam sinned, we sinned. When Adam died, we died. We did in Adam what he did. In the First Adam, all men are constituted sinners, and in the Last Adam, all may be constituted righteous. Hence, these Scriptures set forth the divine principle of federal headship and representation.

Note below concerning this principle:

- All fruit trees were "in" the original fruit tree (Genesis 1:11-13) (seed in itself, the law of reproduction, likeness).
- All animals were "in" the original animals (Genesis 1:20-28) (monkeys, etc.).
- All Levites were "in" Abraham's loins when he paid tithes to Melchisedec (Genesis 14; Hebrews 7:4-10) (cf. also Romans 9:6-7).
- All mankind was "in" Adam when he sinned. Thus, when he sinned, we sinned; when he fell, we fell. We were in his loins as unborn seed and unborn generations.
- All "in Isaac" only counted as the seed (Genesis 21:12).

In nature and creation, this principle of being "in" the original is also illustrated. All the apple trees in the world were in that original apple tree. All animals and birds were in the original animals and birds. All were in that seed. It is the same with the Tree of the Knowledge of Good and Evil. The "seed was in itself"—the seed sin! God also saw the whole of the Levitical tribe and Israel "in Abraham." He saw the entirety of Adam's race "in Adam," when Adam sold out to Satan.

Therefore, when Adam sinned, all sinned. When Adam partook of the Tree of Knowledge of Good and Evil, all partook of it. When Adam disobeyed, all disobeyed. When he fell, all mankind fell with him. When death passed upon Adam, it passed on to all men—the entire human race. We did "in Adam" what he did. Sin is charged to man because he was the seed-bearer; the seed of the human race was in his loins. All members of the human race are seen as "members of the First Adam—the first man, the living soul, the earthly image. All members of the human race are members of the body of Adam (Psalm 51:5; James 1:15). Thus, "in Adam all sinned."

Hebrews 9:27 states, "And as it is appointed unto men once to die, but after this the judgment." Note, however, that II Corinthians 5:17 states, "Therefore if any man be in Christ, he is a new creature: old things are passed away; behold, all things are become new." Death is divine judgment on sin, and sin is the transgression of God's law (I John 3:4; Genesis 2:17; Romans 6:23); yet also note that the believer is a member of the body of Christ and is "in" Christ (Romans 6:3-5).

Verse 13: *"...(For until the law sin was in the world: but sin is not imputed when there is no law."*

A. **"Until the law"**
"Until the law" means until the Law of the Ten Commandments was given to Moses to define sin (Romans 5:14).

B. **"Sin was in the world"**
From Adam to Moses, sin was in the world. It entered by one man, Adam, through the channel of Satan—the source of sin (cf. Romans 5:14).

C. **"Sin is not imputed when there is no law"**
The Amplified New Testament states, "[To be sure,] sin was in the world before ever the Law was given, but sin is not charged to man's account where there is no law [to transgress]." The Bible's definition of sin could be considered here. Sin is the reason for repentance. Note:

1) **Sin is transgression of the law** (I John 3:4). Sin is lawlessness (cf. Exodus 20; Romans 3:20). Adam transgressed the one law given to him in Genesis 2:17. (Note also James 2:8-12.)
2) **The thought of foolishness is sin** (Proverbs 24:9). Satan appealed to Adam and Eve that they would be "as gods knowing good and evil." This thought was foolishness, even as it had been for Satan (Proverbs 16:18; Ezekiel 28: Isaiah 14:12-15).
3) **To know good and to do it not is sin** (James 4:17). Adam knew good and did not do good. This was disobedience to God's Word.
4) **All unrighteousness is sin** (I John 5:14). Unrighteousness is the act of not doing right. Adam was guilty of unrighteousness.
5) **Whatsoever is not of faith is sin** (Romans 14:23). Unbelief in God's Word is sin (cf. Romans 10:17; Genesis 3:1-6; John 16:9-11).

Each of the above apply both to Satan's fall and Adam's fall. Satan was lifted up in pride, covetousness, and unlawful lust to be like God. The very essence of sin was self-will, egotism, and the act of making a god of self. This is the mystery of iniquity. Sin is a spiritual thing and a spiritual law of independence from God. It is the act of doing one's own will.

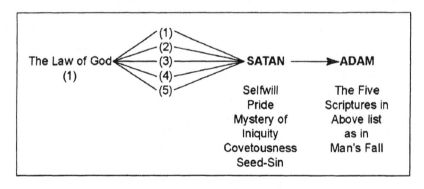

Broken law works wrath (Romans 4:15), and sin can not be imputed if there is no law or no transgression of such. It may then be questioned: since there was no law of given commandments from the time of Adam to Moses, on what basis did God deal with man in this period of time?

- Why did God judge the sin of Cain?
- Why did God judge the wickedness of the world, in the days of Noah, by causing the Flood?

- Why did God judge the Tower of Babel and send tongues of confusion?
- Why did God judge Sodom and Gomorrah?

God did deal with sin by various measures of judgment. However, on what basis did God reckon or impute sin and judge mankind for it? The answer is on the ground of law. The ground is still law but not the law given to Moses in the Ten Commandments. Sin was judged on the ground of the law of conscience (Romans 2:14-15). Man had the law of God, in measure, in his conscience, and the voice of God within man told him right from wrong. Man's conscience became violated, corrupted, and reprobate; nevertheless, God judged sin on the basis of the law of conscience. In the Ten Commandments, Israel was given an external law that clearly defined sin and on which ground God could deal, by wrath, with the transgressors of that given law.

Verse 14: *"Nevertheless death reigned from Adam to Moses, even over them that had not sinned after the similitude of Adam's transgression, who is the figure of him that was to come."*

A. **"Death reigned"**
Death reigned as king over all mankind (cf. Genesis 5, "and he died"). "Grace reigns" (Romans 5:21). Note the use of the word "reign" in Romans 5:14, 17, 21.

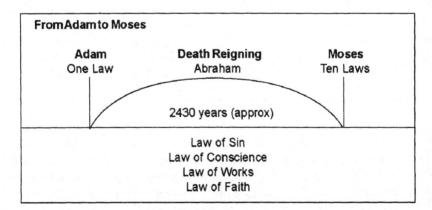

From Adam to Moses

Adam	Death Reigning	Moses
One Law	Abraham	Ten Laws

2430 years (approx)

Law of Sin
Law of Conscience
Law of Works
Law of Faith

B. "Even over them"

The Amplified New Testament states, "Yet death held sway from Adam to Moses [the Lawgiver], even over those who did not themselves transgress [a positive command] as Adam did...." Adam transgressed one given commandment, and therefore, death reigns. From Adam to Moses, death reigned over them, even though no specific commandment or commandments were given to the people of that time. However, those people had the law of conscience, and, on the basis of defiling their consciences, God judged them. Sin was imputed. Note also that, in the Noahic Covenant, laws involving human government were given to Noah.

C. "Who is the figure of him that was to come"

Adam was made in the image of God (cf. I Corinthians 15:45-47), and the image of God is Jesus Christ (II Corinthians 4:4; Colossians 1:15; Hebrews 1:3). Adam was the figure. "Figure" in the Greek is *tupos*, meaning "the type, likeness, representation." Adam was the type, likeness, and representation of the Son of God who was to come. Note below that there are only two "Sons of God" in Scripture in the exact sense:

- Adam (the first)—the created Son of God (Luke 3:38)
- Jesus (the last)—the only begotten Son of God (John 3:16)

"Adam was a type (prefigure) of the one who was to come", in reverse, the former destructive, the latter, saving" (Romans 5:14) (Amplified New Testament) (Genesis 5:5; 7:22; Deuteronomy 34:5).

The Two Results – Condemnation and Justification (Romans 5:15-17)

Verse 15: *"But not as the offence, so also is the free gift. For if through the offence of one many be dead, much more the grace of God, and the gift by grace, which is by one man, Jesus Christ, hath abounded unto many."*

A. "The offence"

Adam's offense brings death. Note "offenses" in Romans 4:25; 5:15-18, 20. Note the words used here:

- Adam's Transgression (Romans 5:14)
- Adam's Offense (Romans 5:15)

- Adam's Sin (Romans 5:12)
- Adam's Disobedience (Romans 5:19)
- Adam's Death (Romans 5:12; 6:23 [wages])

B. "The free gift"

"...[F]reely [Greek: *Gratis*] by His grace..." (Romans 3:24). "...[T]he gift of God is eternal life through Jesus Christ our Lord" (Romans 6:23). "Gift" in the Greek is *doreo*. Note below the word "gift":

- Free Gift (Romans 5:15-16, 18)
- The Gift of Grace (Romans 5:15)
- The Gift (Romans 5:16)
- The Gift of Righteousness (Romans 5:17)
- The Gift of God is Eternal Life (6:23). (Cf. John 4:10 [opposite to what Adam presented us].) (Cf. Romans 4:2-4, wages [earned], gift [unearned].)

C. Through the offense of one, many are dead; through the gift by grace, many have abounded.

Note the sharper contrast of these two men—Adam and Jesus:

Adam – the one man (First Adam). "...[T]hrough the offence of one, many be dead..."

Jesus – the one man, (Last Adam). "...[T]he gift of grace, which is by one man, Jesus Christ, hath abounded unto many."

Verse 16: *"And not as it was by one that sinned, so is the gift: for the judgment was by one to condemnation, but the free gift is of many offences unto justification."*

"Judgment was by one to condemnation, but the free gift is of many"

Adam – the one that sinned unto condemnation (judgment, one offense) (cf. Romans 5:18). (See also the Amplified New Testament.)

Jesus – the righteous One, the free gift, unto justification (many offenses).

Verse 17: *"For if by one man's offence death reigned by one; much more they which receive abundance of grace and of the gift of righteousness shall reign in life by one, Jesus Christ.)"*

A. By one man's offense death reigned, but they that receive the gift of righteousness shall reign in life by Jesus Christ.

Adam – the First Adam. Through one man's offense, death reigned (inherit sin and unrighteousness).

Jesus – the Last Adam. Through one man's righteousness (reign in life), the gift of righteousness may be received by grace.

B. "They which receive"

God, through Christ, makes grace, righteousness, and life available for all men; however, it is available only for those who receive it. "But as many as received him, to them gave he..." (cf. John 1:11-12; 3:16). Jesus must be received by faith.

The Two Acts – Disobedience and Obedience (Romans 5:18-21)

Verse 18: *"Therefore as by the offence of one judgment came upon all men to condemnation; even so by the righteousness of one the free gift came upon all men unto justification of life."*

By the offence of one judgment condemnation came upon all men, but by the righteousness of one can all men have justification to life.

Adam – the First Adam. By the offense of one, judgment came on all men (condemnation, death) (cf. Romans 5:16).

Jesus – the Last Adam. By the righteousness of one, the free gift for all men (justification to life) was received. (Note "judgment" in Romans 5:16, 18; 1:32; 2:1-3, 5, 12, 16.)

Verse 19: *"For as by one man's disobedience many were made sinners, so by the obedience of one shall many be made righteous."*

By one man's disobedience, many were made sinners, but by one man's obedience, many will be made righteous.

Adam – the one man (disobedience, many made sinners).

Jesus – the one man (obedience, many made righteous).

Obedience is the crux of the whole matter. Andrew Murray says, "Christ died to bring us back to the obedience from which Adam fell."

"Obedience," in this verse, is referring to obedience to the Word of the Lord (His will and Word) (Hebrews 5:7-10). Refer to "obedience" in these Scriptures: Romans 1:5; 16:19, 26; II Corinthians 10:5; Philippians 2:8; Deuteronomy 4:30; Isaiah 1:19; I Peter 1:2.

Verse 20: *"Moreover the law entered, that the offence might abound. But where sin abounded, grace did much more abound..."*

A. **"The law entered"**
   Sin entered the world through Adam (Romans 5:12 [in Eden]). Law entered by Moses (Romans 5:20 [Mt. Sinai]; cf. Romans 5:13-14). The purpose of the law is given in Romans 7:7 and 3:20 (refer to notes). The law was given to provide a clear definition of sin and the knowledge of sin. Law and sin are vitally connected (I John 3:4).

B. **"But where sin abounded, grace did much more abound"** (cf. John 1:17)
   Generally, the people of Israel never seemed to understand the prevailing of both law and grace, even though they were under the Mosaic Covenant. A study of Exodus 25-40 reveals this. The moral, civil, and ceremonial laws were continually manifested in Israel in the tabernacle and the temple. Law and grace have always been in God. Law and grace were manifested to Adam (Genesis 2-3). (Cf. John 1:17.) Note below concerning the law and grace in the nation of Israel:
   - The law was given (Exodus 32 and 20-24). The law was given in Israel, as it was to Adam (moral law, civil laws).
   - The law was broken (Exodus 32). Israel broke the law, as did the First Adam (first covenant, "which covenant they broke"). Wrath (Romans 4:15) came on the idolaters, and three thousand were slain. The law works wrath.
   - Grace prevailed (Exodus 33). Moses—mediator of the Old Covenant—made blood atonement (sacrifice, intercession). This is representative of Jesus—the intercessor and mediatory sacrifice of the New Covenant (grace under law).
   - The ark of the covenant (Exodus 25-40) (law and grace). The new table was in the ark of the covenant beneath a blood-stained mercy seat. The Ten Commandments represented the law—the moral law and the civil law (in the book of the law). The blood-stained mercy

seat represented grace (ceremonial law). The unbroken law, (represented by the second set of tables) is typical of the Second Adam—the Lord from heaven, in whose heart the law was perfectly kept and unbroken (Psalm 40:5-9).

If it had not been for the blood on the mercy seat (grace), then Israel would have been exposed continually to the wrath of the broken law (law). Thus, law and grace were even manifested in the Mosaic Covenant. Full coverage of the "law" is given in Romans 7. The abounding sin of man was great; however, the much more abounding grace of God is stronger and greater than sin.

Verse 21: *"...That as sin hath reigned unto death, even so might grace reign through righteousness unto eternal life by Jesus Christ our Lord."*

"Sin hath reigned unto death, even so might grace reign through righteousness"
Note:

- Sin reigns unto death. Death reigns on all men (Romans 5:21, 14, 17).
- Grace reigns unto eternal life, through righteousness (Romans 5:17, 21).

Grace can only reign through righteousness. This practical obedience unto righteousness (Romans 6:16) is dealt with in Romans 6:1-23. If grace is to reign, it can only reign through righteousness. This guards against the abuse of Paul's doctrine of the free grace of God, which is turned into all kinds of lasciviousness. (Note Romans 6:1; 5:20; 3:7-8.)

Summary (Romans 5:12-21)

Note that these verses of Romans 5:12-21 are a series of contrasts (R. Cabe).
Two Men (Romans 5:14)
- Adam (head of the old creation)
- Christ (head of the new creation)

Two Acts
- Adam (one offense, trespass—disobedience) (Romans 5:12, 15, 17-19)
- Christ (one righteous act [Cross]—obedience) (Romans 5:18)

Two Results
- Adam (condemnation, sin, guilt, death) (Romans 5:15-16, 18-19)
- Christ (justification, grace, life) (Romans 5:17-19)

Two Kings
- Sin (reigning through death) (Romans 5:17)
- Grace (reigning through righteousness) (Romans 5:21)

Two States
- Condemned men—slaves of death (by Adam)
- Justified men—reigning in life (by Christ)

Summary (Romans 5)

Two Original Men

Thus, God beholds two original men—federal heads of the human race (the old and new creation races) (I Corinthians 15:47 with Romans 5:14 [marginal]). Adam—the first man, federal head, and representative of the old creation race—delivered mankind over to death. Christ—the second man (the Last Adam) federal head, and representative of the new creation—brings mankind into life. The Cross is the great divider. All are either "in Adam" or "in Christ"(members of one man or the other).

Note the diagram on the following page.

Theological Ramifications

1) God is just and righteous in all He is and all He does.

2) God created man for His glory, to be righteous even as God is righteous.

3) God has manifested His righteousness in two main areas: in the law and in Christ Jesus.

It is important to understand these two areas of God's demonstrated and revealed righteousness: righteousness manifested in the law and righteousness manifested in Christ.

THE FIRST ADAM	THE LAST ADAM
The First Man, Adam, Federal Head	The Last Adam, Federal Head
The First Man, Representative	The Second Man, Representative
The One Man	The One Man
The Living Soul	The Quickening Spirit
Of the Earth, Earthy	The Lord from Heaven, Heavenly
Image of the Earthy	Image of the Heavenly
Sin Entered	Righteousness Entered
Death Reigns	Life Reigns
Upon All Men	Available to All Men
Disobedience, Offense	Obedience, No Offence
Acts of Trespass, Transgression	Acts of Righteousness
State of Sin, Sinners Constituted	State of Righteousness, Righteousness Constituted
Condemnation	Justification
Judgement	Grace Reigns Through Righteousness
Inevitable for All	Available for All
"In Adam"	"In Christ"

A. **Righteousness Manifested in the Law**

Paul's thought of righteousness in Romans is expressed in the law and then in Christ. The relationship (comparison) between the righteousness of the law and the righteousness in Christ is that one is the letter (law), and the other is the life (righteousness in Christ). The law set forth God's righteousness. It condemned sin morally, stopped every mouth, and declared the whole world guilty before God. Exposed sin left man condemned and unjustified. The life of righteousness in Christ did exactly the same as the law. His sinless life condemns sin morally, even as the law did. When the sinner compares himself with the law or with the life of Christ, he stands condemned. Both the law and Christ do the same work in this area.

Thus, God declared His righteousness and demonstrated it both in the law and in Jesus Christ, the righteous One. He gave man a law which was naturally impossible for man to keep; however, He is justified in giving man that law because He brought forth Jesus Christ, a man, in whom that righteous law was kept and fulfilled. The righteous law was kept and fulfilled because of who Christ was (Psalm 40:6-10). The law was a perfect standard of righteousness—holy, just, good, spiritual, and perfect. However, it was just the letter of the law on tables of stone. It pointed out the standard but was unable to give power to any Israelite to live the standard or righteous life.

B. **Righteousness Manifested in the Life of Christ**

God's righteousness has also been manifested in the righteous One— Christ Jesus. There are two special ways it is manifested:

1) **In Christ's Perfect Life—as the Righteous One, Morally Condemning Sin**

(Cf. notes on Romans 5:12-21 [the two Adams].) Note below that Jesus Christ:

- Is the righteous branch (Jeremiah 23:6; 33:15-16).
- Was the righteous servant (Isaiah 53:11; 59:16-17; 63:1).
- Was the righteousness of God manifested in human flesh (in human life) (Isaiah 56:1).
- Was God's righteousness personified (Isaiah 46:13; Malachi 4:2).
- Was born sinless and lived sinless.
- Was perfectly right and holy in thought, word, and deed. All that He was, said, and did was righteous. He was what He was because of who He is (Romans 10:3, Amplified New Testament).

Jesus fulfilled the law; that is, He fulfilled the righteousness of the law, not only externally but also internally, by the Spirit (Romans 8:4). He was all that the law was. There was nothing with the law in itself as a righteous standard. That is, the law was holy, spiritual, just, good, and perfect, and Jesus Christ was all that. Therefore, He was the fulfillment of the law (Romans 10:4; Matthew 5:17-18). The righteousness of the law was fulfilled in Him, for He was the only man who ever walked perfectly after the Spirit. Thus, the righteousness of Christ fulfills the demands of the righteous law. He was the life of righteousness, in contrast to the law, which was the letter of righteousness. However, His life, which fulfills the law, also condemns the sinner in the same way that the righteousness of the law at Mt. Sinai did. His sinless, perfect life condemns sin; it condemns the sinner as much as the law did. It is not His sinless life that saves man first. His sinless life—before the Cross and His death—first condemns man, even as the law condemns him. We are not saved by His life first, but by His death. Only after His death are we saved by His saving life. (Refer again to Romans 5:9-10.)

2) In Christ's Perfect Death—as the Substitutionary One

Not only has God declared and demonstrated His righteousness (as in the righteous law) in Christ's perfect life (the righteous one), God has also declared and demonstrated it in His righteous death.

In Christ's perfectly righteous life, He fulfilled Isaiah 42:21 and "magnified the law, and made it honorable" by keeping it. His righteous life fulfilled the law and in His perfect death, the righteousness of God was also seen. Because Christ alone fulfilled the righteous law (Matthew 3:15), He is the only righteous man and the only righteous life that lived on this earth. He kept the law wholly, perfectly, and unbroken in letter or spirit, and therefore, He alone stands uncondemned.

Law-righteousness was because of life-righteousness. Christ was the perfect man and, by virtue of His righteousness, is heir to eternal life, and all that the Father is He may lay claim to. God can deal righteously with Christ—the righteous One. All mankind, though, is unrighteous, and God, therefore, must deal righteously with man according to His own righteousness (His own character).

Sin has to be dealt with. Jesus Christ is the only righteous man and all others are unrighteous before God. This precipitates Romans 5:14-21. Many were constituted unrighteous because of Adam's sin. Many, by faith, will also be constituted righteous because of Christ's sinlessness.

God must deal righteously with Christ (the perfect One) and give Christ eternal life and inheritance with Himself. God must also deal righteously with the sinful race and punish all with death—judgment on sin. Dealing with sin is the only way God can be righteous. This is seen in Romans 4:25. God does deal with sin. How? He deals with sin in the vicarious sacrifice of Christ. "Vicarious" means "acting or suffering for another, by substitution." This was dealt with in measure under "propitiation," in Romans 3:25. In other words, God took the sins of the whole world, laid them on Jesus Christ, and judged Him accordingly (John 1:29, 36). God made Him to be sin for us (II Corinthians 5:21). The Lord laid on Him the iniquity of us all (Isaiah 53:4-6). For our sin, God judged Christ. God judged Christ instead of us. Christ died for our sins according to the Scriptures (I Corinthians 15:1-3). Christ (the righteous One), when He was made sin, was dealt with by God according to the righteous law. Christ was judged by the death sentence. The death penalty was laid on Him. He became the substitute—the propitiation—for the sins of the whole world (I John 2:2; 4:10). When Christ was made sin by receiving in Himself the penalty of sin (death), the righteousness of God was declared. The righteousness of a holy and just God is displayed in the perfect, substitutionary death of Christ. The wrath of a holy God was poured out on Christ, the sinless Substitute, when He was made sin for us. Christ, who kept the law, suffered the penalty of the law that was broken by mankind (Galatians 3:13). His death was vicarious suffering. Christ died for us.

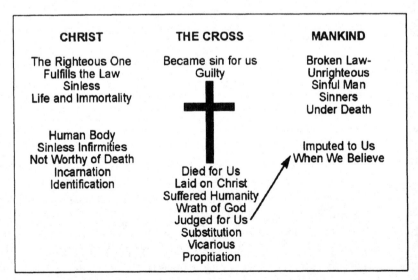

CHRIST	THE CROSS	MANKIND
The Righteous One Fulfills the Law Sinless Life and Immortality	Became sin for us Guilty	Broken Law- Unrighteous Sinful Man Sinners Under Death
Human Body Sinless Infirmities Not Worthy of Death Incarnation Identification	Died for Us Laid on Christ Suffered Humanity Wrath of God Judged for Us Substitution Vicarious Propitiation	Imputed to Us When We Believe

Let us compare the two kinds of righteousness in the law and in Christ: the letter and the life.

The Letter – The Law	The Christ – The Life
• Perfect	• Perfect
• Holy	• Holy
• Just	• Just
• Good	• Good
• Spiritual	• Spiritual
• Righteous	• Righteous
• Written on Tables of Stone	• Written in Tables of Heart (Law in Heart)
• Broken By Israel and Moses	• Unbroken
• No Man Could Keep It	• The Only Man Who Perfectly Kept the Law (He alone sinless)
• Impossible for the Flesh to Keep	• Divine – As a Human, He Kept it
• God's Written Standard of Righteousness Given to Man	• God's Living Standard of Righteousness Sent to Man
• The Law of Righteousness	• The Life of Righteousness
• Condemns Sinful Man	• His Life Condemns Sinful Man
• Leaves Man Hopeless, Helpless	• Came to Help the Hopeless
• Cannot Justify Man	• His Death Can Justify Man
• Not By Works of the Law	• By the Law of Faith
• Externalized Law	• Internalized Law – Written on Flesh Tables of the Heart

Thus, even as Moses demonstrated what Israel had done by breaking the first set of tables, the keeping of the second set of tables in the ark symbolized Christ—the Second Adam, the Lord from heaven who alone perfectly kept the law of God in His heart and life. The law in the ark spoke of the law in Christ—our Ark and blood-stained mercy seat. Thus, in Christ God displayed His righteousness "at this present time" (cf. Romans 11:5).

4) Broken law demands that a penalty be executed (the death penalty).
Man sinned and incurred wrath for transgression of the law.

5) God's law is irrevocable and must be upheld.
If God's law was not upheld, His throne of justice would be at stake.

6) God is love. He is compassionate and longsuffering and waits to be gracious.
God seeks a way to save man from the penalty He imposed by law. Mercy, truth, righteousness, and peace meet together (Psalm 85:10). Mercy rejoices against judgment—not against truth (James 2:13). The problem is how to judge sin and yet save the sinner.

7) God's answer was in the plan of redemption.
The main steps of redemption are reaffirmed here:

A. **Identification with the Human Race**
"Identify" means "to make the same, to treat as being one; to unite or combine in the same state; to become the same; same manner or form, exactly." God desired to identify Himself with His own creation.

B. **Incarnation in the Human Race**
"Incarnation" means "in" and "*carnis*" (flesh). "Incarnation" means "to clothe with flesh, to embody in flesh, invested with flesh, embodied in a fleshly nature and form." Incarnate (speaking in terms of Christ) is "the act of clothing with or the act of assuming a human body and the nature of man, a manifestation."
It was through the incarnation that God in Christ became identified with the human race but was without sin (Hebrews 2:14; John 1:13-18; Luke 1:30-33; Matthew 1:21-23; Hebrews 10:5-8; Galatians 4:4; Romans 1:3). He became one with humanity. God became man. His human body was made of flesh but was sinless and perfect. It still had the same physical infirmities (sinless infirmities) as all other men of Adam's race (hunger, fatigue, weariness, etc.); however, it had no sin.

C. **Substitution for the Human Race**
Christ's identification and incarnation in and with the human race made His substitutionary sacrifice possible. "Substitution" means "the act of putting one person or thing in the place of another; in the room and stead of another, to exchange, interchange, one delegated to act for another."

Jesus Christ—the perfect sinless man—could become a substitute for the human race representatively. The entire race was representatively "in Adam" when Adam sinned and came under the death sentence. When God judged Adam, He judged the whole race representatively in him (in his loins as yet unborn). Jesus Christ—incarnate in the human race (born of it) and partaker of human nature (sin excepted)—could become a substitute and representative of the whole human race Himself. He was the only man ever born of a woman who was sinless because He was God incarnate—the God man. It was man who sinned and man who should die. God cannot sin; God cannot die. For God to deal with sin and death meant that God would have to become incarnate—become a man. God could not redeem man as God. God had to redeem man as man because only a man could die for mankind. This very fact necessitated the incarnation. The virgin birth (incarnation) was God's way of making this possible.

But again, Christ could only die if sin was laid upon Him. He was sinless and, therefore, immortal. When He became our substitute, God laid on Him our sins, and He came under the death penalty. Christ died instead. It may be questioned: "Is the doctrine of substitution just and right?" The answer is in the affirmative because of God's divine nature and character. God is the only One who can deal with sin. He alone knows the full heinousness and hideousness of sin because He is holiness personified.

No fallen sinful creature could ever understand sin as God does. No fallen man can deal with the sin problem. Hence, this means that God alone must, can, and did deal with it. If God was the only One who could deal with the sin problem, then He alone could find a way to deal with it—a way consistent with His divine nature of holiness, love, wrath, and mercy. In the matter of dealing with sin, man is out of the question. God alone must deal with sin, and He must deal with the sin of man as well as the sinner himself. He hates sin, yet loves the sinner. (Refer also to *Strong's Systematic Theology*, p. 752-768.)

God Himself, in Christ, stepped in and became man's substitute. He took man's guilt, sin, and penalty—the very penalty He declared on man—in Himself on the Cross. Christ—one of the divine persons in the Godhead, united with the Judge of sin—took the sentence and judgment in Himself at Calvary. He could do this because He was and is God. By becoming a substitute for man, He fulfills His own sentence of death for the broken law in Himself. It is not sinful man dying for sinful man—no man can (Psalm 49:3-8)—but it is a righteous man (who became sin for sinful men) dying for man. Thus, the law was not overthrown; it was executed. Its demands are now satisfied. It can exact no more than the death sentence. Yes! Substitution is right for God, for He Himself fulfills the law of judgment on man in Himself—in His Son. God, the Judge, voluntarily takes the stead (place) of the judged and condemned man (Romans 5:6-8).

D. **Imputation**

"Imputation" means "the act of imputing, charge of evil, reproach, the act of attributing to one that which really belongs to another." This is exactly what happened at Calvary. The sin and guilt of mankind, with their penal consequences, were attributed to Christ. The sin and guilt were not His; He was the sinless, righteous One. When He voluntarily became our substitute by acting in our stead (in our behalf) to die for us, He took upon Himself our sin in order to suffer its penalty. If He had not taken on this sin, God would not have been just in judging Christ. God can only judge sin. Christ had to take our sins to be judged. When Christ became sin (imputation and substitution), God could justly judge His Son and render the death penalty (II Corinthians 5:21). Sin was imputed (reckoned, ascribed) to Him. It was charged to His account, as he was the author and occasion of it. He had reckoned to Him what was not really His (II Corinthians 5:18-21; Hebrews 2:14; 9:23-28; 8:3; I Peter 3:18; 2:21-24). He died, the just for the unjust, to bring us to God.

E. **Propitiation**

"Propitiation" means "the appeasement; to appease wrath." (Refer back to notes on Romans 3:24-25.) Christ is our propitiation. The wrath of broken law fell on Christ and God's wrath was appeased. Justice remained; holiness was upheld; wrath was appeased.

F. **Resurrection (Romans 4:25)**

The doctrine of substitution indirectly brings some questions to mind. If all this vicarious sacrifice for sin is so (and the Bible plainly declares it to be so), then how can it be? How can an innocent and righteous person (Christ) take another's sin and punishment? Is it right for God to lay hold on Christ and charge to Him the sin, guilt, and punishment of another? How can another be a substitute? How can the sinless die for the sinful? The innocent for the guilty? The just for the unjust? The righteous for the unrighteous? Is vicarious sacrifice right? How can God be just in punishing Christ for my sin? How can another die in the stead (place) of another? Why should Christ endure and suffer the wrath of a holy God against sin—our sin? Is this justice? Was this just for God to do this to His only Son? The answers lie in the fact that Christ, as the perfect man, did not need to come under judgment; however, when He was made sin, He had to be judged. This is divinely and gloriously the case. However, it does not altar the fact that Jesus Christ in Himself was righteous. In Himself, according to moral, civil, and ceremonial law, He was righteous. He Himself was just, yet He died for the unjust (I Peter 3:18).

Christ died for the ungodly. He who knew no sin became sin for us without having sin in Himself. He was made sin. Our Substitute died in our place. As far as man is concerned this fact leaves him free of the guilt and penalty of sin—another has died in his stead. By Christ's death, man is free of the penalty and demands of the broken law. However, for Christ, the righteous One, God must be just in this dealing with the innocent One. How? God proceeded to justify His Son in the resurrection! God raised Him from the dead! When God raised Him from the dead, Christ was justified, and God's righteousness and justice were displayed. Note:

- Justified in the Spirit (spirit) (I Timothy 3:16)
- Quickened by the Spirit. (I Peter 3:18; Romans 1:4)

God is just then in:

- Judging Christ in death when Christ was made sin for us.
- Raising Him from the dead by resurrection because He, in Himself, was an innocent, righteous substitute.

Now, God can be just and can be the Justifier of Him who beleives in Jesus. Christ died for us. Christ was also raised for us. "...[B]y His knowledge shall my righteous servant justify many..." (Isaiah 53:11). God can now present His Son to the world by the gospel that declares what His Son was, what He did, and how He became man's Substitute. Christ identified with mankind. Sin was imputed to Him and judgment noted out on Him. The demands of the law were satisfied in Him. God has dealt with sin in the representative man (Jesus). God's righteousness and justice have been manifested and displayed in Christ, both in His perfect, sinless life and in His perfect, vicarious death. God has justified Christ, the innocent One, by resurrection, and Christ now lives in the power of an endless life.

Christ is the incarnate Substitute—the crucified, buried, resurrected, ascended, and glorified Lord! Because of Him, all men may go free with no wrath of God and no penalty for sin placed on them. God offers a free pardon to men. It is *"gratis"*—for naught. It costs man nothing, but it cost God everything! No one can buy it, earn it, or in any way deserve it. None can work for it. It is freely bestowed; it is all of grace. It is "God's riches at Christ's expense" (Ian Thomas). Man may now be justified and be in right standing with God. Man is redeemed and ransomed, and God in Christ has avenged Satan. All men, judicially and legally, are set free from sin, guilt, and the punishment of sin—death. All may be justified. God Himself is Judge and is also the Justifier of men through Christ. Reconciliation for iniquity has been made (Daniel 9:24). However, all of this can only be received on God's terms—through the channel of faith!

Freedom from Sin (Romans 6:1-23)

Dead to Sin and Alive to God (Romans 6:1-14)

Verse 1: *"What shall we say then? Shall we continue in sin, that grace may abound?"*

"Shall we continue in sin, that grace may abound?" (Romans 5:20; Romans 6:14-15)

Shall we continue in sin that grace may abound? Some false teachers perverted the doctrine of the grace of God and taught others that the more one sins, the more he or she can experience the grace of God. They abused divine grace and used it as a reason to continue in sin. But Paul is quick to answer this false teaching (cf. Romans 3:4-8). Nowhere in the revelation of grace given to Paul in his writings does he make any allowance for continuing to live in sin. Before proceeding in Romans 6 to Paul's reasons why the believer cannot continue in sin, note the following:

- God's grace is freely bestowed on all that believe (Romans 3:24).
- The believer has access into this grace by faith (Romans 4:16; 5:2).
- The believer receives abundance of grace and the gift of grace, which is the gift of righteousness and the gift of eternal life (Romans 5:15, 17; 6:23).

- All men receive death through Adam's sin, but all men may receive life through Jesus Christ and his righteousness. Grace abounded where sin abounded, only much more.
- Grace can only reign through righteousness (Romans 5:21).

The apostle Jude warned against certain ungodly men who crept in sideways, while other were unaware, and turned (perverted and twisted) the grace of God into lasciviousness and all kinds of lusts (Jude 4). Paul told Timothy that the grace of God, which brings salvation, has appeared unto all men, teaching us that we are to:

- Deny ungodly lusts,
- Deny ungodliness,
- Live soberly,
- Live righteously,
- Live godly lives n this present world,
- Look for the blessed hope (Titus 2:11-14).

Any teaching contrary to this is false teaching and the abuse of God's grace, and it will be judged accordingly. God dealt with sin in Christ; otherwise, grace would not be presented to mankind.

Verse 2: *"God forbid. How shall we, that are dead to sin, live any longer therein?"*

A. "God forbid"
   "God forbid" is stated here emphatically as it is in Romans 6:14-15.

B. "How shall we, that are dead to sin, live any longer therein?"
   In this verse and the following verses, the key thought again is "death." Compare:
   - Death on Abraham, Sarah, and Isaac (the body, then resurrection) (Romans 4)
   - Death of Christ (Substitution) (Romans 5)
   - Death now for the believer (Identification) (Romans 6)

If a believer is "dead to sin," it is impossible for him or her to live in sin. If a person lives in sin, then he or she is not dead to it and knows nothing of the true grace of God. In Romans 5 and 6, there are two aspects that the death of Christ revealed (particular to Paul's epistles):

- Christ died for us (substitution, objective truth) (Romans 5).
- We died with Christ (identification, subjective truth) (Romans 6).

Note that the words "death" or "dead" are used about fifteen times Romans 6:2-11, 13, 16, 21, 23. Paul refers to the believer as being "dead to sin." In order to understand and appreciate the full significance of this expression, it is necessary to note the various aspects, meanings, and use of the word "death" in Scripture. Scripture speaks of the following:

1) **Physical Death** – means "the separation of the body from the soul and spirit" (Genesis 2:17; Romans 6:23). Adam died physically within "the day of the Lord" in which He sinned; that is, he died within the "one thousand year day" of the Lord's time. He lived 930 years physically (Genesis 5). Death entered by sin (Romans 5:12-21; I Corinthians 15:21-22). He died, and the death bell tolled for all mankind.

2) **Spiritual Death** – means "the separation of the soul and spirit from God, the source of all life." Adam died in spirit the moment he sinned (Genesis 2:17) (the "twenty-four hour day" of man). Mankind is often spoken of as being "dead in trespasses and sins" while living physically (Ephesians 2:1-3). Mankind is "dead while she liveth" in its present state—dead spiritually, dead in sins, dead to God (I Timothy 5:6; Colossians 2:13; I John 3:14; Ezekiel 18:4-32; 20; Ephesians 2:1-6).

3) **Eternal Death** – (Revelation 2:11; 20:6, 10-15; 21:8). Eternal death is called "the second death" and pertains to eternal, specific separation from God of the spirit and soul of man, as a naked, unclothed (disembodied) spirit being for all eternity. Eternal death is separation from God and His eternal presence and all that that means. This is "the worm that never dies" (Isaiah 66:24; Mark 9:44-48).

Death, in a natural sense, is not annihilation or a state of non-existence. It simply means separation of the various parts of man's triune being. However, there is also the aspect of death as used by Paul in relation to the believer. This aspect of death is also a spiritual state, and is spoken of here as being "dead to sin"; that is, separation from sinful living. The sinner is "dead in sin"—separated from God who is righteousness and life and separated to God from sin and death. Hence, the expression "dead to sin" speaks of the way that the believers' spiritual state is separated unto

God from the sin in which he formerly lived in. Note that Paul never states that "sin is dead to us" but that we are "dead to sin." The law of sin is still present in the believer, but it can be rendered inoperative as the believer walks after the higher law of the Spirit of Life (refer to Romans 8:1-2).

Verse 3: *"Know ye not, that so many of us as were baptized unto Jesus Christ were baptized into his death?"*

A. **"Know ye not"**
   "Know ye not" means "are you ignorant(?)."

B. **"Many of us as were baptized unto Jesus Christ were baptized into his death?"**
   The believer became "dead to sin" by being united with Jesus Christ—baptism into Christ. Baptism is immersion into His death. Note:

   • Baptism (spiritually) – immersion "into Christ," as the new creature, by new birth. The believer is placed "into Christ" as a new creation (II Corinthians 5:17) (regeneration).

   • Baptism (bodily) – immersion into the name of the Godhead bodily (the name of the Lord Jesus Christ) (Acts 2:34-38; Matthew 28:19-20; Mark 16:15-20; Hebrews 6:1-2) (water baptism).

   The believer sees in Calvary not only Christ's death for him or her, but also his or her death with Christ. The believer by spiritual union with Christ, enters into Christ's death, and in water baptism, testifies his or her identification with Christ's death. Thus, this verse, possibly in its fullness, involves baptism in regeneration and then in water baptism.

Verse 4: *"Therefore we are buried with him by baptism into death: that like as Christ was raised up from the dead by the glory of the Father, even so we also should walk in newness of life."*

A. **"Buried with him by baptism"** (Colossians 3:3)
   Baptism is also burial—burial of the old life. The outward symbol of the burial in water points to the real experience of burial in union with Christ. This is the second step (symbolized in water baptism) that should happen spiritually after the believer's union with Christ occurs. Baptism

also involves resurrection. Christ was raised up from the dead by the glory of the Father God. The believer is also raised up out of the water by the glory of God. Christ rose to walk "in newness of life." The believer also rises to walk "in newness of life," not in the oldness of the letter or in the old life.

B. "Baptism into" (cf. Matthew 28:19; I Corinthians 10:1-3)
As Israel was baptized *into* Moses—the mediator of the Old Covenant—so the believer is baptized *into* Christ—the mediator of the New Covenant (Galatians 3:27).

C. "Glory of the Father"
"The glory of the Father" means "the power which God manifested by the Holy Spirit when He raised Christ from the dead."

D. "Walk in newness of life" (cf. John 11:9; I John 1:6; III John 4; Luke 11:33)
"Walk" means "walk about, habitual conduct." Believers walk. (Refer to Ephesians on "walk.") Newness of life is imparted at regeneration.

Verse 5: *"For if we have been planted together in the likeness of his death, we shall be also in the likeness of his resurrection. . ."*

A. Baptism
Thus, baptism is into His:
1) Death (the Cross) (Romans 6:3)
2) Burial (the tomb) (Romans 6:4)
3) Resurrection (the empty tomb) (Romans 6:5). Resurrection comprehends the three days and three nights of the work of the Cross (the sign of Jonah).

B. "Planted"
"Planted" means "as planting and growing together." If in the likeness of His death, we shall also (more fully) be in the likeness of His resurrection, when the time comes for that physically. In this verse, the spiritual is symbolized by the physical (I Corinthians 4:15; Colossians 2:5)—as a seed is planted to come to new life, so we are planted with Christ.

Verse 6: *"…Knowing this, that our old man is crucified with him, that the body of sin might be destroyed, that henceforth we should not serve sin."*

A. **Expressions of Paul Used in Romans, Relative to the Believer**

It is important to understand the various expressions Paul uses in Romans relative to the believer in Christ. Note:

"In Adam" – refers to "the First Adam, the old man; the body of sin, the flesh, the living soul."

"In Christ" – refers to "the Last Adam, the second man; the Lord from heaven, the new man, the Spirit quickening."

"The old man" – Referring to "the Adamic man; the oldest man, or the first man and his nature which is passed on to all men" (Ephesians 4:22-24; Colossians 3:9-10) (cf. John 3:3; Titus 3:5). It also refers to "the old, unrenewed self." Paul figuratively views the Christian, before his union with Christ, as another person.

"The new man" – refers to "Christ, the new nature."

"The Body of Sin" – signifies "a corpse, the body in which sin expresses itself."

B. **"The body of sin"**

Vincent's *Word Studies in the New Testament* has this to say concerning the Greek expression, *"soma tas amartias,"* meaning "body of sin":

- Of the living human body (Romans 4:19; I Corinthians 6:13; 9:27; 12:12-26)

- Of the church as the body of Christ (Romans 12:5; I Corinthians 12:27; Ephesians 1:23; Colossians 1:18) (In the Greek, never *sarz*, meaning "flesh," in this sense)

- Of plants and heavenly bodies (I Corinthians 15:37, 40)

- Of the glorified body of Christ (Philippians 3:21)

- Of the spiritual body of risen believers (I Corinthians 15:44)

Generally, the phrase "the body of sin" speaks of the outward organ for the execution of the good or bad resolves of the will. It denotes "belonging to, or ruled by, the power of sin, in which the members are instruments of unrighteousness" (Romans 6:13). It does not denote the body as containing the principle of evil in our humanity since Paul does not regard sin as inherent in and inseparable from the body (cf. Romans 6:13, II Corinthians 4:10-12; 7:1; Matthew 15:19).

Sin is conceived of as the master—that to which the body belongs as a slave and is obedient to execute its will. The body is to be the slave to Jesus, not the slave to sin's mastery. The flesh itself is not sinful (hands, feet, eyes, etc.) (cf. Matthew 6-7, the Sermon on the Mount). Sin dwells within every person (Romans 7:18). Either the body, or its members, will be slave to sin or to Jesus within.

G.R. Carlson says that there were two kinds of slaves: those captured in war and those born as slaves. Paul uses the figure of those who were born as slaves in this verse. By nature, we were born as slaves to Satan and to sin. Now, we are no longer slaves to Satan but servants of Christ.

C. "Destroyed" (Romans 3:3)

"Destroyed" means "made void, made without effect; loose, bring to naught, fail, vanish away, put away, put down, abolish,· cease, to make inert, or idle, make inefficient, rendered inoperative, or inactive." Just as when the body of Jesus was crucified, died, and was rendered inoperative, inactive, and inert, so the believer's body of sin should be the same because of his or her union with Christ (in His death, no longer serving sin but serving Jesus).

D. "Crucified with Him"

Note again:

- His crucifixion for us (substitution) (Romans 5)
- Our crucifixion with Him (identification) (Romans 6)

Paul's revelation of the Cross is twofold, involving Christ's crucifixion for us ("He died for us" [substitution]) and our crucifixion with Him ("we died with Him" [identification]) (Galatians 2:20; 5:24; Romans 6:6, 11). The old man, the self-nature, is totally depraved and cannot be improved by educational or cultural environment. It has to die. Selfism is the very essence of sin. Love of self and self-will is opposite to God's will. Selfism is making a god of self. G. Christian Weiss, in *The Perfect Will of God* (Chapter 15), says concerning crucifixion:

- Crucifixion is an unnatural death. The flesh, or old man, will not die a natural death or die of old age. It actually resists death. Self will not die. It has to be put to death.
- Crucifixion is a criminal death. It is a death of agony, shame, and judgment. It is never for the innocent or law-abiding citizen but for the unrighteous—not the righteous.

- Crucifixion is a painful death. It is one of the most terrible deaths ever invented. Painless crucifixion is not possible. The more a crucified man resists his inevitable death, the more his suffering and torture will be. He must resign himself to death.
- Crucifixion is a slow death. A man may be crucified and linger for three days or more, reviling, cursing, swearing, pleading, and demanding release. When the Romans crucified a man, the death was recorded that same day, not the actual day when death occurred. A man was "reckoned dead" the moment he was crucified.

Verse 7: *"For he that is dead is freed from sin."*

"He that is dead is freed from sin"
This literally means "he that hath died" in a physical sense. Note that the physical truth points to the spiritual truth. "Freed" means "justified, acquitted, absolved."

Verse 8: *"Now if we be dead with Christ, we believe that we shall also live with him..."*

If we be dead with Him, we shall live with Him.
The believer's identification with Christ (his union with Christ) is noted throughout Romans as seen below:
- Crucified with Him (Romans 6:6)
- Died with Him (Romans 6:3, 8)
- Buried with Him (Romans 6:4)
- Planted Together with Him (Romans 6:5)
- Raised with Him (Romans 6:4-5)
- Alive with Him (Romans 6:8) (cf. also Ephesians 2:5-6 [togetherness]). The believer is alive with him spiritually first, then bodily, and eternally later on.

At the Cross, Jesus Christ took up in Himself every member of Adam's fallen race, and all sin was judged by death. The believer is to see Christ's death not only as substitution (for him or her), but also as identification (with him or her).

As we were all "in Adam" when he came under sin and death, so we were "in Christ" at Calvary's tree. That is:

- When Christ was crucified, the believer was crucified.
- When Christ died, the believer died.
- When Christ was buried, the believer was buried.
- When Christ arose, the believer arose.
- When Christ ascended, the believer ascended.
- When Christ also sat down in the throne with all things being under His feet, the believer also sat down in the throne and all things are under the believer's feet.
- When Christ lives, and as He lives, so the believer lives.

As a member of Christ's body, everything that happened to every physical member of Christ's body shadows forth that which happened, in God's mind, to every believing member of the spiritual body of Christ. This is because the believer is "in Christ" and is the same principle as Romans 5:12. As a sinner "in Adam," man died in sin and inherited "in Adam" all that Adam brought in sin, sickness, and death. As a believer "in Christ," man can die to sin and inherit "in Christ" all that Christ brought in righteousness, health, and life. God sees the whole world in either of these two men—Adam or Christ, the two representative men, and the two federal heads of the old creation race and the new creation race. Men are either "in Adam" or "in Christ." We believe that we shall also live with Him:

- In this life by spiritual resurrection.
- In the life to come by physical resurrection (if physical death takes place).

Verse 9: *"...Knowing that Christ being raised from the dead dieth no more; death hath no more dominion over him."*

"Death hath no more dominion over him"

(Cf. resurrection [II Corinthians 4:10].) Christ lives in the power of an endless life (Hebrews 7:21-27). Death can no longer claim Him; He died to death to die no more. He has the keys of death and hades (Revelation 1:18). He has conquered death, so death has no power over the believer when raised, first spiritually and then physically.

Verse 10: *"For in that he died, he died unto sin once: but in that he liveth, he liveth unto God."*

"He died unto sin once: but in that he liveth"
- "He died unto sin" (negative, death) (Romans 5). He died *for* sin (substitution).
- "He liveth unto God" (positive, resurrection) (Romans 6). He died unto sin (separation).

Verse 11: *"Likewise reckon ye also yourselves to be dead indeed unto sin, but alive unto God through Jesus Christ our Lord."*

A. "Likewise"

"Likewise" means "in similar manner." As Jesus is, so now is the believer.

B. "Reckon"

Note the Greek translations of the word "reckon":
- Greek: *Logizomai* means "to take an inventory (estimate [literally or figuratively]), to conclude, account, etc."
- Greek: *Legos* means "something said (including the thought); by implication, also reasoning (the mental faculty); to count it done, reckon on it." "Reckon" means "to not imagine or count something true that is not true" (cf. Romans 4:17).

Note the following diagrams on "dead to sin" and "alive unto God":

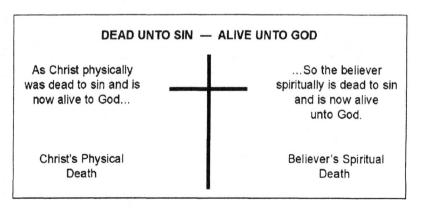

DEAD UNTO SIN — ALIVE UNTO GOD

As Christ physically was dead to sin and is now alive to God...

...So the believer spiritually is dead to sin and is now alive unto God.

Christ's Physical Death

Believer's Spiritual Death

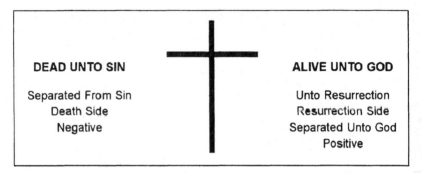

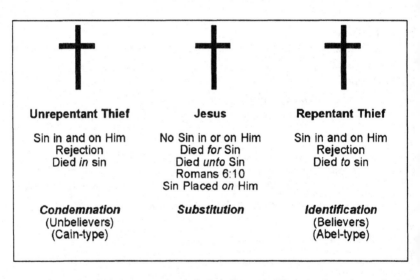

Thus, we have two sides of the Cross. The death side and the resurrection side. As seen above, the three crosses on Calvary illustrate this as well (*Sanctification* by T.C. Hegre).

Verse 12: *"Let not sin therefore reign in your mortal body, that ye should obey it in the lusts thereof."*

A. "Let not sin therefore reign"
    Sin cannot reign as king over us. Note:
    • Death reigned (cf. Romans 5:14, 17).
    • Sin reigned (Romans 6:12).

The believer is to allow Christ, as King, to reign over him or her. (Note "reign in life" in Romans 5:17 and "grace reigns" in Romans 5:21.) Christ, in grace, should be reigning through righteousness in the believer's life. Sin should not be reigning unto death.

B. **"In your mortal body"**
   The mortal body is a "death doomed body." Although Christ Jesus lives in the believer, the believer's body is still mortal and is the "body of our humiliation" (Philippians 3:21) (our vile body, the physical body). The law of sin has not yet been eradicated from the believer. The believer still has a mortal body that is subject to physical death. Physical death is the last enemy to be destroyed. Hence, there is the constant need for the reckoning of one's self "dead to sin" and for not letting sin reign therein. (Romans 8:1-2 will answer this.)
   There are now two laws within the believer. Does the "law of sin" reign in the body and its members, or does the "law of the Spirit of life" reign? The mortal body does not become immortalized until God's appointed time (I Corinthians 15:53-57; I Thessalonians 4:13-18). Mortality will, one day, put on immortality (II Corinthians 5:1-8).

C. **"Obey it in the lusts thereof"** (cf. Romans 7:5, 7, refer to notes)
   All outward or inward expressions of sin can be traced to lust—"an inordinate desire to have that which is forbidden or unlawful to have." Which law are we obeying and allowing to rule and reign in our bodies, bodily members, and bodily appetites?

Verse 13: *"Neither yield ye your members as instruments of unrighteousness unto sin: but yield yourselves unto God, as those that are alive from the dead, and your members as instruments of righteousness unto God."*

A. **Identification with Christ's Death and Resurrection Life**
   Note the order of appropriation in identification with Christ's death and resurrection life.
   "Knowing" – (Romans 6:3, 6, 9) means "not to be ignorant." In Romans 6:3, this word is translated from the Greek word, *agnoite*, meaning "not knowing." In Romans 6:6, it is translated from the Greek word, *ginoskontes*, meaning "to know by experience." In Romans 6:9, it is translated from the Greek word, *eidotes*, meaning "to know by reason of study or observation." "Knowing" is referring to "knowing

truth in its judicial and experiential sides." The fact is done in God's mind at the Cross in Christ. It is a fact there. Faith is the channel of receiving of the Spirit's work. God wants to do in us, by the Spirit, all that Christ did for us at Calvary.

"Reckoning" – (Romans 6:11). In regard to Christ's death and resurrection, "reckoning" is counting on God's Word that it is done at the Cross, accounting it as God's Word spoken.

"Let not sin reign" – (Romans 6:12). This is not the body, but that which law reigns over or in it.

"Yield not" – (Note the use of "yield not" in Romans 6:12-13, 16, 19.) "Yield not" signifies not yielding to temptation, for yielding is sin (Hymn). Temptation is not sin; yielding is. The same members of the body—members which are instruments to be used—once used in the expression of sin and its lusts (appetites of the body), have now become instruments used in righteousness unto God.

Note the comparison below:

Negative:
- Yielding My Members
- As Instruments
- Of Unrighteousness
- Unto Sin
- As Mortal (Dying) Yet Alive

Positive:
- Yielding My Members
- As Instruments
- Unto Righteousness
- Unto God
- As Alive From the Dead

B. **"Yield"**

"Yield" means "put at the service of." (Cf. "present"; cf. Luke 2:22; Acts 9:41; Romans 12:1; Colossians 3:5.) Physical members are a symbol of the moral, of which they are the instruments.

C. **"Instruments"**

The members of the body are instruments for good or evil use (Romans 6:13). The term is used of instruments or tools from earliest times—

ship's tackle, blacksmith tools, implements of war, and (especially in the New Testament) instruments of war (II Corinthians 6:7; 10:4). Instruments of war were used by warring kings (cf. Romans 6:12, 14). "Reign" means "to have dominion over; warfare." Sin is a spiritual law and needs a man, who has a body (an instrument), to express itself. The heart of the whole matter concerns yielding the body's members as an instruments to the reigning law (king)—grace or sin.

D. **"Yield yourselves unto God, as those that are alive from the dead, and your members as instruments of righteousness unto God"**

Myer Pearlman, in *Knowing the Doctrines of the Bible* (p. 108), says that there are five important instincts or laws of man's being. Animals have instincts. Man also has instincts, but also has God given laws to govern those instincts. Man has a conscience which animals do not have. Note the five important instincts of man's being below:

1) The Law of Self-Preservation – warns of danger and enables us to care for ourselves. Sins that are relative to this basic instinct would be selfishness, sensitiveness, anger, and jealousy.

2) The Law of Acquisition – refers to the act of "getting," which leads us to acquire the necessities of self-support—as with Adam in Eden. Sins that are relative to this instinct would be stealing and covetousness.

3) The Law of Appetite – refers to the food-seeking instinct or an impulse that leads to the satisfying of natural hunger. Sins that are relative to this would be gluttony and over-indulgence.

4) The Law of Perpetuation – refers to the law of reproduction; that is, the reproductive instinct in us which brings about the perpetuation of the human race, even as Adam and Eve were given the mandate form God: "Be fruitful." Sins relative to this would be impurity, immorality in all of its forms or perversions. Note that the Lord told man to "be fruitful."

5) The Law of Dominance – refers to instinct dominance, which leads one to the exercise of self-assertion necessitated by one's calling and responsibilities. Adam was to have dominion. Sins that are relative to this law would be tyranny and injustice.

All these instincts are seen in the creation of Adam. Sin is the abuse of all these God given laws or instincts within man. In other words, sin is the wrongful use of instruments to fulfill God-given instincts. The members of the body were used as instruments in taking the forbidden fruit of the Tree of Knowledge of Good and Evil in the Garden of Eden (Genesis 3:1-6). Taking the forbidden fruit was the wrong use of the body's instruments and a violation of the laws of God in man's being. Each of the five senses—hands, feet, ears, mouth, tongue, and mind—were used as instruments of sin in responding to Satan's temptation. Eve yielded her members unto unrighteousness.

These members cannot be and are not evil of themselves. Matthew 5:29-30 confirms this fact when it establishes this principle: "if the eye or the hand or any other member offends you, then cut it off" (paraphrased). However, cutting off a part of the body physically does not solve the problem. It is the law of sin within man that is the problem, not the actual physical members of the body. The members of the body are just instruments.

Note this fact in regards to sex. It can be an instrument for good or evil. "...[P]rofitable for thee that one of they members should perish, and not that thy whole body should be cast into hell" (Matthew 5:27-30; 15:18-19). "...Abstain from fornication: That every one of you should know how to posses his vessel in sanctification and honour..." (I Thessalonians 4:3-5). Amputating a member of the physical body might not solve the problem of lust within.

When Christ died every member of His body died. When He arose every member of His body arose. All His members were alive to God. In like manner, the believer must mortify the members of his or her body and those inordinate desires must be crucified. Then the believer must yield his or her bodily members as instruments unto God. The body then becomes a living sacrifice to do God's will (Romans 12:1). Instead of yielding his or her body members unto unrighteousness, the believer's bodily members become instruments of righteousness. Yielding and presenting ourselves to God needs to become a daily habit, a habit of self-devotion to God once and for all.

Verse 14: *"For sin shall not have dominion over you: for ye are not under the law, but under grace."*

A. **"Sin shall not have dominion over you"**

Paul is clear that the believer can live a victorious life in Christ. Sin does not need to have dominion (reign as king) over the believer. Sin has no need of dominion over the believer; the believer can have dominion over sin instead. This is not to say that the believer is now in a state of "sinless perfection," but rather that the believer no longer needs to be ruled or dominated by sin. If the believer sins, there is an Advocate available with the Father in the person of Jesus Christ and His cleansing blood (I John 1:7-9; 2:1-2). The believer does not have to continually live or practice sin. Sin shall not have dominion over the believer because Jesus Christ has dominion over sin and over the believer.

B. "Not under law, but under grace"

Undoubtedly, one of the most abused, misunderstood, and misused passages of Scripture and of all of Paul's writings is this passage. What does Paul mean when he states that the believer is "not under law, but under grace"? Being under grace has almost become synonymous with being "lawless." The subject of law will be fully dealt with in Romans 7-8.

Sufficient for the present is to say that grace is not lawlessness. The believer is not under the law (that is, the dominion of the law of sin as the context is dealing with). Nor is the believer under the law to Moses (as Romans 7 shows), but the believer is under grace, which is actually being "under the law to Christ" (note I Corinthians 9:20-21). Grace is a higher and stronger law. The laws of the kingdom in the Sermon on the Mount also show this (Matthew 5-7).

Freedom from Sin and Servants of Righteousness (Romans 6:15-23)

Verse 15: *"What then? shall we sin, because we are not under the law, but under grace? God forbid."*

(Refer again to Romans 6:1-2.) Sin is lawlessness (I John 3:4). Shall we sin (be lawless) because we are not under the law (of Moses)? God forbid! Shall we sin because we are under grace and have received the free gift of righteousness? God forbid! The very purpose of grace is to teach us how to live wholly for God in this present evil world (Titus 2:15; II Corinthians 7:1).

Verse 16: *"Know ye not, that to whom ye yield yourselves servants to obey, his servants ye are to whom ye obey; whether of sin unto death, or of obedience unto righteousness?"*

A. **"Servants"**

Note the use of the word "servant" in Romans 6:16-17, 19-20, 22. Every one is someone's servant—someone's slave. Everyone is under some master.

Note the diagram below.

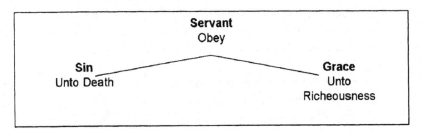

B. **"Obedience unto righteousness"** (cf. Romans 1:5-6; 5:19; 16:26)

By one man's disobedience many were constituted sinners, and by one man's obedience many shall be made righteous. Jesus died to bring us back to the obedience from which Adam fell—back to the obedience of faith. (Note also the word "obey" in Romans 6:12, 16-17; 5:17. Study the following Scriptures on the importance of obedience (Hebrews 5:8-9; II Thessalonians 1:8; Hebrews 2:2-3; Ephesians 5:6; Deuteronomy 11:28; Matthew 7:24; I Samuel 15:22; Exodus 19:5-6; Jeremiah 7:21-28; I Peter 1:2). Christ is the author of eternal salvation unto all who obey Him. If a person fails to live in a state of continual obedience to God and His Word, then he is not accepted by God in faith-righteousness. Obedience is the final test, as it was for Adam in the Garden of Eden.

Verse 17: *"But God be thanked, that ye were the servants of sin, but ye have obeyed from the heart that form of doctrine which was delivered you."*

"Ye were the servants of sin, but ye have obeyed from the heart that form of doctrine which was delivered you"

Man is either a servant to one ethical principal or the other. Whichever one is chosen is the master, and that person becomes the servant or slave of that ethical principle (Matthew 6:24; 7:18). Obedience is the true antithesis of sin, since sin is disobedience and righteousness is life. Note: "...sin unto death, or of obedience unto [life] righteousness?" (Romans 6:16). The choice is between the Tree of Knowledge of Good and Evil and the Tree of Life. Obedience or disobedience determined death or life (Genesis 2:17; 3:1-6). Note:

- Servants of Sin (Romans 6:17)
- Servants of Righteousness (Romans 6:18)

"From the heart"(1:21) – means "internal, not merely the letter or external." Only truth obeyed is truth experienced.

"Form of doctrine" – means "form of teaching" (cf. I Peter 5:3). Note: Pauline type of teaching in contrast to Judaistic teachers (Paul's gospel in Romans 2:16; 16:25).

"Delivered you" – refers to "that to which you were delivered," not "delivered to you" (Vincent). In speaking to the Romans, Paul is referring to being handed over to the educative power of this form of teaching.

Verse 18: *"Being then made free from sin, ye became the servants of righteousness."*

"Made free"
(Refer to notes on Romans 6:7 and 8:1.) "Made free" means "free from the old master (sin); one can now serve the new master (Christ)."

Verse 19: *"I speak after the manner of men because of the infirmity of your flesh: for as ye have yielded your members servants to uncleanness and to iniquity unto iniquity; even so now yield your members servants to righteousness unto holiness."*

A. **"I speak after the manner of men because of the infirmity of your flesh"**
Figures of slaves, bondage, service, etc. are used to convey the truth of what Paul wants to get across. This is on the ground of their imperfect spiritual comprehension (cf. II Corinthians 2:6; I Corinthians 3:1-2).

B. **"For as ye have yielded your members servants to uncleanness and to iniquity unto iniquity; even so now yield your members servants to righteousness unto holiness"**

Note the following words:

"Yielding" – Refer to notes on Romans 6:13, 16, 19.

"Members" – means "the parts of the body, instruments for good or evil use."

"Iniquity unto iniquity" – refers to "a continuing state of iniquity, perverseness, lawlessness" (I John 3:4).

Men are either servants of righteousness—free from sin (Romans 6:18) (unto holiness) or servants of sin—free from righteousness (Romans 6:20). This is determined by which one they yield to.

Verse 20: *"For when ye were the servants of sin, ye were free from righteousness."*

(Cf. Romans 6:18.) Whose servants or slaves are we?

Verse 21: *"What fruit had ye then in those things whereof ye are now ashamed? for the end of those things is death."*

"Fruit" (Romans 1:13)

Bad fruit can only come from a bad tree (Matthew 7:16-20). Death (corrupt fruit) comes from a corrupt tree.

Verse 22: *"But now being made free from sin, and become servants to God, ye have your fruit unto holiness, and the end everlasting life."*

"Ye have your fruit unto holiness, and the end everlasting life"

- "Fruit" – the end—death (sin) (Romans 6:21)
- "Fruit" – the end—everlasting life (holiness) (Romans 6:22; Matthew 7:16-20)

The symbol of a fruit tree is used in either a good or evil sense. Good fruit or corrupt fruit is the evidence of inward righteousness or inward corruption of the tree. If the root is holy, the fruit should be holy. If the root is corrupt, so is fruit. The believer is likened figuratively to a tree—producing either good fruit or bad fruit (Psalm 1; James 3:12).

Verse 23: *"For the wages of sin is death; but the gift of God is eternal life through Jesus Christ our Lord."*

A. **"Wages of sin is death"**

"Wages" means "cooked meat, provisions; money is also seen here" (Vincent). Sin is like a lord who pays his servants wages.

B. **"Gift of God is eternal life"**

(Note: "charisma.") Eternal life is a free gift (in vivid contrast to wages) through Jesus Christ our Lord—Jehovah's anointed Savior. Man receives the wages of sin or the gift of life, depending on whom he serves (Romans 4:4).

Summary (Romans 6)

Romans 6 is referring to sanctification of the believer, Romans 4 is referring to justification, and Romans 5 is referring to identification of Christ in death as our substitutionary sacrifice. Romans 6 is our identification with Him and, therefore, our sanctification—the setting apart of our members to serve Christ. Sanctification is not eradication. Eradication is not the teaching of Scripture (I John 1:8). Sin is not dead to us, but we are to reckon ourselves dead to sin. Sanctification is not suppression either. Sanctification is the operation of the new law of life in us (the higher spiritual laws), which make us free from the law of sin and death. (Refer to Romans 8:1-2 for a fuller exposition.) The fruition of justification is sanctification, and the full fruition of sanctification will be our glorification (Romans 8:26-30).

Freedom from the Law of Moses (Romans 7:1-6)

In this chapter, the key words undoubtedly are "law" (in its various aspects) (23 times), "I" (33 times), and "sin" (15 times). In contrast, the words "Christ" (two times) and "Holy Spirit" (one time) are mentioned only briefly. Thus, the chapter is based upon the struggling "I" in relation to the "law." Paul has already spoken of the law in a number of places in the previous chapters; however, in this chapter and through Romans 8:1-4, the apex of his argument on this matter is found. In Romans 7, Paul gets to the very heart of the problem in man—the law of sin, the sin principle, in relation to other laws.

- Romans 6 – The believer is "dead to sin" (the law of sin) (Romans 6:2).
- Romans 7 – The believer is "dead to the law" (the law of Moses; that is, externalism) (Romans 7:4).

Verse 1: *"Know ye not, brethren, (for I speak to them that know the law,) how that the law hath dominion over a man as long as he liveth?"*

"The law hath dominion over a man as long as he liveth"
Paul, speaking to the Jews who are familiar with the law, says that the law has dominion, reign, and mastery over a person as long as he or she lives.

Verse 2: *"For the woman which hath an husband is bound by the law to her husband so long as he liveth; but if the husband be dead, she is loosed from the law of her husband."*

The Believer Free From the Law
Here, Paul uses the figure of marriage and the law of marriage (as under the law of Moses and before) to illustrate the truth of the believer being free from law. (Note that this analogy must not be pressed too far or beyond the limits of its purpose here.)

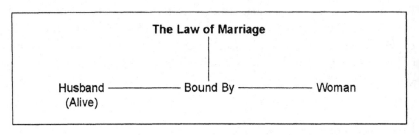

In marriage, each person is bound to the other by the law of marriage. Note how the Jewish mind would be familiar with this figure of marriage. The Old Testament prophets used it much (cf. Isaiah 54:1-2; Jeremiah 3; Ezekiel 16, 23; Hosea 1-3). The marriage of the prophet Hosea was also a symbolic marriage of the Lord God to His people Israel under the law.

Verse 3: *"So then if, while her husband liveth, she be married to another man, she shall be called an adulteress: but if her husband be dead, she is free from that law; so that she is no adulteress, though she be married to another man."*

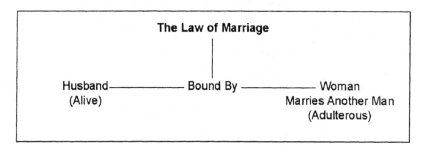

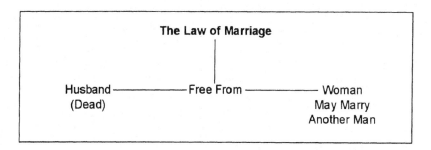

Note:

"Bound" – If the husband is alive, his wife is bound to him (under subject to him).

"Loosed" – If the husband is dead, the wife is free and is released to marry another husband. She is discharged. Her legal connection with him is now annulled (cf. Deuteronomy 23:1-4). If a wife divorces and then marries another man (or gets divorced again), she cannot return to her former husband, for that is an abomination to the Lord (cf. Israel, wife of Jehovah [adulterous and, therefore, He divorced her].)

Verse 4: *"Wherefore, my brethren, ye also are become dead to the law by the body of Christ; that ye should be married to another, even to him who is raised from the dead, that we should bring forth fruit unto God."*

A. The Marriage Analogy

In referring to the analogy of marriage in this verse, Vincent says, "the figure is a bit awkward." This is true, and the analogy should not be pressed beyond its limits. The whole point of the passage is the dissolving of the marriage tie by death. In relating this to the believer being free from the law, questions arise: who or what dies—the law, Christ, or us? The law did not die. Christ died, and we died with Him. Thus, being separated from the former husband of sin, we now can be married to the risen Christ. In relation to the Jews we may say:

- **The old husband is the law of sin.** Israel (the Jews) is bound to the law (of Moses, of sin). Israel is an adulterous person if she is involved with another man. The old husband could also signify the old man.

- **The new husband is the grace of Christ, the risen Christ.** The believer is married to Christ now. The believer died to the law (of Moses, of sin) at the Cross. The believer died to the old husband and the old husband became as dead to her. She is no longer under his dominion or rule. She is under a new rule now. She has a new husband (the new man) and the law of love.

Marriage ties are dissolved by death. The believer died with Christ and identified with His death. So the old husband no longer has claim over the believer. Remember, it does not say "the law died" but "we died to the law." This death dissolves legal obligation. This is the main point of the analogy. *J.F. & B. Commentary* says, "We were crucified with Christ, not the law. This death dissolves our marriage obligation to the law, leaving us at liberty to contract a new relation—to be joined to the risen One, in order to come to spiritual fruitfulness."

Christ died and arose. We died with Him and arose. So now we may be married to each other in spiritual union. The believer is married to Christ, in this sense, even now. The ultimate aspect of the marriage of Christ and the church comes later (Revelation 19:7-8; Ephesians 5:23-32). The whole purpose is to "be married to another," not just to be loosed from a former husband.

B. **"Fruit unto God"**
The whole purpose of marriage is offspring. The figure of marriage is continued as this verse refers to "fruit unto God." The spiritual fruit of such union should be fruit unto holiness. (Note "fruit" in Romans 6:21-22; 7:4-5.) "...Be fruitful, and multiply..." (Genesis 1:26-29). There is fruit unto shame and death (unto death; union with sin and the old husband), and, likewise, there is fruit unto holiness and everlasting life (union with Christ, the new husband) (Galatians 5:22-23; John 15:1-15).

Verse 5: *"For when we were in the flesh, the motions of sins, which were by the law, did work in our members to bring forth fruit unto death."*

A. **"In the flesh"**
"In the flesh" is a much-misunderstood expression. Vincent says the following concerning this expression. It is used:

- In the physical sense (Romans 14:21; I Corinthians 8:13). (Flesh of sacrificed animals, fleshly [II Corinthians 3:3])
- Of our kindred (denoting natural or physical relationships) (Romans 1:3; 9:3, 8; 11:14; Galatians 4:23, 29; I Corinthians 10:18; Philippians 16). (Kindred, or of the same bodily substance)
- Of the whole human body itself (I Corinthians 6:16; 7:28; II Corinthians 4:11; 7:5; 10:3; Romans 2:28; Galatians 6:13). (One body, one flesh [Genesis 2:24; Ephesians 5:28, 31])
- Of living beings, generally (all flesh) (Genesis 6:12; Isaiah 49:26; 66:23; Romans 3:20; Galatians 2:16). (Flesh and blood [I Corinthians 15:50; Ephesians 6:12])
- Of the old man (Greek: *Sarx*, meaning "flesh") (either as a creature in his natural state apart from Christ, or the creaturely side or aspect of the man in Christ). Thus, "the flesh" would seem to be interchangeable with "the old man." Note: flesh has affections and lusts (Galatians 5:24), flesh has a will (Ephesians 2:3; Romans 8:6-7), flesh has a mind (Colossians 2:18), and flesh has a body (Colossians 2:11). "Flesh" is in contrast to "spirit" (Galatians 3:3, 19; 5:16-24; 6:8; Romans 8:4).

Flesh and spirit are, thus, antagonistic. Flesh is the human nature without the divine Spirit (the Holy Spirit). The flesh is the state of the creature before or in contrast with the reception of the divine element whereby he becomes a new creature in Christ. The term "the flesh" characterizes not merely the lower forms of sensual gratification but all the highest developments of the life estranged from God, whether physical, intellectual, or aesthetic (Vincent). Note:

- Paul does not identify flesh and sin. (Cf. "flesh" and "sin" [Romans 8:3; 7:17, 18; II Corinthians 7:1; Galatians 2:20].)
- Paul does not identify *sarx* with the material body, nor does he associate sin exclusively and predominantly with the body. The flesh is the flesh of the living man, animated by the soul (Greek: *Pshueche*), as its principle of life. The spirit, as well as the flesh, is capable of defilement (II Corinthians 7:1).
- Paul does not identify the material side of man with evil. The flesh is not the native seat and source of sin. It is only the organ and the seat of sin's manifestation. Matter is not essentially evil. Logical sense would be that no service to God would be possible if the flesh was evil (Romans 12:1). The flesh is not evil or sinful of itself, but as it has existed from the time of the entrance of sin through Adam, Paul recognizes it as being tainted with sin. Jesus appeared "in the flesh," yet He was sinless (cf. Romans 8:3; II Corinthians 5:21) (Vincent).

B. **"The motions of sins, which were by the law, did work in our members to bring forth fruit unto death"**
   "The motions of sins" – means "movements, sin in actions, motions, emotions or impulses of sin, sinful passions."
   "Did work" – means "wrought" (II Corinthians 4:12; Ephesians 3:20; Galatians 5:6; Colossians 1:29).
   "Which were by the law" – refers to "the law of sin inside us."
   "In our members, bring forth fruit unto death" – means "members of the body, instruments of sins expression" (cf. Romans 6:13, 19). Note: "...fruit...end...death" (Romans 6:21; also 6:22).

Verse 6: *"But now we are delivered from the law, that being dead wherein we were held; that we should serve in newness of spirit, and not in the oldness of the letter."*

A. **"Delivered"**
    "Delivered" refers to "discharged from the old husband or the old wife" (verse 2).

B. **"Held"**
    "Held" refers to "held down." Our old lives have died with Christ at the cross.

C. **"Serve in newness of spirit"** (cf. II Corinthians 3:6)
    We still serve, but we serve the new husband, Christ. The Spirit gives life.

D. **"Newness"**
    Because we are new creatures, all things become new (II Corinthians 5:17). The newness of the Spirit is signified in the *New* Covenant and the *spirit* of the law written on the tables of the heart (Hebrews 8:8-10; II Corinthians 3; Jeremiah 31:31-34).

E. **"Oldness of the letter"**
    "...The letter killeth..." (II Corinthians 3:6). "...Old things are passed away; behold, all things are become new" (II Corinthians 5:17). This phrase refers to the minute particulars of the legal observances of the letter of the law. The oldness of the letter is significant of the *Old* Covenant, and the *letter* of the law is significant of the law written on the tables of stone. (Cf. Romans 2:27; II Corinthians 3; Hebrews 8.)

Freedom from Condemnation (Romans 7:7 - 8:11)

The Law of God (Romans 7:7-12)

Verse 7: *"What shall we say then? Is the law sin? God forbid. Nay, I had not known sin, but by the law: for I had not known lust, except the law had said, Thou shalt not covet."*

(Refer to notes on Romans 3:20. By the law is the knowledge of sin. The law defines sin for man.)

A. Law and Conscience

One of the main purposes of the law was to clearly define sin to man. From Adam to Moses, man was governed by the law of conscience. One man's conscience was not the standard of law for another man's conscience. Hence, God brought in the law which defined sin, regardless of any high or low or corrupted standard of the law of conscience. No man can again argue against the law of God given to Moses at Sinai.

- Conscience: the internal law distinguishing right from wrong, but that is all.
- Law of Moses: the external law; the divine standard of righteousness.

The conscience may be seared, defiled, stifled, etc. Conscience is not the infallible standard for righteousness. Man needs the law—sin defined and God's standard of righteousness for man set forth. Thus, by the law, we have the knowledge of sin, the definition of sin. The law itself is *not sin* (cf. notes on verse 12 with Psalm 19:7-14); the law gives the knowledge of sin.

B. "Not known lust"

Paul's experience here is also representative of every person's experience. The following are various views of this passage under consideration. Some say:

- It is the struggle of the person regenerated endeavoring to overcome sin by his own strength;
- It is the experience of all Christians for their whole lives until they reach heaven;

- It is the experience of all believers until they have the second work of grace and experience "whole sanctification" or "eradication" of the sin principle;
- It speaks of the experience of the devout Jews in their attempt to keep the law which, if they could keep it, would give life.

Undoubtedly, there are measures of truth and application in each of the above views, but the first one is the most consistent view in the proper study of this chapter.

C. **"Lust"**

"Lust" is "coveting, inordinate desire, or desire for that which is not lawful" (cf. Mark 4:19). The word is not just referring to sexual lust, but a general sense of longing for forbidden things.

D. **"Covet"**

"Covet" is used in both a good and a bad sense in Scripture (Luke 22:15; Philippians 1:23; I Corinthians 14:1).

Note here that Paul especially goes back to the Ten Commandments and quotes one of them: the tenth (Exodus 20:1-7; Deuteronomy 5:1-5, 6-21). In these Scriptures, we have the Ten Commandments of the Mosaic Covenant, briefly defined as follows (Deuteronomy 4:10-13):

Man's Relationship to God
1) "Thou shalt have no other gods before me."
2) "Thou shalt not make unto thee any graven image..."
3) "Thou shalt not take the name of the Lord thy God in vain..."
4) "Remember the Sabbath day, to keep it holy."

Man's Relationship to Man
5) "Honour thy father and thy mother..."
6) "Thou shalt not kill [murder]."
7) "Thou shalt not commit adultery."
8) "Thou shalt not steal."
9) "Thou shalt not bear false witness against thy neighbour."
10) "Thou shalt not covet...any thing that is thy neighbour's."

As noted, Paul only quotes the tenth commandment, briefly, "Thou shalt not covet." There is a specific reason for this. When Paul quotes the tenth commandment, he is actually getting the root of the problem, the very law of sin!

The Ten Commandments are basically broken up into two groups, while the last commandment of the second group touches the very root of sin itself.

- The first four commandments deal with man's relationship to God.
- The last six commandments deal with man's relationship to man.

Touching the nine commandments, Paul could testify of his own experience that he was blameless, in external righteousness of the law. "...[T]ouching the righteousness which is in the law, blameless" (Philippians 3:6).

Paul could go down the list of commandments and boast that he had never had other gods beside the one true God (no idolatry), nor had he worshipped images. He had kept the Sabbath and hallowed God's name. In relation to man, he had honored his parents, had not murdered, or stolen, or bore false witness, or committed adultery.

But when Jesus Christ came and Christians multiplied, Paul was exposed to himself for what he was on the inside. It was revealed to him that he had but an external righteousness—Pharisaic righteousness. Hence, it was this tenth commandment which the Holy Spirit especially took up and used with Paul, for it is this tenth commandment that dealt with the very *root* (law, principle) of sin, while the others dealt with the fruit (expression) of sin. The nine broken commandments are simply the fruit of the inner root, the tenth commandment. Note:

- No person would worship other gods if he or she did not covet.
- No person would worship images unless he or she coveted.
- No person would kill, murder, steal, commit adultery, bear false witness, or dishonor his or her parents if that root of *lust* or *covetousness* was not on the inside.

The commandments of Moses deal with the sin outwardly, but the commandments of Jesus deal with sin inwardly. Note this in the Sermon on the Mount (Matthew 5-7). Jesus takes several of the commandments and gets to the very heart of the matter. For example, "Ye have heard that it was said by them of old time, Thou shalt not commit adultery: but I say unto you, That whosoever looketh on a woman to lust after her hath committed adultery with her already in his heart" (Matthew 5:27-28). Moses dealt with the act; Jesus dealt with the thought.

Note the word "lust" in the following Scriptures. Realize, in light of the significance of Paul's statement in verse 7, the reason that he chose the tenth commandment.

- "Lust" – (Greek: *Epithumia*) denotes strong desire of any kind, the various kinds being frequently specified by some adjective.
- "Good desire" – (Luke 22:15; Philippians 1:23; I Thessalonians 2:17, only)
- "Evil desire" – Everywhere else (Romans 6:12, 13:14); lusts of the flesh (Galatians 5:16, 24; Ephesians 2:3; II Peter 3:18; I John 2:16).

(Refer to *Vine's Expository Dictionary* and *New Englishman's Greek Concordance*: Numbers 1937, 1938, 1939, "Lust")

There is nothing wrong with God-given appetites, desires, and natural laws in man's being (refer to notes on "laws of man's being"), but the problem comes when those desires become inordinate and one begins desiring forbidden things. Note below:

- Satan (Lucifer) coveted, lusted to be "like God" (Isaiah 14:12-14; Ezekiel 28); thus, the Fall (John 8:44). Self-will is an expression exercised by the act of the will to satisfy an unlawful desire. In other words: lust. "Then when lust hath conceived..." (James 1:13-15).
- Adam and Eve coveted, lusted (inordinate desire, unlawful desire) after the Tree of Knowledge of Good and Evil. Thus enticed, drawn on by Satan, they lusted after the forbidden tree. The one law, the one commandment was then violated. "...Ye shall be as gods, knowing...a tree to be desired to make one wise...she [coveted, lusted] took" (Genesis 3:1-6).
- Achan saw (coveted, lusted) and took and hid the forbidden things of the spoils of war (Joshua 7).
- David followed the same pattern: coveted, lusted, committed adultery, and met with judgment (II Samuel 11-12).

Thus, each experience listed above contained "...the lust of the flesh, and the lust of the eyes, and the pride of life" (I John 2:16-17). The spirit, soul, and body are all affected by lust and in the examples above, fell. It cannot be over-emphasized that the very root, the very principle, of the law of sin is lust. Lust causes man's will to act contrary to the will and Word of God. Any expression of sin is simply the expression of lust in all its hideous and various evil or respectable forms.

Note again this word "lust" in the following Scriptures: Romans 1:18-32; I Corinthians 6:9-10; Galatians 5:19-21; Ephesians 4:22-32, 5:1-7. Note the lusts of the flesh and of the mind in these references: Romans 6:12, 13:14; Ephesians 2:3; I Timothy 6:9; II Timothy 2:22; Titus 2:12; James 4:1; I Peter 1:14, 2:11, 4:2; Jude 16-17; I Corinthians 10:16; Galatians 5:16.

"But every man is tempted, when he is drawn away of his own lust, and enticed. Then when lust hath conceived, it bringeth forth sin: and sin, when it is finished, bringeth forth death" (James 1:14-15). Thus, it is important to grasp the full meaning of Romans 7:7.

Verse 8: *"But sin, taking occasion by the commandment, wrought in me all manner of concupiscence. For without the law sin was dead."*

A. The Law and Sin

The relation of sin to law, or law to sin, is seen here. The law is not sin, but sin found occasion (Greek: *Aphormen*, meaning "a place to start, a starting point, a base of operations") (Vincent).

Sin took the law as a base of operations. Sin used the law as a point to start. Thus, "...of the Tree of Knowledge of Good and Evil, thou shalt not eat of it..." (Genesis 2:17), the commandment or law was used as a starting point on which sin could work (cf. Genesis 3:1-6). The temptation was when Satan grasped hold of the law (the commandment to Adam) and used it as a fulcrum, a point to stir up lust or "unlawful desire."

"Forbidden things become desirable to man. Because it is forbidden, he feels his freedom is limited and now his lusts rage more violently" (Vincent's quote of Thelouek).

B. "Without the law sin was dead [sin is inactive]"

- "...Where no law is, there is no transgression" (Romans 4:15).
- "...The law entered, that the offense might abound" (Romans 5:20).

Sin entered the world by one man and was in man. When God introduced the Ten Commandments, sin was aggravated into worse action. The law actually exposed man for what he was inside. Sin used the forbidden things, as in the Ten Commandments (as one commandment to Adam), to stir up lust, or unlawful desire, provoking the whole situation.

If a parent gives a commandment to his or her child by saying, "Do not touch the wet paint," that very commandment works on the child, and the law of sin (lust) makes the child want to touch that wet paint. In the same way, Satan used that one commandment of God to Adam and Eve to tempt Eve, to create in her unlawful desire (lust) for that which was forbidden. Without the law, sin was dead. There can be no sin if there is no law to transgress, "...for sin is the transgression of the law" (I John 3:4).

This proposes a problem. Would man have been better off without that law then? Did God have to give Adam and Eve a commandment or any law? Yes! Because God is a God of law, and His very nature commands conformity to law, otherwise there would be lawlessness in His creation, and sin is lawlessness (I John 3:4). The law is as necessary as God Himself is. It is essential to His own being and also to His creatures.

Verse 9: *"For I was alive without the law once: but when the commandment came, sin revived, and I died."*

Note the following statement:

"Referring to time of childlike innocence previous to the stimulus imparted to the inactive principle of sin by the coming of the law, when the moral self-determination with respect to the law had not taken place, and the sin principle was, therefore, practically dead" (Vincent).

Verse 10: *"And the commandment, which was ordained to life, I found to be unto death."*

A. **"The commandment, which was ordained to life"**

The commandment given to Adam was meant to be unto life: the Tree of Eternal Life (Genesis 2:17), and the commandments given to Israel were meant to be unto life. "Ye shall therefore keep my statutes, and my judgments: which if a man do, he shall live in them..." (Leviticus 18:5). "...The man which doeth these things shall live by them" (Romans 10:5). (See also Ezekiel 20:11, 13, 21; Galatians 3:12.) The tragedy was that Israel (man) did not realize his inability to do or keep the perfect law of God. God knew man's inability to keep it, but this was part of the purpose in giving the law to Israel. To expose man to himself and expose his own inability and incapability to keep it. Israel blatantly said, "...All that the Lord hath spoken we will do..." (Exodus 19:7-9, 24:1-8). Thus,

God actually let the nation demonstrate to itself and the whole world
man's utter inability to fulfill the Ten Commandments, and to thereby
inherit life. Thus, it was "death" (verse 11). The law could not give life
because of man's sinful flesh (Romans 8:3; Galatians 3:21).

"The commandment" – means "the specific one." "Thou shalt not
covet" (James 2:8; John 13:34).

B. "Sin revived" (verse 9)
   Sin did not come to life, as it was already there, but it lived again. Sin
lies dormant, until a commandment is given. The law stirs it up.
   G.R. Carlson says that the law reveals the fact (verse 7), the occasion
(verse 8), the power (verse 9), the deceitfulness (verse 11), the effect
(verses 10-11), and the sinfulness (verses 12-13) of sin (p. 57). The law
serves as a mirror to show man's need of washing.
   As noted in the comments on Romans 5:20, the nation of Israel, as a
whole, understood the difference between "grace" and "law."
   Grace was before law, during law, and after law. The deliverance of the
children of Israel was upon the basis of grace and faith. It was the grace
of God expressed in the Abrahamic Covenant that brought Israel forth
out of Egypt, the house of bondage. God sent Moses and Aaron to Israel
in Egypt. Passover, the parting of the Red Sea, the provision of manna
and water from the rock, etc., were all of grace through faith. The people
of Israel could do nothing of themselves to earn deliverance or to deliver
themselves. They could only trust the grace of God. However, when they
finally came to Sinai, they fell from grace to law. They were not satisfied
with grace and faith; they asked for law. They blatantly said, "…All that
the Lord hath spoken we will do…." Thus, God allowed them fifteen
hundred years to demonstrate to themselves and to the rest of the world
their inability to do so. He prepared them for grace personified in Christ
(John 1:17).

Verse 11: *"For sin, taking occasion by the commandment, deceived me, and by it slew
me."*

(Cf. Romans 8:8)

A. **"Sin"**

Sin, using the commandment as a starting point, deceived me into thinking I could keep it, and thus slew me. Sin wrought in me all manner of concupiscence (Genesis 3:1-3, took the commandment for a starting point); that is, all kinds of lusts and unlawful desires.

B. **"Deceived me"**

- Sin, using the commandment, wrought in me all kinds of lusts, evil desires, and unlawful desires.
- Sin deceived me, and by the commandment, slew me (cf. Genesis 2:17).

Note also "beguiled me" (II Corinthians 11:3) and "deceived" (II Thessalonians 2:3).

Verse 12: *"Wherefore the law is holy, and the commandment holy, and just, and good."*

(Also note Romans 7:14 with this verse.) Note Paul's description, and also the Psalmist's, of the law. See the following words:

- Holy
- Just
- Good
- Spiritual
- Perfect, Complete (cf. Psalm 19:7)

The same language is used of the law as of God Himself. The law must be like the Law-giver. God is holy, just, good, spirit, and perfect. Revelation of God's own character is in the law. Thus, it must be clearly stated that there is nothing wrong with the law in itself. This verse answers the query of Romans 7:7: the law is not sin. God forbid. The law is all these things mentioned above, so the problem is not the law of God.

The Law of Sin (Romans 7:13-23)

In this section we get to the very heart of the problem, as far as man is concerned. The problem is not the law of God; the problem is the law of sin in man.

Verse 13: *"Was then that which is good made death unto me? God forbid. But sin, that it might appear sin, working death in me by that which is good; that sin by the commandment might become exceeding sinful."*

A. **"Was then that which is good made death unto me?"**
No! The law is holy, just, good, spiritual, and perfect. So the problem is not with the law. (Note Amplified New Testament.) The law of God did not work death in man—only as the penalty. It was sin that worked death in man. Sin used the law of God, a good thing, as a weapon, in order that through the commandment sin might be clearly shown to be sin, that the extreme malignity and immeasurable sinfulness of sin might plainly appear. "...[H]ath God said, Ye shall not eat of every tree of the garden?" (Genesis 3:1-6; 2:17). Sin used this law as a weapon to start unlawful desires in man.

B. **"Exceeding"**
Greek: *Hyperbole*, literally means "a casting beyond" or "according to excess" (Vincent).

Verse 14: *"For we know that the law is spiritual: but I am carnal, sold under sin."*

A. **"The law is spiritual: but I am carnal"**
There is nothing wrong with the law. The problem is in man. Note:
"The law is spiritual" – The Jew knew the law was spiritual and was more than just the letter (I Timothy 1:8).
"I am carnal" – means "I am sold under sin" (cf. I Kings 21:20, 25; II Kings 17:17). The law is the expression of the Holy Spirit, who is spiritual. Man is carnal (Vincent).

The spiritual man is the man who walks by the Spirit, both in the sense of Galatians 5:16 and in the sense of Galatians 5:25, and he manifests the fruit of the Spirit. He shows evidence of spiritual growth and maturity.
"Carnal" in the Greek: Sarkinos, literally means "made of flesh." An unspiritual, material nature is described as "consisting of flesh." In the Greek the word *sarkitos*, from *sarx*, means "flesh"; it signifies the nature of the flesh (i.e., sensual, controlled by the animal appetites, governed by human nature, instead of the Spirit of God, having its seat in the animal nature, or excited by it). It is also defined as "pertaining to the flesh, bodily, temporal, animal, unregenerate, carnal, fleshly" (*Strongs* [SC4559]).

"Carnivorous" means "flesh eating." Unclean, carnivorous animals are unsuitable types of God's Christ, or His perfect spiritual nature, and are unfit for God's altar, as opposed to herbivorous animals and birds used in sacrifice for God's altar, which are symbolic of the nature of Christ.

B. "Sold under sin"
    "Sold under sin" refers to "sold as a slave, under the power of sin; sold out in and by Adam, as his unborn generations (cf. Romans 5:12 "in Adam"); sold to sin, sickness, disease and death, and Satan's kingdom of darkness."

Verse 15: *"For that which I do I allow not: for what I would, that do I not; but what I hate, that do I."*

A. "Allow"
    "Allow" means "to know."

B. "I," "My," "Me," "Myself"
    Note in this paragraph the use of the egocentric, self-centric personal pronouns.
    "I" – 33 times
    "My" – 5 times
    "Me" – 11 times
    "Myself" – 1 time

C. "For what I would, that do I not; but what I hate, that do I"
    This passage expresses the inner conflict of the believer (and the sinner). Various opinions, as already noted concerning this, deal with whether it refers to Paul's experience before salvation, as a religious Pharisee, or after his conversion. Whether it applies to the sinner, to the believer in Christ, or to the Jew under the law, is questionable (cf. John 3:21).
    The context seems to lend the weight to Paul's experience both under law, as a Jew, and also as a believer in Christ. This is an inward conflict, an inner battle. He did not really know the problem, for the things he did not want to do, the things he hated, he did. This does not sound like the experience of a sinner, but of a religious person, or (as human history confirms) the experience of most believers in Christ, if not all.

Verse 16: *"If then I do that which I would not, I consent unto the law that it is good."*

(Refer to the Amplified New Testament.) If Paul habitually did the good things, which are naturally contrary to his desire, then it means that he acknowledges and agrees with the law that is good (morally excellent), and he takes sides with it.

Verse 17: *"Now then it is no more I that do it, but sin that dwelleth in me."*

"Sin...dwelleth in me"

Here is the whole problem now. It is the *sin principle* within Paul that makes him do what he does. The law of sin within is greater than and stronger than the external law of God written on the tables of stone. Note the reference to "I." "I (ego), my personality proper, my moral self-consciousness which has approved the law (Romans 7:16) and has developed vague ideas for something better" (Vincent).

Verse 18: *"For I know that in me (that is, in my flesh,) dwelleth no good thing: for to will is present with me; but how to perform that which is good I find not."*

A. **"In me"**

"In me" refers to the entire man in whom sin and righteousness struggle, in whose unregenerate condition sin is victor, having its domain in the flesh. Hence, "in me" is considered "carnal" (Romans 7:14).

B. **"Will"**

Another element is introduced here, "the will (wish) to do good." However, it is the flesh that determines one's activity as an unregenerate man (Vincent). (Note: Vincent takes the view of this being the unregenerate.) Though the will (desire or wish) may be there, the flesh (carnal, law of sin) hinders the performance of that which is good (cf. Romans 7:25).

Verse 19: *"For the good that I would I do not: but the evil which I would not, that I do."*

This verse illustrates the conflict of good and evil within. Paul does not do the good, but does the evil (cf. Romans 7:15).

Verse 20: *"Now if I do that I would not, it is no more I that do it, but sin that dwelleth in me."*

The law of sin within is the problem (cf. Romans 7:17 again; Psalm 19:12).

Verse 21: *"I find then a law, that, when I would do good, evil is present with me."*

A. **"I find then a law"**
In the Greek, this actually refers to "the Law."

B. **"When I would do good, evil is present with me"**
This verse could be called "the Tree of Knowledge of Good and Evil" according to Pauline revelation (cf. Genesis 2:1-6, 9, 17). The Tree of Knowledge of Good and Evil, since the moment that man partook of its fruit, is now within man. Man knows good and evil, but can only do that which is evil. This was the deception in eating of the tree, in the temptation of the serpent to the woman, Eve. The verse could be freely translated, "I find then a *tree* (a law), that when I would do *good*, *evil* is present with me," for within the being of every man, woman, and child is the Tree (the law) of the Knowledge of Good and Evil. It is this tree within that is the crux of the problem in Romans 7.

Romans 7 could be called "the Tree of Knowledge of Good and Evil" within man. Before the Fall, the tree was external. After the Fall, the tree entered within man, in the eating of the fruit and within that fruit was the seed, here spoken of as "the Law" of the knowledge of good and evil.

(Note: "good and evil" as in verses 16, 19, and 21, with Genesis 3:1-6, "...ye shall be as gods, knowing good and evil.") Man certainly knows both, but how to perform the good he knows not. He does that which is evil because he is evil.

Verse 22: *"For I delight in the law of God after the inward man..."*

"The inward man"
This phrase refers to the *inner* man of the heart (II Corinthians 3:3). It is really inapplicable to the unregenerate or the unconverted man. Only the one who genuinely desires to serve the law of the Lord has any real delight (rejoicing) to do the will of God.

Verse 23: *"...But I see another law in my members, warring against the law of my mind, and bringing me into captivity to the law of sin which is in my members."*

A. **"Warring against the law of my mind"**

Here we see the conflict of the two laws—the law of God and the law of sin—and the conflict of the law of the mind, which is conscience (Romans 2:14-15). Note the spiritual, inner warfare of the old man, the flesh, and the laws therein (II Corinthians 10:4; II Timothy 2:26; Romans 8:5).

B. **"Law"**

Note the use of the word "law" in this chapter. Also note various other laws mentioned. "Commandment" is used six times.

1) The law (Romans 7: 1, 3-9, 12, 14, 16, 21)
2) The law of her husband (the law of marriage) (Romans 7:2)
3) The law of God (Romans 7:22)
4) The law in my members (Romans 7:23)
5) The law of my mind (i.e., conscience, moral sense of wrong and right) (Romans 7:23)
6) The law of sin (Romans 7:23, 25)

The whole problem is expressed here. There are laws at conflict within the believer, as well as within the sinner. The law of conscience takes sides with the law of God and condemns and convicts man, and the law of sin violates both the internal and external laws.

The law condemns man—conscience, internal, smites him. The external law of God condemns man also, leaving him powerless. The law of sin rules, preventing man from doing the good that he would and the evil that he would not.

C. **"Warring"**

"Warring" means "taking the field against" (Vincent). Warring occurs on the battlefield which is in the mind. "Mind" in the Greek is *nous*. The war is a battle of the mind. (Note II Corinthians 10:1-5.)

D. **"Captivity"**

"Captivity" refers to those taken captive as slaves after the battle (II Corinthians 10:5; Luke 4:18, 21:24). Jesus came to set captives free.

Verses 14-23: *Summary*

In verses 14-23, Paul deals with the heart of the problem. The problem, as noted, is not with the law of God, but within man himself. Man is carnal. Compare man and the law of God below.

The Law of God	The Fallen Man
• The Law is Holy	• Man is Unholy
• The Law is Just	• Man is Unjust
• The Law is Good	• Man is Evil
• The Law is Spiritual	• Man is Carnal
• The Law is Perfect	• Man is Imperfect

Thus, how can man, who is unholy, unjust, evil, carnal, and imperfect, keep that which is holy, just, good, spiritual, and perfect? It is impossible. This is the crux of the whole matter—the total depravity of man in spirit and body. The problem is in *man* himself, *not* in the law of God.

The Cry of the Wretched Man (Romans 7:24-25a)

Verse 24: *"O wretched man that I am! who shall deliver me from the body of this death?"*

(Cf. Romans 8:23)

A. **"O wretched man that I am!"**
   This is the cry of the wretched man. Originally, he became wretched through the exhaustion of hard labor (Vincent). God has been waiting for this cry from man after every self-effort has failed.

B. **"Body"**
   The body here refers to the literal and physical body. The body is the principal instrument which sin uses to enslave and destroy the soul. Instruments of the body are used for the expression of sin, so this is a cry for deliverance from the sin principle within.

C. "The body of this death"

This phrase is also noted as "from this body of death." Some suggest that it refers to the custom of a man who had a dead corpse tied to him and carried it around until exhaustion and death came to release him from that wretchedness. If so, it is a very appropriate figure to use here to illustrate this cry. The body signifies sin, corruption, mortality, death-doomed, stench, and instruments of sin unto death (Philippians 3:21, vile body).

Verse 25a: *"I thank God through Jesus Christ our Lord."*

"I thank God through Jesus Christ our Lord" (Romans 7:24)

This portion of verse 25 is the answer to the cry from verse 24, "Who shall deliver me?" The answer: deliverance certainly does not come through the manner of the sinner outside of Christ. Deliverance can only come through God in our Lord Jesus Christ.

The Law of the Spirit of Life (Romans 7:25b-8:1-11)

Verse 25b: *"So then with the mind I myself serve the law of God; but with the flesh the law of sin."*

A. "With the mind"

With the mind I serve the law of God. The conscience approves the law of God.

B. "With the flesh"

With the flesh I serve the law of sin. Recognize the two laws here, warring within man. This is simply Paul's recognition of the fact of the two laws at conflict here, and the law of sin in the flesh has the victory in the battle, and brings him into captivity, as a slave after the battle. This is not the cry of Paul because he is living sinfully.

What follows in Romans 8:1-2 gives the answer to his deliverance or the answer to the cry of the wretched man from verse 25a.

Romans 8: *The Doctrine of Law*

Because Romans 8 is the climax of the chapters on doctrine in the epistle, and the subject of "law" is the fundamental theme of the book, it will be profitable to digress into a rather full overview of the matter of "law" in the economy of God. It is the key to this epistle. Note that a law is a rule of conduct, or how things function or work.

A. **God Himself is the great Law-giver** (Isaiah 33:22).
God Himself is the source of all law or laws (universal laws, moral laws, etc.). All laws exist naturally in the Creator of the universe. God Himself is essentially law. He Himself is governed by the laws of His own being. These are unchangeable laws of His very nature. The royal law of God's nature is *love* (the law of love). He is governed by the laws of righteousness, holiness, and love. He is the living law.

The Law of Independence
The primary law of God's being is that He is the Self-existent One and, therefore, the Independent One. He does not owe His existence to another, nor does He have to depend on anything or anyone outside of Himself. He is the I Am. The source of life is in Himself. All others—creation and creatures, angelic or human—are absolutely dependent upon Him for their substance and existence. Nothing can exist apart from God. All are eternally dependent on One outside of themselves. All owe their existence to another—God. This is an eternal fact. "In the beginning God..." (Genesis 1:1). His personality, eternity of being, absoluteness, and existence are in and of Himself.

The Law of Opposites
In God also is what may be called "the law of opposites"; that is, God knows good and evil, but does only the good. He cannot do evil because He is good (Genesis 3:21-24).
In God is both hate and love. There can be no love unless there is its opposite, which is hate. God loves the good; He hates the evil. The very fact of good implies its opposite, evil. This principle works in all things. And it is the law of opposites that is in God, as God knows good and evil, but God can only ever be and do the good.

In God there can come forth blessing and cursing, grace and wrath, salvation and damnation, gladness and sadness, peace and storms, life and death, heaven and hell. The law of opposites is seen here.

It was in the creature that brought hell into manifestation. Hell was not meant to be manifested. Hell owes its eternal existence to God. God is love. God is light. Light is also fire. So there is the other side of the nature of God which is manifested when sin manifests itself in the creature: love or hate, grace or wrath, heaven or hell, blessing or cursing.

Of course, these opposites never violate the laws of God's own being, as to His essential or moral attributes: His holiness, love, justice, righteousness, mercy, eternity of being, omnipresence, omnipotence, or omniscience.

God Himself is the Law-giver. He Himself is governed by the laws of His own immutable being; so must His creatures be governed by law. It is the very essence of being.

B. The universe is governed by laws.

The universe (created things) must be governed by laws. There would be total chaos if this were not the case. There would be worlds in collision if God left the universe to "run itself" as it pleased. The universe follows laws as inanimate creation, automatically set in motion at Creation. Science does not create the laws by which the universe runs, it discerns them, discovers them, and may use them. God is the author of law in the universe. The universe is dependent on God and His laws. Thus, the natural kingdom is governed by natural laws, which points to the fact that God's kingdom is governed by spiritual laws.

C. Creatures must be governed by laws.

Henry Drummond suggests in his book, *Natural Law in the Spiritual World*, that there are laws in the spiritual world corresponding to those in the natural world. This seems to be a biblical principle indeed.

Angelic creations are governed by law.

The first law of created beings, be they angelic or human, is "Thou shalt be eternally dependent upon God." This is the law of dependence.

When Satan (Lucifer) fell, it was the result of lawlessness and rebellion (wanting to be a law unto himself). The fallen angels who followed him became lawless, self-governing, and self-directing.

The elect angels, who chose not to follow Satan, remained subject to the law of God. The independent self is the lawless one. The mystery of iniquity is the mystery of lawlessness—the creature taking himself out from under God's authority and becoming an authority unto himself. Sin is lawlessness (I John 3:4). Satan broke that law of dependence by exercising his free will, making an "intelligent" choice, and by choosing self-dependence. Thus, the archangel became the Devil.

When the creatures or created one (the dependent) come out from under the law of dependence upon God (the Creator, the Self-existent One) to become independent, that is sin and lawlessness. It is dependence upon self instead of upon God. Independence is sin—lawlessness. Actually, there is no such thing as independence, for all forever owe their existence to God. Independence is really self-dependence, instead of God-dependence. Satan and the angels who fell with him found this out, but all the angelic hosts were created to be under the law of dependence upon God. It is the first law of creature existence.

Man was created to be governed by law.

When God created man and placed him in Eden, He submitted him to one law, one commandment (Genesis 2:17). It was the law of obedience. It included in itself the law of dependence upon God, to which the angelic hosts were also subject. Man's own physical being is governed by natural laws also; otherwise man's being would become sick and diseased, and he would die. Sickness and disease are the evidence of lawlessness in the human body. God placed man under this moral law—the law of dependence, the law of obedience.

When the Serpent brought about the fall of man, it was by a direct attack against the law of God—God's Word, will, and commandment. He had to get man off of the "ground of faith and obedience and dependence" onto the "ground of unbelief and disobedience." He encouraged man to become lawless, to become a law to himself, or to "do his own thing" (existentialism). "...[B]e as gods, knowing good and evil" (Genesis 3:1-6). In other words, he suggested that they, too, like himself, could be independent, self-dependent, and self-sustaining. It was an appeal to come from the law of dependence to independence.

The law of the mind rose up and overthrew the law of the Lord (II Corinthians 10:1-3). Now, in the fall of man, we see a "chain reaction," like the splitting of the atom, and a number of the laws listed come into operation.

D. Note these laws in their succession and progression:
    • The law of dependence and obedience was broken (Genesis 2:17).
    • The law of sin and death came into being, beginning its deadly work,
      and operating in independent self.
    • The law of conscience began to work. It was undoubtedly inactive
      until the Fall. When man fell, it began to work, accusing and
      excusing their disobedience (Romans 2:15; Genesis 3:1-14). This
      law of conscience operated in man's being from Adam to Moses. It
      was internal law. Guilt came.
    • The law of works was then triggered into operation, in which man felt
      he must do something to make himself presentable to God. The fig
      leaves were used to cover up his shame (Genesis 3:1-10). Man tried to
      justify himself by works (Romans 3:27; I John 2:4; Romans 9:32).
        • The law of conscience – "...I was afraid...and I hid myself"
          (Genesis 3:10).
        • The law of works – "...they sewed fig leaves together, and made
          themselves aprons" (Genesis 3:7).
    • God came in grace and brought in a substitutionary sacrifice that
      revealed another law—the law of faith. This law of faith is in contrast
      to the law of works. The law of works was what man could do to make
      himself presentable to God. The law of faith is what God does in grace
      to make man presentable to Himself.
    • These two laws are exemplified in Adam's first two sons, Cain and
      Abel (Genesis 4; I John 2:4; Hebrews 11:4). Cain illustrates the law
      of works, and Abel the law of faith. This pattern is carried on in the
      lines of the godly and ungodly patriarchs. The patriarchs who were
      under the law of faith, in the covenants of grace and faith, included
      Abel, Enoch, Abraham, Noah, Isaac, Jacob, etc. (Hebrews 11). In the
      lives of Cain and Abel, we see the opposite laws at work, typical of
      the whole human race.
        Cain – The Law of Works. To silence a guilty conscience, Cain felt
          he must do something by self-effort (self-atonement, self-
          salvation, self-dependence). His works were that which he could
          do for himself to make himself presentable to God. So it is for
          all men who follow "the way of Cain."
        Abel – The Law of Faith. Abel accepted God's way of faith in the
          death of another (in a substitutionary sacrifice, the body and
          blood of the lamb). It is what God did for man in grace
          (undeserved, unearned, unmerited). Adam and Eve were saved in

view of their acceptance of the body and blood of the victim slain in their stead. They witnessed the first death, the first blood-shedding, and accepted God as their Priest and Mediator. They are clothed in the skins provided through the death of an innocent animal. They turned from the law of works and self-effort (bloodless fig leaves, what they could do) to the law of faith (the coats of skin, what God had done for them in grace to make them presentable to Himself).

- Thus, in the human race, we now see the "law of opposites" at work, for since man has partaken of the Tree of Knowledge of Good and Evil, he but can only do the evil, which has the power over him. Man, by free will, chose independence. It brought into operation the law of opposites in man's being—a mixture of good and evil, the mystery of godliness, spirit and flesh, all or nothing, yes and no, God and Satan, genuine and counterfeit, health and disease, friendship and enmity, harmony and discord, corruption and incorruption, wisdom and foolishness, truth and error, major and minor kindness and cruelty, perfection and imperfection, obedience and disobedience, etc.

E. **The nation of Israel was under the law.** (Romans 7)

As we have already seen, God delivered Israel out of the house of bondage on the basis of the Abrahamic Covenant, which was of grace through faith in what God could do. Israel could do nothing to bring about its own deliverance except trust the Passover Lamb of God.

From Passover to Sinai, all was done for the people of Israel by the grace of God. They trusted Him. However, at Sinai they fell from the level of the law of faith to the level of the law of works. While the Ten Commandments were in the making, they were also in the breaking (cf. Exodus 19, 20, 24, 32, 33, 34; Deuteronomy 4-5). When Moses broke the tables of stone, he was demonstrating what the people of Israel had already done. God, in His grace and mercy, gave them another set of tables, which were placed "under the blood" in the ark of the covenant. This blood represented the ceremonial law, with priesthood, sacrifices, etc. Only on this basis could God dwell with them.

When the men at Bethshemesh presumed to put aside the blood-stained mercy seat, they were exposed to the ministration of death, and 50,070 were slain (cf. I Samuel 6:19-20; II Corinthians 3).

Israel never did seem to understand the relationship of law and grace as demonstrated in the ark of the covenant. The blood-stained mercy seat was the ceremonial law (grace) which covered the commandments (law). Moral law is equivalent to law. Ceremonial law is equivalent to grace. Both are in God also.

When Israel said, "...All that the Lord hath spoken we will do" (Exodus 19:8), they never realized that the problem was not with the Ten Commandments, but the problem was within themselves; it was internal. This was independence or self-dependence.

Romans 7 defines this for us. The law was holy, just, good, and spiritual. It was also perfect. They were unholy, unjust, evil, carnal, sold under sin. They did not realize that the law of sin within them was stronger than the law of God on tables of stone.

- The law of conscience could not help (cf. Romans 2:14-15; 7:22-23, 12, 16, 19; law of the mind).
- The will could not help them with its resolutions (cf. Romans 7:18).
- The law on tables of stone (external law) could not help them. It told them right and wrong, the conscience convicted them of right and wrong, but neither gave the power to do it, for the law of sin within was stronger than either.

Thus, God let Israel enter into fifteen hundred years of self-effort to demonstrate to themselves, and to the whole world, that they could not keep the law of works because the law of sin was stronger than external law. God gave them something that was impossible to keep perfectly, or spiritually, though in measure externally.

F. **The Law of the Divine Righteousness**
    This has already been dealt with in the theological implications in Romans 5. When Christ Jesus came, He was the law of righteousness *personified*. He kept the law of God in His heart perfectly, unbroken, even as the second tables of the law were placed in the ark of the covenant, unbroken (cf. Hebrews 8:5-10).

    His perfect life condemned men, even as the law of Moses. The reason why Jesus was as a man who fulfilled the law of righteousness was because He was totally dependent upon the Father for the life He lived (John 14:10). He had "a self," but it was not an independent self (not a fallen self) but a self that was dependent on the Father. He was a God-filled self. God is the Independent Self. Man is the dependent self. Christ's perfect life demonstrated this. Thus, the law of righteousness was fulfilled, personified, in Him. He was a man who lived totally by the Spirit. He could say, " 'I do nothing of Myself,' I do only and say only that which my Father shows me.

G. **The Law of the Spirit of Life in Christ Jesus**
   This becomes God's answer to the problem for man. God must bring in another law, a higher and strong law than the law on tables of stone (external law), and the law of conscience (seared or stifled), and the law of sin (internal, as conscience). He did this by bringing in the law of the Spirit of life demonstrated in Christ Jesus.

   This law is Christ living His life in us, for He alone kept the law perfectly. Man, fallen man, is lawless. Redeemed man is under God's law (I Corinthians 9:21; Jeremiah 31:31-34; Hebrews 8).

   In other words, Christ came to save man from himself, from his sin, and from independence and lawlessness! He came to make man Christ-centered, which is God-centered, instead of self-centered (Galatians 2:10). Paul could say, "I [independent self] am crucified with Christ: nevertheless I live [that is, I myself, the God-created self, a new self]; yet not I [independent self], but Christ liveth in me [Christ-filled self]: and the life which I now live in the flesh [the body] I live by the faith of the Son of God, who loved me and gave Himself for me" (Galatians 2:20).

   Thus, the independent self is crucified. The cross has been applied to independence, and the Christ-filled life takes the place of the independent life. This is "...Christ in you, the hope of glory..." (Colossians 1:27). (Refer also to notes on Romans 13:10.) *Love* is the fulfilling of the law.

H. **Summary**
   Before the average Christian is ready for this truth, the painful revelation and truth of "self-discovery" must take place. This is demonstrated in the lives of Adam, Abraham, Isaac, Jacob, Moses, Peter, Paul, and millions of others. (Refer to *Law of Faith*, by Norman Grubb, pp. 30-42, on some of the material above.)

   • God created every self to be filled with Himself, in order that He might fill all things.

   • God created every man with free will, the ability to make a choice, the ability to be independent or God-filled.

   • God allows man to go through a self-discovery process by self-effort, self-fulfillment, and failure.

- God then meets man at the end of this road of self-effort and presents His Son to fill all with Himself, His law of love and righteousness. Man either accepts or rejects it.

Thus, after the cry of the wretched man, at the end of the road of *self-effort*, the believer turns to God to be filled with Christ. Man realizes his bias towards evil—that he cannot rise to the level of conscience that convicts him, nor to the level of the moral law which condemns him. Thus, he turns to Christ, the perfect Law-keeper, to relive His life in his emptied and wretched self.

Independent self has been exposed in its helplessness and guilt by means of the law. Christ is the Law-giver and the Law-keeper in the believer. The Christ-filled self is dependent upon Him. As the Father lived His life in the Son, and the Son was totally dependent upon the Father, so now the Son lives His life in me as I am totally dependent upon Him.

This is the law of the Spirit of Life in Christ Jesus, the higher and greater law. "...Christ in you, the hope of glory..." (Colossians 1:27).

Man can make laws, however, legislation is the best that man can do apart from what God can do. Volumes of laws are passed yearly, by man for man, to protect others and to punish lawbreakers, but legislators are powerless to make people fulfill them. God places His law within us. It is the law of life "in Christ Jesus."

Thus:
- We died to sin—that is, independence.
- We died to self—that is, self-effort, selfishness, self-ism, and egotism.
- We died to law—that is, external commands on tables of stone, telling us what to do, but powerless to help us do it.
- We live in Christ—that is, the internal law of the Spirit of life, the royal law of love in us (Christ reliving His life in us; the Christ-filled self) (Jeremiah 31:31-34; II Corinthians 3; James 2:8; Romans 13:8; Galatians 5:14). We are totally and eternally dependent on Him, filled with Him, as God intended man to be. This is victorious Christian living!

The believer is not *physically* free of the law of sin and death. No law of sin would make death non-existent (cf. the use of three words in I Corinthians 15:51-57: "law," "sin," "death," all linked together). "The sting of death is sin, and the strength of sin is the law" (I Corinthians 15:56).

The universe is governed by laws. The universe would, indeed, be in chaos without laws. Law results in harmony, order, peace in the universe; otherwise, there would be worlds in collision, as already mentioned. Spiritual laws exist also for angelic and human creatures. Natural laws illustrate spiritual laws.

Note:

- The Law of Gravity —"what goes up must come down"; the downward, earthly, gravitational pull. One can never break the law of gravity nor eradicate it. It breaks us if we violate it by jumping out of a window of a fifty-story building. It is no use singing, "I am not under law, but under grace..."
- The Law of Aerodynamics — this is a higher law then the law of gravity. The plane moves in this realm by jet power and propulsion. It does note eradicate the law of gravity. A long as the fuel supply lasts, the plane moves in this higher realm and is "free" from the law of gravity. The law of gravity has no power over it. The law of gravity is rendered inactive and inoperative but not eradicated by this higher law in operation.

Spiritually speaking, we have the counterpart in the laws under present consideration. Note below:

- The Law of Sin and Death — The earthly, downward gravitational pull. It is present in all mankind, and in the believer. It was not eradicated by man's initial salvation. In God's time it will be eradicated.
- The Law of the Spirit of Life — The higher law of "aerodynamics." The Holy Spirit is that higher law. He is "the power." This does not eradicate the law of sin and death, but as long as the believer walks and moves in this higher law, he is "free" from the law of sin and death (John 8:36).

This "law of sin and death" will be eradicated in "the redemption of the body," (Romans 8:23). Thus, Romans 8:2 will be physically true at the redemption of the body, and its glorification, as dealt with in Romans 8:18-25. The law of sin and death will be eradicated eternally then.

Verse I: *"There is therefore no condemnation to them which are in Christ Jesus, who walk not after the flesh, but after the Spirit."*

(Cf. Romans 5:1; 8:1; 12:1.)

A. **"No condemnation"** (cf. Romans 5:16, 18)
   Adam brought condemnation to the race. Christ frees men from that condemnation (i.e., the sentence of condemnation).

   • "Who is he that condemneth?..." (Romans 8:34).

   • "...[B]y the offence of one judgment came upon all men to condemnation..." (Romans 5:16-18).

   • "For if our heart condemn us..." (I John 3:20-22).

   • "...[T]he accuser of our brethren..." (Revelation 12:10-12).

   • "There is therefore now no condemnation to them which are in Christ Jesus..." (Romans 8:1). There is condemnation "in Adam."

   Condemnation came in Genesis 3. Its result was fear, guilt, and a smitten conscience, "in Adam." The cause of condemnation was sin. God dealt with it through Christ. The law also brings condemnation. Believers sometimes live under clouds of condemnation, unforgiveness, and sin. Satan is the accuser of the brethren. We must not give him ground on which to condemn us.
   The believer also must learn to distinguish between satanic condemnation and Holy Spirit conviction.

B. **"To them which are in Christ Jesus"**
   One is either "in Adam" or "in Christ." These are the two federal heads of the human race—the old man and the new creation.

C. **"Who walk not after the flesh, but after the Spirit"**
   Note Galatians 5:16; Romans 6:18, 22; and notes on Romans 8:4.

Verse 2: *"For the law of the Spirit of life in Christ Jesus hath made me free from the law of sin and death."*

   "The law"
   Note the development of the subject of "law" in Romans. In this verse, we see the highest law in relation to the believers—the law of the

Spirit of life in Christ Jesus." To bring into sharper focus the theme of "law" in Romans, find the following list of the main reference to particular laws mentioned in this epistle.

- The Law (Romans 2:12, general use)
- The Law of Conscience (Romans 2:12-15)
- The Law of Works (Romans 3:27)
- The Law of Faith (Romans 3:27)
- The Law of God (Romans 7:22, 25; cf. Exodus 20)
- The Law in My Members (Romans 7:23)
- The Law of My Mind (Romans 7:23; cf. II Corinthians 11:1-3)
- The Law of Sin (Romans 7:23, 25)
- The Law of Sin and Death (Romans 8:2 with Genesis 2:17)
- The Law of the Spirit of Life in Christ Jesus (Romans 8:2)
- The Law of Righteousness (Romans 9:31)
- The Law of Love, the Royal Law, the Law of Liberty (Romans 13:8-10 with James 2:8-12)

(Refer also to the diagram on "dispensational setting of laws.")

Verse 3: *"For what the law could not do, in that it was weak through the flesh, God sending his own Son in the likeness of sinful flesh, and for sin, condemned sin in the flesh..."*

A. What the Law Could Do
- The law could give us the knowledge of sin (Romans 3:20; 7:7).
- The law could condemn is for failing to live up to the divine standard of righteousness.

B. "What the law could not do"
- The law could not justify us (Romans 3:20; Galatians 2:16).
- The law could not give us life (Galatians 3:21).
- The law could not make us righteous (Romans 3:20; Galatians 2:16).
- The law could not make us perfect (Hebrews 7:19).

C. "Weak through the flesh"
Weakness is a problem of the flesh, not of the law (cf. Romans 7:18-22). Again, this is the result of the law of sin inside of man, the law of rebellion. (Refer again to 7:12-24.)

The law is not sin (Romans 7:7). The flesh is the problem, for no good thing dwells in the flesh. The flesh finds it impossible to keep the law.

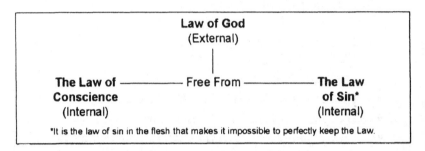

Law of God
(External)

The Law of ——————— Free From ——————— **The Law**
Conscience   **of Sin***
(Internal)   **(Internal)**

*It is the law of sin in the flesh that makes it impossible to perfectly keep the Law.

D. "God sending His own Son in the likeness of sinful flesh" (II Corinthians 5:21; Galatians 3:13)
God did send His Son (John 3:16). Jesus often said that He was sent of the Father. He did not come of His own will (Galatians 4:1-4; John 16:27-28; His pre-existence, then His incarnation).

E. "Likeness of sinful flesh"
Jesus had only the "likeness" of sinful flesh. He did not have sinful flesh, though He was born of a woman. Vincent defines this likeness, "literally of the flesh of sin, not just 'came in the flesh' " (I John 4:2; I Timothy 3:16), for this would not have expressed the bond between Christ's manhood and sin. He did not come in the flesh of sin, which would have represented Him as partaking of sin. He did not come in the likeness of flesh, since He was really and entirely human, but in the likeness of the flesh of sin—really human, conformed in appearance to the flesh whose characteristic is sin, yet sinless.

F. "And for sin"
"And for sin," meaning "by a sacrifice for sin" (marginal). It also means "to atone, to destroy, to save and sanctify its victims" (Vincent). Christ's life condemns sin—morally. His death condemns sin—vicariously. This is the whole work of redemption (II Corinthians 5:21; Galatians 3:13; Romans 5:6-8).

G. "Condemned sin in the flesh"
    "Condemned" means "deposed from its dominion, a thing impossible
to the law, which could pronounce judgment and inflict penalty, but not
dethrone it. Christ's holy character was a condemnation of unholiness"
(Vincent). Sin condemned man in the flesh. Christ condemned sin at the
Cross.

Verse 4:   *"...That the righteousness of the law might be fulfilled in us, who walk not
           after the flesh, but after the Spirit."*

(Cf. verses 4, 2)

Note the chart below:

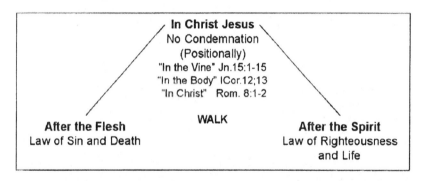

In Christ Jesus
No Condemnation
(Positionally)
"In the Vine" Jn.15:1-15
"In the Body" ICor.12;13
"In Christ" Rom. 8:1-2

After the Flesh   WALK   After the Spirit
Law of Sin and Death   Law of Righteousness
                                           and Life

    Two walks are set before the believer. A person can only walk one path
or the other, one way at a time, not both ways at the same time (cf.
Matthew 7:13-14).

A. "Righteousness of the law"
    "Righteousness" is "moral precepts, righteous requirements." Law is
the expression of the righteousness of God, not just external
righteousness, as in Philippians 3:6, 9; Luke 1:6; Romans 2:26; Hebrews
9:1; Romans 7:12, 14). Righteousness of the law is fulfilled in Christ,
who now is in us, personified in our lives, and thus fulfills that
righteousness.   Positional righteousness must become experiential
righteousness.

B. Christ our Righteousness
    The only One who ever kept the law perfectly is living in us by the

Spirit, and thus the righteousness of the law is fulfilled in us. He keeps His own law within us. Higher law now fulfills the law of God (Romans 13:8). It is written in our hearts, by the Spirit (Jeremiah 31:31-34; Hebrews 8). New covenant laws are in our minds and hearts; thus, there is no conflict between the law and Christ.

Verse 5: *"For they that are after the flesh do mind the things of the flesh; but they that are after the Spirit the things of the Spirit."*

The Mind

"After the flesh" – Meaning "things of the flesh, fleshy things."

"After the Spirit" – Meaning "things of the Spirit, spiritual things" (John 3:6; Galatians 5:22).

Verse 6: *"For to be carnally minded is death; but to be spiritually minded is life and peace."*

The Mind

"Carnally minded" – (carnivorous) results in death

"Spiritually minded" – results in life and peace (Refer to 7:14 on the word "carnal."

The battle is a battle of the mind. One is either minding the flesh or minding the Spirit.

Verse 7: *"Because the carnal mind is enmity against God: for it is not subject the law of God, neither indeed can be."*

The Carnal Mind

"Enmity against God" – a rebel at war against God

"Not subject to the law of God" – lawless

"Neither indeed can be" – resists God (James 4:4; I Corinthians 2:14; battle of the mind)

Verses 5-7: *Summary*

Note the emphasis on the "mind" in verses 5-7. The battle is a battle of the mind (II Corinthians 10:1-4; Romans 12:1-2). The mind is either centered on things of the Spirit or things of the flesh (I Corinthians 2:14). To have "understanding", to "feel", to "think", or to "have an opinion" are all objects of the mind thinking and striving after fleshly things

Verse 8: *"So then they that are in the flesh cannot please God."*

"In the flesh"
"In the flesh" represents a sinful, carnal nature that cannot please God. This phrase compares with "in Adam." In contrast "in the Spirit" refers to walking, moving, and obeying the Spirit of God according to the Word. This phrase compares with "in Christ."

Verse 9: *"But ye are not in the flesh, but in the Spirit, if so be that the Spirit of God dwell in you. Now if any man have not the Spirit of Christ, he is none of his."*

A. **"In the flesh"**
Being "in the flesh" is to follow after the evil desires of the fallen nature.

B. **"In the Spirit"** (Revelation 1:10; 4:2; John 4:34; Galatians 4:6)
Being "in the Spirit" is to follow after the will, thoughts, and desires of the Spirit of God and the Word. These terms are often misunderstood in Christianity. "In the Spirit" is not some "mystical realm." Jesus and the apostles were naturally spiritual and spiritually natural. They were normal men. They lived in the Spirit, and had the life of the Spirit.

C. **"The Spirit"**
Note the emphasis on the Holy Spirit in this verse and the entire chapter. In this chapter, "I" is mentioned two times, "sin" three times, "Lord" nine times, "Holy Spirit" twenty-one times, and "law" four times. In Romans 7, the emphasis is "I." In Romans 8, the emphasis is "the Spirit" (Romans 8:1-2, 4, 9-11, 13-16, 23, 26-27).
- Spiritually (verse 6)
- Spirit of Bondage (verse 15)
- Our Spirit (verse 16)

The Holy Spirit is spoken of as:
- The Spirit (Romans 8:1)
- The Spirit of Life (Romans 8:2, 10)
- The Spirit of God (Romans 8:9, 11, 14; cf. I Corinthians 2:10-12; Ephesians 3:16)
- The Spirit of Christ (Romans 8:9; Galatians 4:6; Philippians 1:19)
- The Spirit of Adoption (Romans 8:15)

All believers have the Spirit:
- By New Birth (John 3:3; Galatians 4:6; "born of the Spirit")
- By Baptism in the Spirit (the Spirit of Christ, the Spirit of the Anointed One, and the same Spirit in us; various titles designate His function and ministry, but the same Holy Spirit)

Let us note the blessings of the Spirit-filled life of victory in this chapter:
- Walking After the Spirit (verses 1, 4)
- The Law of the Spirit of Life (verse 2)
- Minding the Things of the Spirit (verse 5)
- In the Spirit (verse 9)
- Having the Spirit of Christ, the Anointed One (verses 9)
- The Spirit is Life Because of the Righteousness (verse 10)
- The Spirit Quickening our Mortal Bodies: life, healing, health (verse 11)
- The Spirit Indwelling Us (verse 11)
- The Spirit Enabling us to Mortify the Old Desires of the Flesh (verse 13)
- Being Led by the Spirit (verse 14)
- The Spirit as the Spirit of Adoption, of Sonship, not of Bondage (verses 14, 15)
- The Witness of the Spirit (verse 16)
- The Firstfruits of the Spirit (verse 23)
- The Spirit Helping our Infirmities in Prayer (verse 26)
- God Knowing the Mind of the Spirit, the Spirit Making Intercession in Us (verses 26, 27)

(Refer also to Romans 1:4, 9; 2:29; 7:6; 11:8; 12:11; 15:19, 30.) In all, there are twenty-eight references to the word "Spirit" or "spirit" in Romans. The majority of them are in Romans 8.

Verse 10: *"And if the Christ be in you, the body is dead because of sin; but the Spirit is life because of righteousness."*

A. **Dual Indwelling** (John 15:1-10)
   Note:
   - Christ in You (Romans 8:10; Colossians 1:27)
   - You in Christ (Romans 8:1-2; II Corinthians 5:17-18)

B. **"Body is dead"**
   "Body" refers to the believer's body. The body is dead because of sin, because of the law of sin.

C. **"Spirit is life"**
   The Spirit is life because of righteousness or right standing (law of the Spirit in the believer's spirit). The law cannot give life; the Spirit does (Galatians 3:21; II Corinthians 3:6).

Verse 11: *"But if the Spirit of him that raised up Jesus from the dead dwell in you, he that raised up Christ from the dead shall also quicken your mortal bodies by his Spirit that dwelleth in you."*

"Quicken your mortal bodies"
   The same Spirit that raised up Jesus' body from the dead now dwells in us to quicken us and to make us alive (cf. Romans 4:24-25), to give us the resurrection life of the Spirit. God will also make us alive (Ephesians 2:1-6) and quicken our mortal, death-doomed bodies because of the Spirit in us. This verse is one of the greatest verses for divine health and healing.

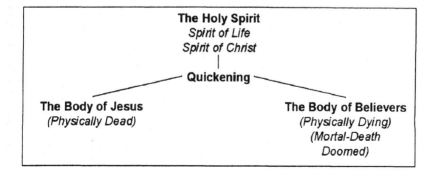

This quickening is physically now, in life, healing, and health (Acts 2:23-24; I Corinthians 6:14; II Corinthians 4:14), and ultimately in the resurrection, if the believer dies before the second coming of Christ.

Freedom from Death (Romans 8:12-39)

The Spirit of Adoption (Romans 8:12-17)

Verse 12: *"Therefore, brethren, we are debtors, not to the flesh, to live after the flesh."*

Not Indebted:
- To the flesh, which brings death,
- But to the Spirit, who gives life (cf. Romans 6:7, 14).

Verse 13: *"For if ye live after the flesh, ye shall die: but if ye through the Spirit do mortify the deeds of the body, ye shall live."*

A. **"Live" or "die"**
- Live after the flesh, and die.
- Mortify the deeds of the body, and live.
- The secret is through the Spirit.

Flesh cannot crucify flesh, or mortify flesh. Flesh cannot cast flesh out. Mortifying the flesh cannot be done through self-effort. It is "through the Spirit" enabling us to do so.

B. **"Mortify"**
To "mortify" is "to make to die, to put to death." One translation says "...habitually putting to death—making extinct, deadening—the [evil] deeds prompted by the body, you shall (really and genuinely) live forever" (Amplified New Testament). A mortuary is a place for the dead. (Also see; Galatians 6:8; Ephesians 4:22; Colossians 3:5.)

C. **"Deeds"**
Deeds are habitual practices (Romans 7:15; John 3:21; Romans 6:12-23).

Verse 14: *"For as many as are led by the Spirit of God, they are the sons of God."*

A. **"Led"**
   We are to be led by the Spirit, not the flesh (cf. Galatians 5:18; Luke 4:1).

B. **"Sons of God"**
   In the Greek, *huioi* means mature, having full sonship, not as children or babes in Christ, as other Greek words imply (cf. John 1:12; Matthew 3:17). Jesus was led of the Spirit, as the Son of God (Matthew 4:1). The Spirit was the One leading in all His life as a Son. So it is for us as well. (Cf. "sonship.")

Verse 15: *"For ye have not received the spirit of bondage again to fear; but ye have received the Spirit of adoption, whereby we cry, Abba, Father."*

A. **"The spirit of bondage again to fear"**
   This phrase refers to the bondage and fear of the law (Hebrews 2:15; Galatians 4:3, 9). The Holy Spirit does not bring us into bondage (II Timothy 1:7; I John 4:18).

B. **"The Spirit of adoption, whereby we cry, Abba, Father"** (Ephesians 1:5; Matthew 6:9)
   "Abba, Father" indicates a close relationship of children to the Father (Isaiah 56:5; Mark 14:36; Galatians 4:5-7). "The Spirit of God, producing the condition of adoption. Setting or placing of a son" (Vincent).
   "Sonship is the process of legal adoption by which the chosen heir becomes not only entitled to the reversion of the property to the civil status, to the burdens as well as the rights of the adopter—became, as it were, his other self, one with him...Roman principle, peculiar at this time to the Romans. It was unknown, to all appearances, to the Jews as it is certainly not found in the legislation of Moses, nor mentioned anywhere as a usage among the children of the Covenant. So the believer, the Roman believers, are adopted sons of God, in an intimate sense one with the Father" (Vincent).

C. **"We cry"**
   To cry is "to express deep emotion." It is a loud cry.

D. **"Abba"**

"Abba" is a Syrian term to which Paul adds the Greek term for Father. This is perhaps a hint at the union of Jew and Gentile in God as Father.

E. **"Adoption"**

(Refer to "adoption," as consummated in Romans 8:23.) Notice the contrasts: not fear of the law, but faith in the Father; not the spirit of bondage, but the Spirit of adoption; not "keep away," but "come near."

Verse 16: *"The Spirit itself beareth witness with our spirit, that we are the children of God..."*

The Witness of the Spirit with Our Spirits (cf. Ephesians 1:13; I John 5:7, 6-10; John 3:1-5)

The Holy Spirit gives the witness to our spirits that we belong to God. It is the testimony of the Holy Spirit to the human spirit. Note the process here:

- Children of God – Greek: *Tekna*, means "to come to full sonship" (John 1:12).
- Sons of God – Greek: *Huici*, means "mature sonship." Note "heirs of God" (Acts 26:18; Galatians 3:29; 4:1-7). The words "inheritance," "inherit," "heir," and "joint heir" are all from the same root in the Greek language. This word appears about fourteen times in the New Testament (Ephesians 1:14, 18; Titus 3:7; Hebrews 6:17; 11:7; I Peter 1:4).

Verse 17: *"...And if children, then heirs; heirs of God, and joint-heirs with Christ; if so be that we suffer with him, that we may be also glorified together."*

A. **"Heirs of God"**

Heirs are entitled to an inheritance.

B. **"Joint-heirs with Christ"**

Joint heirs are entitled to the Father's inheritance for His sons together, not separately. Sons receive their inheritance fully at the adoption.

- Roman law made all children, including adopted ones, equal inheritors.

- Jewish law gave a double portion to the eldest or firstborn son. Roman law was naturally on Paul's mind, suiting his text, where adoption was the basis for inheritance. We have our inheritance in Christ, in God. God and His Son also find inheritance in us (verse 32).

C. "If so be that we may suffer with Him, that we may also be glorified together"
Note the sufferings and the glory to follow (Philippians 1:29):
- In Christ, the Son of God (Matthew 16:21, 27; I Peter 1:11; 2:21-25; 3:18)
- In Christians, the sons of God (Matthew 16:24-26; Romans 5:2-3; I Peter 2:19-20; 4:1-2, 13-19; 5:1, 4, 10; Romans 8:17-18)

We may be surrounded by glory, yet sufferings are part of the process to glory, for Him and for us.

The Hope of the Believer (Romans 8:18-30)

Verse 18: *"For I reckon that the sufferings of this present time are not worthy to be compared with the glory which shall be revealed in us."*

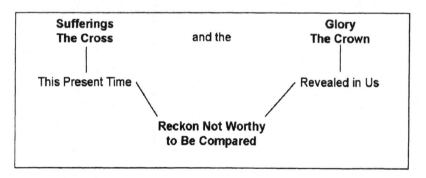

"Sufferings" (II Corinthians 4:17)
While we share the sufferings, we also share the glory. We are not merely suffering for our own stupidity, or otherwise, but suffering for Christ. Note that the theme of Peter's epistles is "suffering and glory."

Verse 19: *"For the earnest expectation of the creature waiteth for the manifestation of the sons of God."*

"For (even the whole) creation (all nature) waits expectantly *and* longs earnestly for God's sons to be made known—waits for the revealing, the disclosing of their sonship" (Amplified New Testament; II Peter 3:13 also).

"Manifestation"
Greek: *Apokalupsis*, means "an uncovering, laying bare, revealing, revelation" (cf. verse 18). Just as creation waited four thousand years for the revelation, (unveiling, manifestation) of *the Son* of God, so it waited six thousand years for the *sons of God.*

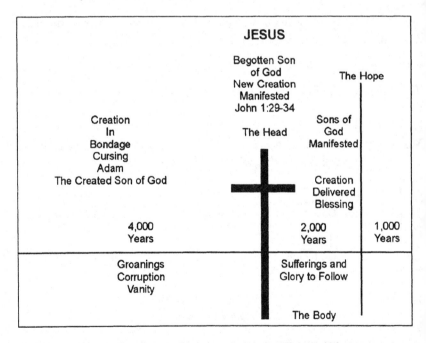

This "manifestation" will come into its fullness at the coming of Christ and the revelation of His redeemed. It involves the events pertaining to the end times, relative to the last years of this present church age.

Verses 20-21: *"For the creature was made subject to vanity, not willingly, but by reason of him who hath subjected the same in hope, because the creature itself also shall be delivered from the bondage of corruption into the glorious liberty of the children of God."*

A. **"The creature was made subject"**

"For the creation (nature) subjected to frailty—to futility, condemned to frustration—not because of some intentional fault on its part, but by the will of Him Who so subjected it. [Yet] with the hope [Ecclesiastes 1:2] that nature (creation) itself will be set free from its bondage to decay and corruption [and gain an entrance] into the glorious freedom of God's children" (Amplified New Testament). (Cf. Genesis 3:19.)

Creation rises and falls with its head—man (Luke 3:38). When Adam, the created son of God, fell, he took the whole of creation under his dominion down with him. When man is restored back to this sonship and dominion through Christ, then the whole creation will rise again to its original Edenic glory, and even greater (Psalm 8; Hebrews 2).

B. **"Hope"** (Romans 5:3-5; 8:20, 24-25; I Peter 1:13; Colossians 1:5; I Timothy 1:1; Hebrews 6:18).

"...Christ in you, the hope of glory..." (Colossians 1:27). Christ in us is also the hope of creation, through restoration to glory, and the hope of redemption, as we are saved by hope. "...[L]ooking for that blessed hope..." (Titus 2:13).

Verse 22: *"For we know that the whole creation groaneth and travaileth in pain together until now."*

A. **"The whole creation groaneth"**

"...[T]he whole creation (of irrational creatures) has been moaning together in the pains of labor until now" (Amplified New Testament). (Also see Jeremiah 12:4, 11; "every creature"[marginal].)

The beasts of creation also fell with man, who was given dominion over the animals he named (Genesis 1:26-31; 2:19-20; Psalm 8; Hebrews 2:5-10). All of creation is groaning, travailing in birth pangs until now:

- The Creation
- The Creatures
- Man also, the Creature Head

One author defines all nature as "the non-rational creation viewed collectively, animated and inanimate" (Vincent).

B. **"Travaileth"** (cf. Revelation 12:2; Galatians 4:19, 27)
"Travaileth" describes the birth pangs of something to be brought forth in the fullness of time.

Verse 23: *"And not only they, but ourselves also, which have the firstfruits of the Spirit, even we ourselves groan within ourselves, waiting for the adoption, to wit, the redemption of our body."*

A. **"Which have the firstfruits of the Spirit"** (cf. II Corinthians 5:5; Ephesians 1:14; James 1:18; John 3:1-5)
"Firstfruits" – The choicest, beginnings given; so it is also in Israel's "firstfruits" (James 1:18; I Corinthians 4:15).
"Earnest" – The "downpayment"; the rest is to follow (II Corinthians 1:22; 5:5; Ephesians 1:13-14).
"Seal" – Genuineness, authenticity, belonging to another (II Corinthians 1:22; Ephesians 1:13-14; 4:30).

The new birth and baptism of the Holy Spirit are simply the "downpayment," "the firstfruits," or "the earnest" of the Holy Spirit's operations in us, of that coming full and total redemption.

B. **"Groan"**
- Creation groans and travails (Romans 8:22).
- The believer groans also (Romans 8:23).
- The Holy Spirit groans within us also (Romans 8:26).

C. **"Waiting for the adoption"**
The adoption is the full placing of children who have come to mature sonship. It is the unveiling. Note:
- The spirit of adoption in our hearts (Romans 8:15)
- The adoption, redemption of our bodies (Romans 8:23)
- To whom pertains the adoption, servants to sons is God's ultimate (Romans 9:4; Galatians 4:1-4)

D. "The Adoption" (Theologically)

The Definition of Adoption

"Adoption" means "to place as a son." Greek: *Huiothesia* is used five times in the New Testament, and each use is by Paul (Romans 8:15, 23; 9:4; Galatians 4:5; Ephesians 1:5). According to custom (Galatians 4:1-2), at a certain time appointed by law, the male child in the family would be formally and legally adopted (i.e, placed in the position of a legal son and given all the privileges of a son). The legal ceremony of adoption did not bring one into the family; it only placed a child of the family as a recognized son in the eyes of Roman law (cf. Genesis 48-49, where Jacob "adopts" the two sons of Joseph into the family of Israel as they were Egypto-Israelitish boys; cf. Exodus 4:22-23, where Israel is spoken of as being "God's son," a many-membered son). This points to the Melchizedecian order of the body of Christ, as priest-sons in ministry. It is the position rather than the relationship. Note:

- New Birth – Born a child (John 1:12-13, 3:3-5). This is regeneration.

- Adoption – God's act of placing a born-again child as a son (Spirit of adoption [Galatians 4:5-6]) (matured by the Spirit [Romans 8:15-19]). The Holy Spirit gives witness of this. The baptism of the Holy Spirit is the earnest of the full inheritance to come, which is given at our adoption. He is called the Spirit of adoption because He comes to bring us to mature sonship. This adoption comes in connection with the redemption of the body. We are predestined to this adoption (Ephesians 1:4-5).

The Time of Adoption

1) Eternity past in the counsels of the Godhead (Ephesians 1:5).
2) By experience at the time of regeneration (Galatians 3:26; 4:1-5; Romans 8:15; John 1:11-12). We are born again as the children of God and receive the Spirit of adoption. We are children that grow up to sonship. The Greek words show the spiritual development of the believer. (Note also I John 2:12-14; Matthew 6:6-10.) Christ is the "pattern son."

   - The Infant (as in the manger), the Babe, the Child (milk-stage) – Greek: *Brephos* means "an infant, babe, young child" (I Peter 2:1-2). Greek: *Nepios* means "not speaking, an infant, minor, simple minded, immature Christian, babe, child, childish" (I Corinthians 3:1; 13:11; Galatians 4:1; Matthew 11:25; 21:16; Romans 2:20).

- The Child (growing up) – Greek: *Teknon* means "child, children, offspring." (For Old Testament Israel, as children growing up, the Tabernacle of Moses, etc. was God's "flannel-graph education.")
- The Son – Greek: *Huice* means "mature sonship, full grown, full sonship."

3) At the coming of Christ (Romans 8:23). At this time our bodies will be delivered from mortality to immortality and made like unto His glorious body (Philippians 3:20-21). "…Thou art my Son, this day have I begotten thee" (cf. Psalm 2; Acts 13:30-33). Sonship is linked with the resurrection of Christ's body in these Scriptures. So it is for the church, the body of Christ, in the ultimate revelation of "the adoption."

The Results of Adoption

1) Deliverance from the law (Galatians 4:4-5)
2) Reception of the Holy Spirit and the witness (Ephesians 3:19; Romans 8:15-16; Galatians 4:6)
3) Reception of the earnest or firstfruits of our inheritance (Romans 8:23; Ephesians 1:11-14)
4) A Father/Son relationship (Galatians 4:6; Romans 8:15; cf. John's gospel, the Father/Son relationship)
5) Walking and living in the Spirit; acting like a son (Romans 8:14; Galatians 5:18)
6) The unveiling of the sons of God to ultimate glory (Romans 8:19-23)
7) The redemption of the body, involving the change, translation, resurrection, and glorification of all believers in the ultimate sense and in His Advent (Romans 8:19-23)

Note the following diagram.

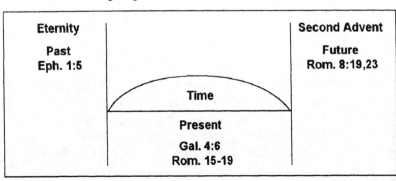

E. **"To wit"**

"To wit" is to know—in other words, if we want to know what the adoption is.

F. **"The redemption of our body"** (Ephesians 1:14; 4:30)

This is the redemption of the purchased possession (Ephesians 1:13-14; II Corinthians 5:2; Luke 20:36; Luke 21:28) or the complete redemption of our bodies.

The last enemy to be destroyed is *death* (I Corinthians 15:51-57, 25-27).

- The believer is redeemed in his spirit (II Corinthians 5:5; John 3:5; Romans 8:16).
- The believer is redeemed, and is being redeemed in his soul, by daily renewing of the mind by the Word (Romans 12:1-2).
- The believer is yet to be redeemed in his body, which is the final part of the redemption (Romans 8:23).

The Fall affected man in spirit, soul, and body. Man needs to be totally redeemed. Man has to come to full glorification in the whole being to be as God intended man to be (I Thessalonians 5:23).

G. **"The Redemption"** (Theologically)

The Definition of Redemption

"Redemption" is "to be bought back; to redeem, to pay a price, to buy back." In the thought of "redemption" there are two aspects involved:

1) Redeem – Hebrew: *Gaal* means "to free by avenging and repaying."
2) Avenge – Hebrew: *Gaal* means "to loose, set free (from blood)" (Numbers 35:12; Deuteronomy 19:6-12; Joshua 20:3-9; Psalm 8:2; 44:16; I Thessalonians 4:6).

The thought of redemption is that of slaves in bondage, having been sold, unable to redeem themselves, and another comes and pays the price of their redemption entirely out of grace; there is nothing deserving in the captive to inspire this favor.

It involves the special laws of redemption in the Old Testament, which especially foreshadowed the Lord Jesus Christ as our "Kinsman Redeemer" (Leviticus 25:23-34). This is what Paul alludes to in Romans

8:24. God has manifested His grace and redemption in Christ Jesus, our Kinsman Redeemer (I Corinthians 1:30; Revelation 4-5).

The picture presented in Romans is that of the whole human race shut up in jail for a life sentence, guilty, helpless, and hopeless, in bondage and slavery, awaiting the death sentence to be executed. The human race is subject to the kingdom of Satan, sold to Satan, sold under sin with no way out, unable to redeem itself (Romans 7:14).

God comes in grace in the person of Christ and redeems man. Man is not beyond redemption. He is not at all irredeemable in this life sentence. Beyond the grave he is. When we speak of the "death sentence," we speak of that which covers the whole man in spirit (spiritual death), soul (death to sin), and body (physical death). The ultimate of all deaths is the "second death" (Revelation 20:11-15).

The Old Testament prophets looked forward to and prophesied of the redemption and the Redeemer to come (Isaiah 41:14; 44:6, 24; 48:17; 49:7, 26; Job 19:25). The prophets recognized that the whole race was in slavery and servitude, sold under sin, to the kingdom of Satan. The whole race was sold in Adam, in whose loins the race was. They looked forward to God's sending of a redeemer who would loose and redeem the race from this captivity (Isaiah 54:5, 8; 59:20; 60:16; 63:16; Jeremiah 50:34; Psalm 19:14; 78:35; Luke 2:38). The prophets, especially the prophet Isaiah, often spoke of "the Lord our Redeemer." Redemption through a kinsman redeemer was the burden of the Old Testament prophets. This could only be by God Himself, as no man could redeem his brother (Psalm 49:5-8).

The Redemption Foreshadowed

The Redemptive Lamb (Exodus 12). Israel was redeemed out of the house of bondage through the lamb (II Samuel 7:23; Deuteronomy 7:8; 13:5; 24:18; I Chronicles 17:21; Micah 6:4; Psalm 111:9; 130:7). Israel's helpless and pitiful condition in Egypt and God's redemption grace, by the blood of the Passover lamb, prefigure the sinner's condition and the full meaning of redemption—a release, a separation, a deliverance, a loosing, a paying of price, an avenging.

The Redemption Money (Exodus 30:11-16; Numbers 3). Every soul numbered in Israel had to be redeemed with a half shekel of silver, the price of the soul, called the "redemption" or the "ransom" money. Peter alludes to this in I Peter 1:18-20. For not bringing the atonement money, God struck Israel with a great plague in II Samuel 24 and I Chronicles 21.

The Laws of Redemption (Leviticus 25; Jeremiah 32:7-8; Ruth 4). These Scriptures show the duties of a kinsman redeemer in relation to his kinsmen, slaves, or lost inheritance. It shadowed that which Adam had lost—the immortality of his body and the inheritance of the planet earth. He needed a kinsman redeemer to be able to buy it back from captivity to Satan.

The Avenging

The thought also in redemption is "to free by avenging and repaying; a separation; to break off; to deliver; to acquire at the forum; to loose by a price; to ransom from captivity; to rescue and deliver from the bondage of sin and its penalties; to avenge."

It refers to taking vengeance on an enemy, to become the avenger of blood. Man's enemy and God's enemy is Satan, the adversary. Satan came and, by subtlety, stole God's creation away from Him, into the slave market, as his subject. God could have dealt with Satan then and there, but He must deal justly, even with Satan. Man, after all, was a freewill creation and freely chose to follow Satan, even if Eve was deceived at the time of choice.

God chose to redeem man in grace and to buy back that which was His by creation. Man is doubly God's now by the right of creation and the right of redemption.

In this act, man is set free—delivered by the right and price of redemption. It is the right of Christ to buy man back to Himself, but also to avenge Satan. Thus, Christ is the Redeemer and the Avenger of blood. At his first coming, He came as the Redeemer. At His second coming, He comes as the Avenger. This is all implied in the word "redemption."

The parties, therefore, involved in redemption are the following:

1) The redeemer—the one who pays the price of redemption.
2) The slave or subject—the one who is freed, bought back from the slave market.
3) The adversary—the one who is to receive vengeance. (The chief thought of Romans, however, is justification. The only reference to Satan is in Romans 16:20; God will bruise Satan finally.)

Summary

To summarize the chief things God has promised in the redemptive process:

1) To redeem us from all iniquities and sins (Psalms 34:22; 71:23; 130:8; Titus 2:14)

2) To redeem our bodies from the curse and death (Job 5:20; 19:25; Galatians 3:13; Romans 8:23; Ephesians 1:7, 14; 4:30)

3) To redeem us out of Satan's kingdom (Psalm 136:24; Colossians 1:13-14)

4) To redeem this world and all of creation from Satan's claims, restoring man's forfeited inheritance (Hebrews 9:12-14; Romans 8:20-24)

Jesus Christ, our Kinsman Redeemer, has paid the ransom price and made possible total redemption. The final set of redemption, as far as the believer is personally concerned, is the redemption of the body.

It is noteworthy that Jesus' body passed through the two stages, which point to what the church in these last days will experience:

1) A Perfect Natural Body (Hebrews 10:5). Jesus had a virgin-born prepared body (Hebrews 10:5; Matthew 1:18-23; Luke 1:30-33). It was a perfect natural body with sinless infirmities (i.e., He could suffer weariness, hunger, thirst; He needed daily sustenance). These were sinless infirmities. He had a body of blood, flesh, and bone, yet it was incorruptible, because it had no sin in it. This body was crucified and buried, but saw no corruption.

2) A Perfect Spiritual Body (cf. I Corinthians 15:44-56). His body was raised incorruptible. It became a flesh and bones body with no blood in it and no sinless infirmities either (i.e., He was no longer hungry, weary, tired, etc). Yet it was the same natural body He had had, only now it was changed into a glorified and spiritual body (Philippians 3:21; I Corinthians 15:43-49). He was not limited but could walk through walls, travel through space, etc. (John 17:5; Luke 24:31, 39; John 20:10, 26; Matthew 17:1-6).

His body is "the firstfruits" sample of what the believers' bodies will be like, in a redeemed and glorified state. (Notice that the unveiling of the sons of God is linked with this redemption of the mortal body. The redemption we seek is from sin and death. Romans 8:2 will be physically true then. The body will be redeemed from sin and, therefore, sickness, disease, and death; thus, it will be free from the law of sin and death [I Corinthians 15:54-57].) There is a natural body, and there is a spiritual body. Once the law of sin has been eradicated, it will be impossible for the believer to die.

(Note: It is possible that there may be a fine distinction between "the redemption" and "the glorification" of the body. The "redemption body" would give man the type of body that Adam had before the Fall. This is what Jesus had in His perfect, natural body, without sin. The "glorified body" would give man the type of body that Christ had after His resurrection—His perfect, spiritual, and glorified body. This glorified body comes to all believers, however, at the sounding of the last trumpet. Meditate on the Scriptures pertaining to this subject (I Thessalonians 4:15-18; II Corinthians 5:1-5; I Corinthians 15:44-58).

Verse 24: *"For we are saved by hope: but hope that is seen is not hope: for what a man seeth, why doth he yet hope for?"*

"For we are saved by hope"
Note:

- This is the hope of total redemption from corruption (Romans 8:20).
- This is the hope of the glory of God (Romans 5:2, 4-5).
- The promises of God give hope. The first promise of hope, to bruise the Serpent's head, was given in Genesis 3:15. (Cf. Romans 16:20 where the hope is fulfilled and we are saved in hope.)

We are saved by faith (I Peter 1:5; Ephesians 2:6-9). We are also saved by hope (Romans 8:24; Colossians 1:5; I Timothy 1:1; Hebrews 6:18). Hope is as an anchor of the soul, in reference to the tabernacle, enters into that within the veil (i.e., the ark for the glory of God, the holiest of all). We are looking for that blessed hope and the glorious appearing of Christ (Titus 2:13). If we already had this hope, we would not need to wait for it. But this hope of the redemption of the body is what we hope for and, therefore, likewise wait for it with patience.

We inherit the promises of faith and patience. Hope against hope may be involved also (Romans 4:18).

Note:

- Hebrews 11 is called "the faith chapter."
- I Corinthians 13 is called "the love chapter."
- Romans 8 may be called "the hope chapter."

There is a place for these three ingredients—faith, love, and hope (I Corinthians 13; Hebrews 11:1; Romans 5:4). God is a God of patience and a God of hope. Hope and comfort may be found in the Scriptures.

Verse 25: *"But if we hope for that we see not, then do we with patience wait for it."*

(Refer to comments on Hebrews 6:11-20.) Faith, patience, and hope are all involved. God gives a promise, which creates hope, and then we must have faith until it comes to pass. Patience is always tested, for God does not often give and fulfill a promise immediately. He works in us patience. (Refer also to Romans 5:1-5.)

Verse 26: *"Likewise the Spirit also helpeth our infirmities: for we know not what we should pray for as we ought: but the Spirit itself maketh intercession for us with groanings which cannot be uttered."*

A. **"The Spirit also helpeth our infirmities"**
The Spirit takes our infirmities, weakness of the flesh, our human limitations, such as ignorance, etc., in the same way that Jesus took our infirmities in Matthew 8:17.

B. **"For we know not what we should pray for as we ought"**
This reflects an ignorance of how to properly pray or a lack of the full or clear mind of God. It is not knowing how to pray according to the need.

C. **"But the Spirit itself maketh intercession for us with groanings which cannot be uttered"**
This type of intercession is "to light upon or fall in with, to go to meet for consultation, conversation, and supplication" (Vincent) (Romans 11:12; Hebrews 7:25).

Thus we have:
- The intercessor in us (in earth, in the believer) (Romans 8:26-27), the Holy Spirit.
- The intercessor for us (in heaven, at the Father's throne) (Romans 8:34), the Son, Jesus Christ.

This completes the cycle of intercession typified in Aaron, his high priestly ministry at the golden altar of incense, and the taking of incense (prayers) of the people of Israel (the saints) and offering them before God (Revelation 5:8; 8:1-5). The Spirit groans along with us.

D. **"Cannot be uttered"**
This phrase can mean either "unutterable," or "unuttered."

Verse 27: *"And he that searcheth the hearts knoweth what is the mind of the Spirit, because he maketh intercession for the saints according to the will of God."*

A. **"And he that searcheth"**
God searches the hearts of His own. The Holy Spirit is one with the Father and the Son in the plan and work of redemption. Thus, He can make perfect intercession according to God's will for that believer and all believers. He is the Heart-searcher.

B. **"The mind of the Spirit"**
The mind of the Spirit is the mind of God. The Spirit is in touch with the Father and the Son continually. There is the unbroken ministry of intercession for the saints—continual incense, perpetually arising to the throne.

Verse 28: *"And we know that all things work together for good to them that love God, to them who are the called according to his purpose."*

A. **"We know"**
We do not just think so, hope so, pray so, but we have a positive knowledge.

B. **"All things work together"**
Note the list of "all things" in Romans 8:31-32 and 35-39.

C. **"For good"**
Whether good or evil, everything is "working" together for good— God's good and the good of the true believer. Divine sovereignty and wisdom make this possible.

Good and evil things can be made to work together (not just separately) for good. This fact is seen in the lives of the saints—Job, Moses, Abraham, Isaac, Jacob, Joseph, the Lord Jesus, Paul, and thousands of others. All of the heroes of faith in Hebrews 11 declare this fact. All suffered evil as well as good, and yet God "worked them all together" for good, for His glory, and for the good of the believers and others.

(Note Nehemiah 13:1-3; Genesis 3:22; 50:20; 42:36.) God can turn the blessings into cursings or the cursings into blessings. All things may seem to be against us. People may mean us evil, but God means us good, for "...all things work together for good to them that love God..."

It is not what happens to the believer that matters; it is his reaction and attitude that counts in it all. Throughout the travail, all is working.

D. **"To them that love God"**
Compare faith, hope, and love (Romans 5:1-8; 8:24-25, 28; I Corinthians 13:13). Love "beareth all things, believeth all things, hopeth all things, endureth all things" (I Corinthians 13:7). Love is the key. God commends His love toward us (Romans 5:8). God sheds His love abroad in our hearts (Romans 5:5). We love God (Romans 8:28).

E. **"To them who are the called"**
We are loved first and then called. Greek: *Kletos* means "the invited."

F. **"According to his purpose"**
Greek: *Prothesis* means "the setting forth of God's plan"; the purpose of God (cf. Romans 9:11; Acts 11:23; Romans 8:28; Ephesians 1:11; 3:11; II Timothy 1:9; 3:10); the eternal purpose of God in Christ Jesus concerning the church (Ephesians 3:1-15).

Verse 29: *"For whom he did foreknow, he also did predestinate to be conformed to the image of his Son, that he might be the firstborn among many brethren."*

A. **"Foreknow"**
This word is used five times in the New Testament. In each case it means "to foreknow" (Acts 26:5; I Peter 1:20; II Peter 3:17; Romans 11:2). It does not mean "foreordain." It signifies pre-science, not pre-election (Vincent). "It is God's being aware of His plan by means of which, before the subjects are destined by Him to salvation He knows whom He has to destine thereto..." (Mayer).

Paul uses "foreknow" distinctly and differently from "pre-destinated." In the Greek, *proegno* means "to foreknow," while *proorisen* means "to predestine." Past, present, and future are all one eternal present to God, the *I Am*. Time is used to accommodate human thought and limitations.

B. **"Predestinate"**

This is a special reference to that which the subjects of His foreknowledge are predestined. "Destination" is "before known, upon the basis of foreknowledge." Foreknowledge is always first, followed by predestination.

C. **"Conformed to the image of his Son"**

His image is the image of His son. This is the "destination" of all who are foreknown of God unto salvation. It is not a matter of some being predestined to heaven and others to hell, but those He foreknew would respond to His call and invitation are predestined to be conformed to the image of His Son. This is the vital point of the passage.

D. **"Conformed"** (cf. Matthew 17:2)

The same Greek word is also translated "transfigured." It means "inner and essential conformity." "...[B]e ye transformed [transfigured] by the renewing of your mind..." (Romans 12:2). (See also II Corinthians 3:18, where the word "changed" is the same Greek word, *metamorphoomai*; Mark 9:2.)

E. **"Image"**

Note the theme of "image" as developed in Scripture also:

- Man was made in the image of God (Genesis 1:26-27).
- Man fell, ruining that image. Man born of man was now in the image and likeness of Adam. His fallen image was marred but still discernible (Genesis 5:1-2).
- Christ is the image of the invisible God (Colossians 1:15; Hebrews 1:3; II Corinthians 4:4).
- All of Adam's race bear the image of the earthly Adam (I Corinthians 15:49; 11:7).
- God forbade Israel to make any images of beasts, man, or any false gods to worship (Romans 1:23).
- The Gentile nations worked and worshipped images (note Daniel 2-3, and the influence of the image of *man* here, for worship).

- God's intention is conform *a man* into His image, the image of the heavenly (1 Corinthians 15:49; Romans 8:29). When the church is like Christ, it will be like God. *The man* in His image and likeness is *the body of Christ*—the church, the redeemed, the manifested sons of God. Note II Corinthians 3:18: "...changed into the same image from glory to glory, even as by the Spirit of the Lord."

"As bird life builds up a bird, the image of itself, so the Christ-life builds up a Christ, the image of Himself, in the inward nature of man" (Vincent).

Thus, this will be God's original and ultimate intention fulfilled. "...Let us make man in our image, after our likeness..." will then be true (Genesis 1:26). This is the whole purpose of redemption—to fulfill that which was apparently frustrated in Creation. It brings man back to the level of God's original will, which seemed to be postponed because of the Fall and the entrance of sin!

It is the "law of conformity to type," as Henry Drummond says in *Natural Law in the Spiritual Worlds*.

F. "First born among many brethren"

The firstborn or the firstfruits were always given directly to God. They represented the choicest and the best. They were also the sample of the rest of the harvest, flock, or family to follow.

Christ is the firstborn, the choicest, the best, but also the representation of the vast family of sons to follow—the many brothers like unto Himself (cf. Revelation 1:5; Colossians 1:15, 18; Hebrews 2:11). He is the heir of God, and the many sons with Him are joint-heirs also (Romans 8:15-17; sonship, of the Head and the body, His church).

Verse 30: *"Moreover whom he did predestinate, them he also called: and whom he called, them he also justified: and whom he justified, them he also glorified."*

Note below under "Verses 26-30 Summary"

Verses 26-30: *Summary*

Note the order of words in this whole passage under consideration. (Refer also to the same words in Ephesians.)
- Intercession – the Spirit's intercession in us (Romans 8:26-27).

- The Will of God – (Romans 8:27; Ephesians 1:1, 5, 9-10; 5:16-18; 6:6-7; Luke 12:41-48).
- The Purpose of God – (Romans 8:28; cf. Ecclesiastes 3:1; Ephesians 1:9, 11; 3:10-11).
- The Foreknowledge of God – (Romans 8:29; Acts 2:23, 30-31; 15:18; I Peter 1:2, 20; Galatians 3:8).
- The Predestination of God – conformed to His image. When we are in the Son's image, we will be in the image of God, for the Son is the express image of God (Romans 8:28-29; Ephesians 1:5-11; Romans 11:2; Acts 17:26).
- The Calling of God – (Romans 8:29; 9:11; 11:5, 7, 28; II Peter 1:10; I Peter 1:2; I Thessalonians 2:12).
- Justification – doctrine of justification (Romans 3; 4; 5; 8:29).
- Glorification – (Romans 8; 8:29; John 17:1, 4-5, 10, 22-24).
- Intercession – the son's intercession for us completes the cycle of the plan of God seen here in the diagram below (illustrated with the circle and cross) (Romans 8:34).

The ultimate of God's purposes is to glorify man, to redeem man with His own glory, to clothe man with His own "light" garment, which man lost in the Fall and became naked. The immortalized resurrection body is the "glorification" spoken of here (cf. John 17:1, 4-5, 10, 22, 24).

The following diagram illustrates the truth dispensationally.

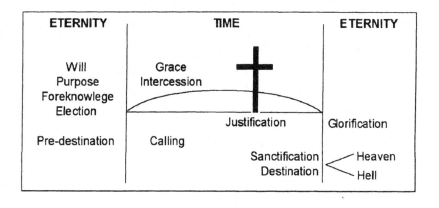

More Than Conquerors (Romans 8:31-39)

In this section (Romans 8:31-39), there are seven questions:

1) "What shall we then say to these things?" (verse 31a).
2) "If God be for us, who can be against us?" (verse 31b).
3) "...[H]ow shall he not with him also freely give us all things?" (verse 32b).
4) "Who shall lay any thing to the charge of God's elect?" (verse 33a).
5) "Who is he that condemneth?" (verse 34a).
6) "Who shall separate us from the love of Christ?" (verse 35a).
7) "Shall tribulation, or distress, or persecution, or famine, or nakedness, or peril, or sword?" (verse 35b).

Verse 31: *"What shall we then say to these things? If God be for us, who can be against us?"*

 A. "What shall we then say?"

  This expression occurs at least seven times in Romans: Romans 4:1; 6:1; 7:7; 8:31; 9:14, 30 and here.

 B. "If God be for us, who can be against us?"

  Though all the things listed in Romans 8:35-39 seem to be against us, nothing is against us when God is for us (refer to Romans 8:28; cf. Numbers 14:9; Psalm 118:6).

Verse 32: *"He that spared not His own Son, but delivered him up for us all, how shall he not with him also freely give us all things?"*

 If God did not spare His best and only beloved Son but delivered *Him* up for our redemption, how much more will He give us everything that is needed to make our redemption complete? If He did not withhold His only beloved Son, will *He* withhold anything else needed to completely redeem us (cf. Romans 5:6, 10; 4:25)? He did not give an angel or mere things to redeem us, but He gave us His best—heaven's best—His only beloved Son. His willingness to give His Son certainly shows His willingness to give all other things, freely. "Freely" in the Greek: *Charizomai* means "gives as an act of grace."

Verse 33: *"Who shall lay any thing to the charge of God's elect? It is God that justifieth."*

A. **"Lay any thing to the charge"**
   Who shall "bring charges," (i.e., call to judicial account)?

B. **"Elect"**
   Those in Christ are the elect, since the rejection of the Hebrew race (I Peter 1:1-2; Colossians 3:12; Titus 1:1; II Timothy 2:10; refer to "election" in Romans 9:10-12).

C. **"It is God that justifieth."**
   Shall God who justifies them bring charges (Isaiah 50:8-9; Revelation 12:10)? God would not bring charges against the very one He is justifying.

Verse 34: *"Who is he that condemneth? It is Christ that died, yea rather, that is risen again, who is even at the right hand of God, who also maketh intercession for us."*

A. **"Who is he that condemneth?"**
   Condemnation came through the First Adam (Romans 5:16, 18). The Devil only has the ground of condemnation on the ground of sin. The law legally condemns man also. But there is no condemnation to them who are now in Christ (Romans 8:1). So who is he that condemns? He is none other than the Adversary, the Accuser of the brothers, the Devil himself (Revelation 12:10).

   "For if our heart condemn us, God is greater than our heart, and knoweth all things" (I John 3:20, also see 3:19, 21). It should be understood clearly that God never condemns. The Holy Spirit convicts, specifically of sins committed, with a view to bringing about cleansing by the blood of Jesus. It is the Devil who accuses and condemns. Distinction should be seen between conviction and condemnation.

B. **"It is Christ that died, yea rather, that is risen again, who is even at the right hand of God, who also maketh intercession for us"** (Job 34:29; Mark 16:19; Colossians 3:1; Hebrews 7:25; 9:24; I John 2:1).

Note the major doctrines implied here:
- Christ died—His crucifixion.
- Christ is risen—His resurrection.
- Christ is at God's right hand—His ascension.
- Christ is interceding—His session. He is the Mediator between God and man and operates in the ministry of intercession.

Note the word "also" (cf. verses 26-27 notes). Thus, the believer has two intercessors: Christ in heaven—for us; and the Holy Spirit in earth—in us.

This chapter shows that the complete Godhead is at work on behalf of the believer:
- God is for us (Romans 8:31).
- Christ is for us (Romans 8:34).
- The Holy Spirit is for us (Romans 8:26).

Verse 35: *"Who shall separate us from the love of Christ? shall tribulation, or distress, or persecution, or famine, or nakedness, or peril, or sword?"*

A. **"Who shall separate us from the love of Christ?"**

Nothing is able to separate the believer in Christ from the love of Christ. After making such a sweeping question, Paul goes on to list two groups of things which, on the surface, seem to separate us from the love of Christ. Indeed, they seem contrary to the love of Christ. But all are part of the "all things" that work together for good in conforming us to the image of God in His Son. (Note Group One below and Group Two under Romans 8:38-39.)

B. **Group One:**
"Shall tribulation" (This word is used about thirty-seven times, indicating Satan's afflictions on the saints.)
"Or distress"
"Or persecution"
"Or famine"
"Or nakedness"
"Or peril"
"Or sword"

By faith, others endured all these things. All the saints of all the ages have experienced some or all of these things, yet faith carried them through as victors (cf. II Corinthians 4:7-18; Hebrews 11:35-40).

Verse 36: *"As it is written, For thy sake we are killed all the day long; we are accounted as sheep for the slaughter."*

(Quoted from Psalm 44:22 and read with II Corinthians 4:10-11.)

"We are accounted as sheep for the slaughter"
Christ was accounted as a sheep for the slaughter and was dumb before His shearers; so should His people be (Isaiah 53:7; Matthew 26:63; Acts 8:32). Our responses will be the same as His. "...[H]e opened not his mouth..." to defend Himself and His innocence or to save Himself (Isaiah 53:7). These things are the "...sufferings of this present time..." (Romans 8:18).

Verse 37: *"Nay, in all these things we are more than conquerors through him that loved us."*

A. **"In all these things"**
In all these things, not outside or apart from them, we are more than conquerors.

B. **"More than conquerors"**
We are not just conquerors, but more than conquerors. We are not just gaining the victory, but also taking the spoils (I Corinthians 15:57; I John 4:4).

C. **"Through him that loved us"**
His love for us and in us (Romans 8:33, 37, 39) will be the conquering power within.

Verses 38-39: *"For I am persuaded, that neither death, nor life, nor angels, nor principalities, nor powers, nor things present, nor things to come, nor height, nor depth, nor any other creature, shall be able to separate us from the love of God, which is in Christ Jesus our Lord."*

A. Group Two:
    "Neither death" – bodily dissolution
    "Nor life" – present life
    "Nor angels" – good or evil
    "Nor principalities" – good or evil (Ephesians 1:21)
    "Nor powers" – good or evil
    "Nor things present" – things in present time
    "Nor things to come" – things in the future
    "Nor height"
    "Nor depth"
    "Nor any other creature"

B. "Shall be able to separate us from the love of God" (cf. Romans 8:35, 37, 39)
    Greek: *Agape* is the love of God, the love of Christ. Of the seventeen things listed in the two groups, none can separate us from God's love in Christ. Notice that these things reach all realms: the physical, the material, the spiritual, the invisible, and the eternal. The one and only thing not listed is *sin!* Sin is the one and only thing in the entire universe that separates the sinner eternally from the love of God in Christ if that redeeming love is rejected in this world.

RIGHTEOUSNESS REJECTED

Righteousness Rejected
(Romans 9:1 - 11:36)

In this section, we move into the great dispensational truth of God's dealings with Israel and the great problem of the setting aside of the nation as a whole and the coming in of the Gentiles.

These national chapters have been greatly misunderstood and misconstrued because of "ultra-national" concepts of the nation of Israel in the plan of God. A careful exposition will help to clarify the "Jewish problem." This is the whole purpose of these chapters—Romans 9, 10, 11. Divine sovereignty in God's calling of Israel is apparent, as well as human responsibility in Israel's rejection of God's salvation.

The Two Israels: Natural and Spiritual (Romans 9:1-13)

The Benefits of Natural Israel (Romans 9:1-5)

Verse 1: *"I say the truth in Christ, I lie not, my conscience also bearing me witness in the Holy Ghost..."*

A. **"In Christ"**
   This is one of Paul's favorite expressions (cf. Galatians 2:4, 16; 3:17; I Corinthians 1:2; II Corinthians 1:21; Galatians 1:22; I Timothy 2:7).

B. **"My conscience also bearing me witness in the Holy Ghost"**
   Notice how Paul's conscience and the Holy Spirit bore witness to the truth. Paul always endeavored to have a clear conscience before God and man (Acts 23:1; Hebrews 9:14).
   The conscience can be seared and defiled. The conscience is not an infallible guide. It must be cleansed by the blood of Christ and brought into alignment with the Holy Spirit. The Holy Spirit works through such a conscience. Thus, Paul could say that his conscience bore him witness in the Holy Spirit. The Spirit brings a man into harmony with the Word of God also. (Refer to these Scriptures on "conscience": I Peter 3:16; Acts 24:16; Romans 2:15; 13:5; II Corinthians 5:11; I Timothy 3:9; Hebrews 9:14; 10:22.)

Verse 2: *"...That I have great heaviness and continual sorrow in my heart."*

(Cf. Romans 10:1; refer to notes.)

"Great heaviness and continual sorrow"
Sorrow and pangs were Paul's lot over his own nation, even though his own nation persecuted him the most. There was no hardness in his heart, only heaviness and continuous sorrow for them. This can only come from a heart of deep love.

Verse 3: *"For I could wish that myself were accursed from Christ for my brethren, my kinsmen according to the flesh..."*

A. "Accursed"
"Accursed" means "separated to destruction" (Galatians 1:8-9; I Corinthians 12:3; 16:22). Paul's cry is equivalent to the cry of Moses (Exodus 33). Moses was willing to have his name blotted out of God's Book of Life in order to save the nation of Israel (Exodus 32:32). "Save them and damn me" is what Moses was saying. Paul is echoing the same desire for the nation in his time. However, Jesus alone was separated and became accursed of God on the Cross (Galatians 3:13) in order that none may be accused.

B. "My brethren, my kinsmen according to the flesh"
Paul is referring to natural Israel after the fleshly birth, not the true Israel after the spiritual birth, as is soon to be seen (Acts 3:12).

Verses 4-5: *"...Who are Israelites; to whom pertaineth the adoption, and the glory, and the covenants, and the giving of the law, and the service of God, and the promises; whose are the fathers, and of whom as concerning the flesh Christ came, who is over all, God blessed for ever. Amen."*

Here Paul lists eight further advantages of the Jews or natural Israel. The things listed show the basic reasons for the choice of the nation by God.

A. The Choice
Scripture reveals that Israel was the nation that God chose to fulfill His own purposes. God took Israel as a nation from the midst of the nations

and made it a great nation by His statues, laws, and judgments (Deuteronomy 4:6-8, 34). In the covenant to Abraham, God said that He would make of him a great nation (Genesis 12:2-3). God also promised Abraham that He would make him a father of many nations (Genesis 17:1-7).

B. The Reason

God chose Israel to be a special people to Himself above all the people on the earth because of His love and because of the covenant that He made with Israel's fathers, Abraham, Isaac, and Jacob (Deuteronomy 7:6-9; 9:1-6). There were a number of things involved in the purpose for this divine choice:

- Israel was chosen to bless all nations (Genesis 9:27; 12:2-3; 17:4-7; 18:18; 22:16-18).

- Israel was chosen to receive the blessing of God (refer to the list to follow here).

- Israel was chosen to be the guardian of the Oracles of God (Romans 3:2; refer to notes).

The list of the blessings bestowed on Israel are set forth with brief explanation.

1) The Adoption – Israel was adopted as God's own firstborn son from among the nations (Genesis 48-49; Exodus 4:22-23; Romans 8:15; Deuteronomy 14:1; Hosea 11:1).

2) The Glory of God – The visible manifestation of the presence of God was evident in the glory-cloud, called "the Shekinah" by the Jews (Exodus 24:16; 40:34-35; Ezekiel 1:28; Hebrews 9:5; I Samuel 4:21; I Kings 8:11).

3) The Covenants – The Abrahamic, the Mosaic, the Palestinian, the Davidic, and finally the New Covenant were made with Israel (Galatians 3:16-17; Ephesians 2:12; Acts 3:25; Matthew 26:26-28).

4) The Giving of the Law – The moral, civil, and ceremonial laws were given to Israel (legislation) (Psalm 147:19; Exodus 20-24; Exodus 25-40; Deuteronomy 4-5).

5) The Service of God – The Tabernacle of Moses, the Tabernacle of David, and the Temple of Solomon with their respective orders of worship were set up in Israel (Hebrews 9:1; Exodus 25-40; Luke 1:74; Philippians 3:3; Levitical services especially).

6) The Promises – The promises of God, particularly as they relate to the seed, the messianic promises (as the sand, then as the stars), and the land, were given to Israel. Natural, temporal, and spiritual promises were involved (Acts 13:32; Ephesians 2:12; Genesis 13; Genesis 15; Genesis 22).

7) The Fathers – Abraham, Isaac, and Jacob, especially, were the three fathers of Israel (Exodus 3:6; Genesis 48:15-16; Deuteronomy 10:15).

8) The Messiah – The line descent of the Messiah, as pertaining to His human nature, came through Israel (Romans 1:3; Luke 3:23-38; Jeremiah 23:5).

9) The Oracles of God – The Word of God, the Holy Scriptures were given to Israel.

The summation of these show that the choice of Israel as a nation was to receive and to be the guardians of the written Words and to be the progenitors of the living Word through whom all nations would be blessed.

The True Israel of God (Romans 9:6-13)

Verse 6: *"Not as though the word of God hath taken none effect. For they are not all Israel, which are of Israel..."*

(Cf. Numbers 23:19)

A. **"Taken none effect"**
This phrase literally means "fallen out or failed." The Word of God never fails but accomplishes that which it is sent to do, in spite of the failures of men (Isaiah 55:10-11).
Paul is quick to add this statement, lest any feel that God's giving of all these benefits to Israel had been in vain or of no effect.

B. **"For they are not all Israel, which are of Israel"**
Nothing could be clearer or plainer than this statement. It specifically shows that there are really two Israels—the natural and the spiritual (John 8:39; Galatians 6:16).

Paul then proceeds to demonstrate or illustrate the two Israels by several groups of twos, which set forth the natural and the spiritual.

Verse 7: *"...Neither, because they are the seed of Abraham, are they all children: but, In Isaac shall thy seed be called."*

A. **"The seed of Abraham"**

Here Paul refers to "the seed of Abraham." By referring to the accounts in Genesis, we find that Abraham had other "seed" besides Isaac:

- Ishmael was Abraham's seed by Hagar, the Egyptian handmaid. Ishmael was a child of the flesh (Genesis 16).
- Isaac was Abraham's seed by Sarah, the proper wife. Isaac was the child of the promise (Genesis 21).
- After the death of Sarah, Abraham married again, and by his second wife, Keturah, there came at least six sons. These were also the seed of Abraham (Genesis 25:1-6).

Thus, there are other nations who can claim Abraham as their father, and the people of those nations can claim to be the seed of Abraham; that is, after the natural birth. However, the Scripture is clear that these are not counted for *the seed.* Only "...in Isaac shall thy seed be called" (Galatians 4:23; Genesis 21:12), not "in Ishmael," etc. That is to say, only the nation that could trace its birth and genealogy through to Isaac, Abraham's only begotten son, could, in God's sight, be counted for *the seed.*

B. **"In Isaac"**

"In Isaac" of the Old Testament pointed to "in Christ" of the New Testament. This was the great conflict in the gospel of John (John 8) between Jesus and the Jews. Jesus acknowledged their claim as the seed of Abraham by the natural birth, but He repudiated their claim as the seed of Abraham by reason of their lack of spiritual birth (John 8:33-40). Thus, the Ishmaelites, the Midianites, and the Edomites could all be counted as Abraham's seed if this was not so.

Verse 8: *"That is, They which are the children of the flesh, these are not the children of God: but the children of the promise are counted for the seed."*

"They which are the children of the flesh"

Thus, the children of the flesh, Hagar's son, Ishmael, and the sons of Keturah, though Abraham's seed, are not counted as the children of God. Only the children of the promise are counted before God (Galatians 4:23-28). These simple diagrams show the two seed lines that Paul is referring to.

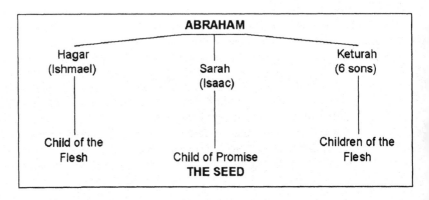

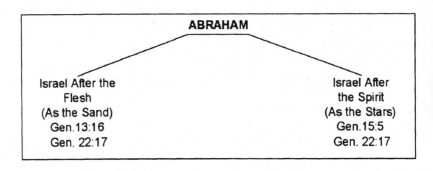

Verse 9: *"For this is the word of promise, At this time will I come, and Sarah shall have a son."*

(Galatians 4:23-28)

"And Sarah shall have a son" (Genesis 18:10, 14)

Any seed outside of Sarah's son, Isaac, is not counted as *the* seed in God's mind. Isaac pointed to Jesus, who was Abraham's seed in the truest sense of the word (Galatians 3:16; Romans 9:10-13).

Verses 10-13: *"And not only this; but when Rebecca also had conceived by one, even by our father Isaac; (for the children being not yet born, neither having done any good or evil, that the purpose of God according to election might stand, not of works, but of Him that calleth;) it was said unto her, The elder shall serve the younger. As it is written, Jacob have I loved, but Esau have I hated."*

A. God's Choice of Seed

Here Paul introduces his next illustration concerning the choice of a particular seed involving Isaac's wife, Rebecca, and their twin sons, Jacob and Esau (Genesis 25:21).

God promised Rebecca, before the sons were born, neither having done good or evil, that the elder, Esau, should serve the younger, Jacob (Genesis 25:23). Years later, through the prophet, Malachi (Malachi 1:2-3), God could say that He loved Jacob and hated (a Hebraism for "not chosen") Esau (John 3:20; James 3:16; Jeremiah 49:10; Matthew 6:24; Luke 14:26). All this could be done on the basis of God's foreknowledge (cf. Numbers 23:10; 7, 23; 24:5; 20:14-21).

In fact, Romans 9 really illustrates Romans 8:28-30, in relation to the words "will," "purpose," "foreknowledge," "predestination," and "calling." Again, we see the choice between two seed lines, through Isaac, as the following diagram shows.

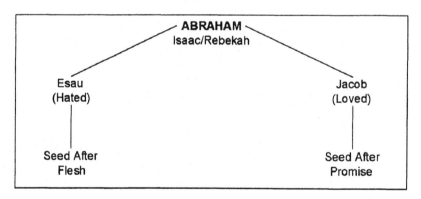

God's choice here was not on the basis of the children having done good or evil, as they had not yet even been born. It was on the basis of His foreknowledge. "For whom he did foreknow, he also did predestinate...them he also called..." (Romans 8:29-30). Thus, we have "will," "purpose," "foreknowledge," "predestination," and "calling" involved here.

Paul introduces another word, "election," in relation to "purpose" and "calling." Thus, the words may be arranged as follows:

- Will
- Purpose
- Foreknowledge
- Election
- Predestination
- Calling (Romans 4:17)

God had a purpose in His election (choice) of Jacob in preference to Esau, and hence, He called Jacob to be *the* seed. There are two important words used here, and subsequently through these "national chapters." These two words are the following: (1) "election," and (2) "calling." It would be appropriate to consider these (Romans 9:11).

B. **Election**

"Elect" in the Hebrew: *Bawkheer* means "to select, to choose; the person chosen." "Elect" in the Greek: *Eklektos* means "picked out; chosen (by God)." "Election" in the Greek: *Ekloge* means "selection, choice; the act of picking out; the person chosen."

- "...God's elect..." (Romans 8:33).
- "...[T]he purpose of God according to election..." (Romans 9:11).
- "...[T]here is a remnant according to the election of grace" (Romans 11:5).
- "...[T]he election hath obtained it..." (Romans 11:7).
- "...[A]s touching the election, they are beloved..." (Romans 11:28).

In its simplest meaning, this word refers to the intention, process, and result of making a choice. It refers to an act of the will, but more specifically, in the Scriptures, it refers to an act of the divine will.

- Christ is God's elect (Luke 23:35; I Peter 2:4-6).
- The angels are God's elect (I Timothy 5:21; contrast fallen angels).
- Israel was God's elect (Isaiah 45:4).
- The church is God's elect (Matthew 20:16; 22:4; 24:22; 24:31, 24; Mark 13:20, 22, 27; Luke 18:7; John 15:16, 19; Romans 8:33; 11:5, 7; I Corinthians 1:27-28; Ephesians 1:4; Colossians 3:12; I Thessalonians 1:4; II Timothy 2:10; Titus 1:1; I Peter 1:2; 2:9; II Peter 1:10; Revelation 17:14).

This term is applied both corporately (see above) and individually (Psalm 106:23 – Moses; Acts 9:15 – Paul; Romans 16:13; Rufus).

There are two major aspects of election that must be kept distinct:
1) Election of Time – temporal purpose, whether positive or negative
2) Election of Eternity – eternal destiny, on the basis of grace

The election of time refers to God's choosing of individuals or nations to fulfill His purposes in relation to time. Such was the case with Pharaoh (who resists), Moses (who accepts), Cyrus, Israel, Assyria, and Babylon. This involved privilege and responsibility. Election of eternity refers to the eternal destiny of all freewill, moral agents.

In relation to the choice (election) of Isaac above Ishmael, and Jacob above Esau, it was first of all an election of time with temporal purposes, as far as the nation of Israel was concerned. Above and beyond this, there were things involving the eternal purposes of God, as far as the redemption of mankind was concerned. However, this is not to say that God elected Isaac and Jacob to be saved and Ishmael and Esau to be damned. Neither does this imply that God elected all members of natural or national Israel to be saved and other nations to be damned. Both the Old and New Testaments clearly show that even in national Israel, there were those who were sons of Belial. There were those who said "they were Jews and were not" but belonged to the synagogue of Satan, or as Paul said in verse 6, "...For they are not all Israel, which are of Israel." In other words, there are two Israels: the natural and the spiritual. These involve the two aspects of election: the election of time and the election of eternity.

- Election is a sovereign act of God, whereby certain persons are chosen from among mankind for Himself (John 15:19). God was under no obligation to elect anyone, since all have lost their standing before Him.

- Election is wholly of grace, apart from human merit (Romans 9:11; 11:5-6). He chose those who were utterly unworthy of salvation. Man deserved the exact opposite, but in His grace, He chose to save some.

- Election is only applicable to those "in Christ." God could not choose man based on himself because of his sinfulness and ill-deserving state; therefore, God could only choose man based on the merits of another.

- Election is according to and soundly based on God's foreknowledge (I Peter 1:1-2). God chose only those whom He foreknew would accept Christ.

C. **Election and Foreknowledge**

Greek: *Proginosko* means "to know beforehand," to foreknow. Greek: *Prognosis* means "a knowing beforehand," foreknowledge.

These words simply refer to a knowing beforehand. The first is used twice of human knowledge (Acts 26:5; II Peter 3:17), but both are otherwise used of divine knowledge, referring to God's ability to perfectly know the future.

- Christ was foreknown (Acts 2:23; I Peter 1:20 [Authorized King James says, "foreordained"]).
- Israel was foreknown (Romans 11:2, as God's earthly people).
- The church was foreknown (Romans 8:29; I Peter 1:2).

Notice the related words, "foresee" and "foretell." They, along with "foreknowledge," are connected with God's omniscience. Foretelling refers to prophecy, and as such, is not connected to predestination, but to foreknowledge. God foresaw, and foreknew, and thus, He foretold through the mouth of the prophets. The Scriptures definitely base God's election on His foreknowledge.

- "For whom he did foreknow, he also did predestinate..." (Romans 8:29).
- "Elect according to the foreknowledge of God the Father..." (I Peter 1:2).

Because Scripture repeatedly teaches that man is responsible for accepting or rejecting salvation, we must conclude that the basis of God's election is man's reaction to the revelation God has made of Himself. Since man is hopelessly dead in trespasses and sins and cannot do anything to obtain salvation, God graciously restores to all men sufficient ability to make their own choices as to whether or not they will submit to Him. In His foreknowledge, He sees what each man will do with this restored ability, and He elects men to salvation in harmony with His knowledge of their choice of Him.

God's foreknowledge did not stem from His election or predestination. Before He created anything, He foresaw that sin would enter the universe, yet He decided to let it happen. Before He created man, He foreknew how far man would depart from holiness and who, specifically, would depart from it, and in the light of this knowledge, He thought it good to create man and to permit such a departure from the right way. Even though God foresaw the entrance of sin and allowed it to happen, still He did not cause it. So also, God is able to foresee man's choices without violating man's freewill, by causing man to choose according to His foreknowledge.

D. **Election and Predestination**

Greek: *Pro-orize* literally means "to previously mark out by a boundary line, to predetermine, to decide beforehand." This word is used to refer to a determination made previous to its actual coming to pass and which carries with it the power to make it come to pass. Thus, it is an action of will, only attributed to God Himself. Predestination, then, is the effective exercise of the will of God by which things determined by Him are brought to pass.

- The work of the Atonement was predestinated (Acts 4:28; 1 Corinthians 2:7).
- Saints are predestinated:
  1) To be conformed to the image of Christ (Romans 8:29-30).
  2) To become the children of God (Ephesians 1:5).
  3) To bring praise and glory to God (Ephesians 1:11-12).

Although election and predestination go hand in hand, notice the following distinction:

- Election – God has decided to save those who accept His Son.
- Predestination – God has fixed the destiny beforehand of those who are and are not of His election. Thus, predestination can be viewed as the bringing to pass of God's election. While election looks back to foreknowledge, predestination looks forward to destiny. Both are based on God's foreknowledge; neither violates man's freewill choice.

E. **Election and Calling**

Greek: *Kaleo* means "to call into one's presence, to invite, to call by name." Greek: *Kletos* means "called, invited." Greek: *Klesis* means "a calling to, an invitation to." Greek: *Proskaleo* means "to call to oneself, to bid to come to oneself."

These words all imply a calling or an inviting, and when used in relation to God as the One who calls or invites, they point to one of two major areas:

1) A call to participation in the privileges of the gospel—a call to salvation

2) A call to participation in the function of the gospel—a call to ministry

Notice how the word "call" is used in the present discussion and in these chapters:

- "...[T]he called according to his purpose" (Romans 8:28).
- "...[D]id foreknow...did predestinate...called..." (Romans 8:29-30).
- "...In Isaac shall thy seed be called" (Romans 9:7).
- "...[N]ot of works, but of him that calleth..." (Romans 9:11).
- "...[W]hom he hath called, not of the Jews only, but also of the Gentiles" (Romans 9:24).
- "...I will call them my people..." (Romans 9:25).
- "...[R]ich unto all that call upon him" (Romans 10:12).
- "For whosoever shall call on the name of the Lord..." (Romans 10:13).
- "How then shall they call on him..." (Romans 10:14).
- "For the gifts and calling of God are without repentance" (Romans 11:29). (Refer to *Strong's* numbers 2564, 2821.)

Thus, we have in this progression: grace, election, election and foreknowledge, election and predestination, and then election and calling.

God's calling is based on predestination, which is based on foreknowledge, which is based on the essential attribute of God called "omniscience." Again, calling may involve temporal and/or eternal purposes; thus, God "calls" Gentile kings and nations to purpose or to fulfill His purposes. Man must respond to this call. It is not of works. Man cannot call himself. He can respond to God's choice and call.

In relation to the choice of Israel, we see the election of race (*ethnos*, nation) (Romans 9:11; 11:28), and we see also the election of grace (Romans 11:5, 7).

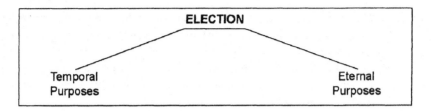

God call men first to repentance (Matthew 3:2; 4:17; Mark 1:15; Acts 2:38; 17:30; II Peter 3:9), and secondly to faith (Mark 1:15; John 6:29; 20:31; Acts 16:31; 19:4; Romans 10:9; I John 3:23). His calling is to all men, to "whosoever," to "all the ends of the earth" (Romans 9:30; Matthew 11:28; John 3:16; Revelation 22:17; Isaiah 45:22; Matthew 28:19; Mark 16:15; I Timothy 2:4; II Peter 3:9; Matthew 22:9). God's desire is that all men might be saved. Only man's free will becomes the obstacle to his salvation. The means of the call are various. God uses the following:

- The Word of God—the Gospel (Romans 10:17; II Thessalonians 2:14)
- The Spirit of God to Convict (John 16:7-11; Genesis 6:3; Hebrews 3:7-8)
- The Servants of the Lord (II Chronicles 36:15-16; Jeremiah 25:4; Romans 10:14-15)
- Providential Dealings of God (Romans 2:4; Jeremiah 31:3; Isaiah 26:9; Psalm 107:6)

While election, predestination, and foreknowledge relate to eternity, more specifically, calling relates to time. God's call has been sounding throughout the ages of time and will continue to sound in the "space given to repent" to man in this plan of the ages.

It should be noted that God called Isaac, Jacob, and the nation of Israel to fulfill His purposes, touching both temporal and eternal realities. It was not that Israel was predestined to salvation eternally. while other nations were predestined to damnation eternally. For, in the work of the Atonement, Paul has made it clear that salvation is available for all men, be they Jew or Gentile.

God has atoned for man in Christ, the debt has been paid, and reconciliation is available for all men. The Atonement has been made available for all. However, the question will arise: if the Atonement is for all, then are all actually saved? The answer to this question is found by considering this Atonement in its two distinct parts: the provision and the application.

Since Christ has rendered penal satisfaction to the Father, He alone has the right to declare the terms upon which the benefits of His death and resurrection are to be bestowed. Just as He was not obligated to die for any man in the first place, neither is He now obligated to save everyone. As He was moved by grace to provide salvation, so He is moved by grace to lay down the conditions on which salvation may be experienced. This is for Jew or Gentile. It is this delicate balance in theology which must be kept in view when considering these "national chapters" concerning the casting off of Israel and its acceptance again into the olive tree.

These two columns will show the delicate balance between the provision and application of the Atonement, whether for Jew or Gentile, circumcised or uncircumcised.

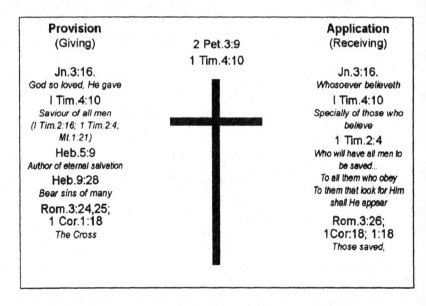

Provision (Giving)	2 Pet.3:9 1 Tim.4:10	**Application** (Receiving)
Jn.3:16. *God so loved, He gave*		Jn.3:16. *Whosoever believeth*
I Tim.4:10 *Saviour of all men* *(I Tim.2:16; 1 Tim.2:4;* *Mt.1:21)*		I Tim.4:10 *Specially of those who* *believe*
Heb.5:9 *Author of eternal salvation*		1 Tim.2:4 *Who will have all men to* *be saved...*
Heb.9:28 *Bear sins of many*		*To all them who obey* *To them that look for Him* *shall He appear*
Rom.3:24,25; 1 Cor.1:18 *The Cross*		Rom.3:26; 1Cor:18; 1:18 *Those saved,*

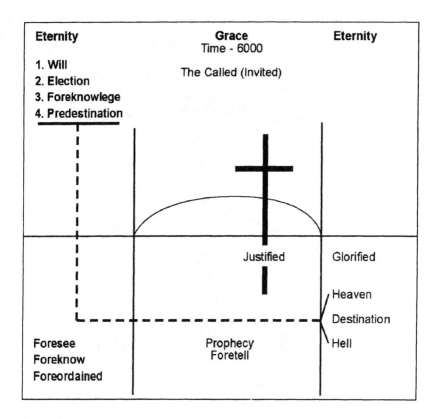

(Refer also to Theissen's *Systematic Theology*, p.341.)

If a person goes to one extreme on this, he or she will become fatalistic (the belief that there is no need to try), or if a person goes to the other extreme he or she will fall into the trap of legalism (works of self-effort). Faith is essential in order to be one of God's elect (Titus 1:1). This became the stumbling block to Israel, the elect nation.

Note the diagram on the following page.

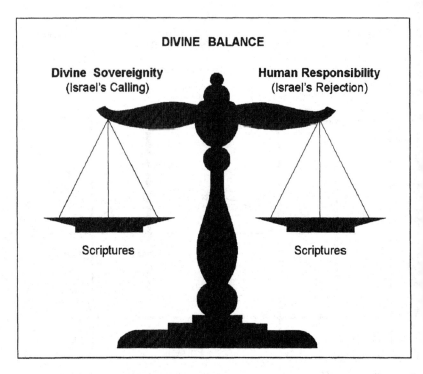

Refer to diagram concerning "Provision" and "Application" and apply Scriptures to the above scales.

Vessels of Wrath and Vessels of Mercy (Romans 9:14-29)

The Mercy of God (Romans 9:14-18)

Verse 14: *"What shall we say then? Is there unrighteousness with God? God forbid."*

Paul anticipates the Jews' reaction to God's elective purposes. The Jews would charge God with wrongdoing, for choosing persons before birth, before they had done neither good nor evil, and before they had any say in the matter. The Scriptures show that there is no unrighteousness with God. God is just in all His dealings, even with His creatures (Deuteronomy 32:4; Job 8:3). He cannot do anything with His creatures that is inconsistent with His character, and His moral attributes cannot be violated.

Verse 15: *"For he saith to Moses, I will have mercy on whom I will have mercy, and will have compassion on whom I will have compassion."*

This was spoken to Moses concerning Israel at a time when God would have destroyed the nation had it not been for the intercessory prayer of Moses, their mediator (Exodus 33:16-19).

Verse 16: *"So then it is not of him that willeth, nor of him that runneth, but of God that sheweth mercy."*

In this verse, we get to the word and the very cause behind "election." That is "mercy"—the mercy of God. Notice the use of the words in these verses.

A. **"Willeth"**
God will have mercy on whom He will have mercy (verse 15). It is not of man's self will (verse 16).

B. **"Runneth"**
"Runneth" reflects strenuous effort as in a fast race (cf. I Corinthians 9:24-26; Galatians 2:2; 5:7; II Thessalonians 3:1). Thus, it is not human will or human work.

C. **"Mercy"** (verses 15-16, 18, 23)
Mercy is the pity of God.
- "...I will have mercy on whom I will have mercy..." (Romans 9:15).
- "...God that sheweth mercy" (Romans 9:16).
- "Therefore hath he mercy on whom he will have mercy..." (Romans 9:18).
- "...[V]essels of mercy..." (Romans 9:23).
- "...[H]ave now obtained mercy..." (Romans 11:30).
- "...[T]hat through your mercy they may obtain mercy" (Romans 11:31).
- "...[T]hat he might have mercy upon all" (Romans 11:32).

God can have pity on whom He chooses. Mercy arises out of grace (Romans 11:5-6). There is nothing in fallen and sinful man that deserves or merits the grace and mercy of God. Hence, if man is to receive mercy, it must come spontaneously from the heart of God. And this is what happens. God can choose to have mercy and compassion on whom He will. It is His will or wish to do so. He wishes to have mercy upon all, but not all will respond to his mercy (Romans 11:32; Ephesians 2:5-10; Titus 3:4-6).

The balance is seen again in the sovereign will of God (John 6:37; 1:12; Acts 13:48; Romans 9:15; Ephesians 1:4-5; II Thessalonians 2:13; II Timothy 1:9; I Peter 1:2; Romans 8:29-30) and the free will of man (as Adam was free to choose) (John 3:16; 5:40; Romans 3:22-23; Revelation 22:17).

Verse 17: *"For the scripture saith unto Pharaoh, Even for this same purpose have I raised thee up, that I might shew my power in thee, and that my name might be declared throughout all the earth."*

(Exodus 9:16; Exodus 4:21; 5:2; 7:3, 4)

Another dual is brought in here by implication, to illustrate God's choice in His elective purposes. This involves two nations, Moses with Israel, and Pharaoh with Egyptians. The very thing God raised up (created thee, preserved him alive) Pharaoh for was that so His power and His Name might be declared throughout the then known world. God's power and Name would be manifested in both Egypt and Israel, one, in a negative way, judgment; and the other, in a positive way, mercy.

It is important to understand that which pertains to Pharaoh, expressly as it is stated in the next verse. Note the diagram below.

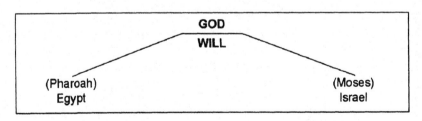

Verse 18: *"Therefore hath he mercy on whom he will have mercy, and whom he will he hardeneth."*

"Hath he mercy on whom he will have mercy, and whom he will he hardeneth"

In this verse, we touch upon another principle of God's dealings with mankind. God will have mercy on whomsoever He will, but He hardens His heart toward those who resist His mercy. The same sun that melts also hardens. There are a number of Scriptures that deal with the hardening of the heart. These Scriptures flow into two streams. One stream shows man hardening his heart, and the other stream shows God hardening the heart of man. The principle is best defined for us in Psalm 18:25-26, which states: "With the merciful thou wilt shew thyself merciful; with an upright man thou wilt shew thyself upright; with the pure thou wilt shew thyself pure; and with the froward thou wilt shew thyself froward."

- "...[C]ondemning the wicked, to bring his way upon his head..." (I Kings 8:32).
- "Surely he scorneth the scorners: but he giveth grace unto the lowly" (Proverbs 3:34).
- "Then will I also walk contrary unto you..." (Leviticus 26:23-24, 27-28; read also I Samuel 2:30).

In other words, God will be to us what we are to Him. God will harden His heart if we harden our hearts. The following Scriptures are applicable to Pharaoh and all who follow his obstinacy:
- "A wicked man hardeneth his face..." (Proverbs 21:29).
- "...[H]e that hardeneth his heart shall fall into mischief" (Proverbs 28:14).
- "He, that being often reproved hardeneth his neck, shall suddenly be destroyed, and that without remedy" (Proverbs 29:1).
- "...[T]hy hardness and impenitent heart..." (Romans 2:5).
- "...[T]he hardness of your hearts..." (Matthew 19:8; 10:14-15; 16:4; Acts 19:9).

It is plainly stated in Scripture that Pharaoh was often reproved, but hardened his heart and was finally cut off. Because Pharaoh hardened his heart, God further hardened Pharaoh's heart. "...[W]hom he will he hardeneth" (Romans 9:18). Vincent states, "In Exodus the hardening is represented as self-produced (Exodus 8:15, 32; 9:34), and as produced by God (Exodus 4:21; 7:3; 9:12; 10:20, 27; 11:10). Paul here chooses the latter representation."

The words "harden" and hardened" are used twenty times in the book of Exodus in the Amplified Version. In the Hebrew, there are three different root words used:

1) *Strong's* number 2388 – Hebrew: *Chazaq* means (1) "to tie fast, to bind"; (2) "to hold fast, to stick fast, to persist, to be constant, to be earnest or assiduous"; (3) "to make firm, to strengthen, to be hardened, to be obstinate" (Malachi 3:13); (4) "to be urgent, pressing" (Gesenius). This word is used in Exodus 4:21; 7:13, 22; 8:19; 9:12, 35; 10:20, 27; 11:10; 14:4, 8, 17. Every one of these occurrences involves the Lord acting upon Pharaoh (Exodus 7:22; 8:19; 9:35; these merely express the condition of the heart, and it is questionable whether the Lord or Pharaoh acted here).

2) *Strong's* number 7185 – Hebrew: *Qashah* means (1) "to be hard"; (2) "to be heavy" (used of the hand of God in punishment); (3) "to be difficult, hard" (Gesenius). This word is only translated "harden" once in Exodus 7:3 (literally, "I will cause to harden"), concerning the Lord acting upon Pharaoh, but the same word is used in Exodus 13:15, meaning "Pharaoh would hardly let us go." (It literally means "hardened to let us go" and is used twice, once of the Lord upon Pharaoh, and once of Pharaoh upon himself.)

3) *Strong's* numbers 3513 and 3515 – Hebrew: *Kabad* or *Kabed* means (1) "to be heavy, indolence, dullness"; (2) "to harden" (Gesenius). This word is translated "hardened" six times in Exodus. One time it is used of the Lord acting upon Pharaoh (Exodus 10:1). Three times it is used of Pharaoh hardening his own heart (Exodus 8:15, 32; 9:34). Twice it merely states the condition of Pharaoh's heart without indicating whether it was as a result of the Lord or of Pharaoh's own will. Three times in Exodus 14:4, 17-18, this same word is translated, "I will be honored upon Pharaoh," concerning the Lord acting upon Pharaoh.

According to the Hebrew text there are fourteen instances of the Lord acting upon Pharaoh, four instances of Pharaoh hardening his own heart, and five instances that express the condition of Pharaoh's heart.

God, who dealt with Pharaoh, showed His forbearance and long-suffering by giving him opportunities to repent. To them that loved Him, He showed mercy; to them that hated Him, He showed judgment (cf. I Samuel 6:6 with these Scriptures also).

In considering the fact of God hardening the heart of Pharaoh, the whole context of biblical revelation must be taken into consideration. God never capriciously hardens men's hearts. God is just, righteous, and holy in His being and in all His ways, as noted previously. God cannot and will not do anything with His creatures which is inconsistent with His character; God, for He is love and grace personified, does not harden men because of His own whims and fancies. There was some obstinacy in the heart of Pharaoh. There was resistance to the mighty plagues and miracles, and though he seemed to repent, it was but a temporary remorse for the trouble that Egypt was in. As soon as one plague was removed, he hardened his heart again, which in turn evoked another plague. God could justly harden Pharaoh's heart because of this vacillating attitude.

"We cannot charge God with cruelty and injustice, or anything that is inconsistent with His own righteous character and laws. To do so is to make God the author of sin, and promoter of evil. It is to contradict other passages of Scripture (I Timothy 2:14; James 1:13; II Peter 3:9) and also to contradict the facts in Pharaoh's own case, for, God gave Pharaoh abundant warning, instruction, and calls and inducement to repentance" (Vincent). Note the following diagram in relation to a balance.

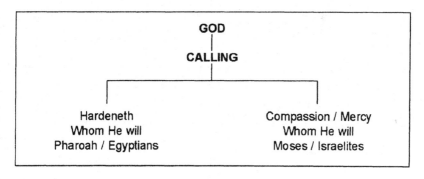

The Divine Potter (Romans 9:19-29)

Divine sovereignty and human responsibility are here in delicate balance in this "hardening" realm.

Verse 19: *"Thou wilt say then unto me, Why doth he yet find fault? For who hath resisted his will?"*

Paul anticipates another reaction of the Jews to his statement on the will of God showing mercy or hardening the heart. If God does according to His will, then why does He yet find fault? None can resist His counsel or his deliberate determinations (Daniel 4:34; II Chronicles 20:6).

It should be remembered that there are two Greek words for "will." One, *thelo,* refers to "wish or desire," and the other, *boulomai,* refers to "resolve, council, or deliberate determination." In Romans 9:18, the word "*thelo*" is used twice. In Romans 9:19, the word "*boulomai*" is used.

Verse 20: *"Nay but, O man, who art thou that repliest against God? Shall the thing formed say to him that formed it, Why hast thou made me thus?"*

A. **"O man, who art thou that repliest against God"**

In response to Jewish reaction against God's sovereign will, Paul reproves them for answering for and daring to dispute with God—the creature arguing with the Creator. The real issue is that God can do what He wishes or wills with His own creation. Of course, His attributes show us that He will not do anything with His creatures that would be inconsistent with His moral attributes.

B. **"Shall the thing formed say to him that formed it, "Why hast thou made me this"**

Paul introduces here the figure of the potter and the clay, with a quotation from Isaiah 29:16 and 45:9. What right has the clay to question the potter, who is making of the clay a vessel? No right at all! The potter is the creator, and the clay is the created one.

However, the analogy here must not be taken to the extreme, for man, though created by God and for God, is not a shapeless, senseless, will-less lump of clay. God made man an intelligent, responsible, and freewill being.

Verse 21: *"Hath not the potter power over the clay, of the same lump to make one vessel unto honour, and another unto dishonour?"*

(Read I Peter 3:7; Matthew 12:29; Acts 9:15.) All human beings can be vessels of God, for honor or for dishonor.

Verses 22-24: *"What if God, willing to shew his wrath, and to make his power known, endured with much longsuffering the vessels of wrath fitted to destruction: and that he might make known the riches of his glory on the vessels of mercy, which he had afore prepared unto glory, even us, whom he hath called, not of the Jews only, but also of the Gentiles?"*

A. **"Longsuffering"** (Romans 9:22 with II Peter 3:9)

"The Lord is...long-suffering toward us and is not willing that any should perish, but that all should come to repentance" (II Peter 3:9).

B. "Vessels of wrath . . . vessels of mercy"

The figure of the potter making clay vessels was a very familiar one to
the Jewish mind. Jeremiah 18:1-6 is an example of the Israel nation as a
clay vessel to be used in the hand of the potter (also Genesis 2:7; Isaiah
64:8).

Individuals and nations are spoken of as clay vessels. God, who is the
great Potter, can make whatever type of vessel He pleases and can use this
vessel for whatever purposes He has in mind. However, in all the passages
that deal with the figures of the potter and clay, there are injunctions and
exhortations that deal with man's free-will. For man is not a lump of
senseless or will-less clay. He can respond or resist the Potter's touch. In
the following, we see the divine Potter making two types of vessels: vessels
of wrath and vessels of mercy. The vessels of wrath were fitted (Greek:
Kataptismena literally means "adjusted, or fitted themselves to God's
destruction" [I Thessalonians 2:15-16]; also note "perdition" [as in John
17:12]), and the vessels of mercy were prepared for glory (Psalm 2:9;
Exodus 33:18).

This simple diagram on the following page brings into focus the
dominant features of this chapter expounded thus far:

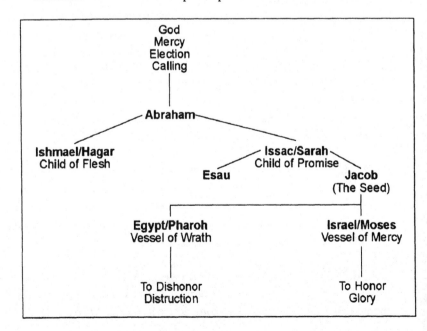

C. **"The riches of his glory"**
Note also:

- "...[T]he riches of the glory..." or "...the riches of his glory..." (Colossians 1:27; Ephesians 1:18; 3:16).
- "...[T]he riches of his goodness..." (Romans 2:4).
- "...[T]he riches both of the wisdom and knowledge..." (Romans 11:33).
- "...[T]he riches of his grace..." (Ephesians 1:7; 2:7).
- "...[T]he unsearchable riches of Christ..." (Ephesians 3:8).

D. **"Afore prepared unto glory"** (Ephesians 2:10; Matthew 25:34; Romans 8:30).

E. **"Called, not of the Jews only, but also of the Gentiles"**
Here, Paul takes his thought of the vessels to mean the present calling of God; that is, the calling out of both Jew and Gentile into God's mercy as revealed in Christ. Just as God could, on the basis of His mercy, choose Isaac, Jacob, and Israel and make them vessels of honor and mercy, so He could choose believing Jews and believing Gentiles to be the same. Also, as He chose Ishmael, Esau, and Pharaoh to be vessels of dishonor and wrath, so He could make unbelieving Jews and unbelieving Gentiles like vessels (Romans 3:29).

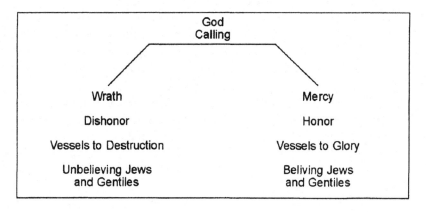

Verses 25-26: *"As he saith also in O see, I will call them my people, which were not my people; and her beloved, which was not beloved. And it shall come to pass, that in the place where it was said unto them, Ye are not my people; there shall they be called the children of the living God."*

Two quotations are taken here from the prophet Hosea (Hosea 2:23 and 1:10). In the context of the book of Hosea, we find that Hosea's marriage and the children born therein were symbolic. The names of his children were especially prophetic. They were "signs and wonders" in Israel (cf. Isaiah 8:18).

The briefest facts of Hosea's marriage and his sign-children need to be understood in measure to appreciate Paul's quotation of these two passages in relation to the calling in of believing Gentiles. Hosea himself typified Jehovah. Gomer, his wife, typified Israel, the wife of Jehovah. His second child, a daughter, was named "Loruhamah," which meant "I will no more have mercy upon the house of Israel." His third child, a son, was named "Lo-ammi," which means "for ye are not My people," and "I will not be your God" (Hosea 1:6-9).

Both of these sign-children signified the rejection and setting aside of the house of Israel by the Lord God; God would not have mercy on them, and they would no longer be His people.

This historically took place about 721 BC during the Assyrian captivity, as far as the house of Israel was concerned. However, the same prophet, Hosea, prophesied of a time to come when the very people who were not God's people would become the sons of the living God (Hosea 1:10). Also, God said that He would have mercy on them who had not obtained mercy, they would become the people of God, and He would be their God (Hosea 2:23).

The apostles, Paul and Peter, take up these verses of Scripture and show that they find their fulfillment in the New Covenant in Christ (compare I Peter 2:10; 1:1 with Romans 10:15-21; 11:30-32).

Paul's use of these verses also shows that they had a much fuller implication that the natural and national Israel, rejected and cast off, would come back and become God's people. Though interpreted to mean natural Israel, yet these verses become applicable and predictive of the Gentiles, who were not God's people and who would become such by the new birth under the New Covenant, by the mercy of God extended to both Jew and Gentile.

Under the Old Covenant, Israel forfeited the mercy of God and actually became "Gentilized." Under the New Covenant, the mercy of God is extended to both Jews and Gentiles (Isaiah 49:22). This was taking place in Paul's time; hence, his use of the prophetic passages from Hosea's sign-children.

The Jews could not complain of the mercy of God made available for Gentiles, or for Jews, for it was, if they would accept it in and through Christ Jesus, God's channel of receiving mercy.

Verse 27: *"Esaias also crieth concerning Israel, Though the number of the children of Israel be as the sand of the sea, a remnant shall be saved..."*

(Cf. Isaiah 10:22-23 and Romans 1:15)

"Crieth" (refer to Luke 18:39; John 7:28, 37; Acts 19:28; 23:6)

Verses 28-29: *"...For he will finish [close the account] the work, and cut it short in righteousness: because a short work will the Lord make upon the earth. And as Esaias said before, Except the Lord of Sabbath had left us a seed, we had been as Sodoma, and been made like unto Gomorrha."*

(Cf. Isaiah 10:23 with Isaiah 28:21-22.)

Here, Paul quotes from the prophet Isaiah for the nation's own Hebrew prophets foretold Israel's rejection, their casting off, and then their subsequent restoration through the New Covenant.

It will be noted that several covenants are involved here, these being the Abrahamic, Mosaic, and the New Covenants. Under the Abrahamic Covenant, God promised that the seed of Abraham would be "as the sand of the sea" (Genesis 13:16; 22:17; Hosea 1:10). The sand is symbolic of the earthly, the natural, national Israel. God could never break the covenant with Abraham, even though He may reject and cast Israel off as if they were not His people. Even though the greater part of the elected nation would be unbelieving, yet there would be a faithful remnant.

"...[A] remnant shall be saved" (Romans 9:27). Notice the use of the word "remnant" in Romans 9:27 and 11:5. God has always preserved unto Himself a believing remnant. (Refer to notes on Romans 11:1-7 with Isaiah 10:20-22.) (On the word "saved," refer to comments on Romans 10:1, 9, 13; 11:14, 26.)

In Romans 9:28, there seems to be an allusion to the quick work of the gospel. God will finish the work (i.e., close the account). He will fulfill His Word. The period of Messiah's ministry, especially, was indeed "a short work" before the Jews, as a nation, rejected it. The prophet Habakkuk said, "Behold ye among the heathen, and regard, and wonder marvellously: for I will work a work in your days, which ye will not believe, though it be told to you" (Habakkuk 1:5; Acts 13:41; Isaiah 28:21; 29:13-14).

The subject of the "remnant" is confirmed again in Romans 9:29, where Paul quotes a further passage from the prophet Isaiah. Isaiah uses the word "remnant," while Paul uses the word "seed." God preserved a remnant, or a seed, in old times, in the midst of apostasy. It is interesting to note the reference to Israel becoming as Sodom and Gomorra. So corrupt had Israel become in Isaiah's time (salvation of Jehovah, type of Jesus) that God refers to His own people as "...rulers of Sodom...people of Gomorrah" (Isaiah 1:1-4, 9-10). The Bible tells us what happened to Sodom and Gomorrah for their wickedness. They were totally destroyed by fire and brimstone. The same thing would have befallen God's chosen nation had it not been for the godly seed, the faithful remnant. The Jews had nothing to say in defense or criticism of the wrath or the mercy of God. Their own nation's history had proved that they themselves did not even deserve mercy (Genesis 18-19).

Thus, Paul brought in two of their prophets, Hosea and Isaiah, who foretold the mercy and grace of God in the midst of wrath (Habakkuk 3:2).

Faith-Righteousness: The Stumbling Stone (Romans 9:30-33)

Verses 30-31: *"What shall we say then? That the Gentiles, which followed not after righteousness, have attained to righteousness, even the righteousness which is of the faith. But Israel, which followed after the law of righteousness, hath not attained to the law of righteousness."*

(Cf. Romans 1:17; 4:11; 10:3; Galatians 5:5)

This is the crux of the whole matter. The Gentiles have obtained the righteousness of faith, even though they were not seeking it. The Jews have not attained it, even though they were seeking after it. Why? The answer is given in the following verse. The tragedy was in the fact that the Jews did not see that God's mercy and elective purposes not only included themselves but also the Gentiles. They expected the Gentiles to come to the gates of Judaism, whereas both Jews and Gentiles were to enter God's gate—Christ Jesus.

Verse 32: *"Wherefore? Because they sought it not by faith, but as it were by the works of the law. For they stumbled at that stumblingstone..."*

The issue of faith versus works comes into play again: a righteousness by faith or a righteousness by works (Romans 3:27; I Corinthians 1:23). (The issue of faith versus works-righteousness has been fully dealt with in chapters 3-5, as seen there.) The only faith righteousness that is acceptable to God is that which He Himself provides, by grace, through faith, in Christ. Man's righteousness is as filthy rags (Isaiah 64:6).

Works-righteousness of the law is but as refuse (Philippians 3:6-9). Faith-righteousness alone is acceptable to God (I Corinthians 1:30). Jesus Christ is God's righteousness personified. He is Jehovah-Tsidkenu, the *Lord* my righteousness (Jeremiah 23:5-6; refer also to notes on Romans 10:3-4).

Verse 33: *"...As it is written, Behold I lay in Sion a stumblingstone and a rock of offence: and whosoever believeth on him shall not be ashamed."*

A. "Lay in Sion"
   (Cf. the Old Testament Mt. Zion, where the Tabernacle of David was pitched.) This is the foreshadowing of the true and the heavenly Mt. Zion—the New Jerusalem, the city of the living God (Hebrews 12:22-24; Psalm 87).

B. "A stumblingstone and a rock of offence"
   Here is the reason that Israel failed to obtain faith-righteousness. The stumblingstone was *faith*. *Faith*-righteousness was also a rock of offense to them. However, the same stone that was a stumblingstone to the Jews became a stepping stone to the Gentiles.

The Jews just did not want to believe in Jesus Christ. They did not want to receive freely the righteousness of God as in Christ. They would rather earn or work for righteousness. They would rather endeavor to earn life from God by works of the law, by self-righteousness, than to receive it as a free gift.

So Jesus Christ was a great stumblingstone to the Jews. He was the rock of *offense* (cf. Matthew 16:23). Furthermore, because this righteousness was made available for all who would believe, by the work of the Cross, the stumblingstone was sharpened (I Corinthians 1:22-24). Note (The Cross):

- Christ Crucified (a stumblingstone)
- Faith-righteousness (a stumblingstone)

The theme of "the stone" or "the rock" is a very prominent one in both testaments. (Refer to these Scriptures: Psalm 118:22; Isaiah 8:14; 28:16; Matthew 21:42; I Peter 2:6-8; Acts 4:10-12.)

The same stone is *the foundation stone* to those who believe (Isaiah 28:16; I Peter 2:6-8). Stumblingstone or foundation stone? It all depends on the heart attitude—faith or unbelief!

C. **"Whosoever believeth on Him"** (cf. John 3:16)
   "Whosoever" applies to the Jew or Gentile. Believing is the channel for the reception of God's righteousness, imputed righteousness through Christ.

D. **"Shall not be ashamed"** (cf. Romans 11:11; Isaiah 28:16; 49:23)
   "Ashamed" means "confounded." This phrase can also mean "shall not make haste, or flee hastily."

Romans 9: *Summary*

The diagram on the following page summarizes the exposition of Romans 9, which also illustrates Romans 8:28-30.

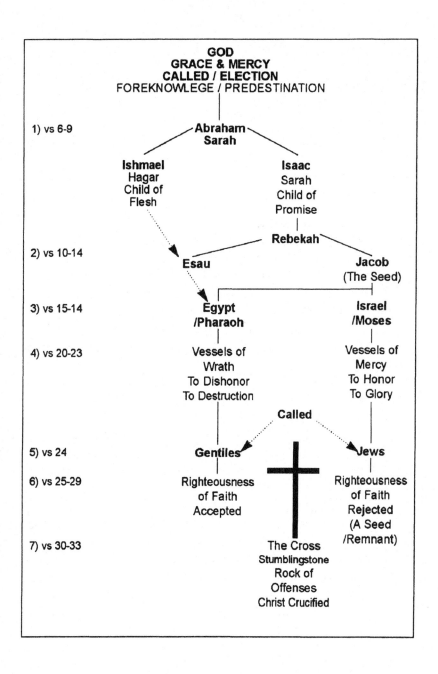

Faith-Righteousness (Romans 10:1-21)

Faith-Righteousness Recognized (Romans 10:1-4)

Verse 1: *"Brethren, my heart's desire and prayer to God for Israel is, that they might be saved."*

(Cf. notes on Romans 9:1-3.)

"That they might be saved"

Paul's desire, out of the good will of his heart, his prayer for Israel, was that they might be saved. Notice the word "saved" and the Scriptures which teach that the only way for Israel (and the Gentiles as well) to be saved is through Christ. There is not one way for the Jews and another way for the Gentiles (John 14:1-6). Compare the following verses:

- "...[A] remnant shall be saved..." (Romans 9:27).
- "...[P]rayer to God for Israel is, that they might be saved" (Romans 10:1).
- "...[I]f thou shalt confess...and believe...thou shalt be saved" (Romans 10:9).
- "...[U]nto salvation" (Romans 10:10).
- "For whosoever shall call upon the name of the Lord shall be saved" (Romans 10:13; cf. Joel 2:32 with Acts 2:21). Salvation comes in and through the name of the Lord Jesus Christ (Acts 2:47; 16:30-31).
- "And so all Israel shall be saved..." (Romans 11:26). "...[T]hey are not all Israel, which are of Israel..." (Romans 9:6). How shall "all Israel be saved"? By calling on the name of the Lord, in and through the Lord Jesus Christ (refer to Romans 10:13-14).
- "He that believeth and is baptized shall be saved..." (Mark 16:15-16; cf. I Peter 3:21).
- "For by grace are ye saved through faith..." (Ephesians 2:5, 8).
- "... [L]est they should believe and be saved" (Luke 8:12).
- "...[T]hat the world through him might be saved" (John 3:17).
- "Look unto me, and be ye saved, all the ends of the earth..." (Isaiah 45:22).

- "…[S]ave some of them" (Romans 11:14).
- "…[S]aved from wrath through him…saved by his [death and] life" (Romans 5:9-10).

Verse 2: *"For I bear them record that they have a zeal of God, but not according to knowledge."*

"They have a zeal of God"

"Zealous" means "to be hot, to boil over." Paul himself was an example of this zeal. Now his attitudes and zeal were pointed in the right direction. Ignorant zeal is wasted (I Timothy 1:13).

It is possible to be zealous for God, but not according to knowledge. This is misguided and misdirected religious zeal (cf. Acts 21:20; 22:3; Galatians 1:14; Acts 26:9; Philippians 3:6).

It is a tragic thing to be exceedingly zealous, and then find that this zeal is unfounded and misdirected. So many false cults today have such zeal.

Verse 3: *"For they being ignorant of God's righteousness, and going about to establish their own righteousness, have not submitted themselves unto the righteousness of God."*

A. **"Ignorant of God's righteousness"** (cf. Romans 1:17; 9:30-31)

They were ignorant of the law of righteousness (Romans 3:22-30). For the religious leaders, and the Jews in general, it was willful ignorance.

B. **"Going about to establish their own righteousness"**

"Establish" means "to set up" (cf. Philippians 3:9; Romans 9:32). They tried to establish their own righteousness by works of the law, works of self-effort, the law of works (Romans 3:27-28). Ignorance leads to works.

C. **"Have not submitted themselves unto the righteousness of God"**

They were not submitted to Christ, Jehovah Taidkenu, "the Lord our righteousness" (I Corinthians 1:30; Jeremiah 23:3-6; Romans 4; 1:16-17; 3:20-22). Notice the order: ignorance, works, and lack of submission! This is the same for Jews or Gentiles.

Verse 4: *"For Christ is the end of the law for righteousness to every one that believeth."*

"Christ is the end of the law for righteousness to every one that believeth"
Christ is the end (the aim) of the law for righteousness to every one that believeth, Jew or Gentile (Matthew 5:17; Galatians 3:24). Vincent defined "end" in the following ways:
1) Aim (Galatians 3:24)
2) Fulfillment (Matthew 5:17)
3) Termination (Galatians 2:16; 3:2-4) (Vincent prefers this third one.)

Myer Pearlman likened the law to a train. In making a journey, we use the train as a means to an end. We have no intention of making the train our home; when we get to our destination, we leave the train. The self-satisfied Jews refused to move from the seats of the Old Covenant train, even though they were at the end of the line (*Romans, Teacher's Manual,* p. 74.)
The law of righteousness (as a righteous standard) pointed to Christ-righteousness. Both the law and Christ were the righteousness of God; one was the letter, and the other was the life.

- Law-righteousness – externalized; tables of stone; the letter standard
- Christ-righteousness – internalized; personified; tables of the heart; the life standard; the embodiment of righteousness

The law was a schoolmaster to bring us to Christ (Galatians 3:24).

Faith-Righteousness Received (Romans 10:5-13)

Verse 5: *"For Moses describeth the righteousness which is of the law, That the man which doeth those things shall live by them."*

(Refer to notes on "the law of works," Romans 3:27.)

"The man which doeth these things shall live by them"
Notice here again, "...keep my statutes...if a man do, he shall live in them..." (Leviticus 18:5; Nehemiah 9:29; Ezekiel 20:11; Galatians 3:12) Do and live. The law of righteousness was "doing, then living," doing to gain eternal life.

The gospel is exactly the opposite—living, then doing! The law could not give life because man could not do the things in the law because of the law of sin in the flesh (Romans 7). How can a *dead* man, a man dead in trespasses and sins, *do* righteousness? He needs life, God-life, to enable him to do righteousness. The gospel does this.

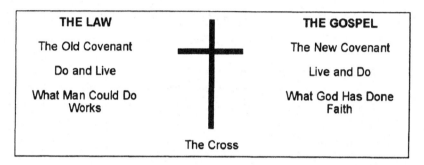

THE LAW	THE GOSPEL
The Old Covenant	The New Covenant
Do and Live	Live and Do
What Man Could Do Works	What God Has Done Faith

The Cross

Verses 6-7: *"But the righteousness which is of faith speaketh on this wise, Say not in thine heart, Who shall ascend into heaven? (that is, to bring Christ down from above:) or, Who shall descend into the deep? (that is, to bring up Christ again from the dead.)"*

Faith-righteousness speaks on this wise, in contrast to that which law-righteousness says. Paul again quotes, but this time from Moses (Deuteronomy 30:11-14), showing that Moses spoke not only of law-righteousness (*do and live*), but also of faith-righteousness (believe, live, and do). Thus, as all under the law pointed to Christ, so do these Scriptures point to faith-righteousness. Paul applies this secondary meaning to Christians.

- Argument: If Christ is righteousness, and He is up in heaven, then who will ascend to heaven to bring Him down? Or, if Christ came down, and He died and descended to the regions of the dead, then who can descend to bring Him up again from the dead?
- Answer: No man could ascend into heaven to bring Christ down. He has come down by means of the incarnation. No man could descend into the deep (i.e., the abyss). He has risen up from the grave and hades by means of the resurrection. The cycle of the Father's will is completed.

Christ did descend from heaven into the lower parts of the earth. He died for our sins to become our righteousness, God raised Him from the dead, and now He has ascended and gone back to heaven. Notice the theme of "descending and ascending" in these Scriptures: Genesis 28:12; John 1:51; Psalm 68:18; Proverbs 30:4; Ephesians 4:8-10.

Verse 8: *"But what saith it? The word is nigh thee, even in thy mouth, and in thy heart: that is, the word of faith, which we preach..."*

"Even in thy mouth, and in thy heart"

Our response should be that the Word of the Gospel is near us (cf. "heart and mouth" in these Scriptures: Romans 10:8-10; Acts 8:37; Luke 12:8; Matthew 10:32; 12:34).

- In the mouth
- In the heart

"...[O]ut of the abundance of the heart the mouth speaketh" (Matthew 12:34; Deuteronomy 30:14; Exodus 13:19; Deuteronomy 6:6-9). What word? The word in our mouth and heart, the *Word* of *Faith*, the Word which we preach (Matthew 4:17; II Peter 2:5). The mouth and the heart are vitally connected.

Verse 9: *"That if thou shalt confess with thy mouth the Lord Jesus, and shalt believe in thine heart that God hath raised him from the dead, thou shalt be saved."*

A. **"Confess"**
   Greek: *Homologeo* means "to assent. i.e., covenant, acknowledge"; it is translated as "confess," "profess," "confession is made," "give thanks," "promise" (*Strong's* number 3670; refer also to Matthew 7:23; 10:32; Luke 12:8; John 12:42; Romans 10:9-10; I John 4:2-3, 15; II John 7).

B. **"With the mouth"**
   "With the mouth" also implies "from the heart." (Refer to "heart and mouth.")

C. **"The Lord Jesus"** (cf. Romans 10:12-13; Luke 12:8; Acts 7:59-60; 8:37; 9:5-6, 17)

This phrase shows Jesus as *Lord*. The emphasis is on His lordship (I Corinthians 12:3). "...[I]f we believe on him that raised up Jesus our Lord from the dead..." then we will be saved (cf. Romans 10:1 and notes on 4:23-25).

Verse 10: *"For with the heart man believeth unto righteousness; and with the mouth confession is made unto salvation."*

Thus, salvation comes through confession and faith (mouth and heart) in the resurrection of the Lord Jesus (Romans 4:23-25).
- The heart believes unto righteousness.
- The mouth confesses unto salvation.

Verse 11: *"For the scripture saith, Whosoever believeth on him shall not be ashamed."*

The Scripture says, "...Behold, I lay in Sion a stumblingstone and rock of offence: and whosoever believeth on him shall not be ashamed" (Isaiah 28:16; 49:23; Jeremiah 17:13; Romans 9:33).

Verse 12: *"For there is no difference between the Jew and the Greek: for the same Lord over all is rich unto all that call upon him."*

A. **"For there is no difference"**
   There is no difference, or distinction, between the Jews or the Greeks. "...[F]or there is no difference: for all have sinned, and come short of the glory of God..." (cf. Romans 3:22-23).
   "And God, which knoweth the hearts, bare them witness, giving them the Holy Ghost, even as he did unto us; and put no difference between us and them, purifying their hearts by faith" (Acts 15:8-9).
   If God puts no difference between the Jew and the Gentile in the way of salvation, then we cannot make any difference in the way each should be saved. There is no difference; there is but one way for all. The only thing that makes a difference between mankind is the blood of Jesus Christ, our Passover Lamb (Exodus 9:4, 6, 26; 10:23; 11:6-7; 12:13).

B. **"The same Lord"**
   The same *Lord* (Jesus, Romans 10:9) over *all* is rich (in mercy) to all who call upon Him (Acts 15:9; 10:36; I Timothy 2:5; Romans 3:22, 29-31; Ephesians 1:7; 2:4,7).

Verse 13: *"For whosoever shall call upon the name of the Lord shall be saved."*

A. **"Whosoever"** (Romans 9:33; 10:11, 13)
   "Whosoever" means Jew or Gentile.

B. **"Call upon the name of the Lord"**
   Those who call on the name of the Lord, in the *Lord* Jesus Christ, shall
   be saved (Joel 2:32; Acts 2:21, 9:14).

C. **"Shall be saved"**
   Those who call on Him will be saved from wrath through Him
   (Romans 5:9) (saved by His life [Romans 5:10], saved [Romans 10:1]).
   How can a Jew or a Gentile be saved if not by calling on the name of
   the Lord (cf. Matthew 14:30)?

Faith-Righteousness Rejected (Romans 10:14-21)

Verses 14-15: *"How then shall they call on him in whom they have not believed? and
how shall they believe in him of whom they have not heard? and how shall they
hear without a preacher? and how shall they preach, except they be sent? as it
is written, How beautiful are the feet of them that preach the gospel of peace,
and bring glad tidings of good things!"*

A. Four Questions Asked:
   1) **"How then shall they call on Him in whom they have never
      believed?"** – Notice the word "call" in verses 12-14. Man many invoke
      Him as Lord. God calls man. Man calls upon God. Thus, the
      distinction between sovereignty and responsibility emerges (Joel 2:32).
   2) **"And how shall they believe in Him on whom they have not heard?"**
   3) **"And how shall they hear without a preacher?"** (Titus 1:3).
   4) **"And how shall they preach except they be sent?"**

   There is a logical progression here in the saving gospel (Matthew
   10:16; Mark 4:29).

B. **"As it is written, How beautiful are the feet of them that preach the gospel of peace, and bring glad tidings of good things!"**
"Feet" (Acts 5:9; Romans 3:15; Ephesians 6:15; Nahum 1:15; Isaiah 52:7).
"Gospel of peace" (Romans 5:1; Ephesians 2:14; Colossians 1:20; refer to "gospel" in notes on Romans 1:9, 15-16).
"Glad tidings of good things" (Luke 2:10). The gospel is glad tidings, good news of good things, in contrast to the law, which is bad news to the violators.

Verse 16: *"But they have not all obeyed the gospel. For Esaias saith, Lord, who hath believed our report?"*

A. **"Not all obeyed the gospel"**
The Gospels and the book of Acts reveal this (Romans 5:19; Acts 5:29). Following Isaiah 52:7, Isaiah 53:1 says, "Who hath believed our report?" (cf. Acts 13:46-48; Romans 1:16).

B. **"Who hath believed our report"**
Marginal notes say, "Who had believed the hearing of us, or the preaching?"
Only the remnant, the seed, heard and believed God's report (Romans 9:27-29) and were saved by calling on the name of the Lord (Acts 2:21; 37-47).

Verse 17: *"So then faith cometh by hearing, and hearing by the word of God."*

"Faith cometh by hearing"
This is the foundational verse to the whole revelation of faith in the Scriptures (I Thessalonians 2:13; Hebrews 11). All had received a Word (*rhema*) from God that created faith. It is impossible to have faith apart from a Word from God. However, the Jews had that Word in the Writings, but did not allow it to create faith. They did not really hear it (Hebrews 4:1-2). Note the progressive order of the Word in verses 14-17.
1) Sending – by God
2) Preaching – by ministers
3) Hearing – by sinners (cf. verse 16, margin, verse 17)
4) Believing – by repentance
5) Calling – by repentance and faith
6) Saving – by God

Verse 18: *"But I say, Have they not heard? Yes verily, their sound went into all the earth, and their words unto the ends of the world."*

A. **"Their sound"**
"Their sound" can mean "plummet line." "Sound" can also be a musical chord. This is also alluding to the gospel as it went forth into the entire known world under the early glory of the book of Acts. The Jews had the Old Testament in their synagogues but did not listen (John 6:44; Acts 13:26-27; 15:21).

B. **"Unto the ends of the world"**
This means to the ends of the Gentile world especially (cf. Psalm 19:1-4). It also refers to the gospel in the heavens, in the Word of Creation, of which all the world has witness (Romans 1:19-20; Matthew 24:14; Colossians 1:6, 23; Acts 17:6; Matthew 4:8).

Verse 19: *"But I say, Did not Israel know? First Moses saith, I will provoke you to jealousy by them that are no people, and by a foolish nation I will anger you."*

A. **"Did not Israel know?"**
The answer is yes. Israel did know and had its own prophetic Scriptures that should have created faith for the coming Messiah. The Jews need not have crucified Him (cf. Acts 13:27). They did not want to accept free and universal salvation. National bigotry and pride of election blinded them.

B. **"First Moses saith"**
Paul now brings in Moses and Isaiah as witnesses against unbelieving Israel. Both had prophesied the conversion and the coming in of the Gentiles.
Moses came first in the order of writing (Deuteronomy 32:21; Romans 11:11, 14; I Corinthians 10:22).

C. **"I will provoke you to jealousy"**
The coming in and acceptance of the gospel by the Gentiles provoked the Jews to jealousy and anger, as seen in the book of Acts (Acts 13:46-48; 17:1-15; I Thessalonians 2:13-16).

D. **"By them that are no people"**
The Jews felt that the Gentiles were not a people, but foolish nations, while the Jews themselves were the people—the select and elect nation. Yet they rejected the gospel after they had heard it, and the Gentiles responded to it. God endeavored to use this very thing to provoke His own people to respond to the gospel as the Gentiles had responded. The Jews themselves—not God—were responsible for their own rejection. God foreknew and foretold it, but the Jews were responsible for it all.

Verse 20: *"But Esaias is very bold, and saith, I was found of them that sought me not; I was made manifest unto them that asked not after me."*

"I was found of them that sought me not"
(This verse is quoted from Isaiah 65:1.) So the Gentiles found Christ, when they had not been looking for Him, and His glory was manifested to the Gentiles when they had not even asked after Him (refer again to Romans 9:30). Israel refused to "behold Him," but the Gentiles beheld Him and looked and lived.

Verse 21: *"But to Israel he saith, All day long I have stretched forth my hands unto a disobedient and gainsaying people."*

(This verse is quoted from Isaiah 65:2 [refer again to Romans 9:31].) Isaiah 65:1-16 could be read in connection with the acceptance of the gospel by the Gentiles and the rejection of such by the Jewish nation as a whole. Paul, by the inspiration of the Holy Spirit, clearly interprets this prophecy of Isaiah for us, which, undoubtedly, during the prophet's time was enigmatic. The apostle was not bringing in any new doctrine. He used Israel's own prophetic Scriptures to show how it had been foreknown and foretold that the Jews would reject the Messiah and the Gentiles would accept Him.

"Gainsaying people"
"Gainsaying" means "word resisting, contradicting." The Jews became a willfully disobedient and Word resisting people. Israel knew, but did not obey, the gospel and, thus, were unjustified.

Verses 15-21: *Summary*

Comparisons:
- Romans 10:15 with Isaiah 52:7
- Romans 10:16 with Isaiah 53:1
- Romans 10:18 with Psalm19:4
- Romans 10:19 with Deuteronomy 32:21
- Romans 10:20 with Isaiah 65:1
- Romans 10:21 with Isaiah 65:2

The Election of Grace (Romans 11:1-10)

The Remnant (Romans 11:1-6)

Verse 1: *"I say then, Hath God cast away His people? God forbid. For I also am an Israelite, of the seed of Abraham, of the tribe of Benjamin."*

A. **"Cast away"**
   "Cast away" means "to shove or thrust" (Philippians 3:5).

B. **"I also am an Israelite"**
   Anticipating Jewish reaction again, Paul is quick to say that he himself is an example of the fact that God has not totally cast away His people (I Peter 2:9; Acts 13:17).

C. **"Of the seed of Abraham, of the tribe of Benjamin"**
   Paul is an Israelite, of the chosen nation, of the seed of Abraham, of the father of all who believe, of the tribe of Benjamin (cf. Jeremiah 31:37; I Samuel 12:22; II Corinthians 11:22; Philippians 3:1-5). He is a part of the remnant, the seed saved. The rejection is only partial, not total; temporal, not eternal (Vincent).

Verse 2: *"God hath not cast away his people which he foreknew. Wot ye not what the scripture saith of Elias? how he maketh intercession to God against Israel, saying..."*

Paul uses an example out of Old Testament national history that took place in the days of Elijah. He speaks of Elijah's intercession against Israel, his complaint against them before the Lord God. He should have made intercession for them (cf. Romans 8:26, 28, 34).

A. "His people which he foreknew" (cf. Romans 8:29)

B. "Wot ye not"
   In other words, do you not know?

Verse 3: *"...Lord, they have killed thy prophets, and digged down thine alters; and I am left alone, and they seek my life."*

(Cf. I Kings 19:10, 14.)

This was Elijah's prayer at the close of the three and a half years of drought. It was certainly a foreshadowing of Christ's three and a half years of ministry, too.

Verse 4: *"But what saith the answer of God unto him? I have reserved to myself seven thousand men, who have not bowed the knee to the image of Baal."*

God told Elijah that even in this time of national apostasy and unbelief, He had reserved a faithful and believing remnant in Israel. There was a true Israel within natural Israel (I Kings 19:18).

Verse 5: *"Even so then at this present time also there is a remnant according to the election of grace."*

"According to the election of grace"
(Refer to notes on "election" in Romans 9:11; Galatians 5:4; Deuteronomy 9:4-5.)

It has already been noted that there are two aspects of election, namely:
1) The election of persons or nations in time for temporal purposes.
2) The election of persons for eternal purposes, things pertaining to redemption.

The election of grace is the sovereignty of God in grace whereby He chose, in Christ Jesus, for salvation all those whom He foreknew would accept Him.

The charts below illustrates the election of a remnant in Elijah's time and the present election in Paul's time.

Elijah – Israel (Old Testament)

• Elect	• The Remnant
• The Nation	• Faithful 7000
• Idolatrous	• Election of Grace
• Natural Israel	• True Israel
• Seed of Abraham after the Flesh	• Seed of Abraham after the Spirit

Paul – Israel/Judah (New Testament)

• The Elect Nation	• The Remnant
• Unbelieving	• Believing
• Seed of Abraham	• Seed of Abraham
• Natural Israel (John 8)	• True Israel
• Blinded	• Eyes Opened
• Hardened	• Election of Grace

Verse 6: *"And if by grace, then is it no more of works: otherwise grace is no more grace. But if it be of works, then is it no more grace: otherwise work is no more work."*

Grace Verses Works

Here, the subject of grace versus works emerges again (Romans 4:4-5; Deuteronomy 9:4-5; Galatians 5:4). The grace and mercy of God brought salvation and righteousness to man in Christ. It cannot be grace and law together, nor can it be works and faith. No man can be saved by works of the law, as has been already noted. Note:

- Grace (Romans 3:24; 4:16; 5:2, 17, 21)
- Works (Romans 4:2-4; 3:27; 9:32)

Grace is not grace if it is by works, and works are not works if they are by grace.

We remind ourselves again of the definition of grace, as seen in previous chapters of Romans. Grace is the undeserved, unmerited, and unearned favor of God bestowed upon sinful man. It is undeserved because all we deserve is wrath; it is unmerited because nothing we are deserves it; and it is unearned because nothing we do can earn it.

It was God who took the initiative to redeem man. Once Adam sinned in Eden, it was God who came seeking Adam, not Adam who came seeking God. The Atonement was God's idea, not man's (Romans 3:10-12; 5:8, 10; John 15:16; 6:44). Man could not initiate the provision of the Atonement and neither can he initiate its application. God has taken the initiative and has manifested His grace to all men (Titus 2:11), so that all men are without excuse (Romans 1:20). The Jews could not and would not accept God's grace in Christ (John 1:14-17). They would rather, in their foolish pride, seek to be justified by works of the law.

The Blinded Nation (Romans 11:7-10)

Verse 7: *"What then? Israel hath not obtained that which he seeketh for; but the election hath obtained it, and the rest were blinded..."*

(Refer to "election" notes [Romans 9:10-13].)

A. "Israel hath not obtained that which he seeketh for"
    Thus, the people of Israel, as a whole, failed to obtain the righteousness they were seeking for. The election of grace (verse 6), the seed, or the remnant received it because they accepted it by faith. The rest of the nation was blinded (marginal reference says "hardened") like Pharaoh (refer to Romans 9:15-18 again).

B. "The rest were blinded" (refer to Romans 11:25)
    This means "blindness in part" (Mark 3:5; Isaiah 29:10; Psalm 69:22-23; Deuteronomy 29:4).

Verse 8: *"...(According as it is written, God hath given them the spirit of slumber, eyes that they should not see, and ears that they should not hear;) unto this day."*

(Quoted from the messianic prophet, Isaiah; cf. Isaiah 29:10-12; Deuteronomy 29:4; Isaiah 6:9; Jeremiah 5:21; Ezekiel 12:2; Matthew 13:14; John 12:40; Acts 28:26.)

A. "The spirit of slumber"
   The marginal reference for "slumber" says "remorse."

B. "Eyes that they should not see, and ears that they should not hear"
   The Jew shows his blindness in the reading of the Old Testament. The veil is on the heart. Hardness of the heart leads to blindness of the eye, spiritual slumber, stupor (II Corinthians 3:13-16). There is none so blind and deaf as the one who does not want to see or hear.

Verses 9-10: *"And David saith, Let their table be made a snare, and a trap, and a stumblingblock, and a recompense unto them: let their eyes be darkened, that they may not see, and bow down their back alway."*

Messianic Psalm of the Cross

These verses are quoted from Psalm 69:22-23. It is worthy to note that this was recognized as a messianic Psalm of the Cross (refer to Romans 11:20-21, 26, 8-9). With the rejection of their own long-promised Messiah, the Jewish table (significant of feasting and material prosperity, as table of shewbread, Passover table, etc.,) became a snare and a trap to them. Their spiritual eyes became darkened, indeed (refer to verse 8 and references), and they came into servitude to their enemies, bowing their backs as slaves. Note:

- "A snare"
- "A trap"
- "A stumblingblock"
- "A recompense" means "retribution."

The Good Olive Tree (Romans 11:11-32)

Salvation to the Gentiles (Romans 11:11-12)

Verse 11: *"I say then, Have they stumbled that they should fall? God forbid: but rather through their fall salvation is come unto the Gentiles, for to provoke them to jealousy."*

Compare the following verses:

- God has not totally cast His people away (Romans 11:1-2).
- God has not totally allowed the nation to stumble into ruin (Romans 11:11).

The very fact of the believing remnant shows this. God has capitalized on the Jew's unbelief and used it to bring in the Gentiles unto salvation (cf. Acts 13:46; 18:6; Romans 10:19-21).

Verse 12: *"Now if the fall of them be the riches of the world, and the diminishing of them the riches of the Gentiles; how much more their fulness?"*

If the lapse of the Jewish nation has been the enriching of the world and the enriching of the Gentiles, with salvation, then what can be expected with the restoration of the Jews?

The Apostle to the Gentiles (Romans 11:13-16)

Verse 13: *"For I speak to you Gentiles, inasmuch as I am the apostle of the Gentiles, I magnify mine office..."*

Paul himself was a Jew, a Benjamite, and an Israelite, yet he was not sent especially to the Jews, but to the Gentiles. Paul is a Jew talking to Gentiles about his own nation's blindness and the blessing on the Gentiles; hence, he emphasizes his own ministry to them (Acts 9:15; Galatians 1:16; Ephesians 3:8; I Timothy 2:7; Romans 11:1).

Verse 14: *"...If by any means I may provoke to emulation them which are my flesh, and might save some of them."*

Paul magnified his apostolic ministry to the Gentiles to try to provoke his own people to jealousy and to save some of them, if he could not save all of them (Romans 11:1; 10:1,13; I Corinthians 9:22; I Timothy 4:16; James 5:20).

Verse 15: *"For if the casting away of them be the reconciling of the world, what shall the receiving of them be, but life from the dead?"*

Notice Romans 11:11-12, 15:

- By Jewish stumbling, salvation has come to the Gentiles.
- By Jewish falling, the world and Gentiles have been enriched.
- By Jewish casting away, reconciliation is available for the world.

But when the Jewish people are restored, they will be enriched. It will be as life from death (Ezekiel 37), the resurrection of a nation, the valley of dry bones resurrected.

Verse 16: *"For if the firstfruit be holy, the lump is also holy: and if the root be holy, so are the branches."*

Here, Paul brings in two familiar Hebrew figures or symbols.

A. **"If the firstfruit be holy"**
   The firstfruit of the dough was holy (Leviticus 23:10-17; James 1:18; Exodus 23:16; Numbers 15:17-21). Under the law, the firstfruit of the dough was offered to God. The firstfruit was holy, as was the whole total of the dough. The firstfruit represented the whole. The same truth was applicable to the truth of the firstborn. Thus, "the remnant," "the seed," "the election of grace" saved in Acts in early church history were a kind of "firstfruit" to God. They represented the "fullness" or the complete number of the Jewish elect which would be offered to God through Christ in due time. The rest of the dough would be those of Romans 11:26 who will be saved and become holy to God in Christ. In another sense, the patriarchs were the "firstfruit" of the whole nation.

B. **"If the root be holy"**
   The root and branches of the olive tree were holy (Jeremiah 11:16; Psalm 52:8). The Scriptures speak of Israel under the symbol of an olive tree. The olive tree was the oil tree, the source of oil used in the anointing of prophets, kings, and priests. (Cf. Psalm 80; Isaiah 5; Ezekiel 15.) So Israel was the only nation in which God placed the anointing of His Holy Spirit, and raised up His ministries. Israel was the Lord's anointed. The root (Abraham, of verse 18) was holy, so the branches (the nation that

sprang from him, the faithful) were also holy. (Refer to Scriptures on the olive tree: Judges 9:8-15; Romans 11:16-24; Matthew 21; John 15:1-5.)

The vine, the fig tree, and the olive tree are all symbols of Israel, in covenantal, material, national, and spiritual blessings on the nation. Note the diagram below.

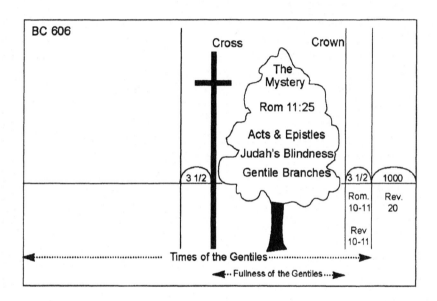

Note:

- The Root – Abraham
- The Trunk – The United Nation of Israel
- The Two Main branches – The House of Israel and Judah
- The Wild Branches – The Gentiles Grafted In

(This is the same thought as the firstfruit and the whole lump of dough.)

The Wild Olive Branches Grafted In (Romans 11:17-24)

Verses 17-18: *"And if some of the branches be broken off, and thou, being a wild olive tree, wert graffed in among [for] them, and with them partakest of the root and fatness of the olive tree; boast not against the branches. But if thou boast, thou bearest not the root, but the root thee."*

Here again, another thought is brought in concerning the stumbling, fall, or casting away of the Jews. Some of the branches, but not all, are broken off. This is seen in the three thousand, the five thousand, and the multitudes of the Jews in Acts who did accept Christ. These branches were not broken off. They remained in the good olive tree, partaking of the root and the fatness of the tree.

The Gentiles are likened to "a wild olive branch." Broken off from their former source of life, they are now to be grafted in amongst the Jewish natural branches and to partake of a new sap-life. Hence, they are not boasting against the Jewish branches who were broken off. They must remember that the root upholds the branches, not the branches the root.

Abraham is the root in this tree, Israel is the trunk, and the branches are the believing ones of the tribes (Acts 2:9-11; Ephesians 2:12-13; I Corinthians 10:2; Matthew 24:32; Mark 11:8).

The Gentile believer must never forget that he owes much to the Jewish nation of Israel as God's elect people in the Old Testament, especially the Scriptures and the Messiah, who brought salvation to all who would believe.

Verse 19: *"Thou wilt say then, The branches were broken off, that I might be graffed in."*

Gentile boasting would say this. However, it is only part of the truth— part of the reason, not the full reason.

Verse 20: *"Well; because of unbelief they were broken off, and thou standest by faith. Be not highminded, but fear..."*

(Cf. 12:16; Proverbs 28:14; Isaiah 66:2.)

Paul warns the Gentiles against prideful boasting. The Jewish branches were not just cast off to allow the Gentiles to be grafted in, but they were cast off because of *unbelief.* Whether Jew or Gentile, all stand by *faith.* Therefore, the believing Gentile needs to have a healthy fear and not become conceited or lifted up in pride. God will do to unbelieving Gentiles what He has done to unbelieving Jews, as they are but a graft and not the original stock.

God did not spare the unbelieving people of Israel when they backslid into unbelief. Neither will He spare the Gentiles if they follow suit.

Verse 21: *"...For if God spared not the natural branches, take heed lest he also spare not thee."*

This is just a logical sequence of thought. If God broke the natural Jewish branches off because of unbelief, so He will, much more, break off the wild olive branches if they do not abide in faith. All stand only by faith.

Verse 22: *"Behold therefore the goodness and severity of God: on them which fell, severity; but toward thee, goodness, if thou continue in his goodness: otherwise thou also shalt be cut off."*

(Cf. I Corinthians 5:2; Hebrews 3:6; John 15:2; Luke 13:7.)

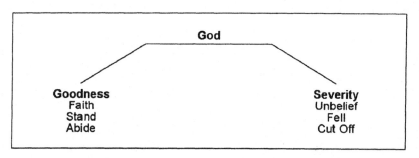

The rejection of Israel shows the severity of God. On the other hand, the goodness of God is shown towards the Gentiles being grafted in. The severity of God is seen in the destruction of Jerusalem in AD70 and the terrible things that happened to them in that siege.

Verse 23: *"And they also, if they abide not still in unbelief, shall be graffed in: for God is able to graff them in again."*

(Cf. II Corinthians 3:16.)

"If they abide not still in unbelief"
The whole Jewish problem is stated here in one word, "belief." It is used four times in verses 20, 23, 30, 32. The moment a Jew (or Gentile)

comes out of unbelief, he is grafted into the good olive tree, which is the true Israel of God. God is able to graft the Jew back in again, but only in faith (verse 24).

There are only two areas of "abiding":
1) Abiding or continuing in faith (verses 20, 22; note the word "if")
2) Abiding or continuing in unbelief (verses 20, 23, 30, 32; note the word "if")

Verse 24: *"For if thou wert cut out of the olive tree which is wild by nature, and wert graffed contrary to nature into a good olive tree: how much more shall these, which be the natural branches, be graffed into their own olive tree?"*

It is easier for God to graft the Jewish branches back into their olive tree than to graft in wild Gentile branches. It is much more natural to graft a branch back into the original tree from which it was cut.

Note the chart below.

The Unbelieving Jews	The Believing Jews and Gentiles
• Blinded/Snared/Trapped/ Stumblingblock	• Jewish Remnant – Election of Grace
• Cast Away	• Not Cast Away
• Branches Broken Off	• Branches Abide in the Olive Tree, Gentiles Grafted in Amongst them
• Because of Unbelief	• Stand By Faith
• Spared not Natural Branches	• Spared - If Abide in Faith, Otherwise Cut Off
• Severity of God on Them Which Fell	• Goodness of God on Them Which Continue
• God Able to Graft These in Again If they Abide not Still in Unbelief	• So All Israel Shall be Saved
• Blindness in Part on Nation Until "The Mystery"	• Fullness of Gentiles Come in, "The Mystery" Jew/Gentile one olive tree
• To Obtain Mercy	• Have Obtained Mercy

The Mystery of Israel's Blindness (Romans I 1:25-32)

Verse 25: *"For I would not, brethren, that ye should be ignorant of this mystery, lest ye should be wise in your own conceits; that blindness in part is happened to Israel, until the fulness of the Gentiles be come in."*

(Cf. Romans 12:16; II Corinthians 3:14; Revelation 7:9.)

A. **"I would not, brethren, that ye should be ignorant of this mystery"**
   Paul was a steward of the mysteries of God (I Corinthians 4:1-2). There were many mysteries revealed to him, and, as a faithful steward of God, he wrote of them in his epistles.

   The word "mystery" does not mean "secret" or "hidden," but that which was concealed and has now been revealed, that which is brought out and disclosed; "that which can only be known to the initiated" (*Strong's, Young's*).

B. **"Not…that ye should be ignorant"**
   This is a Pauline expression, particularly (cf. I Corinthians 10:1; 12:1; I Thessalonians 4:13). Sins of ignorance are covered by the blood of Jesus. It is the ministry of the Holy Spirit to enlighten our ignorance by the revelation and illumination of the Word of God.

C. **"Wise in our own conceits"** (cf. verses 18, 20)
   The Gentiles are in danger of their own spiritual pride, the pride of knowledge apart from the love of God. Knowledge puffs up (I Corinthians 8:1-2).

D. **"Blindness in part is happened to Israel"**
   This mystery of Israel's blindness, or hardness of heart, and the fullness of the Gentiles must not be confused with the times of the Gentiles (Luke 21:24-25).

   The first has to do with the full number of the Gentiles coming into salvation during this period of time when God is taking out of the Gentiles a people for His name (Acts 15:15-18).

   The latter has to do with the period of time when Jerusalem is trodden down of the Gentiles and when Jewish people are under the domination of Gentile powers.

The first more specifically ends at the beginning of the three and a half years' tribulation period; the latter more specifically ends at the close of the three and a half years' tribulation period at the second coming of the Lord Jesus Christ (Revelation 11:1-3; 19:11- 15).

Verse 26: *"And so all Israel shall be saved: as it is written, There shall come out of Sion the Deliverer, and shall turn away ungodliness from Jacob..."*

(Refer to notes on 9:27; 10:1-9; 9:6.)

A. **"All Israel shall be saved"**
It should be remembered that they "...are not all Israel which are of Israel..." (Romans 9:6). Thus, when it says "...all Israel shall be saved...," it simply means that all those of Israel who are going to be saved will be saved. There never has been a time in Israel's history when every individual member of the nation was "saved" in the biblical sense of the word.

Undoubtedly, there will come an outpouring of the Holy Spirit on the Jewish nation in the last days before the Messiah comes again. The people of the nation, as a whole, will have their eyes opened to behold their Messiah. The blindness and hardness will be taken away. But, this is not to say that every individual of the nation will accept Christ by faith. All those whom God foreknows, and who are of the election of grace, will be saved, thus completing "the lump of dough" and "the root with the grafted-in-again branches" before the Lord (note also Zechariah 11-14 in relation to the above remarks).

B. **"There shall come out of Sion the Deliverer"**
Deliverance will come out of Zion (cf. Romans 9:32-33). The Deliverer who comes out of Zion is the Foundation Stone laid in Zion, the Lord Jesus Christ Himself (Psalm 14:7; Isaiah 59:20). He was the Stumblingstone and the Rock of Offense in His first advent. The Hebrew thought is *goel* or "kinsman redeemer," the nearest "kinsman" (cf. Deuteronomy 25:5-10; Job 19:25; Ruth 3:12-13; 4:1-10), and also the "avenger of blood."

Verse 27: *"For this is my covenant unto them, when I shall take away their sins."*

(Cf. Isaiah 27:9; Jeremiah 31:31-34; Hebrews 8:8.)

A. **"For this is my covenant unto them"**
   This covenant is none other than the *New* Covenant. This New Covenant was made by the Lord Jesus, the Deliverer, the Stumblingstone, the Rock of Offense, the Foundation Stone in Zion, when He broke the bread and blessed the wine with the twelve apostles in Jerusalem before His crucifixion (Matthew 26:26-28).

B. **"When I shall take away their sins"**
   Under the New Covenant, their sins could be taken away by the blood of the cross. Under the Mosaic Covenant, their sins were remembered against them, and animal blood could never take away sin (Hebrews 10:1-4). As long as the Jew rejects the New Covenant, he remains under the curse of the Mosaic Covenant (Old Covenant). Only the blood of Jesus, that innocent blood by which they invoked a curse on themselves and their unborn generations, can lift that curse upon acceptance (Matthew 27:25; Numbers 35). Thus, has the Jewish people suffered untold agonies amongst the nations, where they have been wandering, driven, and scattered, because of this self-imposed curse of "the innocent blood." This curse cannot be lifted until they humble themselves and accept the blessing of that blood of Jesus. Witness the millions slain in this dispensation of the Holy Spirit. Consider the six million Jews killed under Hitler in the Holocaust of World War II.

Verse 28: *"As concerning the gospel, they are enemies for your sakes: but as touching the election, they are beloved for the fathers' sakes."*

(Cf. Deuteronomy 7:8; 6-8; Romans 15:8; 9:5.)

   The Jewish nation was beloved for the fathers' sakes: Abraham, Isaac, and Jacob. We must not forget that "salvation is of the Jews" (John 4:22) and that through them we have the Holy Oracles (Romans 3:1-2) given to the world. But as far as the gospel is concerned, they were the real enemies to their own countrymen, as well as to Gentile believers. They became anti-Christian (cf. I Thessalonians 2:14-16)! Note the diagram on the following page.

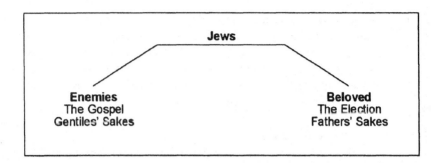

Verse 29: *"For the gifts and calling of God are without repentance."*

A. **"The gifts and calling"**
   The gifts and calling of God to Israel as a nation are given in Romans 9:4-5. God did not repent or change His mind concerning these things. He gave these things to the nation and allowed their purpose to be fulfilled.

B. **"Without repentance"**
   "Without repentance" means "not subject to recall, irrevocable" (II Corinthians 7:10; Numbers 23:19).
   Man may fall out of line with God's gifts and calling, but God does not change His mind as to His having given that gift or calling. Samson, King Saul, Gideon, and Judas are examples of individuals, while Israel and Judah are examples on a national scale.
   Individuals and nations may fall from the purposes of God by transgression (cf. Romans 11:11, 20-32), but God's mind is the same, even though He is saddened by such a fall and judges the ones involved.

Verses 30-31: *"For as ye in times past have not believed God, yet have now obtained mercy through their unbelief: even so have these also now not believed, that through your mercy they also may obtain mercy."*

   The Gentiles, in times past, did not obey God, yet God had mercy on them through the unbelief and disobedience of Israel. The converse can be true also. The people of Israel at present do not believe God, yet God will have mercy on them too, as He did on the Gentiles in their disobedience (cf. Ephesians 2:2; Colossians 3:7).

Verse 32: *"For God hath concluded them all in unbelief, that he might have mercy upon all."*

A. **"God hath concluded"**
Marginal notes say, "shut them all up together" (Galatians 3:22-23).

B. **"All"**
Compare the following verses:
- "...[A]ll under sin..." (Romans 3:9).
- "...[A]ll the world may become guilty before God" (Romans 3:19).
- "...[T]here is no difference..." (Romans 3:22).
- "For all have sinned, and come short of the glory of God..." (Romans 3:23).
- "...[A]ll in unbelief that he might have mercy upon all" (Romans 11:32).

Jew or Gentile, *all* are in unbelief, and *all* are in disobedience, and *all* are in need of the mercy and grace of God. Thus, all are on the same level before God. Hills and mountains are brought low, valleys are raised up, and all is leveled out before Almighty God. Oh, that the Gentiles and the Jews would recognize the fact and accept God's free grace and mercy in Christ, and be clothed in His freely offered faith-righteousness! Mercy is the foundation of unmerited salvation.

The Wisdom of God (Romans 11:33-36)

Verse 33: *"O the depth of the riches both of the wisdom and knowledge of God! how unsearchable are his judgments, and his ways past finding out!"*

(Cf. Psalm 36:6; Job 11:7; Psalm 92:5.)

This passage is just pure praise from Paul's heart. When one attempts to contemplate God's grace and mercy, His foreknowledge and election, His purposes in creation and redemption, after all that is said and written by man, these attributes of God are still so rich, so deep, so inscrutable, so untraceable for finite man to grasp. Man can only bow and worship!

"**Depth**" – (I Corinthians 2:10)

"**Riches**" – (Refer to Romans 9:23)

"**Wisdom**" – Means "the best thing to do in light of all the facts; all wise" (Proverbs 9:10; Ephesians 1:17).

"**Knowledge**" – Means "omniscience, all knowing, having all facts before Him" (I Corinthians 12:8; Colossians 2:3).

"**Unsearchable**" – means "inscrutable."

"**Judgments**" – means "decisions, opinions, assessments" (Psalm 119:7).

"**Ways**" – (Cf. Psalm 103:7.)

"**Past finding out**" –Means "untraceable" (cf. Ephesians 3:8).

Verse 34: *"For who hath known the mind of the Lord? or who hath been his counsellor?"*

(Cf. I Corinthians 2:16; Job 15:8; Isaiah 40:13; Jeremiah 23:18; Job 36:22.)

No man is able to comprehend the mind of God in order to be His "fellow counselor" and to help Him make decisions. Known unto God are all His works from the beginning of the world, even from eternity to eternity. Omnipotence, omnipresence, and omniscience—finite man can only bow before such and worship. These things touch the essential attributes of God. We are ignorant apart from God's revelation to us.

Verse 35: *"Or who hath first given to him, and it shall be recompensed unto him again?"*

No man has given to God, and no man need be repaid by God. God alone is sufficient (Job 35:7; 41:3).

Verse 36: *"For of him, and through him, and to him, are all things: to whom be glory for ever. Amen."*

(Colossians 1:16; Hebrews 13:21; Revelation 1:6)

A. "**Of him**"
Greek: *Ek* means "out of, proceeding from, as the source, beginning, originator, the First, the Alpha."

B. **"Through him"**

Greek: *Dia* means "be means of, as maintainer, preserve, ruler, channel, course, flowing forth and through."

C. **"To him"**

Greek: *Eis* means "unto." He is the point to which all tends (I Corinthians 15:28)—the consummation, the ultimate, the end, the Last, the Omega.

This completes the divine cycle and intention, involving the Godhead as Father, Son, and Holy Spirit; *of* the Father, *through* the Son, and *by* the Holy Spirit. "In the beginning God..." (Genesis 1:1), and in the end, God. "...[T]hat God may be all and in all" (I Corinthians 15:28).

- "All come from Him; all lives by Him; all ends in Him" (Moffatt).
- "For the universe owes its origin to Him, was created by Him, and has its aim and purpose in Him" (Weymouth).
- "For from Him everything comes; through Him everything exists; and in Him everything ends" (Goodspeed).
- "Source, guide, and goal of all that is" (New English).

RIGHTEOUSNESS REVEALED

Righteousness Revealed
(Romans 12:1 - 16:27)

Priestly Presentation to God (Romans 12:1-2)

In this section, Paul now takes the doctrinal into the practical, the precept into practice, imputed righteousness into outworked righteousness (cf. II Corinthians 10:1; I Peter 2:5; Hebrews 10:20).

Verse 1: *"I beseech you therefore, brethren, by the mercies of God, that ye present your bodies a living sacrifice, holy, acceptable unto God, which is your reasonable service."*

A. **"Beseech"**
   Greek: *Parclea* means "to call aside, appeal to (by way of exhortation, entreaty, comfort, or instruction)." On the basis of all that has gone before, Paul entreats the believer by the *mercies* of God—the motive for our obedience (Romans 9:15-16, 18, 23).

B. **"Present"**
   "Present" means "yield" (Romans 6:13, 19; Luke 2:22). This is the technical term for presenting the Levitical victims and offerings (Vincent).

C. **"Bodies"**
   The body is now the temple of the Lord, bought with the price. It is not the "body of sin," for that has been crucified—reckoned dead. Paul does not want that body, but the body now surrendered to God, to another. That body is now raised to walk in newness of life. That body is now presented to Him (I Corinthians 6:20).

D. **"A living sacrifice"**
   Compare living sacrifices to the presentation of the Old Testament animals, slain sacrifices, given to God at His altar (Leviticus 1-7). "Presenting, presentation" as in the priestly ministration unto the Lord.

E. "Holy"
   The Old Testament sacrifices had to be holy before being presented to the Lord. This is typified in the pure lamb "...without blemish and without spot....," holy to the Lord (Ephesians 5:23-26; I Peter 1:19-20), consecrated, dedicated, devoted.

F. "Acceptable unto God"
   To be acceptable to God is to be well pleasing, fit for His acceptance, just as all Old Testament sacrifices. The believer-priest now offers his body to God as a New Testament sacrifice, not an animal body.

G. "Reasonable service"
   "Reasonable service" is "spiritual service, rational service, reasonable worship, spiritual service; an act of intelligent worship." (Refer to the Amplified New Testament and Phillips; Romans 9:4.)

Verse 2: *"And be not conformed to this world: but be ye transformed by the renewing of your mind, that ye may prove what is that good, and acceptable, and perfect, will of God."*

Note conformed verses transformed.

A. "Conformed"
   "Conformed" means "fashioned, imitate." "Do not be conformed to this world—this age, fashioned after and adapted to its external, superficial customs...." (Amplified New Testament).

B. "Transformed"
   Greek: *Metamorphoomai* means "to change the form" (Matthew 17:2); it is translated as "transfigured."
   A few years ago an article appeared in LIFE magazine. It was most enlightening when spiritually applied to the renewing of the mind. For many centuries, biologists had wondered what could possibly cause a caterpillar to change to a butterfly. At last, one biologist discovered a very significant thing. He found that this remarkable transformation was caused by a hormone in the tiny brain of the caterpillar. He found that, if the hormone was removed, the caterpillar would remain a caterpillar until death, but if the hormone was left in the brain, the caterpillar would

change to a beautiful butterfly. To prove this theory, he joined five caterpillars together, removing the hormone from the brains of the first four and leaving it in the brain of the last one. The first four remained as they were, while the last changed to a butterfly. He then reversed the process, leaving the hormone in the head of the first worm, and removing it from the last four. To the amazement of all, the whole five changed to butterflies, or shall we say, became the same as the head one. The spiritual significance of this remarkable discovery cannot be overlooked, for it is God's Word in His creation, teaching us that, as a worm is transformed to a celestial creature by a tiny cell in its mind, so also are we transformed by receiving the mind of Christ.

C. **"Renewing of your mind"**
Mind renewal involves new ideals and new attitudes that mold the mind. Only the Word of God, as applied by the Holy Spirit, can renew the mind (II Timothy 1:7; Philippians 2:5; II Corinthians 10:1-4; Romans 1:28; Luke 10:27; Isaiah 26:3; Romans 8:5-7). The object is to obtain the mind of the Spirit.

D. **"Prove"**
"To prove" is "to discern or learn by experience."

E. **"Good, and acceptable, and perfect, will of God"**
Note the following:
"Good"
"Acceptable" – well pleasing
"Perfect" – Greek: *Telios* means "reached its end, nothing beyond" (Matthew 6:9-10; Romans 8:27; Ephesians 1:5, 9, 11; 5:17; Luke 12:47-48).

Verses 1-2: *Summary*

These two verses really present a priestly scene:
* The believer is a priest.
* His body is the sacrifice.
* Presenting it is his priestly worship.
* The will of God is the most important thing in the universe.

Compare also Christ Jesus in the following Scriptures:

Hebrews 10:5-10	Romans 12:1-2
• Christ Jesus – High Priest	• The Believer-Priest
• Body Prepared	• Body Bought With a Price
• Presented to God as a Sacrifice	• Presented to God as a Living Sacrifice
• To Do God's Will	• To Do God's Will

Responsibilities of the Righteous (Romans 12:3-13:14)

To the Church (Romans 12:3-21)

In this section, we see the practical outworking of righteousness. Imputed and judicial righteousness must become outworked and in-wrought righteousness. Legal righteousness must be seen in practical righteousness.

Verse 3: *"For I say, through the grace given unto me, to every man that is among you, not to think of himself more highly than he ought to think; but to think soberly, according as God hath dealt to every man the measure of faith."*

A. **"Grace"**
Greek: *Charis* is the grace-gift of apostleship to the Gentiles given to Paul (cf. Romans 1:5; Ephesians 3:8; Galatians 2:9). The believer is not to overestimate himself or his value, or to think too highly of himself. He is not to go to either extreme of underestimation or overestimation of himself before God or men. He must think sanely, soberly, according to the measure of faith that God has given him (Proverbs 25:27; Ephesians 4:7). He is not to be high-minded or conceited.

B. **"Measure of faith"** (cf. verse 6; refer also to notes on "faith" in Romans 1:17)
All believers are given a measure or a degree of faith, according to their place in the body of Christ. This verse is not written to sinners, but to

believers in Christ. The reference here is not referring particularly to "saving faith," but to the "measure of faith" given to one to function in his or her gift in the body of Christ, as verses 4-8 show. (Note also the word "measure" in Ephesians 4:13-16.)

Verses 4-5: *"For as we have many members in one body, and all members have not the same office: so we, being many, are one body in Christ, and every one members one of another."*

(Cf. Ephesians 4:16; I Corinthians 12:12-27.)

A. **"Office"**
"Office" means "various functions, offices." Office is literally a mode of acting (Vincent).

B. **"Body"**
It is worthy to note the various aspects of the word "body" in Romans. In 6:6-12, Paul deals with the mortal body as being the body of sin. In 8:10-11, that same body is to be reckoned dead to sin in its members. In 12:1-2, we are exhorted to present these bodies to God as a living sacrifice. Now, in 12:4-5, Paul moves into the aspect of the believer as a member of the spiritual body of Christ—the church (Romans 7:4).

In Chapter 11, the Jew and Gentile are seen as branches in the same olive tree, to produce good fruit unto the glory of God. In Chapter 12, the Jew and Gentile are seen as members of the same body—the body of Christ—to function as healthy members in that body (Ephesians 3:1-6).

I Corinthians 6:15 says, "Know ye not that your bodies are the members of Christ?" This shows the connection between the spiritual body—the body of Christ—and the believers' mortal or physical bodies presented to God. The visible points to the mystical. The visible is the expression of the spiritual. The only way that a believer can demonstrate, on a practical level, that he is a member of the body of Christ is to yield the members of his physical body to the good service of the Lord (I Corinthians 6:15-20; Romans 6:12-13; I Corinthians 12:12; Acts 2, 10, 11). The church, composed of Jew and Gentile, is symbolized by the human body. The whole purpose of a body is to be the vehicle of expression for the indwelling person and his nature, character, and will.

The body of Christ is to be the vehicle of expression for the Spirit of Christ who indwells the believer. In this body, He desires to reveal His nature, character, power, and will to the whole world.

The human body is the union of many parts or members, and each member in its particular office and function sets forth that union of the members of the body of Christ. First the natural, then the spiritual is God's order. Each member is interdependent, and each needs the others, for all are part of the whole. We work from the part to the whole and from the whole to the part. We are members of the body of Christ (corporately) and members in particular (individually).

Verses 6-8: *"Having then gifts differing according to the grace that is given us, whether prophecy, let us prophesy according to the proportion of faith; or ministry, let us wait on our ministering: or he that teacheth, on teaching; or he that exhorteth, on exhortation: he that giveth, let him do it with simplicity; he that ruleth, with diligence; he that sheweth mercy, with cheerfulness."*

A. **"Having then gifts differing"**

As in the natural body, so in the spiritual body. God has placed different gifts in the different members of the body according to His place and function for them in the body. "...[I]mpart unto you some spiritual gift..." (cf. Romans 1:11).

Greek: *Charisma* and *Charis* are "grace gifts." Consider the use and connection of these two words in these Scriptures: Ephesians 4:7; Romans 12:6. Thus, the gifts differ in the members:

- Grace is given in measure to all the members.
- Grace is given according to the gift given.
- The gift is given by God according to the member's place in the body and how God intends that member to function.
- The gift in the members and the grace given makes the member a functioning member.

The list given here in Romans 12 is by no means exhaustive. It should be related to the other lists of "gifts" in the body of Christ given by Paul in I Corinthians 12 and Ephesians 4. Set out in columns as follows:

Romans 12:6-8	I Corinthians 12:4-11	Ephesians 4:11
1. Prophesying 2. Ministering 3. Teaching 4. Exhorting 5. Giving 6. Ruling 7. Mercy showing	1. Word of Wisdom 2. Word of Knowledge 3. Faith 4. Healing 5. Miracles 6. Prophecy 7. Discerning of Spirits 8. Tongues 9. Interpretation of Tongues	1. Apostles 2. Prophets 3. Evangelists 4. Pastors 5. Teachers

B. **"Whether prophecy, let us prophesy according to the proportion of faith"** (cf. I Corinthians 12:4-11)

Prophecy is one of the nine gifts of the Holy Spirit. All believers may prophesy (I Corinthians 14:1, 3-5, 31). Prophecy upon men and women is a sign of the last days' outpouring of the Holy Spirit on all flesh (Joel 2:28-32). Guidelines for prophecy are given in I Corinthians 14:3:

- Edification – "to build up"
- Exhortation – "to stir up"
- Comfort – "to bind up"

All prophetic utterances must be tested by the infallible Word of God and by the Spirit also. Distinction should also be noted in the following:

- The Gift of Prophecy (I Corinthians 12:10).
- The Office of a Prophet (I Corinthians 12:29; Ephesians 4:11-12).
  - All who prophesy are not prophets (cf. Acts 21:8-11).
- The Spirit of Prophecy (Revelation 19:10).
- The Prophecy of Scripture, the Infallible Word of God (II Peter 1:20).

The first three must be checked against the fourth.

Prophecy also must be according to the proportion or the measure of faith given—not going beyond into presumption. (Note also verse 3.) The above gives the guidelines and safeguards for the use and operation of this gift and its various limitations according to a person's place in the body.

C. "Or ministry, let us wait on our ministering"

Greek: *Diakonia* means "the service rendered by a *diakonos*; the ministry of serving, or service; practical service or serving others as a deacon." To wait on their service is like an attendant waiting on others, the ones that they are serving (Philippians 1:1; I Timothy 3:10, 13).

Notice those who "ministered" to Jesus and the apostles (Matthew 20:26; Mark 10:43; Romans 16:1-2; Luke 10:40).

Notice the Old Testament Levites who "served" the tabernacle and the priesthood, as well as the people. All of God's people should have the servant Spirit of Christ—serving one another by love. However, there will be those who are expressly called as deacons or servants to the Lord, the ministry, the churches, and the people of God.

D. "Or he that teacheth, on teaching"

The teacher is one of the five-fold ascension gift ministries in the body (I Corinthians 12:28-29; Ephesians 4:9-12; James 3:1; Matthew 23:8). He also must give himself to the ministry in prayer, study, and meditation in the Word and the anointing of the Holy Spirit (I John 2:20, 27). He must be armed with understanding for his times (I Chronicles 12:32; II Chronicles 15:3). Elders are apt to teach. Also, there are varied levels, degrees, or measures of the teaching ministry—touching and reaching all age levels of the body, from children and youth to adults.

E. "Or he that exhorteth, on exhortation"

Greek: *Paraklesis* means "to call aside, appeal to (by way of exhortation, entreaty, comfort, or instruction); ministry or exhortation needed to 'stir up' the people of God, those who hear, encouraging them to practical godliness" (Acts 15:32; 2:40).

This ministry is aimed at the heart and the will. Barnabas, "son of consolation and exhortation," had this ministry also (Acts 4:36).

F. "He that giveth, let him do it with simplicity"

The ministry of giving is to be done with liberality, with a generous heart—not stingy or mean, even as a spendthrift, but wise and charitable, giving to those in genuine need.

"Giveth" – imparting, sharing with (II Corinthians 9:7, 11, 13; Luke 3:11)

"Simplicity" – single eye to the glory of God; not giving as the Pharisees (Matthew 6:22; II Corinthians 8:2)

G. **"He that ruleth, with diligence"**
   This ministry gift is any position involving superintendence or presiding over. The ministry of ruling, or presiding, should be done with zeal and diligence, not haphazardly or lazily, but in earnestness.

H. **"He that sheweth mercy, with cheerfulness"**
   This is the ministry of showing mercy. Acts of mercy or pity should be done with a cheerful attitude. Kenneth N. Taylor calls this the "gift of kindness" to others (Proverbs 31:26). Cheerfulness is equal to hilarious (II Corinthians 9:7).

I. **Summary**
   All of these gifts are expressions of "Christ in you"—of Christ in the members of the body. All are manifested perfectly in Him and all are to be seen functioning in the church, which is His body. These are His ministries at work in the members. All are needed. All flow through the redeemed personality of the individual, and as the believer's personality is cleansed, purged, and refined by the indwelling Spirit of Christ, then these things will have a more perfect expression and more effective operation to the blessing of those in the body of Christ and to those in the world.

Verses 9-21: *"Let love be without dissimulation. Abhor that which is evil; cleave to that which is good. Be kindly affectioned one to another with brotherly love; in honour preferring one another; not slothful in business; fervent in spirit; serving the Lord; rejoicing in hope; patient in tribulation; continuing instant in prayer; distributing to the necessity of saints; given to hospitality. Bless them which persecute you: bless, and curse not. Rejoice with them that do rejoice, and weep with them that weep. Be of the same mind one toward another. Mind not high things, but condescend to men of low estate. Be not wise in your own conceits. Recompense to no man evil for evil. Provide things honest in the sight of all men. If it be possible, as much as lieth in you, live peaceably with all men. Dearly beloved, avenge not yourselves, but rather give place unto wrath: for it is written, Vengeance is mine; I will repay, saith the Lord. Therefore if thine enemy hunger, feed him; if he thirst, give him drink: for in so doing thou shalt heap coals of fire on his head. Be not overcome of evil, but overcome evil with good."*

A. **Practical Outworking of Righteousness**

Following, we have twenty-three injunctions to practical righteousness.

"Let love be without dissimulation" – Love must be genuine, sincere, unfeigned, or without hypocrisy (I Timothy 1:5; John 5:20; Matthew 23:13; I John 3:18).

"Abhor that which is evil; cleave to that which is good" – Abhor or hate evil (negative). Love or cleave to the good (positive). Regard evil with all horror; cling to the good (Joshua 23:8; II Kings 18:6; Psalms 34:14; 97:10).

"Be kindly affectioned one to another with brotherly love" – "Love one another with brotherly affection" (RSV). Greek: *Philadelphia* means "brotherly love, love of a brother." Brotherly affection should be shown at all times (Hebrews 13:1; I Peter 1:22). As in a family natural affection is expressed, so also should affection be expressed in the family of God, as love between a mother and children.

"In honor preferring one another" – Honor and show respect to each other. Go before as a guide (I Peter 2:17; 5:5; Philippians 2:3).

"Not slothful in business" – Slothfulness or laziness in work, secular or spiritual, is not a characteristic of righteousness. Business requires diligence or zeal.

"Fervent in spirit" – Be on fire, aglow with the Spirit (cf. Acts 18:25).

"Serving the Lord" – Greek: *Douleuo* means "to serve as a bondman; serving as a love-slave to his master" (Exodus 21:1-6).

"Rejoicing in hope" – Be joyful in hope, not having hope and being sad with it (Luke 10:20; Romans 5:2, notes). There is great place for "hope" in the Christian's life (I Corinthians 13:7; Matthew 10:22) because of the blessed hope of His coming.

"Patient in tribulation" – Sufferings, afflictions, and trouble are all part of character training (Luke 21:19). Tribulation works patience (Romans 5:3) (James 1:2; II Corinthians 12:10). Endurance, steadfastness will support the believer through all trials. Note: Romans persecutions of the saints. (See also Romans 8:25; 15:4,5.)

"Continuing instant in prayer" – Continue is steadfast, persistent, persevering prayer (Luke 18:1; Acts 1:14; 2:42, 46-47).

"Distributing to the necessity of saints" – Greek: *Koinonea* means "distributing, communication" to the saints' needs; sharing the necessities (I Corinthians 16:1; Romans 15:27). Note "necessities," not always wants!

"Given to hospitality" – The believer is to show and practice hospitality, kindness to strangers (Hebrews 13:2; I Timothy 3:2; Titus 1:8; I Peter 4:9).

"Bless them which persecute you; bless, and curse not" – The believer has power, in his hand and in his tongue, to bless or curse his persecutors (Matthew 5:44). This is the Spirit of Christ to bless those who persecute us (John 5:16; Luke 6:27-28).

"Rejoice with them that do rejoice, and weep with them that weep" – This is the mental disposition with which an act is performed (cf. I Corinthians 12:26). When the believer is in the company of those who are happy and joyful, he should enter into their joys, or if he is in the company of sadness and sorrow, he should enter into that by a proper disposition. This does not mean he is to become a professional mourner or joker. Jesus had joy; Jesus wept.

"Be of the same mind one toward another" – "The same mind" is "one mind, harmony with each other (Philippians 2:2; I Corinthians 1:10), brotherly sympathy with one another."

"Mind not high things, but condescend to men of low estate" – "Men of low estate" are the "lowly ones." Marginal notes say, "Be contented with mean things." The believer is not to be haughty, ambitious, or puffed up in his mind. He is to be humble-minded and willing to come down to the level of ordinary, humble people. He is to "be carried away with the lowly." It is easy to get caught up in the "proud crowd" (Romans 11:20; Jeremiah 45:5).

"Be not wise in your own conceits" – The believer must not be conceited (Proverbs 3:7; Romans 11:2-3; Proverbs 26:12). He must not think too highly of himself or his own opinions, thinking he knows everything. Knowledge puffs up (I Corinthians 8:1-3).

"Recompense to no man evil for evil" – The believer should not have the letter of the law, which is "...An eye for an eye, and a tooth for a tooth...," or injury for injury, or evil for evil (Matthew 5:38-39; Exodus 21:24; Leviticus 24:20; Deuteronomy 19:21). He is not to do to others what they have done to him. He is doing to others what he would want to have done to him in a specific situation (Romans 12:14). Grace goes beyond the spirit of the law (Colossians 3:13).

"Provide things honest in the sight of all men" – "Take thought for things honorable (good and beautiful) in the sight of all men" (II

Corinthians 8:21 [paraphrased], Proverbs 3:4). The believer is not to aim for anything less than that which is honorable in all his dealings with people.

"If it be possible, as much as lieth in you, live peaceably with all men" – The believer should, as far as it is his responsibility and as far as it is possible, endeavor to live in peace with all men (Hebrews 12:14; Romans 14:19). It always takes two to make a war. The true believer, at times, can even make his enemies to be at peace with him by his attitude (Proverbs 16:7). He is a peace-maker, not a peace-breaker (Matthew 5:9).

"Dearly beloved, avenge not yourselves, but rather give place unto wrath: for it is written, Vengeance is Mine; I will repay, saith the Lord" – The believer is not to take vengeance into his own hands. He is to let God, in His time and His wrath, bring retribution (cf. Leviticus 19:18; Deuteronomy 32:35; Hebrews 10:30; Luke 18:3; Acts 7:24). God will recompense His way. His wrath is poured out in absolute righteousness. God restrains His wrath at the moment to bring men to repentance. The believer must link up with God's attitude on this. (Refer to notes on "wrath" in Romans 1:18; 2:4-5, 8; 4:15.) The broken law works wrath, but the believer is not to function in the letter of the law in this age of New Covenant grace.

"Therefore, if thine enemy hunger, feed him; if he thirst, give him drink: for in so doing thou shalt heap coals of fire on his head" – The believer, under New Covenant grace, can learn to love his enemy and demonstrate it practically by giving him food or drink, if needed (cf. Matthew 5:43-48; I Corinthians 13:3; Proverbs 25:21-22). An Old Testament example of this is found in II Kings 6:18-23 when the Israelites were charged to give food and drink to their enemies, the Syrians. Coals of fire are symbolic of the burning sense of shame (Psalm 18:13).

"Be not overcome of evil, but overcome evil with good" – The believer is not to be conquered by evil, but is to conquer evil with good. He can get the better of evil by doing good, conquering darkness with light, not letting the darkness or evil conquer him. Jesus demonstrated this principle.

B. **Correspondence to the Sermon on the Mount**
    There are a number of correspondences in Romans 12:9-21 with "The Sermon on the Mount" as in Matthew 5-7. This could be called Paul's

Sermon on the Mount. It deals with practical righteousness. The following are the most prominent correspondences and allusions to Christ's Sermon the Mount.

- Alms and Prayer (Romans 12:13with Matthew 6:1-15)
- Blessing and Cursing (Romans 12:14 with Matthew 5:44, 11-12)
- Evil and Good (Romans 12:17 with Matthew 5:38-39)
- Blessing Your Enemies (Romans 12:20 with Matthew 5:43-47)
- Overcoming Evil with Good (Romans 12:21 with Matthew 5:39-42)

To the Government (Romans 13:1-7)

In this section, Paul deals with the Christian's responsibility to the government. The points outlined are very important to understanding the believer's relationship to civil authority and government, which he is under, and the responsibilities to the same. This would be very important to the Christians suffering under Roman authorities and governmental power.

Verse 1: *"Let every soul be subject unto the higher powers. For there is no power but of God: the powers that be are ordained of God."*

A. **"Let every soul be subject unto the higher powers."**
The believer is to be subject to the higher authorities or powers. Subjection and submission is to the authorities over him in the country of which he is a citizen.

B. **"For there is no power by of God"**
The believer should recognize that there is no power but of God. The authorities or government superiors are all subject to God (Daniel 2:21). God rules in the affairs of men. All authority comes from God, and only exists with His permission. He established the existing authorities. (Cf. (Luke 7:8.)

C. **"The powers that be are ordained of God"**
The believer should understand that the powers that be are ordained (ordered) of God. All authority is of God, is ordained of God, and is subject to God. He is the highest authority. Though the use of the office may be abused, there is nothing wrong with the office itself.

Thus, Herod, Pilate (cf. John 19:10-12; Luke 22:53), Nebuchadnezzar, Caesar, etc., could have "no power except it were given to them" from above regardless of the form of man's government that placed them in office.

Verse 2: *"Whosoever therefore resisteth the power, resisteth the ordinance of God: and they that resist shall receive to themselves damnation."*

A. **"Whosoever therefore resisteth the power, resisteth the ordinance of God"**
   The believer who resists or withstands the power or sets himself in array against it is resisting a divine ordinance, for it is God who orders authority in government. One must not set himself in opposition to God ordained and appointed authority by becoming a rebel.

B. **"And they that resist shall receive to themselves damnation"**
   "Damnation" means "judicial sentence." The believer (and also the unbeliever), who resists God's divine institutions, will bring judgment on himself. God must punish those who resist authority. Sentence, penalty, and punishment will be meted out. (Cf. Titus 3:1.)

Verse 3: *"For rulers are not a terror to good works, but to the evil. Wilt thou then not be afraid of the power? do that which is good, and thou shalt have praise of the same..."*

The believer must realize that only those who do evil need to be afraid of the powers that be. Good only merits praise. (Read the Amplified New Testament.) Civil authorities are meant to bring a healthy fear to law-breakers (I Peter 2:14). The law is made for the lawless (I Timothy 1:9).

Verse 4: *"...For he is the minister of God to thee for good. But if thou do that which is evil, be afraid; for he beareth not the sword in vain: for he is a minister of God, a revenger to execute wrath upon him that doeth evil."*

The believer must recognize that the civil authorities are also God's ministers. Greek: *Diakonos* means "a servant of God." As an authority, he is also under authority. Thus, a civil authority is what follows:
- A Minister of God

- A Bearer of the Sword of Justice
- A Revenger to Execute Wrath on One who Does Evil—An Avenger (cf. Romans 12:19)

Under the Noahic Covenant, civil law, or rather, human government, was given to man. God delegated authority to men and placed civil government in the hands of men. That covenant is still in effect today, though man may try to abrogate it.

Also under the Mosaic Covenant, civil law—the amplification of the moral law—was placed in the hands of judges and elders of Israel. When the laws were violated, the evil doer was judged by these ministers of God's government in Israel, and thus, punished by the sword or by other means of retribution.

Verse 5: *"Wherefore ye must needs be subject, not only for wrath, but also for conscience sake."*

(Cf. I Peter 2:19; Ecclesiastes 8:2.)

The believer must submit to civil authorities, not just through fear of punishment or penalty, but having and maintaining a clear conscience before God, who is the highest authority over all the authorities He has ordained. The believer must submit based on principle, not just fear, (Romans 2:15; 9:1; Acts 23:1) whether to a monarchy, democracy, or dictator.

Verse 6: *"For this cause pay ye tribute also: for they are God's ministers, attending continually upon this very thing."*

The believer should not avoid paying taxes to the government, for the very civil powers are servants of the people, and they are in their office to attend to the protection of the people from evil workers. The government, therefore, has to be supported by the people it protects (Luke 20:22-25; 23:2). The authorities are official servants. Nero was emperor at this time, and his was an absolute monarchy, making life and death edicts.

Verse 7: *"Render therefore to all their dues: tribute to whom tribute is due; custom to whom custom; fear to whom fear; honour to whom honour."*

A. **"Tribute to whom tribute is due; custom to whom custom; fear to whom fear; honour to whom honour"**

"Honor" means "respect." The believer is obligated to give the civil powers whatsoever is due them in their respective offices. He must give that which is due for public ends (cf. Matthew 17:25-27; 22:21; Luke 20:25). Paul confirms Jesus' teachings on the tribute or tax money. Render to Caesar those things which are Caesar's.

B. **Delegated Authority**

The subject of delegated authority, as in this section, is a very vital one. It sets forth some basic principles of authority. Note the diagram.

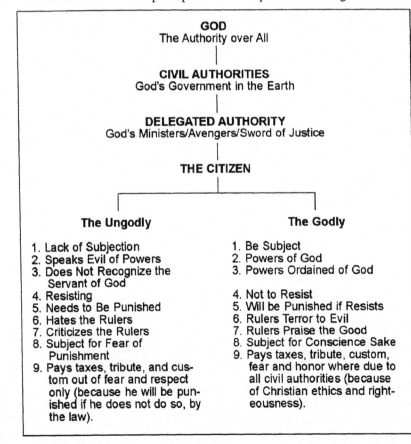

GOD
The Authority over All

CIVIL AUTHORITIES
God's Government in the Earth

DELEGATED AUTHORITY
God's Ministers/Avengers/Sword of Justice

THE CITIZEN

The Ungodly	The Godly
1. Lack of Subjection	1. Be Subject
2. Speaks Evil of Powers	2. Powers of God
3. Does Not Recognize the Servant of God	3. Powers Ordained of God
4. Resisting	4. Not to Resist
5. Needs to Be Punished	5. Will be Punished if Resists
6. Hates the Rulers	6. Rulers Terror to Evil
7. Criticizes the Rulers	7. Rulers Praise the Good
8. Subject for Fear of Punishment	8. Subject for Conscience Sake
9. Pays taxes, tribute, and custom out of fear and respect only (because he will be punished if he does not do so, by the law).	9. Pays taxes, tribute, custom, fear and honor where due to all civil authorities (because of Christian ethics and righteousness).

The teaching of the Scripture is clear on the believer's attitude and actions in the country where he is a citizen and under the government to which he is subject. Joseph, Daniel, Jesus, and Paul all confirm the believer's submission to government—foreign or domestic. The one and only time a believer disobeys the immediate authorities above him is when they ask him to do things contrary to God's Word or contrary to God Himself. Then the believer comes directly under God's highest authority, and suffers the penalty of the civil authority, which is delegated authority. Here, he can submit or disobey (cf. Daniel 3, the three Hebrew children submitted to the king but refused to worship the image).

However, God will deal with the civil authority if they go beyond their delegated authority and try to usurp or violate the authority of God. Several examples of this are Daniel, when he prayed to God three times a day (Daniel 6), the Hebrew youths, when they did not bow to the image of the king, and Peter and John, when they were forbidden by the ecclesiastical powers to preach the name of Jesus (Acts 4:18-21). All of them obeyed God rather than men (Acts 5:27-29). Paul did exercise his right as a Roman citizen when necessary and appealed to a law that was higher than Jewish law (Acts 23).

A believer can be submissive to such authority and let those in charge do what they will, but he need not obey them. Daniel, Shadrach, Meshech, Abednego, Jesus, Peter, John, and Paul exemplify this. They submitted to the government and suffered accordingly, but they could not obey the commands of the government, which were contrary to the supreme authority—God Himself. Believers cannot incite anarchy, or be lawless, or violate laws, even though they are citizens of heaven also.

To Others: Believers or Unbelievers (Romans 13:8-10)

Verse 8: *"Owe no man any thing, but to love one another: for he that loveth another hath fulfilled the law."*

(Cf. Galatians 5:14; I Timothy 1:5.) There is no law against love.

Verse 9: *"For this, Thou shalt not commit adultery, Thou shalt not kill, Thou shalt not steal, Thou shalt not bear false witness, Thou shalt not covet; and if there be any other commandment, it is briefly comprehended in this saying, namely, Thou shalt love thy neighbour as thyself."*

A. **"Thou shalt not commit adultery"** (seventh commandment, Exodus 20:14; Matthew 19:18)

B. **"Thou shalt not kill"** (sixth commandment on murder, Exodus 20:13; Matthew 19:18)

C. **"Thou shalt not steal"** (eighth commandment, Exodus 20:13; Matthew 19:18)

D. **"Thou shalt not bear false witness"** (ninth commandment, Exodus 20:16; Matthew 19:18)

E. **"Thou shalt not covet"** (tenth commandment, Exodus 20:17; refer to Romans 7:7-12 notes again)

F. **"And if there be any other commandment, it is briefly comprehended in this saying, namely"**
   "Comprehended" means "summed up." See following:

G. **"Thou shalt love thy neighbor as thyself"** (Leviticus 19:18; Mark 12:31; James 2:8; Matthew 22:39)

Verse 10: *"Love worketh no ill to his neighbour: therefore love is the fulfilling of the law."*

(Cf. Matthew 22:34-40.)

This present subsection on love is the climax of Paul's revelation on the subject of "law" in Romans, and it clarifies Romans 7-8 pertaining to the law that the New Testament believer is under. It is the *law of love; love fulfills the law.* It is important to understand the matter of law, here, in relation to the believer. Under the Old or Mosaic Covenant, as noted in earlier chapters of this epistle, the law was divided into three main areas:

A. **The Moral Law**

The moral law consisted of the Ten Commandments, which were written on two tables of stone and placed in the ark of the covenant. It was given three times before it found its place in the ark, beneath the bloodstained mercy seat. It was given:

1) Orally to the nation (Deuteronomy 4-5).
2) On tables of stone, written by the finger of god (Exodus 32-33) and broken by Moses.
3) On the second tables of stone, placed in the ark of god (Exodus 34).

B. **The Civil Law**

The civil law was the amplification of the moral law and was written in the book of the covenant—the book of the law—which was placed at the side of the ark (Exodus 24; Deuteronomy 32-33).

C. **The Ceremonial Law**

The ceremonial law included laws pertaining to cleansing and purification from sin or transgression of the moral and civil laws. Moses was the mediator of this covenant. This ceremonial law involved the laws of the priesthood, the tabernacle, the feasts, the sacrificial system, and the laws of purification (Exodus 25-40; Leviticus 1-7, 9-10, 16, 23). It was the handwriting contained in ordinances. God's grace was typified in the ceremonial law.

D. **The Work of the Cross and the Law**

It is also important to understand what happened through Christ at the Cross in relation to these three areas of law. The following diagram helps us to summarize these main points.

In His life, He alone fulfilled and kept the moral law perfectly: morally, civilly, and also ceremonially (Psalm 40:8; Hebrews 10:5-10; Matthew 5-7). He kept and fulfilled the very spirit of the law. In relation to the Cross, we see: (Note the diagram on the following page)

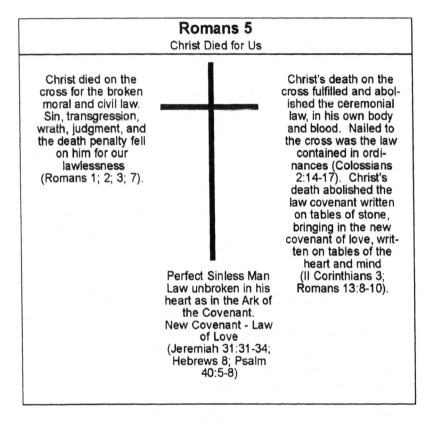

Romans 5
Christ Died for Us

Christ died on the cross for the broken moral and civil law. Sin, transgression, wrath, judgment, and the death penalty fell on him for our lawlessness (Romans 1; 2; 3; 7).

Christ's death on the cross fulfilled and abolished the ceremonial law, in his own body and blood. Nailed to the cross was the law contained in ordinances (Colossians 2:14-17). Christ's death abolished the law covenant written on tables of stone, bringing in the new covenant of love, written on tables of the heart and mind (II Corinthians 3; Romans 13:8-10).

Perfect Sinless Man Law unbroken in his heart as in the Ark of the Covenant. New Covenant - Law of Love (Jeremiah 31:31-34; Hebrews 8; Psalm 40:5-8)

Jesus, when challenged as to which was the greatest commandment, quoted Deuteronomy 6:5; 10:12; 30:6 as the greatest commandment, and then added quotations from Leviticus 19:18 for the next commandment.

- "...Thou shalt love the Lord God with all thy heart, and with all thy soul, and with all thy mind." This is the first and greatest commandment.

- "And the second is like unto it, Thou shalt love thy neighbour as thyself. On these two commandments hang all the law and the prophets" (Matthew 22:34-40).

The Ten Commandments were written on two tables of stone. They can be divided into two groupings. The first four laws have to do with man's relationship to God. The last six have to do with man's relationship to man. Each group can be summarized in the two commandments of Jesus. The first four commandments will be fulfilled if one truly *loves* God with all his heart, soul, mind, and strength. The last six commandments will be fulfilled if one truly *loves* man as he loves himself.

Therefore, *love* is the fulfilling of the law! Man will not have any other gods before God if he loves Him. Man will not make any graven images, or take God's name in vain, or break God's rest if he loves Him. Love fulfills the commandments involving our relationship to God.

The same follows with the other commandments. If one really loves his neighbor as himself, he will honor his parents, he will not commit adultery, steal, kill, lie, or covet. Love for one's neighbor fulfills the law. The law of love is called "the royal law of liberty" according to James (James 2:8-12).

In Romans 13:9, Paul quotes five of these commandments dealing with man's relationship to man. A believer, if he truly loves his neighbor as himself and if this love is shed abroad in the heart by the Holy Spirit (Romans 5:3-5), will not violate any of these commandments. By loving his neighbor as himself, he fulfills the law.

The difference should be seen also in the moral and ceremonial law in relation to Calvary's work.

Note the diagram on the following page.

Thus, on these *two commandments* hang *all* the law and the prophets. *Love* fulfills the *law!* The believer is not under the law of Moses, but he is under the law of Jesus (I Corinthians 9:21). Notice that the two fulfill the ten, in the spirit, not merely by the letter.

All or any of these violations of the commandments are working ill to one's neighbor. "Who is my neighbor?" The answer is spelled out clearly in Luke 10:25-37.

Thus, *love* sums up in one word the Ten Commandments. The Old Covenant commandments were written by the finger of God on tables of stone under the Old Testament Pentecost. The New Covenant commandments are written by the Spirit of God on fleshly tables of the heart under the New Testament Pentecost (II Corinthians 3; Romans 8:1-4).

It is worthy to note that the Ten Commandments are written in the New Testament, except the fourth commandment, which Paul deals with in two passages of his epistles. The moral law was holy, just, good, and spiritual, and it is fulfilled in principle and in spirit in the two commandments of Jesus—in loving God and loving my neighbor.

The Moral Law	The Ceremonial Law
The 10 Laws or Commandments Spoken by God, direct to the people of Israel from Mt. Sinai in the 3rd month (Deuteronomy 4:12-13; 5:20; Exodus 19:1).	**The Law Contained in Ordinances** Spoken by God to Moses from above the Mercy Seat in the Tabernacle. Set up in the first month of the second year (Exodus 25:22; Leviticus 1:1-2).
Written By God on Tables of Stone (Exodus 24:12)	**Written By Man in a Book** (Deuteronomy 31:24; 25:58)
Placed in the Ark (Exodus 25:16)	**Placed in the Side of the Ark** (Deuteronomy 31:26)
Is Perfect (Psalm 19:7; 119)	**Made Nothing Perfect** (Hebrews 7:19)
To Stand Forever (Psalm 111:7-8)	**Was Nailed to the Cross** (Colossians 2:14)
Was Not Abolished By Christ (Matthew 5:17-18)	**Was Abolished By Christ At Calvary** (Ephesians 2:15)
Established By Faith (Romans 3:31)	**Added Because of Transgressions Till the Seed** (Christ) Should Come (Galatians 3:19)
Written By the Finger of God (Exodus 31:18)	**Engraved (Chiseled) in Stone By Joshua** (Deuteronomy 27; Joshua 8:30-35; II Corinthians 3:6-12). The law on tables of stone was abolished and is now written in the heart and mind by the Spirit (finger) of God.
Law Is Holy, Just, Good, Spiritual (Romans 7)	**Spiritual Now in the Heart.**

Thus:

Relationship to God	1. Do Not Have Any Other Gods 2. Do Not Make Any Images 3. Do Not Take God's Name in Vain 4. Keep the Sabbath 5. Honor Your Parents	Love God	On These 2/10
Relationship to Man	6. Do Not Kill 7. Do Not Commit Adultery 8. Do Not Steal 9. Do Not Bear False Witness 10. Do Not Covet	Love Neighbor	One Word **Love** One Word **Love**

Note the Ten Commandments in the New Testament:
1) One God (I Timothy 2:5)
2) No Idolatry (I Corinthians 10:7, 14; I John 5:21)
3) No Profanity (Colossians 3:8; Matthew 6:33; II Timothy 2:19)
4) The Sabbath (dealt with in Colossians 2:16-17; Romans 14:5-6; Galatians 4:10-11; refer to notes; this commandment is not once repeated in the New Testament)
5) Honoring Parents (Ephesians 6:2)
6) No Murder (I John 3:14-15)
7) No Adultery (Ephesians 5:3-5; Galatians 5:19)
8) No Stealing (Ephesians 4:28)
9) No False Witness (Ephesians 4:25; I Corinthians 13)
10) No Coveting (Ephesians 5:3)

Thus, grace is not lawlessness. The believer is under the law of Christ (I Corinthians 9:21; Matthew 5-6-7). The law is written on the fleshly tables of his heart by the Spirit (by the finger) of God in the New Testament Pentecost (II Corinthians 3). It is fulfilled by the life in the Spirit. "...That the righteousness of the law might be fulfilled in us, who walk...after the Spirit" (Romans 8:1-4). Note the following diagram.

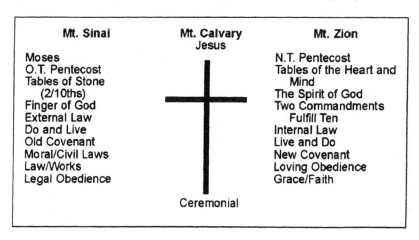

Mt. Sinai	Mt. Calvary Jesus	Mt. Zion
Moses		N.T. Pentecost
O.T. Pentecost		Tables of the Heart and
Tables of Stone		Mind
(2/10ths)		The Spirit of God
Finger of God		Two Commandments
External Law		Fulfill Ten
Do and Live		Internal Law
Old Covenant		Live and Do
Moral/Civil Laws		New Covenant
Law/Works		Loving Obedience
Legal Obedience		Grace/Faith
	Ceremonial	

To God: Allotted Time (Romans 13:11-14)

Verse 11: *"And that, knowing the time, that now it is high time to awake out of sleep: for now is our salvation nearer than when we believed."*

A. **"The time"**
Greek: *Kairos* means "season" (I Corinthians 15:34; Ephesians 5:11-14; I John 2:18). It is high time, the hour to awake, or wake up from sleep.

B. **"Sleep"**
(Note "sleep" in Matthew 24:1-13; I Thessalonians 5:1-10; Luke 9:32; Mark 13:32; 14:33-42.) The believer should recognize the "times and seasons" in which he is living (I Thessalonians 5:1; Ecclesiastics 3:1).

C. **"Salvation nearer"**
This is referring to the final deliverance or full salvation. We are saved, are being saved, and are yet to be saved. It is a salvation ready to be revealed at the last time, the salvation of our bodies (1 Peter 1:5; Romans 8:22-26).

Verse 12: *"The night is far spent, the day is at hand: let us therefore cast off the works of darkness, and let us put on the armour of light."*

A. **"The night is far spent, the day is at hand"**
Sin is the rule of the night (Ephesians 5:11-14; 6:13). Righteousness is the rule of the day (Hebrews 10:25 [the day]; II Peter 3:9-10; Philippians 4:5).

B. **"Cast off"**
"Cast off" means "as one puts off night garments and dresses for the day." Armor includes weapons of light. Notice the idea of putting off and putting on in verse 14. Negative and positive are both involved here. It is of no use to put off the negative unless one puts on the positive.

Verse 13: *"Let us walk honestly, as in the day; not in rioting and drunkenness, not in chambering and wantonness, not in strife and envying."*

(Cf. Proverbs 23:20; I Corinthians 6:9; James 3:14.) "Honestly" means "honorably, decently." The believer is a child of light, in contrast to the children of darkness. The two kingdoms of light and darkness are in conflict. The two kingdoms have their particular characteristics, as these verses show by contrast. Note the diagram on the following page.

KINGDOM OF LIGHT	KINGDOM OF DARKNESS
The Day	The Night
Put on the Armour of Light	Cast Off the Works of Darkness
Walking Honestly/Decently	Indecent Walking
Awake	Asleep
Knowing the Time and Hour	Not Knowing the Seasons
Put on the Lord Jesus Christ	Rioting-Reveling, carousing. 1Pet. 4:3
	Drunkenness-Lk. 21:34; Jn. 2:10
	Chambering-Lewdness, Prostitution, Sexual Promiscuity.
	Wantonness-Indecency, Lasciviousness-Mk. 7:22 and debauchery, sensuality.
	Strife-Quarrelling.
	Envying-jealousy- Ja. 3:14
Jesus Christ - Armour of Light No Provision for the Flesh	The Works of the Flesh- Gal. 5:19-21

Verse 14: *"But put ye on the Lord Jesus Christ, and make not provision for the flesh, to fulfil the lusts thereof."*

(Cf. Galatians 3:27; Ephesians 4:24; Galatians 5:16.)

"Put ye on the Lord Jesus Christ"

To "put on" is to clothe yourselves, as with a garment, with the Lord Jesus Christ, who is the new and divine nature. We must replace what we put off by putting on positive qualities.

*   The Positive – "Put on" the new nature (Romans 12:12, 14; Ephesians 4:22-32; Colossians 3:10-16).
*   The Negative – "Put off" the flesh or the old nature (Romans 12:12-14; Ephesians 4:24; Colossians 3:8-9).

Bishop Moule says, "Put on, clothe, and arm yourselves with the Lord Jesus Christ. We can put Him on as *Lord*, surrendering ourselves to His absolute sovereignty and will. We can put Him on as *Jesus*, clasping the truth that He, our human brother, yet divine, saves His people from their sins. We can put Him on as *Christ*, our Head, anointed without measure by the eternal Spirit, and sending that same Spirit into His Body members so that we are indeed one with Him and receive into our being the resources of His life."

Attitudes to Weaker Brethren (Romans 14:1-12)

Concerning Meats and Days

Verse 1: *"Him that is weak in the faith receive ye, but not to doubtful disputations."*

"Weak in the faith"
To be weak in faith is not necessarily to be weak in Christian doctrine. Perhaps Paul is referring to a Jewish class of Essenes (celibate, and ascetic, vegetarians and Sabbatarians here). Others may be stronger in ("in," not "the") faith. All are to be received—weak or strong. The weak are not to be received to "doubtful disputations" or "criticizings." Believers are not to have disputes over some of the scruples of others (marginal notes say, "not to judge his doubtful thoughts").

Verse 2: *"For one believeth that he may eat all things: another, who is weak, eateth herbs."*

(Cf. 1 Corinthians 8:1-13; 10:19-33; Titus 1:15.) One should remember that oftentimes meats were offered to idols, and Jewish brothers would not eat this meat. The Jewish people (or the people of Israel) were forbidden by the law to eat certain meats, as God said they were unclean, according to His commandments (Leviticus 11; Daniel 1).

(Refer also to comments on Romans 14:13-23.) For the present, however, notice that, in the early church, meats forbidden by the law, or meats offered to idols, were controversial as to whether or not they should be eaten. Some would not eat any meat at all, only herbs, according to the Edenic state before man's fall. Meats were not eaten between the time of Adam and Noah. Under the Noahic Covenant, the Lord permitted meats to be eaten, but the blood had to be poured out. Under the Mosaic Covenant, "clean and unclean" meats were specified for the nation of Israel (refer further to verses 14-23).

Verse 3: *"Let not him that eateth despise him that eateth not; and let not him which eateth not judge him that eateth; for God hath received him."*

(Cf. Colossians 2:16.)

Meat-eating is a non-essential when it comes to the fundamental doctrines of the faith. It does not strike at the foundational truths; therefore it should not act as a point of controversy amongst believers (Hebrews 13:9; I Timothy 4:1-4; I Corinthians 8:1-13). God does not make it a point of issue or a point of fellowship in the New Testament (I Corinthians 8:8). I Corinthians 6:13 says, "Meats for the belly and the belly for meats: but God shall destroy both it and them...." Neither should believers take issues over these things. If God received them as they were in verse 3, then we should also receive them, as in verse 1.

Verse 4: *"Who art thou that judgest another man's servant? to his own master he standeth or falleth. Yea, he shall be holden up: for God is able to make him stand."*

(Cf. James 4:12.)

All believers, weak or strong in the faith, are God's servants. He is their Master, and all stand or fall and are accountable to Him. God is able to uphold the weak and to make them stand. Therefore, we are not to judge or criticize God's servants with regard to meat-eating or no meat-eating.

Verse 5: *"One man esteemeth one day above another: another esteemeth every day alike. Let every man be fully persuaded in his own mind."*

(Cf. Galatians 4:10; Colossians 2:14-17.)

Another area of disputation in the early church was concerning the keeping of "Sabbath days" or other special days (Exodus 31:12-18; Leviticus 23; Numbers 28; Leviticus 5).

The Jews especially esteemed the Sabbath day above any other day of the week. The feast days, or high days, were also special. To the Gentiles, generally speaking, every day of the week was alike. They were not concerned about keeping sacred days. Again, with the transition from the keeping of the Sabbath to the keeping of the first day of the week, there was doubtfulness. There is no express command concerning the keeping of a particular day in the New Testament. It seems evident enough that during the transition period in Acts, some kept the Sabbath and some the first day of the week (cf. the Sabbath day in Acts 17:1-4; 14:1; 16:13; 19:8; the first day of the week in Acts20:7; I Corinthians 16:2; Revelation 1:10).

It is worthy to note that under the Mosaic Covenant, even while the Jews were keeping the Sabbath, they kept the first day of the week also on special days, thus foreshadowing the New Testament keeping of the first day of the week.

Old Testament Type:

1) The Sheaf of Firstfruits was kept "...on the morrow after the sabbath...," i.e., the first day of the week (Leviticus 23:9-14).
2) The Feast of Pentecost was also kept "...unto the morrow after the seventh sabbath...," which was the first day of the week (Leviticus 23:15-22).

New Testament Anti-type:

These two feasts find their fulfillment in the New Testament in Christ and the church.

1) The Sheaf of Firstfruits shadowed forth Christ's resurrection, which took place on the first day of the week (cf. I Corinthians 15:20-23; Matthew 28:1; Mark 16:1-2; Luke 23:54-56; John 19:31; 20:1).
2) The birthday of the church took place at Pentecost, the first day of the new week. The Holy Spirit was outpoured on this day (Acts 2:1-4).

Hence, the two most important events in the foundation of the New Testament church took place, not on the Old Testament Sabbath, but on the *first day* of the week. The Son of God was resurrected and the Holy Spirit was outpoured on the first day, by-passing the Hebrew Sabbath. It was indicative that the prophecy of Hosea 2:11 was being fulfilled, when God said that He would cause "...to cease...her sabbaths..."

The New Testament also shows two other things that took place on this day, confirming the fact that the Old Testament Sabbath was abolished at the Cross.

1) The disciples met together to break bread on the first day of the week (Acts 20:7 with I Corinthians 11:23-32).

2) The offerings for the saints were set aside on the first day of the week (I Corinthians 16:1-2).

The believers found true Sabbath rest "in Christ" (Matthew 11:28-30; Hebrews 4). The Holy Spirit is the *seal* of the *New* Covenant. The *Sabbath* was the sign and seal of the *Old* Covenant. The believer is not under the *Old* Covenant. God never took any of the seals of previous covenants and placed them on the New Covenant. The New Covenant has its own distinctive seal in the baptism of the Holy Spirit. All other covenants and their seals pointed to the New Covenant and seal. To add the Sabbath day on to the New Covenant is to bring in mixture of law and grace, mixture of Old and New Covenants—a day in with the Holy Spirit.

We are not to judge one another with regard to meat or drink, holy days, new moons, or Sabbath days, as all were the shadows of things to come (Colossians 2:14-17). Everyone should be fully persuaded in their own minds. They should have reached convictions on these things. It is evident that God is not especially concerned about special or sacred days.

The Christian serves God every day of the week. He also realizes that the human body does need a day of rest each week, for "...The sabbath was made for man, and not man for the sabbath..." (Mark 2:27-28). The Sabbath, as part of the ceremonial law, was nailed to the cross. The fourth commandment was really a ceremonial law, not a moral law!

However, though the Sabbath belongs to the Old Covenant, and the believer is not obligated to a day, yet he will avail himself of some day when he will gather with the body of Christ for fellowship.

The early believers gathered together on the resurrection day, and the Pentecost day, the first day of the week. The Christian does not keep a day (perhaps Sunday) because he has to from a legal point of view, but from love, because he loves to. He does it unto the Lord.

Verse 6: *"He that regardeth the day, regardeth it unto the Lord; and he that regardeth not the day, to the Lord he doth not regard it. He that eateth, eateth to the Lord, for he giveth God thanks; and he that eateth not, to the Lord he eateth not, and giveth God thanks."*

The whole point, here, concerning days or meats, is the attitude to the Lord. Whether one keeps days or not, or whether he eats meats or not, thanking God for his food, as unto the Lord, is what God accepts.

"Whether therefore ye eat, or drink, or whatsoever ye do, do all to the glory of God" (I Corinthians 10:31).

Verse 7: *"For none of us liveth to himself, and no man dieth to himself."*

(Cf. I Corinthians 6:19-20; Galatians 2:20; I Thessalonians 5:10; I Peter 4:2.)

No one is totally independent of others. No one can live and die "in his own little world." Each one is affecting someone else all the time, in life or death.

Verse 8: *"For whether we live, we live unto the Lord; and whether we die, we die unto the Lord: whether we live therefore, or die, we are the Lord's."*

In life or in death, we belong to the Lord and are responsible and accountable to Him.

Verse 9: *"For to this end Christ both died, and rose, and revived, that he might be Lord both of the dead and living."*

(Cf. II Corinthians 5:15; Acts 10:36, 42; I Thessalonians 4:15-18; I Peter 4:5.)

As it is for us in verse 8, so it is for Christ in verse 9. Whether we live or die, we belong to the Lord. He lived and died and rose again to be *Lord* over the dead and the living. He will "...judge the quick and the dead" (I Peter 4:5).

Verse 10: *"But why dost thou judge thy brother? or why dost thou set at nought thy brother? for we shall all stand before the judgment seat of Christ."*

(Cf. Matthew 25:31; II Corinthians 5:10.)

A. **"Judge"**
   "To judge" is "to criticize" your brother (verses 3-4).

B. "Set at nought"
   "To set at nought" is "to despise" your brother (Romans 13:3; Luke 18:9; 23:11).

C. "For we shall all stand before the judgment seat of Christ"
   All are to stand before the judgment seat of Christ (of God), but not all will stand before the great white throne of judgment, which is for the ungodly (Revelation 20:11-15). This judgment is as to works, and rewards, not as to eternal salvation. This judgment determines a believer's place, reward, and position in the kingdom to come, as well as the measure of glory of the resurrection (I Corinthians 15:40-42).

Verse 11: *"For it is written, As I live, saith the Lord, every knee shall bow to me, and every tongue shall confess to God."*

(Cf. Isaiah 45:23.)

A. "Every knee shall bow to me"
   Knees shall bow (Philippians 2:10).

B. "Every tongue shall confess to God"
   Tongues shall confess (Philippians 2:11). So it was for Joseph, and so it is for Jesus—the beloved, rejected, exalted, and enthroned Son (Genesis 41:43).

Verse 12: *"So then every one of us shall give account of himself to God."*

(Cf. Matthew 12:36; 18:23; Galatians 6:5; I Peter 4:5; Luke 16:2; Acts 19:40; Romans 9:28; Hebrews 13:17.)

A. "We shall all stand before the judgment seat of Christ" (verse 10)

B. "Every one of us shall give account of himself to God"
   We shall give account of ourselves, not the other person, to God. This is a sobering thought. We will answer for our own actions, not the other person's actions.

Attitudes to Weaker Brethren (Romans 14:13-15:6)

Concerning Meats, Charity, and Faith (Romans 14:13-23)

Verse 13: *"Let us not therefore judge one another any more: but judge this rather, that no man put a stumblingblock or an occasion to fall in his brother's way."*

(Cf. I Corinthians 8:9.)

In light of the fact that we are all to be judged by our own accounts at the judgment seat of Christ, we should not judge one another any more with regard to nonessentials—days and meats. We must not put a stumbling block (occasion of falling [Romans 9:32; 14:20]), or a scandal (obstacle, hindrance [Romans 9:33]) in our brother's way. Criticism and harsh and unkind judgment becomes a stumbling block and a scandal to weaker brothers. By such, we judge our brother, causing him to stumble, and thus, come under judgment ourselves. "Judge not, that ye be not judged...." (cf. Matthew 7:1-5).

Verse 14: *"I know, and am persuaded by the Lord Jesus, that there is nothing unclean of itself: but to him that esteemeth any thing to be unclean, to him it is unclean."*

(Cf. I Corinthians 10:25.)

Paul give his persuasion (this from a believing Jew) by the Lord Jesus that there is nothing ceremonially unclean (common, unclean, defiled, profane) (Acts 2:44; 10:14) in or of itself, in the Levitical sense.

It is sin alone that makes a thing clean or unclean, and God's Word distinguishes such. Meats offered to idols were not unclean. The meat was nothing; it was the spirit behind the idol that made the meat "clean or unclean." Those who know the truth concerning meats (I Timothy 4:1-5) need not fear uncleanness—only unclean and defiling to those who believe it to be such. Doctrines of devils command us to take away or totally abstain from meats. It is not what enters a man that defiles, but what comes out (Mark 7:14-23).

Verses 1-14: *Summary of Bibliography on "Meats"*

- God made the animal kingdom and called it "good" (Genesis 1:24-28).

- Adam's food under the Edenic and Adamic Covenants was fruit and herbs. There is no mention of meats—clean or unclean (Genesis 1:29-31). After sin, there is still no mention of meats (Genesis 2-3).

- God told Noah to take in all manner of food for his family and for the animals (Genesis 6:19-22).

- The first mention of meats as clean and unclean was to Noah when he was commissioned to build the ark (Genesis 7:1-9).

- Noah sacrificed clean animals to God (Genesis 8:15-22).

- God allowed meat to be eaten here; not distinguishing "clean or unclean" as far as eating was concerned. However, the blood had to be poured out (Genesis 9:1-4).

- The Mosaic Covenant to Israel made a distinction between clean and unclean meat by certain signs (Leviticus 11). From Adam to Noah, no meats were eaten. From Noah to Moses, meats clean and unclean were eaten. From Moses to Jesus, only meats defined as "clean" were to be eaten.

   What made the animal "unclean" after God said it was "good" in Genesis? The answer is sin (God's word)! No animal has sinned. There is no defilement in the animals (Leviticus 20:25-26). Out of clean or unclean animals, the firstborn were given to God (Exodus 13:1-2). Leviticus chapters 1-7 show that the "clean" animals signified Christ's offering. Thus, God did not take any carnivorous or wild animal for his altar to typify His Son, but the domestic and herbivorous animals were the only suitable types of His Son's nature, character, and submission to the Father's will (Leviticus 10:12-15; 6:16-18; 7:11-15). Certain portions of the animals were given to God, to the priests, or to the one who was doing the offering. Only clean meats were offered to the Lord (Leviticus 27:11). "But ask now the beasts, and they shall teach thee..." (Job 12:7-9). (Refer to the epistle of Barnabas, chapter 9 also.) Not the meats themselves, but the spiritual truth symbolized therein (Hebrews 9:9-10) were imposed on Israel until the time of reformation came with Jesus Christ.

- The New Testament revelation was that nothing was unclean of itself (Romans 14:14). The believer must eat all in faith (Romans 14:23) and must not judge weaker brothers who do not eat meat. "...Meats for the belly, and the belly for the meats: but God shall destroy both it and them..." (I Corinthians 6:12-13). Neither eating meat nor not eating meat makes us worse or better before God (I Corinthians 8). Whatever we do, we must do all to the glory of God. The custom in Paul's time was to offer meats, or parts, to idols and to also give some to the idol temple priests (I Corinthians 10:15-33). Christian Jews especially felt that they could not partake of such meat sold in the market after this. They put the same fears into Gentile believers (Exodus 34:15; Leviticus 17:7). However, God had cleansed things through the Cross, and the believer was to be occupied with grace, not with meats (Hebrews 13:9). We are not to judge one another on meats (Colossians 2:15-17). Jesus said that it is not meat that defiles (Mark 7:14-23). The kingdom of God is not meat or drink (Romans 14:17). It is the doctrine of devils to abstain from all meats (I Timothy 4:1-6). God created them to be received with thanks.

- God used animals to symbolize Christ, believers, as well as Israel and Gentile nations. Peter's vision of "clean and unclean animals" confirmed this (Acts 10:9-29; Acts 11). (Refer to Daniel 7-8; Revelation 13; I Peter 5:8; Daniel 4:28-33, 16; 5:21; Psalms 49:12-13, 20; 73:22; Ecclesiastes 3:18-21; II Peter 2:12; Jude 10; Titus 1:12; Revelation 1:17; 14:99-11; 17.) All these Scriptures teach that beasts are symbolic of fallen human nature. All beastly things will come to their end at the coming of Christ.

- The believer's true meat is to do the will of God (John 4:32-34; 6:27, 55; Hebrews 5:12, 14; I Corinthians 3:2; 10:3). It is spiritual meat and drink (I Corinthians 10:18; Hebrews 13:9-13; I Corinthians 9:13-14; 11:20-34; Matthew 24:24; Psalms 104:27; 147:15), meat in due season. Thus, animals were used as symbols, food, clothing, sacrifices for sin, pleasure, and work. When they have finished all of these purposes, then there will come an end of all flesh.

Verse 15: *"But if thy brother be grieved with thy meat, now walkest thou no charitably. Destroy not him with thy meat, for whom Christ died."*

If a weak brother is caused to stumble or is offended or grieved (hurt or feels pain) by your meat-eating, then you are not walking in love (cf. 13:8, 10). The stronger brother must not destroy the weaker brother because Christ died for him also (refer also to verse 20).

Verse 16: *"Let not then your good be evil spoken of..."*

"Evil spoken of" also means "blasphemed." What is good for the stronger must not become a reproach to others. It may be right for you, but do not let it be a point of stumbling for a weaker believer (I Corinthians 8:8-9).

Verse 17: *"For the kingdom of God is not meat and drink; but righteousness, and peace, and joy in the Holy Ghost."*

(Cf. I Corinthians 8:8.)

A. **"For the kingdom of God is not meat and drink"**
   The kingdom of God is not a matter of food or drink, or eating or drinking. The rule and reign of God is over the hearts of men. It is based on righteous principles, not what a person eats or drinks, foods, which are all to perish with the using.

B. **"Righteousness, and peace, and joy in the Holy Ghost"**
   Melchisedec is King of Righteousness and King of Peace (Hebrews 7:1-4; Psalm 85:10; John 16:33; Isaiah 32:17). His kingdom, rule, and reign will be the same as Himself—a kingdom of righteousness, peace and joy in the Spirit (refer to Romans 1:17; 5:1-2; righteousness, peace, and rejoicing).
   Each is interdependent and dependent on the other. There can be no joy apart from peace, no peace apart from righteousness, and no righteousness apart from faith in God through Christ and His atoning work.
   Thus, God, Christ, faith, righteousness, peace, and joy are all interconnected (Romans 12:17; 14:17, 19; 15:13, 33; Galatians 5:22). The characteristics of those born into the kingdom of God will be such.

Verse 18: *"For he that in these things serveth Christ is acceptable to God, and approved of men."*

If a believer serves Christ in this charitable way, he is acceptable, or well pleasing (Romans 12:1) to God, and wins the approval of his fellowmen (II Corinthians 8:21).

Verse 19: *"Let us therefore follow after the things which make for peace, and things wherewith one may edify another."*

(Cf. 12:18; Hebrews 12:14.)

Two good test questions on all that we do would pertain to peace (concord) and edification:
1) Does it make for peace, concord, unity, harmony?
2) Does it edify and build up or tear down and destroy (I Corinthians 8:1; 14:12; I Thessalonians 5:15; Acts 20:32)? Edification is one of the essential tests on all that we do or say (I Corinthians 14).

Verse 20: *"For meat destroy not the work of God. All things indeed are pure; but it is evil for that man who eateth with offence."*

(Refer to verses 15 and 20.)

A. **"For meat destroy not the work of God"**
  - Do not destroy a brother by meat disputations (verse 15).
  - Do not destroy the work of God by meat issues (verse 20).

B. **"All things indeed are pure"**
  All things are pure to those who inwardly know the truth. There is no food that is ceremonially unclean. It becomes impure or evil to the one—the weaker brother—who eats with a guilty conscience, or to the one who eats it so as to deliberately put a stumbling block in the way of other brothers, strangers, or believers (Matthew 15:10-20; I Corinthians 8:9; Titus 1:15).

Verse 21: *"It is good neither to eat flesh, nor to drink wine, nor anything whereby thy brother stumbleth, or is offended, or is made weak."*

(Cf. I Corinthians 8:1-13.) This verse puts in summary what the attitude of the stronger and more mature believer should be. We should be willing not to eat meat, drink wine, or do anything that would cause our brothers to stumble or to be weakened. That is, we should be willing to become vegetarians or teetotalers for the brothers and for the work of God. A study of the whole tenor of Scripture, with regard to wine, shows that the negative far outweighs any positive. Priests and elders were not to be wine drinkers. (Refer to a concordance for the weight of Scripture concerning this matter. Also refer to the following Scriptures: Titus 1:7; Leviticus 10:9; Deuteronomy 29:5-6; Proverbs 20:1; 23:29-32; 31:3-7; Isaiah 28:7; Luke 1:15; Numbers 6:2-3; I Timothy 3:3a.)

Verse 22: *"Hast though faith? have it to thyself before God. Happy is he that condemeth not himself in that thing which he alloweth."*

(I John 3:21)

If a person has faith that there is nothing unclean before God, then he can keep these convictions to himself and the Lord, but he may not criticize or cause a brother to stumble over these things. A person is happy if he does not feel condemned over food or day issues. If he does not have qualms, bad conscience, or misgiving about these issues, he can be happy, but he should consider his brother.

Verse 23: *"And he that doubteth is damned if he eat, because he eateth not of faith: for whatsoever is not of faith is sin."*

(Cf. Titus 1:15.) If a person has doubts ("discerns and puts a difference") about the food and day issues, he condemns himself if he eats or violates the day. If a person's conscience, because he has doubts, is not clear before God, then he becomes self-condemned. All eating must be done in faith. Anything that is not of faith is sin. "...For whatever does not originate and proceed from faith is sin—that is, whatever is done without a conviction of its approval by God is sinful" (Amplified New Testament).

(Refer also to I John 5:14; 3:4; James 5:17; Proverbs 24:9; and other Scriptures which define sin.) The principle laid down concerning meats and days is applicable to all other non-essential areas of the faith or anything that does not attack the fundamental doctrines of salvation.

Note:
- We must recognize that there are weaker and stronger brothers, according to cultural and religious background.
- We must accept and receive one another, weaker or stronger, as God has received us.
- We must not make issues and disputes with weaker brothers over foods or days.
- We must keep certain convictions to ourselves.
- We must remember that we are all accountable to God for all that we do.
- We must consider our brothers in all that we do, and we must not use our liberties as a stumbling block to them in any way.
- We must test all that we do as to peace, edification, and love.

Verses 15-23: Summary

To summarize:
- In essentials, unity
- In non-essentials, liberty
- In all things, charity

Concerning Pleasing Others (Romans 15:1-6)

Verse 1: "We then that are strong ought to bear the infirmities of the weak, and not to please ourselves."

(Cf. Galatians 6:1; Romans 14:1.) The strong believer should bear with the weaknesses of the weak and immature believer; he should not insist on doing what he pleases.

Verse 2: *"Let every one of us please his neighbour for his good to edification."*

Let everyone of us do this (I Corinthians 10:33; Romans 14:19). The strong believer will seek to please his neighbor, to do him good, and to build him up in the Lord. "How can I help" and "please" will be the motivating questions to edifying others.

Verses 3-4: *"For even Christ pleased not himself; but, as it is written, The reproaches of them that reproached thee fell on me. For whatsoever things were written aforetime were written for our learning, that we through patience and comfort of the scriptures might have hope."*

(Matthew 26:39; Psalm 69:9; John 3:16; I John 4:2; John 8:29) (Cf. I Corinthians 10:6, 11.)

A. **"Christ pleased not himself"**

Note the correlation between Christ and the manner in which the strong believer should live:

- Christ pleased not Himself; the strong believer should not please himself.

- Christ bore the infirmities of the weak; the strong believer should bear the infirmities of the weak.

- Christ edified others; the strong believer should build others up.

- Christ bore the reproaches of God on Himself; the strong believer should be willing to bear the reproach for others and for Christ.

B. **"Whatsoever things were written aforetime were written for our learning"**

The Old Testament Scriptures were written also for our admonition, to give us patient endurance, comfort, and hope.

These verses are very strong supportive Scriptures for the use of the Old Testament Scriptures for instruction, admonition, and example to the New Testament church. It is worthy to note that there are many quotations, references, and allusions from the Old Testament found in this epistle of Paul, thus demonstrating, by his own use of such, the truth of this verse. (Refer to a concordance to see how many Old Testament references are used in this epistle.)

Verse 5: *"Now the God of patience and consolation grant you to be likeminded one toward another according to Christ Jesus..."*

A. **"The God of patience and consolation"**

God is the source of all fortitude and encouragement. Note:

- The God of patience and consolation (comfort) (verses 4-5)

- The God of hope (joy and peace) (verse 13)
- The God of peace (verse 33)

B. **"Like-minded"**
"Like-minded" means "one minded" (I Corinthians 1:10; Philippians 2:1-5).

C. **"According to Christ Jesus"**
This means "in accordance with the example of Jesus Christ."

Verse 6: *"...That ye may with one mind and one mouth glorify God, even the Father of our Lord Jesus Christ."*

"With one mind and one mouth" (I Corinthians 1:9-10)
"One mind" – thinking the same thing
"One mouth" – speaking the same thing

Unity of speech is dependent on unity of thought; having the mind of Christ (Acts 2:1; 4:24). Being of one accord is possible only through total submission to the Spirit.

Thus, as members of the body of Christ, we are to seek to please and to edify each other, speaking the same thing, having the same mind, and glorifying God together.

The Gentile Believers (Romans 15:7-13)

The Mercy of God on the Gentiles (Romans 15:7-12)

Verse 7: *"Wherefore receive ye one another, as Christ also received us to the glory of God."*

(Cf. Romans 14:1-3; 5:2.)

God has received us. Therefore, we should receive one another in like manner (cf. Matthew 18:5; 10:40-42). To receive another who is of Christ is to receive Christ, and to receive Christ is to receive the Father.

Verse 8: *"Now I say that Jesus Christ was a minister of the circumcision for the truth of God, to confirm the promises made unto the fathers..."*

Paul resumes the subject matter of the Gentiles, here.

- In chapter 2, he deals especially with the Jew.
- In chapter 15, he deals more specifically with the Gentile.
- In chapters 9-11, he deals with both Jew and Gentile grafted into the same olive tree.

A. **"Jesus Christ was a minister of the circumcision"** (Matthew 15:24; John 1:11; Acts 3:25; Galatians 2:7-9; refer also to Romans 2:28-29; 4:9-12)
   Jesus went to the Jew first, to the lost sheep of the house of Israel.

B. **"For the truth of God"**
   The purpose of Jesus ministry to the Jews was to vindicate God's truthfulness.

C. **"Confirm the promises"**
   Jesus came to the Jews to make valid the promises of God given in the covenants (Romans 9:4-5; II Corinthians 1:20; Mark 16:15-20; Hebrews 2:1-4 with Daniel 9:27). Christ confirmed the Abrahamic Covenant with the Jews for three and a half years in His ministry.

D. **"The fathers"** (cf. 9:5)
   "The Fathers" are Abraham, Isaac, and Jacob, in whom the covenant promises of redemption were founded.

Verse 9: *"...And that the Gentiles might glorify God for his mercy; as it is written, For this cause I will confess to thee among the Gentiles, and sing unto thy name."*

A. **"The Gentiles might glorify God for his mercy"** (John 10:16; Romans 9:15-18; 11:30-32)
   This quotation is from David in Psalm 18:49. "The heathen" of the Psalms are "the Gentiles" in Romans (II Samuel 22:50). This is very similar to the messianic quotation of Psalm 22:22 in Hebrews 2:12.

B. **"Confess"**

This is referring to a confession of faith in the Lord Jesus, "to give praise" (Romans 14:11). Note that the Greek word, *psallo*, means "song with instrument."

C. **"Sing unto thy name"** (cf. James 5:13)

Here is evidence of the Gentiles glorifying God for His mercy in songs of the Lord.

Verse 10: *"And again he saith, Rejoice, ye Gentiles, with his people."*

(Partial quotation from Deuteronomy 32:43)

"The nations" of Moses' prophecy become "the Gentiles" in Romans. Thus, Gentiles and Jews rejoice (literally "merry-making") together in Christ (Luke 12:19; 15:23-24).

Verse 11: *"And again, Praise the Lord, all ye Gentiles; and laud him, all ye people."*

(Quotation from Psalm 117:1)

Again "the nations" are "the Gentiles," and with the people of God (Israel), they praise and exalt God through the Lord Jesus Christ.

Verse 12: *"And again, Esaias saith, There shall be a root of Jesse, and he that shall rise to reign over the Gentiles; and in him shall the Gentiles trust."*

(Quotation from Isaiah 11:10 and 42:1 basically)

The Root is the Lord Jesus Christ (Revelation 5:5-10). He reigns over the kingdom of God, into which the Jew and Gentile are born again (John 3:1-5), and the Gentiles trust in Him (Matthew 12:18-21). He is the Nazarene, the Root, the Offspring, the Shoot out of Jesse (Isaiah 11:1-5; Revelation 22:16).

Blessing (Romans 15:13)

Verse 13: *"Now the God of hope fill you with all joy and peace in believing, that ye may abound in hope, through the power of the Holy Ghost."*

(Refer to notes on verses 5 and 33.)

Notice how these words work together: "God," "hope," "joy," "peace," "believing," "hope," "Holy Ghost" (Romans 14:17; 5:1-5; 12:12).

The Gentile Churches (Romans 15:14-33)

The Offering Up of the Gentiles (Romans 15:14-29)

Verse 14: *"And I myself also am persuade of you, my brethren, that ye also are full of goodness, filled with all knowledge, able also to admonish one another."*

(Cf. II Peter 1:12; I John 2:20, 21, 27; I Corinthians 8:1.)

A Threefold Commendation of the Church at Rome
1) "Full of goodness" (Romans 3:12)
2) "Filled with knowledge" (Ephesians 1:17-18; I Corinthians 8:1)
3) "Able to admonish one another" (Acts 20:31)

Verse 15: *"Nevertheless, brethren, I have written the more boldly unto you in some sort, as putting you in mind, because of the grace that is given to me of God..."*

Paul's boldness in this letter was because of the grace of apostleship given him as the Apostle to the Gentiles, even though he himself was a Jew, an Israelite, of the tribe of Benjamin. His authority was a spiritual authority, not a dictatorial authority (Romans 1:5; 12:3; Galatians 1:1-3, 15).

Verse 16: *". . . That I should be the minister of Jesus Christ to the Gentiles, ministering the gospel of God, that the offering up of the Gentiles might be acceptable, being sanctified by the Holy Ghost."*

(Cf. Romans 11:13; Galatians 2:7-9; I Timothy 2:7; II Timothy 1:11.)

A. **"I should be the minister of Jesus Christ to the Gentiles"**
   - Jesus Christ was a minister of the circumcision (verse 8).
   - Paul was a minister of the uncircumcision (verse 16). The meaning in the Greek indicates his ministry as a priest.

B. **"Offering up of the Gentiles"**
    Offering them up is sacrificing them to God as an offering by Jesus Christ, the great High Priest, and sanctifying them by the Holy Ghost (cf. Isaiah 66:20; Philippians 2:17; Malachi 1:11; Romans 12:1-2).
    As in the Old Testament, when sacrifices were offered by the priest and made acceptable by the blood and the oil, so Paul was acting as a New Testament priest, presenting, through Christ, the Gentiles as an offering to God, sanctified by the blood of Jesus and the oil of the Holy Spirit.
    This is typified in Leviticus 2 and 23. The offering (i.e., the meal offering or wave loaves offering) was placed on the altar.

Verse 17: *"I have therefore whereof I may glory through Jesus Christ in those things which pertain to God."*

The result of Paul's ministry was the seal of his apostleship before the Lord. He could boast in Christ as to these things (Hebrews 2:17; 5:1). Things pertaining to God are the functions of worship as a ministering priest.

Verse 18: *"For I will not dare to speak of any of those things which Christ hath not wrought by me, to make the Gentiles obedient, by word and deed. . ."*

(Acts 21:19; Galatians 2:8; Romans 1:5; 16:26)

Paul's boasting was not in what others had done, but in what Christ had done through him. The evidence was the Gentile churches he founded and their obedience in word and deed, theory and practice.

Verse 19: *"...Through mighty signs and wonders, by the power of the Spirit of God; so that from Jerusalem, and round about unto Illyricum, I have fully preached the gospel of Christ."*

Evidence of Apostolic Ministry

"Signs and wonders" – the results of the ministry (Matthew 11:20)

"The power of the Holy Spirit" – the resource and source of the ministry

"From Jerusalem to Illyricum" – the scope of the ministry

"Fully preached the gospel of Christ" – the Word of the ministry (Acts 19:11; II Corinthians 2:12)

Verse 20: *"Yea, so have I strived to preach the gospel, not where Christ was named, lest I should build upon another man's foundation..."*

A. **"Not where Christ was named"**

This was a new territory where Christ had not been named. It was a new area of ministry.

B. **"Lest I should build upon another man's foundation"**

Not building on another man's foundation proved the success of the ministry (II Corinthians 10:13-16).

Verse 21: *"...But as it is written, To whom he was not spoken of, they shall see: and they that have not heard shall understand."*

(Cf. Isaiah 52:15, 13-14.)

This quote from Isaiah is a messianic prophecy which speaks of the Messiah sprinkling many nations (not just the Israel nation) and the Gentiles seeing, hearing, and believing the Good News.

(Contrast the blindness and deafness of the Jews as in Romans 11:7-8, 25. Note the prophetic passages, from David, the Psalms, Moses in Deuteronomy, and the messianic prophet Isaiah concerning the Gentiles, which are quoted by Paul in this chapter in verses 9-12, 21. Paul quotes more from Isaiah's prophecies of the coming in of the Gentiles than does any other apostle.)

Verse 22: *"For which cause also I have been much hindered from coming to you."*

(Cf. Romans 1:13; I Thessalonians 2:17.)

Satan hinders at times, yet God permits such over and above all in His sovereign will and time. God's will for Paul hindered him from going to Rome as yet (refer also 15:32).

Verse 23: *"But now having no more place in these parts, and having a great desire these many years to come unto you..."*

(Cf. Acts 19:21; Romans 1:11.)

God's will and time must go together. Paul was feeling, by now, that his ministry to the Gentiles in those areas (i.e., Corinth; refer to the postscript) was coming to a close. He had for years felt he would come to Rome (refer to notes on Romans 1:8-13 again).

Verse 24: *"...Whensoever I take my journey into Spain, I will come to you: for I trust to see you in my journey, and to be brought on my way thitherward by you, if first I be somewhat filled with your company."*

(Cf. Acts 15:3.)

Perhaps Paul never did get to Spain (verse 28). God's will and time was for Paul to get to Rome where he would, in time, die for the faith of Christ. In Rome, however, God would give Paul the "last fruits" in the gospel, right in the household of Caesar.

Verses 25-26: *"But now I go unto Jerusalem to minister unto the saints. For it hath pleased them of Macedonia and Achaia to make a certain contribution for the poor saints which are at Jerusalem."*

(Cf. Acts 19:21; 24:17.)

"Contribution"
Greek: *Koinonian* means "contribution" (cf. I Corinthians 16:1; II Corinthians 8:1; Acts 2:42).

Verse 27: *"It hath pleased them verily; and their debtors they are. For if the Gentiles have been made partakers of their spiritual things, their duty is also to minister unto them in carnal things."*

(Cf. Romans 11:7; I Corinthians 9:11; Galatians 6:6.)

Jews and Gentiles:
- Spiritual Things – Partakers – Carnal Things
- The Gospel – Minister – Debtors

In Romans 13:6, almsgiving is a priestly service, as an act of worship.

Verse 28: *"When therefore I have performed this, and have sealed to them this fruit, I will come by you into Spain."*

(Philippians 4:17, 15-19)

"Fruit"
The ministry of relief offerings to the saints is "fruit" unto God also.

Verse 29: *"And I am sure that, when I come unto you, I shall come in the fulness of the blessing of the gospel of Christ."*

(Cf. Romans 1:11.)

Every minister of the gospel of Christ should come in order to bless the saints in the fullness of blessing. If he does not come, then he cannot bless the saints.

Paul's Request for Prayer (Romans 15:30-33)

Verse 30: *"Now I beseech you, brethren, for the Lord Jesus Christ's sake, and for the love of the Spirit, that ye strive together with me in your prayers to God for me..."*

Paul asks for prayer.
Paul, with all his grace, ability, and knowledge, still asks the saints at Rome to strive with him in prayer.
"For the Lord Jesus Christ's sake"
"For the love of the Spirit" (Philippians 2:1; II Corinthians 1:11; Colossians 4:12)

Verses 31-32: *"...That I may be delivered from them that do not believe in Judea; and that my service which I have for Jerusalem may be accepted of the saints; that I may come unto you with joy by the will of God, and may with you be refreshed."*

A. **The Four Requests of Paul**
    "That I may be delivered from them that do not believe in Judea" – That he might be delivered from the unbelieving (disobedient) Jews (I Thessalonians 2:14-18; Romans 10:21).
    "That my service which I have for Jerusalem may be accepted of the saints" – That the offering of the Gentles to the Jerusalem saints would be accepted by them (II Corinthians 8:4), or that the Jews, independent or proud, would not hate to receive anything from the Gentiles.
    "That I may come unto you with the joy by the will of God" – That he might come to them with joy in the will of God (note Romans 1:8-13 with "I will" of Romans 15:24, 28).
    "May with you be refreshed" – That he and they together might be spiritually refreshed (that they might rest) (Romans 1:10; Acts 18:21; I Corinthians 4:19; Matthew 11:28; James 4:15; I Corinthians 16:18; II Corinthians 7:13; II Timothy 1:16; Philemon 7, 20).

Verse 33: *"Now the God of peace be with you all. Amen."*

(Refer to verses 5, 13; 16:20; I Corinthians 14:33; II Corinthians 13:11; Philippians 4:9; I Thessalonians 5:23; II Thessalonians 3:16; Hebrews 13:20.)

"God of peace"
Patience, hope, peace—all are needed by the saints in Rome, then and today!

Saluting the Saints (Romans 16:1-6)

The following are a number of salutations and greetings to various saints, brothers, and sisters in Christ. Some of them are mentioned only here; others are briefly mentioned elsewhere in the New Testament as workers in the gospel. Most of them have some brief commendable quality mentioned in the salutation or greeting. It is always good to mention some commendable quality of the brothers and sisters.

We all will be greeted by the Lord Jesus in "that day" when the saints meet together to be forever with the Lord, and He will mention our names and qualities which are to be commended (I Thessalonians 4:15-18).

Phebe: The Deaconess (Romans 16:1-2)

Verses 1-2: *"I commend unto you Phebe our sister, which is a servant of the church which is at Cenchrea: that ye receive her in the Lord, as becometh saints, and that ye assist her in whatsoever business she hath need of you: for she hath been a succourer of many, and of myself also."*

Paul's Commendation (Cf. Acts 18:18; Philippians 2:29; III John 5, 6.)
This is no imposition of Phebe (meaning "bright"), a sister in the Lord.
"A servant" – Greek: Diaknonos means a deaconess of the church, not one who rules, but one who serves.
"A succourer" – "Succourer" means "patroness, official position." She is a patroness of many and also of Paul. She is a servant of the ministry.
"That ye receive her in the Lord, as becometh saints" – Do not despise her because she is a woman.
"That ye assist her in whatsoever business she hath need of you"

Vincent says, concerning widows or sometimes virgins, that they had the following duties:

- To take care of the sick and the poor
- To minister to the martyrs and confessors in prison
- To instruct in the catechism
- To assist in the baptism of women
- To exercise general supervision over the female church members (I Timothy 5:3-16).

In the Gospels, during the ministry of the Lord Jesus Christ and the apostles, there were a number of "deaconesses" who ministered unto Him, serving Him and the apostles with him.

Many Other Saints Saluted (Romans 16:3-16)

Verses 3-4: *"Greet Priscilla and Aquila my helpers in Christ Jesus: who have for my life laid down their own necks: unto whom not only I give thanks, but also all the churches of the Gentiles."*

(Cf. Acts 18:2, 18-26; I Corinthians 6:19; II Timothy 4:19.)

The Jews had been driven from Rome under Claudius' decree; thus, Aquilla and Priscilla must have returned to Rome at this period of time.

Only eternity will tell the story of how Priscilla and Aquila saved Paul's life in all the threats against him by Jews and Gentiles in the cities of Asia Minor. Paul gave them, as well as the Gentile churches, thanks. Notice here that the woman's name seems to always precede the man's name, as they shared in ministry together. They, with Paul, were of the tent-making trade.

Verse 5a: *"Likewise greet the church that is in their house."*

Apparently these two were back in Rome and had a church in their house, as did many houses in early church history. There were not special "church buildings" in those days, but many of the saints, who had larger houses, opened their homes for church meetings. Thus, the "church in the house" was quite common in those days.

House churches:
- The House of Aquilla and Priscilla (I Corinthians 16:19).
- The House of Nymphas (Colossians 4:15).
- The House of Philemon (Philemon 2).
- Possibly these saints also had *ekklesia*, meaning "called out ones," in their houses (Romans 16:14-15).

Verses 5b-15: *"Salute my wellbeloved Epaenetus, who is the firstfruits of Achaia unto Christ. Greet Mary, who bestowed much labour on us. Salute Andronicus and Junia, my kinsmen, and my fellowprisoners, who are of note among the apostles, who also were in Christ before me. Greet Amplias my beloved in the Lord. Salute Urbane, our helper in Christ, and Stachys my beloved. Salute Apelles approved in Christ. Salute them which are of Aristobulus' household. Salute Herodion my kinsman. Greet them that be of the household of Narcissus, which are in the Lord. Salute Tryphena and Tryphosa, who labour in the Lord. Salute the beloved Persis, which laboured much in the Lord. Salute Rufus chosen in the Lord, and his mother and mine. Salute Asyncritus, Phlegon, Hermas, Patrobas, Hermes, and the brethren which are with them. Salute Philologus, and Julia, Nereus, and his sister, and Olympas, and all the saints which are with them."*

Here, Paul lists the saints whom he wants to name and salute.

A. **"Salute my well-beloved Epaentus, who is the firstfruits of Achaia unto Christ"** (cf. I Corinthians 16:19, 15; Colossians 4:15; Philemon 2)

(Refer to the Old Testament "firstfruits," special offerings to God, representative of the harvest to come.) (Cf. James 1:18; Revelation 14:4; Leviticus 23:17; Exodus 23:16-19; Numbers 15:17-21.)

"Epaenetus" – means "praised."

B. **"Greet Mary, who bestowed much labour on us"**

Mary is another sister in Christ who is serving the ministry (cf. Luke 8:2-3; Matthew 27:55; I Timothy 5:10).

"Mary" – a Jewish name, as Miriam, which means "obstinacy, rebelliousness."

C. **"Salute Andronicus and Junia, my kinsman, and my fellowprisoners, who are of note amongst the apostles, who also were in Christ before me"** (Galatians 1:22).

- Kinsman
- Fellowprisoners
- Of Note Among the Apostles
- In Christ

"Andronicus" – means "man conqueror."

"Junia" – means "youth" (could be masculine or feminine).

D. "Greet Amplias my beloved in the Lord"
"Amplias" – means "large."

E. "Salute Urbane, our helper in Christ, and Stachys my beloved"
Urbane was a helper. Stachys was beloved (Galatians 1:22).
"Urbane" – means "of a city, polite."
"Stachys" – means "ear of corn."

F. "Salute Apelles approved in Christ."
"Apelles" – means "called" or "approved."

G. "Salute them which are of Aristobulus' household" (marginal reference says, "friends").
"Aristobulus" – means "best counselor."

H. "Salute Herodion my kinsman."
"Herodion" – means "heroic."

I. "Greet them that be of the household of Narcissus, which are in the Lord" (marginal reference says, "friends").
"Narcissus" – means "narcotic."

J. "Salute Tryphena and Tryphosa, who labour in the Lord."
Both were possibly sisters in the Lord.
"Tryphena" – means "to live luxuriously; shining."
"Tryphosa" – means "shining."

K. "Salute the beloved Persis, which labored much in the Lord."
Persis was beloved and labored in the Lord.
"Persis" – means "Persian."

L. "Salute Rufus chosen in the Lord, and his mother and mine."
Rufus might have been the son of Simon of Cyrene (Mark 15: 21).
"Rufus" – means "red."
"His mother and mine" – refers to perhaps a spiritual mother in Israel (cf. II John 1; Judges 5:7).

M. "Salute Asyncritus, Phlegon, Hermas, Patrobas, Hermes, and the brethren which are with them."
"Asyncritus" – means "incomparable."
"Phlegon" – means "burning."
"Hermas" – means "Mercury."
"Patrobas" – means "paternal."
"Hermes" – means "Mercury."

N. "Salute Philologus, and Julia, Nereus, and his sister, and Olympus, and the saints which are with them."
"Philologus" – means "learned."
"Julia" – means "soft-haired" (feminine of Julius).
"Nereus" – means "lamp; brightness."
"And his sister" – refers to Nereus' sister.
"Olympas" – means "heavenly."

Verse 16: *"Salute one another with an holy kiss. The churches of Christ salute you."*

(Cf. I Corinthians 16:20; II Corinthians 13:12; I Thessalonians 5:26; I Peter 5:14.)

"Holy kiss"
This is not a "Judas kiss" (Luke 22:47-48; II Samuel 20:9; Psalms 41:9; 55:13; Matthew 26:47-49). The kiss in western culture has become associated with lust or sex, but not so in the early church. Notice the words of endearment and commendable qualities mentioned in these verses (1-16):
Endearments
1) Commend
2) Greet (verses 3, 5-6, 8, 11)
1) Salute (verses 5, 7, 9, 10-16, 21-23)
2) Kinsman
3) Fellowprisoners
4) Well beloved (verse 5)
5) Beloved (verses 8-9, 12)
6) Saints (verses 2, 15)
7) Firstfruits (verse 5)

Qualities
1) Servant (*diakonos*) (verse 1)
2) Succourer (verse 2)
3) Helpers (verses 3, 9)
4) Laborers (verses 6, 12)
5) Approved (verse 10)
6) Chosen (verse 13)

All saints should have these qualities and endearments.

Marks of Divisionaries (Romans 16:17-20)

Verse 17: *"Now I beseech you, brethren, mark them which cause divisions and offences contrary to the doctrine which ye have learned; and avoid them."*

A. **"Mark them which cause divisions and offences"**
   After saluting and greeting the saints and commending them and their qualities before the Lord, Paul now warns of those who would be divisionaries amongst them, dividing the body of Christ.

   Two-fold admonition and exhortation concerning these divisionaries:
   - Mark them.
   - Avoid them. Turn aside from them (I Corinthians 5:9; II Timothy 3:5).

   Two-fold evidences of divisionaries:
   - They cause divisions.
   - The cause offenses contrary to the doctrine which they had learned.

   Divisions have two main sources:
   - Divisions of Satan and of the Carnality of Men (I Corinthians 1:10; 3:3; 11:18; Acts 14:4; 23: 7)
   - Division of God over the Issues of the Truth of God in Christ (Exodus 8:23; Luke 12:51; John 7:43; 9:16; 10:19; Luke 11:18; Matthew 12:25)

   Note the author of division:
   - Satan caused division in heaven amongst the angelic hosts over self-will.

- Satan caused division in earth between God and man over sin in the Garden of Eden (Genesis 3).
- Satan caused division in the godly line also. The nation of Israel was divided in the purposes of God.

Jesus Christ, God's truth, brought division everywhere He went. In His day, those who refused to hear and receive the truth became the divisionary ones, not Jesus!

B. "Doctrine"
"Doctrine" means "teaching, to teach the substance." It is absolutely important to maintain true and pure doctrine, the doctrine of God, the doctrine of Christ, and the doctrine of the apostles (Acts 2:42; I Timothy 6:1-3; 3:10; 4:1-4; Titus 2:10; Hebrews 6:1-2; 5:11-12). We must watch out for doctrines of devils and doctrines of men that make the Word of God of no effect (Mark 7:1-10).

Verse 18: *"For they that are such serve not our Lord Jesus Christ, but their own belly; and by good words and fair speeches deceive the hearts of the simple."*

A. Two-fold Characteristics of Divisionaries
- They serve not our Lord Jesus Christ, but their own bellies (Philippians 3:17-19; I Timothy 6:5).
- They deceive the simple (the innocent), beguiling them by good words and fair speeches (Colossians 2:4; II Timothy 3:6).

Verse 19: *"For your obedience is come abroad unto all men. I am glad therefore on your behalf: but yet I would have you wise unto that which is good, and simple concerning evil."*

A. "Your obedience is come abroad unto all men"
The faith and obedience of the church at Rome was spoken of throughout the whole known world (cf. Romans 1:8; Matthew 10:16). Paul rejoiced for this testimony. His exhortation was that they would be wise to the good and simple, or harmless, to the evil.

B. "Wise unto that which is good"
This means having knowledge, understanding, and wisdom on everything that is good and pleases God.

C. **"Simple concerning evil"**

"Simple" refers to "harmless." It does not hurt to be ignorant concerning evil. Knowledge of the evils of foreign religions, occult practices, and immoral rites does not necessarily help a believer. Often that kind of information, and so-called education, is dangerous and cultivates the evil responses in man. Man has partaken of the Tree of Knowledge of *Good* and *Evil,* and he does not need to feed upon that tree and its fruit anymore. In Christ, the believer moves to the Tree of *Life* (Genesis 2:17; 3:1-6)!

Verse 20: *"And the God of peace shall bruise Satan under your feet shortly. The grace of our Lord Jesus Christ be with you. Amen."*

(Cf. Genesis 3:15; Romans 15:33.)

A. **"Peace"**
- The Peace of God
- Peace with God
- The God of Peace

Peace between God and man was broken by the Serpent in Eden (Genesis 3). The woman was deceived, and division came by the doctrine and speech of Satan (Romans 16:16-18), by his fair words and speeches to deceive the heart of the innocent woman. The woman was simple and gullible to these words and doctrine (I Timothy 2:12-15; II Corinthians 11:1-3).

B. **"Bruise Satan under your feet"**

The ultimate fulfillment of the bruising of Satan's head is through the church, the bride of Christ (Ephesians 5:23-32).

The promise of the bruising of the head of Satan was given to the woman, Eve. She typified the church. God often used a woman to crush the head of the enemy in the book of Judges (cf. Judges 4-5; 9:50-55). Thus, Deborah, Jael, and "the certain woman" typified the church.

To bruise is to tread Satan under foot. To bruise the Serpent's head (the head being the source of power and intelligence, governing the whole body of the Serpent) is to totally destroy his power, pride, mind, and will.

This will be the final ministry of the church, and it is set forth in Revelation 12.

C. **"The grace of our Lord Jesus Christ be with you. Amen"** (I
Corinthians 16:23).
This is Paul's apostolic benediction by the gospel of the grace of God.
The grace of God in Christ is the full source of the final bruising of
Satan. "Amen" means "so be it, let it, sure, true, verily, it shall come to
pass."

Salutations and A Benediction (Romans 16:21-24)

Verses 21-23: *"Timotheus my workfellow, and Lucius, and Jason, and Sosipater, my*
kinsmen, salute you. I Tertius, who wrote this epistle, salute you in the Lord.
Gaius mine host, and of the whole church, saluteth you. Erastus the
chamberlain of the city saluteth you, and Quartus a brother."

Here are further salutations by Paul's companions.

A. **"Timotheus my workfellow, and Lucius, and Jason, and Sosipater, my**
kinsmen, salute you."
"Timotheous" – means "honoring God." He was Paul's workfellow
(Acts 16:1; Hebrews 13:23) and a son in the faith.
"Lucius" – means "morning born" (Acts 13:1).
"Jason" – means "healer" (Acts 17:5).
"Sosipater" – means "father saved" (Acts 20:4).

B. **"I Tertius, who wrote this epistle, salute you in the Lord."**
Tertius was Paul's amanuensis (cf. Galatians 6:11).
"Tertius" – means "third."

C. **"Gaius mine host, and of the whole church, saluteth you"** (Acts 19:29;
20:4; I Corinthians 1:14, possibly the same one).
"Gaius" – means "lord."

D. **"Erastus the chamberlain of the city saluteth you, and Quartus a**
brother" (Acts 19:22; II Timothy 4:20).
A chamberlain was a land steward or administrator of city lands.
"Erastus" – means "beloved."
"Quartus" – means "fourth." Paul refers to him as a brother.

Verse 24: *"The grace of our Lord Jesus Christ be with you all. Amen."*

(Romans 16:20; I Coronations 16:23; I Thessalonians 5:28) This is another apostolic benediction.

The Final Benediction (Romans 16:25-27)

Verse 25: *"Now to him that is of power to establish you according to my gospel, and the preaching of Jesus Christ, according to the revelation of the mystery, which was kept secret since the world began. . ."*

A. **"Power to establish you"** (I Peter 5:10)
   There was a need to stabilize the saints, to settle them so they would not be carried about by every wind of contrary doctrine (Ephesians 4:9-16).

B. **"My gospel"** (refer to notes on Romans 1:1; 2:16)

C. **"Revelation of the mystery"** (refer to Romans 11:25; Ephesians 3:1-10, 20)
   This mystery, which was distinctly given to Paul, is the mystery of the church, the body of Christ, composed of Jew and Gentile.
   Disclosure of the secret was given to Paul, even though it had been kept secret (kept hidden away, kept silent) in the mind of God since the world began (Ephesians 1:9; Colossians 1:25-27).

Verse 26: *". . .But now is made manifest, and by the scriptures of the prophets, according to the commandment of the everlasting God, made known to all nations for the obedience of faith. . ."*

A. **"Manifest"**
   "Manifest" means "revealed, made known, disclosed" (Ephesians 1:9; Acts 6:7).

B. **"By the scriptures of the prophets"**
   The Old Testament prophets actually foretold the mystery of the church, though they did not perceive it (Romans 1:1-3). The Old Testament prophets did not fully understand their own utterances, especially those pertaining to the Messiah, His kingdom, and the coming in of the Gentiles to the kingdom (I Peter 1:10-12; II Peter 1:19-21;

Romans 15:4; I Corinthians 10:6,11). Paul quotes much, even in Romans, from the Old Testament Scriptures. By them he shows the revelation of the church, hidden in the Old Testament, yet clearly made manifest in the revelation of the mystery of the body of Christ made up of Jews and Gentiles, as given to him.

Hence, although the church was not specifically seen by the prophets, it was typified and prophesied of throughout the Law, the Psalms, and the Prophets.

This gives us justification for using the Old Testament Scriptures to help us in teaching the mystery, in illustrating the doctrines by types and shadows from the Old Testament, and in confirming the doctrine by the clear New Testament Scriptures.

Paul's quotations of Old Testament Scriptures, concerning the Gentiles coming into blessing through the Messiah, confirms these things. However, it was given to Paul that the Jews and the Gentiles together would be the one body and would be in the one olive tree (Romans 11; I Corinthians 12:12).

It was God's commandment that this mystery should be made known (Ephesians 3:1-20) to all nations, not just to the chosen Israel nation, as in times past.

C. "Obedience of faith" (Acts 6:7)
   Faith and obedience are like two sides of the same coin. Faith without obedience is dead (James 2:17).

Verse 27: "...To God only wise, be glory through Jesus Christ for ever. Amen."

A. "God only wise" (Cf. Jude 25; Romans 11:33-36)
   God is all wise, the source and fountainhead of all wisdom, knowledge, and understanding. The wisdom of God in His redemptive purpose is manifested through His grace in Christ, and He alone is worthy of glory.

B. "Amen"
   So be it; so it is.

Postscript: "Written to the Romans from Corinthus, and sent by Phebe, a servant of the church at Cenchrea."

Bibliography

Boyd, James P. *Bible Dictionary*. Uhrichsville, Ohio: Barbour Publishing, Inc.

Carlson, G. Raymond. *Romans, Teacher's Manual*. Springfield, Missouri: Gospel Publishing House.

Griffith Thomas, W. H. *St. Paul's Epistle to the Romans*. Grand Rapids, Michigan: Wm. B. Eardman's Publishing Company, 1946.

Grubb, Norman. *God Unlimited*. Fort Washington, Pennsylvania: Christian Literature Crusade, Inc., 1972.

Grubb, Norman. *Touching the Invisible*. Fort Washington, Pennsylvania: Christian Literature Crusade, Inc., 1975.

Haldane, Robert. *Romans: Banner of Truth Commentaries*. Grand Rapids, Michigan: Kregal Publications.

Kenyon, E. W. *Two Kinds of Righteousness*. Lynnwood, Washington: Kenyon Gospel Publishers.

Pearlman, Myer. *Knowing the Doctrines of the Bible*. Springfield, Missouri: Gospel Publishing House, 1937.

Thiessen, Henry C. *Systematic Theology*. Grand Rapids, Michigan: William B. Eerdmans Publishing Company.

Vincent, M. R. *Word Studies in the New Testament*. Grand Rapids, Michigan: William B. Eerdmans Publishing Company, 1957.

Weiss, G. Christian. *The Perfect Will of God*. Chicago, Illinios: Moody Press.

Other Resources Available by Kevin J. Conner

Kevin J. Conner

Church in the New Testament
The Book of Acts
Interpreting the Book of Revelation
Interpreting the Symbols & Types
The Epistle to the Romans
Feasts of Israel
Foundations of Christian Doctrine
The Tabernacle of Moses
The Tabernacle of David
The Temple of Solomon

Kevin J. Conner & Ken Malmin

The Covenants
Interpreting the Scriptures
New Testament Survey
Old Testament Survey

Ask for these resources at your local Christian bookstore.

City Bible Publishing
9200 NE Fremont
Portland OR 97220
503-253-9020
1-800-777-6057
www.citybiblepublishing.com

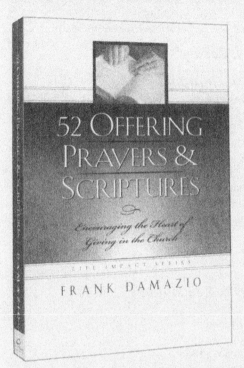

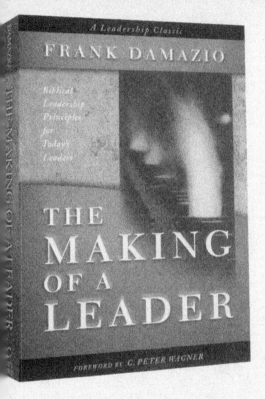

CPSIA information can be obtained
at www.ICGtesting.com
Printed in the USA
FSOW04n1937100516
20323FS